HARVARD EAST ASIAN STUDIES 7

The East Asian Research Center at Harvard University administers research projects designed to further scholarly understanding of China, Korea, Japan, and adjacent areas.

CH'ING
ADMINISTRATIVE TERMS

六部成語註解

任以都譯註

Ch'ing Administrative Terms

A Translation of The Terminology of the Six Boards with Explanatory Notes

Translated and edited by

E-tu Zen Sun

HARVARD
UNIVERSITY PRESS

Cambridge

Second Printing, 1973

Distributed in Great Britain

by Oxford University Press, London

Preparation of this volume was aided
by a grant from the Ford Foundation

Library of Congress Catalog Card Number 61-15279

SBN 674-12725-0

Printed in the United States of America

With this book
the translator pays tribute to
Vassar College
on the occasion of its
centennial

CONTENTS

Contents

Contents

Chapter V. THE BOARD OF PUNISHMENTS
          (Hsing-pu 刑部)

Chapter VI. THE BOARD OF WORKS
          (Kung-pu 工部)

Contents

SUPPLEMENT

INTRODUCTION

As the world becomes more bureaucratized, the Chinese example of bureaucracy becomes more interesting, whether today or under the Ch'ing Dynasty of the years 1644 to 1911. Those who work with Ch'ing documents are constantly fascinated by their quantity and orderliness. Never in premodern history have so many official communications been so thoroughly organized for examination by a hard-worked posterity. Inevitably, one who studies these voluminous sequences of documents becomes interested in the men and mechanisms which produced them and which, in the same process, governed the largest single unit of mankind.

The present dictionary of administrative terms was compiled by clerks for the use of clerks. It thus emanates from a somewhat different level of the Ch'ing administration than the memorials and state papers which form the usual fare of modern readers of Ch'ing documents. The clerks were not scholar-officials but did the daily work of copying, collating, revising, filing, recopying, condensing, listing, distributing, archiving, and otherwise generally processing the documents written by scholar-officials. In this position, responsible for the day-to-day operations of the bureaucratic machine, the clerks had to know the essential purport of the documents they handled, if only to keep the machine on its track and themselves from being run over by it.

Introduction

Their problem was complicated by the fact that at Peking the Ch'ing administration was a dyarchy (or, as some have called it, a synarchy) in which Manchus and a few Mongols constituted about half the personnel, appointed to work in tandem with Chinese. Hence arose the need for Manchu-Chinese phrase-books and dictionaries, among which one of the most widely used was the original 1742 progenitor of the present work. As Dr. Sun's Preface indicates, the Chinese portion of this Manchu-Chinese work was annotated in the late nineteenth century by an unknown and not-too-knowledgeable (presumably clerkly) compiler to make a volume of Chinese terms with explanatory notes. Japanese scholars of the early twentieth century, having found this work of value in understanding the Ch'ing bureaucracy and its activities, produced a revised edition in 1940. Twenty years later still, we now publish this English translation in the belief that it will be helpful to specialists in Ch'ing history.

Because of its origin, this phrase-book is both an aid to research, like any dictionary, and an historical document in itself. As a dictionary of technical administrative terms, it is by no means complete, and even contained in its late-nineteenth-century form a number of errors. Its selection of terms is a representative one, however, and they are rather usefully arranged in topical sequences which Dr. Sun has been able to elucidate by her insertion of section headings. Of the errors, some were noted by the Japanese editor of the 1940 edition, and a few remaining have been pointed out by the present translator and the specialists who have advised her.

One special fascination of this volume's phrase lists is the attention devoted to the evils of bureaucratism--the innumerable terms for malfeasance, defalcation, forgery, wrong reporting, bribery, collusion, subornation, and other illegal practices, the names for all of which the users evidently wanted to have at their finger tips. (See, for example, the entries beginning with no. 1066 concerning corruption in the salt monopoly administration.) Another point of interest is in the terms for technical processes such as the minting of copper coins (no. 1104). Of all the sections, it will also be observed, that on the Board of War contains the smallest number of technical terms, as though the literocratic disesteem of the military was shared in practice by the yamen clerks. In these and other ways, I believe this volume will afford insight into the operations of the Ch'ing bureaucracy, which are being studied from other angles by other projects of this Center, particularly in the forthcoming book by Ch'ü T'ung-tsu on Local Government in China under the Ch'ing.

This English edition of the Liu-pu ch'eng-yü chu-chieh, and the insight which readers of Ch'ing documents may derive from it, have been made possible by the special qualifications of the translator-editor. E-tu Zen Sun secured her college education at the National Southwest Associated University (formed by Nankai, Peking National, and Tsing Hua universities) in wartime Kunming and in the United States at Vassar (B. A. 1944) and at Radcliffe (Ph. D. 1949). She has taught Far Eastern history at Goucher

Introduction

College and Pennsylvania State University and has been a research
fellow at the Johns Hopkins University and at Harvard. Her
publications already include a number of articles and book reviews,
two bibliographical volumes, a monographic study of Chinese
Railways and British Interests, 1898-1911 (New York 1954), and
a volume of translations, with John DeFrancis, entitled Chinese
Social History (Washington, D.C., 1956). Only an historian of
thoroughly bicultural capacity, sound training, and preternatural
perseverance could have carried this present work through to
completion.

John K. Fairbank

TRANSLATOR'S PREFACE

This is a dictionary of terms and phrases which were used
in the conduct of official business in the Six Boards (or Ministries)
at Peking during the Ch'ing dynasty. The present translation is
based on the edition published in Japan in 1940, but before that
date the work had had an interesting history during two centuries:[1]
first it was a manual widely used by government clerks in China
from the middle of the eighteenth century, and later it served
Japanese scholars as a source of information in their studies of
Chinese institutions and history. This translation has been undertaken with a view to extending the book's latter function as a research
aid to serve current Western scholarship in Chinese history. It
will prove of use in three respects: to provide the meaning of terms
one encounters in Ch'ing documents, to offer English equivalents for
these terms, and to indicate something of bureaucratic procedure
and practice, particularly as seen at the clerks' level.

By and large the entries in this dictionary fall into two
major groups. One is the administrative and technical terminology
that constitutes the greater part of the work; the other consists of
nontechnical phrases and terms that were frequently used in

---

1. An informative account of the origin and evolution of the Liu-pu
ch'eng-yü is to be found in the Introduction by Mr. Naitō Kenkichi
内藤乾吉　to the Japanese edition, Rikubu seigo chukai 六部
成語註解 (Terminology of the Six Boards with explanatory notes;
Kōbundō, Kyōto, 1940), 149 pp., plus an index of 25 pp.

connection with government activity, but actually were samples of plain Chinese. Under the first group one may list the following categories: official titles, and terms of reference to officials; all sorts of official acts--ranging from the collection of taxes to the observance of mourning for one's parents; various aspects of the actual operation of the administrative machinery in all its major branches; and the standards for and disciplining of bureaucratic behavior. The second group includes some conventional phrases in documentary Chinese, together with certain common literary expressions that obviously were placed in this dictionary for the benefit of clerks, especially Manchu clerks, who might have found them difficult to understand. The total impression that might be gained from these varied types of content is that of a cross-sectional view not only of what the Ch'ing bureaucracy did, but also of what it was; and beyond that, a glimpse of the social and economic environment that sustained this government.

To the student of history, therefore, the present volume will be of interest not as a dictionary of terms alone, but also because of the light it sheds on the institutional history of the Ch'ing era. It is plain that this work yields information on government activities in the economic, educational, social and political life of the country; but above all it is useful in furnishing the reader with a rich store of clues to possible lines of inquiry into the nature of the Ch'ing bureaucracy. The numerous items dealing with all sorts of illegal acts and official misconduct, as pointed out by Professor Fairbank in his Introduction, for example, are

a clear indication of the presence of control mechanisms--operating
with varying degrees of efficacy, to be sure--within the bureaucratic system itself (see especially Sections 6, 13, 14, and 15 in
Chapter I).   Further study along this line may enlighten us as to
the place of the bureaucracy in premodern society: what the ideal
goal was for its members, what were the deficiencies and pitfalls,
and how the delinquent members were chastised and the meritorious
rewarded, in order that the system might not collapse through
inability to fulfill its role of public administration.   In other words,
further understanding of Ch'ing institutions may be gained through
an evaluation of the role, both ideal and practical, of the individual
official in the system.

As the Manchu rule in China came into its heyday, the task
of administering the country called for a facile knowledge, particularly on the part of government clerks, of the equivalent Chinese
and Manchu expressions and terms used in the conduct of official
business.   When Manchu-Chinese dictionaries began to be published,
starting in the K'ang-hsi period (1622-1722), their contents usually
included sections devoted to the established terminology of government offices.   An early work of this kind was published in 1693,
the [T'ung-wen] Kuang-hui ch'üan-shu [同文] 廣彙全書
(A compendium of the Manchu and Chinese languages), and it
was followed some thirty years later by Ch'ing-wen pei-k'ao
清文備考   (A reference book of the Manchu language;
1722).   The former was a dictionary of words and phrases, the
latter a combination grammar and dictionary, while in each of

them certain chapters were given over to the terminology of the
Six Boards which formed the core of the administrative structure
at Peking.   A third work, <u>Ta Ch'ing ch'üan-shu</u> 大清全書
(A complete Manchu-Chinese dictionary; 1683), also contained
among its contents several hundred items concerning the Six Boards.

The above were the forerunners of the <u>Liu-pu ch'eng-yü</u>
(Terminology of the Six Boards), which was first published anony-
mously under that title in 1742 (Ch'ien-lung 7).   It contained material
selected from all three of the earlier dictionaries, and included both
the Manchu and the Chinese versions of the terminology.   The book
was widely circulated, for within the next century and a half it went
through several additional printings, including one in 1816 (Chia-
ch'ing 21).   The latter and the original 1742 version, both available
in Japanese libraries, are the two old editions used by Mr. Naitō
in editing the Japanese publication of 1940.[2]

The "explanatory notes," that is, interpretations of the
meaning of the individual items, were added to the Chinese part
of the original work toward the last part of the Ch'ing dynasty by
an unknown compiler who was active, as internal evidence indicates,
either late in the T'ung-chih period (1862-1874) or during the Kuang-
hsü period (1875-1908).   The result of his labor was separately

---

2.   In the notes supplied by Mr. Naitō in the text, these are
referred to as the Ch'ien-lung edition 乾本 and the Chia-ch'ing
edition 嘉本 , respectively, when they are mentioned separately.
When referred to together, however, they appear under the designation "Manchu-Chinese edition."

published in a new edition,[3] for which the precise date of
publication is not stated. It was an improved language aid, an
it were, for Manchu functionaries in government offices. This
was the Liu-pu ch'eng-yǔ chu-chieh 註解 (Terminology of the Six
Boards with explanatory notes), which is the subject of the present
translation.

This dictionary first drew the attention of Japanese specialists for a non-academic purpose concerning Formosa. After that
island passed under Japanese jurisdiction in 1895, a government
agency known as the Rinji Taiwan Kyūkan Chosakai (Temporary
Commission of the Taiwan Government-general for the Study of
Old Chinese Customs) was established to conduct research on
Chinese institutions which would be useful to the colonial administration,[4] and the Liu-pu ch'eng-yǔ chu-chieh was among the
sources of information consulted by the scholars taking part in
the project, with far-reaching consequences. Among them, for
example, Azumagawa Tokuji later utilized the Liu-pu ch'eng-yǔ
chu-chieh in compiling his Tenkai 典海 (A dictionary of
institutional phrases); and among the persons who took back to

---

3. Mr. Naitō refers to this in his notes as the "annotated
edition" 註本.

4. See John K. Fairbank and Masataka Banno, Japanese
Studies of Modern China (Rutland, Vermont, and Tokyo:
Tuttle, 1955), p. 10.

Japan hand-written copies of this work was Professor Kato
Shigeshi, who decades later promoted the idea of putting out
a collated edition of it in Japan.

In editing the 1940 edition, Mr. Naitŏ made a careful
textual comparison between the late-Ch'ing edition and a number
of previous versions; he also used other late-Ch'ing compilations
that contain official terminology such as the Ch'eng-yŭ chi-yao
成語輯要 (A collection of [official] terminology), which was
produced in the Kuang-hsŭ period. As a result he was able to
point out a number of discrepancies. Among them, the discrepancies found in the various editions of the Liu-pu ch'eng-yŭ
themselves are mentioned in notes added to his text. Mr. Naitŏ's
edition, though published in Japan, is in the original Chinese, not
a translation. Only his Introduction is in Japanese.

Some of the terms and their interpretations give definite
evidence of their early Ch'ing origin, having reference to
situations that had been current prior to the first publication
of the book. Entry 245, a reference to the capture and delivery
of fugitives from the Eight Banners, is a clear-cut example. On
the other hand, the imprint of later ages is not lacking; entry 458,
for instance, mentions likin, a mid-nineteenth-century innovation
in the tax system.

The translation has followed the exact order of the original
arrangement as to chapter and content, and no reorganization of
the main body of material has been attempted, save for the
division of each chapter into a number of sections, with added section

headings. The Supplement (pu-i 補遺) that follows the last chapter of Mr. Naitō's 1940 edition has been rendered as given, in a separate unit; the Amendments (ting-cheng 訂正) that come near the end of the Japanese volume, however, have now been incorporated by me into the main chapters, so that the amended version is placed immediately under the item it amends, and both are plain to the English reader at a glance.

Two passages reproduced in the Japanese 1940 edition have been excluded from this translation. They are first, at the beginning of Chapter I, nine pages containing explanations concerning the Peking Gazette, procedures with regard to daily audiences and special audience, and the methods of memorializing the throne; and second, at the end of Chapter III, eight pages giving the early Ch'ing texts of congratulatory memorials presented to the Emperor, the Empress, and the Heir-Apparent on their respective birthdays. In addition, an Addendum on Textual Comparisons (Chiao-k'an pu-i 校勘補遺, pp. 147-149 of the 1940 edition), compiled by Mr. Naitō, is likewise not included in the present volume. These omitted pages, of course, have value for students of the subjects they concern, but seem inappropriate for the present already lengthy reference volume.

In the course of my work on the present translation I have been deeply indebted to Professors John K. Fairbank and Lien-sheng Yang of Harvard for their helpful advice and friendly encouragement, which I gratefully acknowledge. I owe special thanks to Mr. T'ung-tsu Ch'ü, who has kindly read my draft, and

called my attention to necessary corrections in my renderings.
I wish to thank Professor W. Franke of the University of Hamburg,
as well as Professor Charles O. Hucker of the University of
Arizona and Miss Judy Feldman of Cambridge, Massachusetts,
who have sent me suggestions and comments as specialists. Miss
Sally Ch'eng of the Center for East Asian Studies, Harvard
University, has helped me greatly in the preparation of the
manuscript from the very beginning to the finish, for which I
express my sincere thanks. I alone, of course, am responsible
for the imperfections that remain in the translation.

E-tu Zen Sun

December 1958

TRANSLATOR'S NOTE ON GENERAL PROCEDURES

1. Each individual term or phrase and its interpretation are translated as closely to the sense of the original text as possible without doing great injustice to the English idiom. Very literary Chinese, however, is sometimes simplified for the sake of clarity.

2. Square brackets indicate additional words or further explanations inserted by the present translator for clarification of the text, including cross references to other entries. They also denote my own renderings of official terms.

3.   Parentheses denote one of three things , depending on the context: Original notes in the text which were supplied by the Japanese editor, Mr. Naitō, in the 1940 edition, and which are so indicated by an asterisk preceding the note; or words supplied by the present translator which are implied but not expressed in the Chinese text; or renderings of official titles that follow the version given in Brunnert and Hagelstrom.

4. Errors found by the present translator in the text are first translated as given, then corrected in notes appended to the entry concerned.

5. At the beginning or the end of a number of items there are in the original Chinese text brief phrases explaining the meaning, or giving the equivalents, of certain key words in Chinese. Since this is often useless for our present purpose--the meaning of the words being manifest in the interpretation itself-- these phrases have been omitted where such omission will not

detract from the comprehensibility of an item. Where this has been done it is indicated by three dots enclosed in square brackets.

6. Translations of official titles generally follow those given in the standard manual of Ch'ing official titles, H.S. Brunnert and V.V. Hagelstrom, Present Day Political Organization of China, translated from the Russian by A. Beltchenko and E.E. Moran (Shanghai: Kelly and Walsh, 1912). When a different rendering has seemed necessary, or when a term has not been found in Brunnert, I have sought to establish a reasonable English equivalent after comparing the terms used by various modern scholars; when that has been unavailing, I have tried to devise my own renderings. When it appears for the first time an English translation that follows Brunnert is placed in parentheses, thus: yü-shih 御史 (provincial censor); renderings of my own choice for items not found in Brunnert are placed in square brackets. Major differences from Brunnert are explained in footnotes. When more than one version is given in Brunnert for the same term, the version I use is further indicated by the letter B with the number in Brunnert, for example (B.190).

7. In some cases the Chinese terms already have generally accepted English versions that are widely used, such as governor, governor-general, or local constable (for hsün-fu 巡撫 , tsung-tu 總督 , and ti-pao 地保, respectively). I have followed such general usage without further ado.

8. In the original the contents of each chapter fall into more or less definite blocks, each of which centers around a

central core of subject matter. To facilitate the use of this volume I have divided each chapter into sections on the basis of these blocks, and have supplied numbered headings for them. It needs to be pointed out, however, that the lines between the original blocks were not very strictly drawn, nor was the presentation of material within each block always finely schematized. As a result the present superimposed pattern of sections cannot avoid having many flaws. It is hoped that the reader will not be too dismayed to find that occasionally a few items have appeared in places where they do not seem to belong. The Indexes will help in locating specific items.

9. P'in chi 品級 is translated as "rank and class" (after Brunnert). Chi by itself is also "class," as in "reduction of salary by two classes" 降俸二級 . Teng 等 , on the other hand, denotes a unit in any given system of gradation, and is translated as "grade."

10. 石 as a measurement of volume is simply rendered as tan (or shih), rather than as "a picul," the latter being a weight of 100 catties or 133 lbs.

11. Transliteration of Chinese words in this work follows, to the best of the translator's knowledge, the Wade-Giles system.

E. Z. S.

CH'ING ADMINISTRATIVE TERMS

CHAPTER I

THE BOARD OF CIVIL APPOINTMENT

[[1]] Categories of appointment and transfer. Nos. 1-26

1. TA HSÜAN 大選 Regular appointment

> The ordinary order 班次 of appointment of officials to vacant posts [see note under 2].

> The names of officials awaiting appointments are entered in books at the Board of Civil Appointment. When a vacancy occurs the appointment is made according to the listed order (of names). This is known as the regular order of appointments. In addition, (appointment by) recommendation 保舉 is also practiced [see 33]. Aside from the ordinary order of appointments there are also many others, each known by a special term. These are individually explained in detail in the following items.

2. CHI HSÜAN 急選 Expedited appointment

> Receiving appointment sooner than others who belong to the same list 班. [The Kuang-hsü hui-tien (Shanghai: Commercial Press, 1908, hereafter KHHT), 9:1, gives the following definitions for ta hsüan and chi hsüan: "The system of making monthly appointments is regularized (by the Board of Civil Appointment); those made in the even months are called ta hsüan, and those in the odd months, chi hsüan." It goes on to explain that when the system was first drawn up ta hsüan involved the candidates on the list of regular designations [ch'u-pan 除班] and the list of advancements [sheng-pan 升班], while chi hsüan dealt with the list of expectant officials [pu-pan 補班]. In the course of time, however, changes were made in these compositions.]

3. AI HSÜAN 挨選 Appointment in proper order

> Receiving appointment according to the order (of names) on the list to which one belongs.

Civil Appointment

4. TING HSÜAN 頂選 Top of the list

   (One's own name is) now the first one on the waiting list.

5. HOU HSÜAN 候選 Awaiting appointment

   This is a general term for officials awaiting appointment to posts.

6. HOU CH'ÜEH 候缺 Awaiting a vacancy

   Same as [5]. Also refers to an official waiting to fill some particular office 補缺.

7. HOU PU 候補 Expectant

   Waiting to fill a specific office, in a government agency either in the capital or in the provinces.

8. CHIEN PU 間補 Alternated appointment

   Each expectant official is placed on one of many different waiting lists. When a vacancy occurs, one from list A is appointed; when another occurs, one from list B will be appointed--for example, appointing a person on the Regular Graduates List 正途班 [see 11] to a first vacancy, and appointing one on the Purchasers List 捐班 [see 14] to a second vacancy, etc.

9. CH'AO T'UI 朝推 Court selection

   Selected by the Emperor himself.

   [Amended, p. 141:] (An official) selected by joint action of the Court officials.

10. CH'ÜAN HENG 銓衡 Just selection

    The order in which appointments are made.

    [Amended, p. 141:] The system of making official appointments, meaning that the selections are made as justly as are the scales of measuring standards, without undue weight or favor.

11. CHENG-T'U PAN 正途班 Regular Graduates List

    (Composed of) persons possessing the degrees of provincial graduate (chü-jen 舉人) or metropolitan graduate (chin-shih 進士).

-2-

12. PAO-CHÜ PAN 保舉班 List of recommended names

    (Persons) recommended to expectant ranks on account of meritorious service.

13. I-HSÜ PAN 議敘班 Evaluation list

    (Persons who,) having completed their compiling jobs in the Kuo-shih Kuan 國史館 (State Historiographer's Office) or other tasks in government agencies, are referred to the Board (of Civil Appointment) for evaluation, and are given expectant ranks.

14. CHÜAN PAN 捐班 Purchasers List

    Persons who have purchased expectant ranks with silver.

15. CIIIN-HSIEN PU-YUNG PAN 儘先補用班 Expectant Officials' priority list

    Persons to be given priority among expectant officials in being appointed to substantive posts, owing either to meritorious service or to contributions of silver.

16. SHENG YUNG 陞用 Promotion

    Being promoted to (a higher) official post.

17. TIAO PU 調補 Transfer

    A substantive official in locality A being transferred to a substantive post of corresponding rank in locality B. [The text (p. 11) reads <u>kuan-jen kuan</u> 官任官 , which is an error for <u>shih-jen kuan</u> 實任官 .]

18. T'I PU 題補 Proposed appointment

    When a vacancy occurs, the superior official selects (one person) either from the list of expectant officials or among those due for promotion, and memorializes the throne (for permission) thus to fill the post.

19. YÜAN CH'ÜEH 員缺 Vacancy

    An unfilled government post.

20. NEI SHENG 內陞 Promotion to the capital

    Officials serving in the provinces being promoted or appointed to positions in the capital.

Civil Appointment

21. WAI CHUAN 外轉 Reassignment to the provinces

   Officials serving in the capital being transferred to
   provincial posts.

22. TS'AI CH'ÜEH 裁缺 Reduction in force

   Abolition of existing government offices.

23. KAI PU 改補 Change of post

   An official originally appointed to one post is shifted to
   another.

24. K'AO HSÜAN 考選 Appointment by examination

   Appointment to official posts is made on the basis of a
   test of the officials' abilities.

25. CHIEN HSÜAN 揀選 Appointment by selection

   Among those due for promotion to a certain post, the
   best are selected and presented to the Emperor, and (the
   appointment) is decided (thereafter) by imperial decree.

26. CHIEH PU 借補 Appointed to different rank

   An expectant official of high rank is temporarily appointed
   to a minor government post [cf. 81].

[[2]] References to titles and merits. Nos. 27-38

27. HSIEN-CH'ÜEH [HSIANG-TANG] 衔缺相當
    Corresponding posts

   An official's original position being one of the same rank
   as the present vacancy (under consideration); these are
   called corresponding posts.

28. CHIH-HSIEN 職衔 Rank and title

   The rank and class 品級 of an official post.

   [Amended, p. 141:] An official's substantive rank 實職
   and brevet rank 虛衔.

29. TA HSIEN 大衔 Great titles

   The rank and title of a high official.

30. CHIA HSIEN 加銜 Nominal rank

Title given as honorary or brevet rank 虛銜 in addition to one's formal official title (s).

31. CHIH MING 職名 Office and name

The office and personal name of an official.

32. PAO-T'I 保題 Memorialize for recommendation

Memorial written to make recommendations.

33. PAO-CHÜ 保舉 Recommendation

A meritorious official being recommended by his superior for additional [promotion] 酌加. [Pao-chü also could be used interchangeably with chü-chien 舉薦, the recommending of specially noteworthy talent for official posts. See Oda Yorozu 織田萬, Shinkoku gyōsei hō 清國行政法, translated into Chinese by Cheng Ch'ih, Ch'en Yü-nien, and Liang Shih-tung (Shanghai, 1906), p. 13.]

34. I-HSÜ 議敍 Evaluation

(A meritorious official) being evaluated by the Board of Civil Appointment as to the extent of his merit, and rewarded accordingly.

35. YU-HSÜ 優敍 Special rewards

After evaluation, rewards are doubled (for a meritorious official).

36. CHIA-CHI 加級 Additional grade

To be advanced one grade 等 above one's original rank and class.

37. CHI-LU 紀錄 Records of merits

Registration of an official's deeds and accomplishments in a book for the (government's) record.

38. CHI-LU WU-TZ'U 紀錄五次 Recorded five times

Every official (usually) receives advancement in grade and has his merits recorded more than once, depending on the extent of his achievements. The number (of recordings of merits) therefore varies, for example, four, five, six, or seven times.

[[3]] Procedures in the capital for an appointee. Nos. 39-52

39. SHUANG-YÜEH PAN 雙月班 Even months list

(*The Manchu-Chinese editions of this manual omit "list. ")

The Board of Civil Appointment maintains different appointment lists. Some are of persons to be appointed only to vacancies occurring in the even months, others are for the odd months, and still other lists are of persons who could be given appointments regardless of the months. The even months are the second, fourth, sixth, eighth, tenth, and twelfth; the odd months are the first, third, fifth, seventh, ninth, and eleventh.

40. CHIH-CHIEH 職揭 Personal manifest

An official reporting his presence [see 41] to the Board of Civil Appointment is required to submit first in writing to the Wen-hsüan Ssu 文選司 (Department of Selection) his name and present official title. This is known as a personal manifest.

The Department of Selection is a department in the Board of Civil Appointment whose special function is the processing of appointments.

41. T'OU-KUNG 投供 Reporting one's presence

An official due to receive appointment to a post is called to the Board of Civil Appointment, where he is asked to write out a copy of his own record of career 履歷 [cf. 95] and present it (to the Board) for inspection.

42. CH'IN-KUNG 親供 Personally penned report

An official's record of career written by his own hand.

43. YEN-TAO 驗到 Checking arrival

Officials from the provinces who come to the capital for presentation to the Emperor 引見 must, on reaching Peking, report their arrival immediately to the Board of Civil Appointment, where the Board officials will check their age and likenesses. This is known as checking arrivals.

44. KUO-T'ANG 過堂 Triennial inspection

Once every three years all the officials of the Six Boards are individually inspected by the chief executives 堂官 of the Board of Civil Appointment. This is known as the triennial inspection. [T'ang-kuan 堂官 and ssu-kuan 司官 (45): here they have been rendered as "chief executives" and "administrative staff" respectively, which are more specific than B. 304. T'ang-kuan in the present context include the Board presidents and vice-presidents; ssu-kuan are the other Board officials subordinate to them. Cf. W. F. Mayers, The Chinese Government (Shanghai, 1896), pp. 18, 19.]

45. TIEN-MAO 點卯 Roll-call

Every month the clerks and runners of all the Boards are individually inspected by the administrative staff 司官 (of their respective Boards) once or twice, or three times. This is known as roll-call. [Ssu-kuan 司官 : see note under 44.]

46. YEN-LI 演禮 Rehearsal of ceremonies

An official should go to the Board of Civil Appointment on the day preceding that on which he is due for presentation to the Emperor, there to learn and practice the ceremonial rituals.

47. CH'E (CH'IH)-CH'IEN 掣簽 Drawing of lots

The destinations of officials of expectant or apprentice 學習 statuses, who are appointed to provincial or various (metropolitan) offices, are determined by drawing of lots at the Board of Civil Appointment. [The Hsüeh-hsi

Kuan   (Sub-officer) in B. 708 and 711 does not fit the present context.]

48. CH'IEN-T'UNG 籤筒 Lottery holder

Shaped like a writing-brush container 筆筒 , this vessel holds bamboo sticks on which are written the names of (individual) provinces. When officials are due to be dispatched, the chief executives of the Board of Civil Appointment decide their exact destinations by drawing the sticks.

49. LING P'ING 領憑 Receiving the certificate

An official going from the capital to his provincial post must first receive a written certifying document 文牒 , which upon arrival at the province is submitted to his superior for official inspection.

50. CHI YU 給由 Furnishing data

When an official deserves promotion, his superior must first communicate with the Board of Civil Appointment to check into his record of service, and whether or not he has been penalized 處分 . The Board will assemble such information and (forward it to the inquiring official) in its reply to the communication.

51. TANG-T'ANG 當堂 In the presence of the chief executives

Such procedures as receiving the certificate [see 49] and drawing of lots [see 47] are all carried out in the presence of the chief executives (of the Board of Civil Appointment).

52. TUI-YÜEH LING P'ING 對月領憑 Receiving the certificate by monthly rotation

There are fixed rules which designate the particular months in which certificates [see 49] for specific provinces are to be issued by the Board of Civil Appointment. Officials (appointed to provincial posts) must each await their turns, and receive certificates in the months properly designated for their respective provinces.

[[4]] The appointee assumes office. Nos. 53-76

53. TAO JEN 到任 Arrival at the post

The official has arrived at his post, received the seal of office, and taken over the administration.

54. JU CHING 入境 Entered the area

The official has entered the area that is under the juris-diction of his office.

55. JEN-SO 任所 Seat of office

The place where the office is located.

56. SHOU SHIH 受事 Assume office

Taking over the office and attending to the administration thereof.

57. HUI SHU 回署 Return to office

The return of an official to his own office upon the com-pletion of a journey undertaken on a government mission.

58. TSE-JEN 責任 Official duties

All matters that lie within the jurisdiction of an official that should be directed or administered 管辦 by him.

59. HSIEN JEN 現任 Current post

The post currently occupied (by an official).

60. YU JEN 優任 Better position

To be preferentially employed by being appointed to a higher position.

61. YUAN JEN 原任 Former post

The positions held previously by those who have resigned or are retired 辭職退閑之人.

62. HSIN JEN 新任 New incumbent

One who has newly arrived at a post.

63. CH'IEN JEN 前任 Former incumbent; predecessor

One who previously served at the post.

64. CHIEH JEN 接任 Taking charge of a post

The official duties [cf. 58] of a government post are turned over by the former incumbent to the new incumbent.

65. SHENG-SHOU 生手 New hand

One who has had no previous experience with his present government position, nor carried out his present functions, and is doing the work for the first time, is called a new hand.

66. SHU-SHIH 署事 Acting (official)

When the incumbent official is away on a government mission, his post is left in the hands of an official appointed to act (for him during his absence).

67. CHIAO-TAI 交代 Handing over

The former incumbent turning over all unfinished business of the office and the granaries, treasury, and tax funds to the new incumbent.

68. CHIAO P'AN 交盤 Delivery of inventory

At the time of the handing over [cf. 67], the new official will accept (the inventory) only when he is satisfied, after weighing and checking (*probably misprint here), that the contents of the treasury are in agreement (with the accounts). [Apparently referring to the word p'ing 枰, a misprint for ch'eng 秤, to weigh.]

69. KUAN-LI 管理 In charge

To supervise and administer certain specific matters.

70. CHING-KUAN 經管 Directly in charge

To be personally in charge of a certain matter.

71. SHU-LI 署理 Acting

To administer an office in an acting capacity [see 66].

72. CHIEH-SHU 接署 Take charge as acting (official)

   To take office in an acting capacity.

73. HU-LI 護理 Temporarily in charge

   When a superior official is away for only a short period on government business, a subordinate will have custody. of his seal of office and act in his behalf.

   [Amended, p. 141): In all government offices, when an official of lower rank acts in behalf of one higher, or when minor personnel act in behalf of superior personnel, then they have custody of the seal and are known to be "temporarily in charge." The term "acting" (shu-li) applies to officials who act for those of equal rank and title.

74. TSAN-LI 贊理 Assistant; to assist

   To assist in the administration (of an office).

75. TU-LI 督理 Directing; director; to direct

   To direct and lead one's subordinates in the carrying out of a function.

76. CHAN-LI 暫理 Temporarily acting

   To administer temporarily.

   [Amended, p. 141:] Chan-hsing shu-li 暫行署理 : To be an acting (official) temporarily.

[[5]] Scrutiny of officials. Nos. 77-96

77. I-TENG CH'EN-CHIH 一等稱職 First class: "fully competent for the office"

   All civil officials in both the capital and the provinces 京外文官 (have their records of service) examined once every three years, and are divided into three classes according to (each person's) diligence or negligence in the performance of duty. There is a special designation for each class, that for the first [i.e., highest] being "fully competent for the office." (Those belonging to this

-11-

class) may win promotion to a higher post.

78. **ERH-TENG CH'IN-CHIH** 二等勤職 Second class: "diligent in office"

The special designation for those belonging to the second class is "diligent in office."

79. **SAN-TENG P'ING-CHIH** 三等平職 Third class: "equal to the office"

The special designation for those belonging to the third class is "equal to the office."

Officials placed in the second and third classes may remain in their present posts.

80. **FENG-TS'AI KAI-TIAO** 奉裁改調 Abolition of post and transfer (of incumbent)

(*Tiao 調 "transfer" originally read pu 補 "appoint.")

When a certain post is abolished by imperial decree, the official thus deprived of his present position is appointed to a post at another place.

81. **CHIEH-P'IN TIAO-PU** 借品調補 Appointment to a different rank

If, for instance, an official of the fifth rank is temporarily appointed to a post of the sixth rank, he later still ought to be reappointed to a post of the fifth rank [cf. 26].

82. **TUI-P'IN TIAO-YUNG** 對品調用 Mutual transfer at equal rank

Exchange of positions between officials of the same rank and class.

83. **TUI-P'IN TIAO HSIEN-SAN YUNG** 對品調閑散用 Transfer within the same rank to a leisurely (post)

If an official is somewhat incompetent (for his present work), he is to be assigned to a less demanding post of the same rank.

84. CHAO-CHI TIAO PIEH-HSIANG TSA-CHIH YUNG 照級調別項雜職用 Transfer to another post of the same rank

If a chief official 正印官 is incompetent, he is to be transferred to another post of the same rank but which is of an assistant nature, or is a minor post 佐雜缺. [For tso tsa 佐雜 Brunnert (858A) gives the general term "petty officials." I have rendered the tso and tsa separately, since each designates a different category of officials, i.e., the tso is tso-erh 佐貳, sub-prefects and assistant magistrates of departments and districts; tsa is tsa chih 雜職, such as postmaster, granary keeper, and un-classed minor officers. KHHT, 5:1; 6:5a-b; 8:4-5.]

85. I HSIANG-TANG YŬAN-CH'ÜEH LÜEH-CHIA SHENG-YUNG 以相當員缺略加陞用 Slight promotion to a suitable official post

To raise an official's position slightly by appointing him to a suitable post.

86. K'AO-CH'ENG 考成 Scrutiny of achievements

Superior officials examining the performance of their subordinates to see the extent of the latter's achievements.

87. K'AO-MAN 考滿 Time due for scrutiny

There are time limits to (the interval between) scrutinies of achievements [see 86]. In some cases three years constitute the time period.

88. YIN-CHIEN 引見 Presentation to the Emperor

Officials due for promotion or appointment are presented to the Emperor by the Board of Civil Appointment.

89. PI-CHIEN 陛見 Imperial audience

High officials of the provinces coming to the capital for audiences with the Emperor.

90. CH'ING PI-CHIEN 請陛見 Request for an imperial audience

According to regulations, high officials in the provinces

should request audience with the Emperor once every
three years.

91. **CHING-CH'A** 京察 Metropolitan inspection

Civil officials in the capital are inspected once every
three years; this is known as "metropolitan inspection."

92. **TA-CHI** 大計 Great accounting

Officials serving in the provinces are inspected once in
three years; this is known as the "great accounting."
[The governors-general and governors, however, are
included among the metropolitan officials for appraisal in
the metropolitan inspection (see 91). See Oda, Shinkoku
gyōsei hō, p. 165.]

93. **CHI-TIEN** 計典 Matters of (great) accounting

Events pertaining to the great accounting.

94. **CHIEH-CH'I** 屆期 At the designated time

The previously designated time has arrived.

95. **LÜ-LI** 履歷 Record of career

An official's history of entry into a public career 出身
the places where he has held government posts, the manner
in which he has been recommended, etc., are all termed
"record of career."

96. **SSU-CHU** 四柱 The four columns

(*The Manchu-Chinese editions read ssu-chu ch'ing-ts'e
四柱清冊 , "the four-columned record book.")
Four-columned books are used during metropolitan
inspections [cf. 91], and entries are made in them by the
superior officials as to the merits or demerits (of the
inspected officials). [Ssu-chu ch'ing-ts'e was also a
standard term used in bookkeeping; see Board of Revenue,
552, 1118.]

[[6]] Impeachment and punitive measures. Nos. 97–138

97. CHÜ HO 舉劾 Recommendation and impeachment

At the completion of the metropolitan inspection, the better (officials) are recommended, and the inferior ones are impeached.

98. CH'ÜAN CHENG 勸懲 Exhortation and warning

Recommendation and impeachment [see 97] are resorted to, in order that the diligent may be encouraged and the negligent warned.

99. SHIH-SHIH 事實 Biographical facts

Actual deeds done during one's lifetime, such as (being) a chaste woman, a famous scholar, a filial son, and the like.

100. SHIH-CHI 事蹟 Past deeds

Things that one has done.

101. LIEH CHI 劣蹟 Bad deeds

Bad acts performed by a person.

102. CHI-TS'AN 計參 Impeachment after great accounting

Impeachment (of an official) is made on the basis of factual findings of a great accounting [cf. 92].

103. TS'AN-KO 參革 Dismissal after impeachment

(An official) is dismissed from office after being impeached in a memorial.

104. TS'AN-FA 參罰 Penalty for the impeached

The penalty for an impeached official is decided on.

105. CH'IEN-TS'AN 前參 Initial impeachment

Department and district officials 州縣官 are often impeached more than once for various causes. In such cases the first impeachment lodged (against an official) is referred to as the initial impeachment.

106. TS'AN-HOU 參後 Conduct following impeachment

An official's conduct following his impeachment should also be observed by his superior.

107. LU CHANG 露章 Memorial of exposure

A memorial containing an impeachment of other officials is called "memorial of exposure."

108. CHIU-TS'AN 糾參 Investigation and impeachment

To examine the faults of an official and then impeach him.

109. CHIEN-CHÜ 檢舉 Self-impeachment

(An official) uncovers his own mistakes, and memorializes to impeach himself.

110. CHE-TS'AN 摘參 Impeachment on specific charges

To impeach an official by specifying his faults.

111. CH'U-FEN 處分 Penalty

The proper punishment.

112. I-CH'U 議處 Deliberation on penalty

After an official has been impeached, his offenses are referred by imperial decree to the Board (of Civil Appointment) for discussion and sentence.

113. HUI-I 會議 Joint conference

(Officials from) several government agencies meeting to discuss a matter jointly.

114. I-KUAN 議官 The conferring officials

Officials who should participate in a conference.

115. CHO-TING 酌定 To deliberate and decide

To weigh the factors of a given situation and then come to a decision.

116. PO-HSING 駁行 Written rejection

When a document bearing an impeachment that is to be

memorialized by the Board (of Civil Appointment) is not in line with the established rules, the Board will reject it through written communication.

117. KAI-CHENG PO-HUI 改正撥回 Returned for correction

When a matter has been discussed and decided by the Board to be out of order, it is referred back to the place of origin and (the authorities there) are ordered to make the proper corrections.

118. CHU-CH'IH 逐斥 Dismissal with reprimand

The continuation of an official in a certain post is un-desirable, and he is dismissed.

119. KO-CHIH 革職 Dismissal from office

To relieve an official of his post and title.

120. NA-WEN 拿問 Arrest for questioning

When an official is guilty of a serious crime, he is to be arrested after having been relieved of his post, and held for trial and fixing of penalty.

121. CHE YIN 摘印 Surrender of seal

When an official has been dismissed from office by imperial order, his superior will dispatch an agent to get the seal of office from him.

[Amended, p. 141:] When an official is guilty of an offense 犯事 and must be instantly relieved of his post--thus being unable to wait for the arrival of the duly appointed person to take over the office--the governor-general (and/or) governor is to dispatch an agent immediately and ask the official to surrender the seal of office, so that he can depart from his post.

122. LI JEN 離任 Departure from the post

When an official leaves his post, either because of the observance of mourning for a parent or on account of impeachment, it is known as "departure from the post."

123. CHIEH JEN 解任 Relieved of duty

When an official is guilty of an offense and must be summoned for questioning, he is to be relieved of his official duties for the duration 暫停其職守.

124. CHIANG-CHI 降級 Lowering of rank

An official guilty of offense (s) is to be demoted from his (present) position by one, two, or three classes.

125. HSIEH SHIH 卸事 Handing over the office

Handing over one's administrative duties to be performed by another person.

126. FA FENG 罰俸 Forfeit of salary

An official guilty of a minor offense is punished, as decided by the Board (of Civil Appointment), by forfeiting his salary up to one, or two, or three years.

127. CHIANG TIAO 降調 Demotion and transfer

After being demoted (an official) is transferred to a different position of corresponding [i.e., the demoted] rank.

128. LIU JEN 留任 Retained at post

An official guilty of a minor offense who has been demoted or deprived of title may stay on at his original post.

129. CHU FENG 住俸 Withholding of salary

When an official is (absent owing to) the death of a parent, or to some disciplinary action, his salary from the first day of absence is computed and withheld from him. [Text: K'ai-ch'üeh chih jih wei-shih 開缺之日為止；止 is a misprint for shih 始 .]

130. HSING FENG 行俸 Field salary

The regular salary of a [metropolitan] official traveling on government mission is paid in the capital, while he personally receives another sum as salary in the province. This is called "field salary." (*Also known as "withholding salary" 住俸 [sic?].)

131. CHIANG-FENG 降俸 Reduction of salary

The salary of a demoted official is also reduced accordingly.

132. T'ING FENG 停俸 Stopping of salary

The salary of an official absent owing to illness or to his being in mourning for parent's death is stopped. [Cf. 129.]

133. CH'U FENG 除俸 Elimination of salary

When an official is deprived of office for some cause, his salary is eliminated [from the government payroll].

134. T'ING SHENG 停陞 Temporary exclusion from advancement

An official's minor offense is placed on record, and he is excluded from advancement for three months.

135. CHIANG-FENG ERH-CHI 降俸二級 Reduction of salary by two classes

The salary of a guilty official is reduced to the level of two classes below (his present position).

136. CH'ANG-CH'UAN TAI FENG 常川帶俸 Continuation of original salary

High officials commanding defense forces on the Western frontier [concurrently] hold their respective metropolitan posts, and continue to receive their regular salaries for these posts even though they have been appointed to offices in the provinces. [Text: Hsi-yü 西域. This clearly refers to the frontier areas such as Sinkiang, and not to the Western Regions of traditional history.]

137. FU-KUO HUAN-CHIH 附過還職 Restored to office but bearing record of demerit

In case an official (is guilty of a misdeed and) should be dismissed from office, his superior [may] take into consideration the fact that he is ordinarily diligent and prudent 勤謹, and restore him to his office after placing his demerits on record.

138. HUAN-CHIH 還職 Restored to office

Same as above [137] but without recording the demerit.

[[7]] Avoidance; retirement; further punitive measures.
Nos. 139-150

139. HUI-PI 迴避 Avoidance

When (members of the same family such as) father and
son, uncle and nephew, older brother and younger brother,
and other relations become officials in the same province,
the one(s) of lower rank is required to practice avoidance
by serving in another province. [This is a simplified
statement in explanation of a vastly elaborate system that
prescribes the rule of avoidance for members of the
same extended family. Not only the official rank of the
individual members but their mutual kinship relations are
also taken as the basis to decide who ought to avoid whom.
Kuang-hsü hui-tien, 10:3a-b. Similar rules in some
instances prevail among persons who come from neighboring districts or provinces, and those who bear tutor-
disciple relationships toward each other. Avoidance is
observed not only in appointments to office, but also in
the public examinations. See KHHT, 10:3a-b, 33:3; and
Kuang-hsü hui-tien shih-li, ch. 35, 47.]

140. P'ING-HSING 平行 Equal rank

(Officials) of the same rank and class, who therefore do
not have the responsibility of supervising one another, are
known as of "equal rank."

141. HSIU-CHIH 休致 Retirement

When an official has become aged and useless his superior
will memorialize for his retirement with retention of his
latest rank.

142. KUEI-NUNG 歸農 Retire to the farm

To resign from one's post and return home to tend the

family farm.

143. CHIANG-CHIH ERH-CHI 降職二級 Demoted by two classes

That is, actual demotion by two classes.

144. CHUNG-YANG 終養 Care (of parents) until the end

Provincial officials who have aged parents are permitted to ask for leaves of absence, so that they may go home to care for their parents. They may be reappointed to posts after the parents' deaths.

145. YÜAN-KUAN CHIH-SHIH 原官致仕 Retire with the original official title

(*See below) [146].

146. KAO-PING CH'I-HSIU 告病乞休 Request for retirement due to ill health

An aged and sick metropolitan or provincial official is permitted to petition in his own behalf for retirement due to ill health. His superior, after verifying the facts and considering the official's record of performance, will memorialize in his behalf, and ask for retention of his original official title while he is relieved of his official responsibilities. To those with the highest merit a half salary may be granted for life.

147. CHIA I-CHI CHIANG ERH-CHI CHIN CHIANG I-CHI TAI-TSUI T'U-KUNG 加一級降二級今降一級戴罪圖功 Advanced one class but demoted two classes, now [therefore] demoted one class; bearing guilt in anticipation of merit

If an official was first advanced one class for merit, but now should be demoted two classes on account of some offense, the Board will let one of the latter cancel the advancement, and still lower his rank by one class. He is then ordered to work for new merit while bearing the record of his offense.

148. T'ING CH'I SHENG-CHUAN TAI-TSUI T'U-KUNG 停其陞轉戴罪圖功 Excluded from advancement, bearing guilt in anticipation of merit

If an official is guilty of a very minor offense, he need
not be lowered in rank, but is to have the offense placed
on record and be excluded from advancement in office for
three months. The rest is the same as above [147].
[Text: ch'i-ch'ing 其輕 ; 其 is a misprint for shen 甚 .]

149. SUI JEN-NEI YU TS'AN-FA I-YU CHI-LU 雖任內有
參罰亦有紀錄 During (an official's) term of office
there were recordings of merit as well as impeachments
and penalties

Example: at the end of a district magistrate's term of
office his superior official is to give his performance a
general evaluation as to its merits and demerits. If during
the term (the magistrate) has been advanced in grade and
awarded recordings of merit as well as having been subject
to impeachment and forfeit of salary, the merits and
demerits may be considered as of equal weight and allowed
to cancel each other. (*The value of one recording of
merit is slightly less than that of an advancement in grade.)

150. YÜ HSIN-JEN-NEI FA-FENG I-NIEN 於新任內罰俸
一年 Forfeiture of one year's salary in the new post

Example: if an official was sentenced to forfeiture of
two years' salary in his previous post, but after one year
is promoted or transferred to a new office, then one year's
salary of the latter will still be forfeit to make up the
two-year penalty.

[[8]] Absence; mourning. Nos. 151-163

151. YIN KUNG CH'U-CHING 因公出境 Away from the area
on a government mission

[For example,] a local official, upon arrival at his post,
is sent by his superior to (a place) outside the area under
his jurisdiction.

152. YÜAN SHIH CH'U-CHING 緣事出境 Away from the area
for cause

Same as above [151], or away on personal business.

153. FENG-WEI KUNG-CH'U 奉委公出 Away on a government mission

Same as above [151 only].

154. WEN-FU 聞訃 Receiving news of death

Receiving news of father's or mother's death while one is away from home at an official post.

155. TING-YU 丁憂 Mourning for parents

Period in which one wears mourning for parents; also known as "mourning in distress" [ting chien 丁艱].

156. SHOU CHIH 守制 Observance of mourning

The same as mourning for parents [155].

157. TING NEI-CHIEN 丁內艱 Mourning for mother's death

To be in mourning for one's mother is called "mourning for mother's death"; (for father it is called "mourning for father's death" [ting wai-chien 丁外艱]).

158. FU-CH'ÜEH 服闋 Completion of mourning period

According to usage, when (an official) has completed his observance of the prescribed three-year mourning period for a parent he should return to his official career.

159. CH'I-FU 起復 Return to official career

When an official has completed his period of mourning he is to report to the superior official in his home province 本籍上司 and ask for a notification to the Board (of Civil Appointment), whence he is to receive appointment to a post.

160. KUEI-CH'I SHOU-CHIH 歸旗守制 Return to the Banner for observance of mourning.

While a Chinese official observes a mourning period at his home, a Manchu official does so by returning to his own Banner.

161. KUEI TSANG 歸葬 On leave for parents' interment

When an official, whose parents have previously died
but could not be interred [e. g.] owing to the lack of
burial ground, hears from his family, while serving in
another province, that the burial ground has been
arranged for, he is customarily allowed to obtain leave
and return home for the parents' burial.

162. HSING CH'IN 省親 Visiting parents

An official in a province near his home, or serving in
such posts as Chu-k'ao 主考 [Chief examiner], Hsüeh-
cheng 學政 [Provincial Director of Education], etc.,
may, at the end of his term of office while returning to
Peking, obtain a leave of two or three months for a return
home to visit his parents. [In Brunnert "Chief Examiner"
is the rendering for Chu-shih Kuan 主試官 (B. 652 F.).

163. TO-CH'ING CH'I-FU 奪情起復 Return to official career
by curtailing sentiment

When a high official of the provincial government or a high
ranking military officer suddenly receives news of his
parent's death, the Emperor [may] order him to observe
mourning at his post without leave; or if he has already
departed on leave for his home district and the Emperor
desires his service, he may be ordered to proceed to his
appointed post before completing the prescribed period of
mourning; this is called "return to official career by
curtailing sentiment. "

"Curtailing sentiment" refers to the curtailment of one's
filial piety. [Tu fu ssu tao 督撫司道: B. 837 contains
the abbreviated rendering of these designations that I am
using, and enumerates the following officials as those
included in the term: governor-general, governor,
lieutenant-governor, judicial commissioner, salt controller,
and grain intendant.]

[[9]] Legal documents. Nos. 164-165

164. YIN-CHIEH 印結 Sealed bond of guaranty

[For example,] any person coming to Peking for the public examinations, or to obtain an official post by purchase, must offer a sealed bond of guaranty secured by a metropolitan official from his own province. The seal used is that of [one of] the Six Boards.

165. KAN-CHIEH 甘結 Signed receipt; affidavit

When a government office has passed sentence on a case [of litigation], and any property or the like is to be returned to its owner, the latter is ordered to sign a deposition or affidavit indicating his willingness to accept the judgment.

[[10]] References to officials. Nos. 166-201

166. YU-SSU 有司   The authorities concerned

All officials having jurisdiction over the people are called "the authorities concerned."

167. CHIH-SHIH 執事 Official in charge [cf. 69]

An official charged with the conduct of certain specific matters is known as being in charge of such matters. [The Chih-shih Kuan 執事官 given in Brunnert are military and examination officials, and therefore do not fit the present item.]

168. SHANG-SSU 上司 Superior (official)

All those who have the right to control a given official are the latter's superiors.

169. T'UNG-LIAO 同僚 Colleagues

All those who are of equal rank serving together (in a government office) are "colleagues." Also termed "fellow-officials" 同寅 . [T'ung-liao simply means "colleagues" or those who serve at the same time; it is not a term limited to persons of the same rank.]

170. SHU-YÜAN 屬員 Subordinate (official)

Lesser officials under the control of a higher one are called (the latter's) subordinates.

171. PU-LANG 部郎 Department directors of Boards

The yüan-wai-lang 員外郎 (assistant department directors, B. 291) of the Six Boards.

[Amended, p. 141:] The lang-chung 郎中 (department directors, B. 290) and assistant department directors of the Six Boards.

172. CHIN-SHIH KUAN 近侍官 Court officials

All officials, whether high or low, who function at the Court 內廷 are known as "Court officials"--such as [those in offices like] the Grand Council 軍機處 , the Grand Secretariat 內閣 , and so on.

173. NEI-CH'AI 內差 Dispatched from the Court

Officials dispatched from the Court to carry out missions in various offices

174. CH'AI-KUAN 差官 Official agent

A minor official dispatched by a higher one to carry out missions in various places.

175. CH'IN-LIN SHANG-SSU 親臨上司 Immediate superior

The superior official having the closest immediate control (over a subordinate), such as a prefect's controlling a district magistrate.

176. WAI LI 外吏 Outside official

Department and district (magistrates) 州縣(官) in the provinces are also known as "outside officials." [Since this term seems not to include the higher provincial authorities, I have translated it literally and not as "provincial officials," which is usually what it means in common parlance.]

177. AI TZU-FENG 挨資俸 In order of seniority

When officials are [considered for] promotion, the number of years of each person's government service is reviewed, with those showing the most years enjoying seniority. The order in which promotions are made is decided on the basis of the relative seniority (among) the officials.

178. CH'ÜAN-FENG KUAN, PAN-FENG KUAN 全俸官, 半俸官 Full-salaried official; half-salaried official

Those apprentice officials [cf. 47] of the Six Boards in the Capital who, at the end of the three-year period (of apprenticeship), are retained for employment in their respective Boards, are to be given half salaries until they are appointed to (substantive) posts, when full salaries are paid.

179. LI FU-FENG, LI PIEN-FENG 歷腹俸, 歷邊俸 Interior posts; border posts

Among provincial authorities there is a distinction between those serving in (the empire's) border areas and those serving in China proper. After completing three years of service in border areas the officials' chances of promotion will be ten times better than that of the officials who have served in China proper.

180. LIU KUAN 流官 Ranked officials

(*The Ch'ien-lung edition gives liu-nei kuan 流内官 [officials within the ranks]; nei is omitted in the Chia-ch'ing edition.)

Officials who possess rank and class. Liu means ranks and gradations.

181. LIU-WAI KUAN 流外官 Unranked officials

Minor officials who are without rank and class, such as (those known as) "unclassified officials" 未入流.

182. FU TSO 府佐 Assistants to the prefect

Officials who assist a prefect in carrying out his functions, such as the t'ung-chih 同知 (first class sub-prefect,

B. 849) and t'ung p'an 通判 (second class sub-prefect,
B. 849A).

183. TSO-ERH KUAN 佐貳官 Assistant magistrates [of
prefectures, departments, districts]

A general term for officials who help in the work of
prefects and magistrates of the various classes 府州縣
[see B. 856B], meaning (one who works in an) assistant
and secondary capacity. [More specifically, these include
the sub-prefects first and second class (t'ung-chih 同知
and t'ung-p'an 通判 respectively), assistant department
magistrates (chou t'ung 州同 and chou-p'an 州判), and
assistant district magistrates (hsien-ch'eng 縣丞).]

184. FENG-HSIEN KUAN 風憲官 Disciplinary officials

Officials who memorialize on matters learned through
intelligence, and who uphold and maintain the fundamental
laws of government 法度 ; that is, the yü-shih 御史
(provincial censors, B. 213).

185. KUAN-TAI KUAN 冠帶官 Cap-and-sash officials

An official who has been awarded the imperial gifts of
cap and sash. For example, when a new metropolitan
graduate (chin-shih 進士) is appointed to a post he is
always given a garment and a cap.

186. CHENG-YIN KUAN 正印官 Chief magistrate

The chief official in a prefecture, department, or district,
who has custody of the seal of office.

187. FANG-MIEN KUAN 方面官 Territorial officials

Intendants and prefects are known as "territorial high
officials" 方面大員 . [The territorial officials refer
to those who have the authority to govern a territory; i.e.,
the governor-general, the governor, and the intendant;
prefects are not included.]

188. MU-YÜAN 幕員 Official adviser

Among (an official's) personal advisers 幕友 , one who
occupies a formal official position is called an "official
adviser."

189. TSA-CHIH 雜職 Minor posts

> Those who are not chief magistrates [cf. 186] are termed
> [holders of] minor posts; that is, posts of an assistant
> nature. [Text reads: chi tso-erh yeh 即佐貳也.
> This is in contradiction to the definitions as given in
> Hui-tien, in which "tsa chih" and "tso-erh" are two
> distinct official categories. Cf. 84.]

190. CHENG-T'U CH'U-SHEN 正途出身　Holder of regular
graduate ranks

> Those who hold the regular graduate degrees by passing
> the public examinations are called "holders of regular
> graduate ranks." [Cf. 11.]

191. CHIEN-HSÜAN CHÜ-JEN 檢選舉人 Selected provincial
graduates

> (*Chien 檢 [to inspect] is probably a misprint for chien
> 揀 [to select].)

> Those among provincial graduates (chü-jen 舉人)
> who are selected for their knowledge of public affairs
> and appointed to such posts as district magistrates.
> [The procedures known as chien-hsüan were the means by
> which provincial graduates who failed to pass the metro-
> politan examinations were selected to fill various posts.
> An individual provincial graduate was eligible for such
> appointment after failing once, if he was from a province
> remote from the capital; and, if from a nearby province,
> after three times. Such selection took place in Peking and
> was generally referred to simply as chien-hsüan, as is the
> case in the present entry. There was another form,
> however, known as ta-t'iao "grand selection" or ta-t'iao
> chien-hsüan, which was conducted in the provinces by
> specially commissioned officials, and should be distinguish-
> ed from the selection done in the capital. The posts filled
> by the persons selected through either procedure were
> those of district magistrates or instructors in government
> academies; those selected in the capital, however, also
> might be appointed to minor posts in the National College
> of Letters, district assistant magistracy, etc. KHHT,

7:3-4; Ch'ing-shih kao, 117:12b; Wang Ch'ing-yün, Shih-ch'ü yü-chi (1890 ed.; hereafter SCYC), vol. I, chap. "On the Appointment of Provincial Graduates to Official Posts."]

192. CHIAO-HSI KUNG-SHENG 教習貢生 Teaching senior licentiates

Those among the imperial students (kung-sheng 貢生 who are selected for their literary excellence and appointed to teaching positions at the various (government) academies.

193. YAO-MO HSIAO-LI 么麼小吏 Insignificant minor official

When presenting written memoranda to his superior officials, an official of low rank often refers to himself as "insignificant minor official." Yao-mo 么麼 means tiny and humble.

[Amended, p. 141:] Yao-mo means a tiny thing. The term originated in the Han dynasty with Pan Shu-p'i's 班叔皮 [Pan Piao 班彪] Discourse on Royalty [Wang-ming Lun 王命論]. The phrase "insignificant minor official" is used by minor officials when addressing higher ones as a gesture of humility.

194. SO-TSAI KUAN-YÜAN 所在官員 Officials at the said place

Persons at a distant place refer to officials here as "officials at the said place."

195. T'UNG-CH'ENG KUAN-YÜAN 同城官員 Officials of the same city

Those who serve in government posts in the same city are called "officials of the same city."

196. PU-HSI T'UNG-CH'ENG 不係同城 Not of the same city

Those not holding posts in the same city.

197. CHUNG HSING P'ING PO 中行評博 Secretarial and technical staff

These include the chung-shu 中書 (secretaries [clerical], B. 137), hsing-jen 行人 [emissaries],

p'ing-shih 評事 (assistant secretaries, B. 216) and
po-shih 博士 (mathematicians or doctors, B. 229, 412A).
The post of hsing-jen existed still in the Ch'ien-lung period,
but is now defunct.

198. T'I-T'ANG 提塘 Provincial courier

All provincial (governments) maintain officials in the
capital who are charged with the transmission of official
documents. These are called "provincial couriers."
[Cf. 402.]

199. CH'ENG-CH'AI 承差 Deputy in charge

The deputy 委員 who has been assigned to carry out a
certain duty. [Ch'eng-ch'ai 承差 as defined in KHHT,
12:4, is a category of clerks in a governor-general or
governor's office. The text in Hui-tien reads: "...Second,
ch'eng-ch'ai: in addition to the shu-li [also clerks], the
governors-general and governors also have ch'eng-ch'ai..."
The present interpretation therefore appears to be a
variant.]

200. CH'ENG-HSING SHU-PAN 承行書辦 Clerk in charge
of correspondence

The clerk 書吏 who has been ordered by his superior to
take charge of official correspondence.

201. CHING-CHIH 經制 In control

(An official) having the authority to manage and control
[a certain matter] is styled "in control."

[[11]] Administration of tribal areas. Nos. 202-208

202. SHE LIU 設流 Establishment of ranked officials

The setting up of new (posts of) civil officials
who possess rank and class in frontier regions.

203. KAI T'U KUEI LIU 改土歸流 Change from tribal to
regular government

In the native regions of Yunnan, Kweichow, Kwangtung

and Kwangsi, the posts of prefect, etc. , are usually filled
by the local chiefs; these hold hereditary titles and are
known as tribal officials 土官 . As they are often guilty
of willful tyranny, the (posts of) tribal officials are frequently abolished [by the imperial government] and replaced by posts for ranked officials.

204. T'U-CHIH CH'ENG-HSI 土職承襲 Inheritance of
tribal chieftainship

After the death of a tribal official in such provinces as
Yunnan, Kweichow, Kwangtung and Kwangsi, his position
is customarily inherited by his son. This matter is
handled by the Board of Civil Appointment. [The incoming
tribal official's position is formalized by the Board of Civil
Appointment, which confers on him a charter [hao-chih
號紙] stating the post which is being inherited, the
official's genealogy, and the date on which he assumes
office. The old charter held by his predecessor must be
turned in to exchange for the new one. The tribal officials
are "accorded the same treatment by the government as the
ranked officials, " that is, they are "rewarded for their
merits, punished for their misdeeds, given ranks of honor
when they merit imperial favor, and accorded posthumous
awards when they die (in military service). " KHHT,
12:2a-b.]

205. CH'IN-KUNG T'U-TS'E 親供圖冊 Personal report, map
and file

Before the son of a tribal official assumes his inherited
post he is called for a personal interrogation by the high
local authorities, who will submit his [the young chief's]
personal report, together with the map and population
register of his domain to the Board (of Civil Appointment)
for examination.

206. TING-PEI TSUNG-T'U TSUNG CHIH T'U-TS'E 頂輩宗
圖宗支圖冊 Patrilineal chart; lateral kinship chart

The son of the (late) tribal chief is also ordered to draw up
a chart showing his forefathers that had preceded him in this
hereditary post; this is the "patrilineal chart. " He is also

ordered to make a chart depicting all the branches in his clan, as well as write out a copy of the current census of the clan.

207. **TSU-MU LIN-FENG KUNG-CHIEH** 族目鄰封公結
Joint bond by clan leaders and neighboring tribal officials

The son of the (late) tribal chief is also ordered to obtain a joint bond given by the leaders in his own clan and by the tribal officials of neighboring areas. (This bond) together with the above-mentioned charts is forwarded to the Board of Civil Appointment, which will permit (the chief's son) to inherit the post after a thorough examination (of these documents). [The term t'ou-mu 頭目 has been used in more than one context in items 203-207. In the present case it refers not to tribal chiefs but to men of leading status within the chief's family clan.]

208. **T'U-JEN HSIN-FU CH'IN CHIH T'U-SHE CH'ENG-HSI**
土人信服親枝土舍承襲 Inheritance by closely-related tribal leader trusted by the tribal commoners

If a tribal official dies without leaving an heir who can inherit his post, a member of a closely related branch of his clan who is trusted by the tribal commoners is selected, and the Board (of Civil Appointment) is petitioned for permission to inherit the post.

In the Miao territory the ordinary people are termed "tribal commers" 土人, and the ruling class are known as "tribal leader" 土舍.

[[12]] Conventional opening phrases in official documents. Nos. 209-214

209. **TSUN-CHIH CHU-CHIEN SHIH** 遵旨逐件事 In reference to the matter investigated according to imperial command

(*The following [i.e., 209-214] are the formal opening phrases of official communications (from other government offices) to the Board of Civil Appointment.)

When another government office has completed investigation of a certain matter requested by the Board of Civil Appointment according to a previous imperial command, "In reference to the matter investigated according to imperial command" is the phrase used to begin the official communication containing the answer to the Board.

210. FU-KUAN CHIH LIU-P'IN TENG SHIH 服官之流品等事 With reference to the public career, rank and other matters (pertaining to X)

If the Board of Civil Appointment has asked a provincial government to check the public career record of a certain official and this has been done accordingly, (the provincial authorities) will reply to the Board using as the opening phrase "With reference to the public career, rank, and other matters (pertaining to X). "

211. YU-SSU K'AO-CH'ENG WU LI TENG SHIH 有司考成無例等事 With reference to the matter of appraisal of achievements by the authorities concerned, there are no fixed precedents

The prefectural and district officials in the provinces are periodically 每 checked by their superiors for their achievements in office [cf. 86]. There is, however, no fixed precedent as to how soon an official should be appraised, and what method should be employed for checking. Sometimes when the Board of Civil Appointment makes inquiries in the provinces regarding the appraisal of achievements, this (sentence) is the answer given by the provincial authorities.

212. K'EN EN HSIANG-T'I SHENG-PU TENG SHIH 懇恩詳題陞補等事 With reference to the matter of petition for advancement by imperial favor

When an official in some government office is due for advancement, the said office customarily will make the decision and then report to the Board of Civil Appointment. The latter will memorialize for imperial approval of the promotion. This is the opening phrase of the report presented by the said office to the Board.

213. K'EN EN HSIANG-CH'ING T'I FU HSING-SHIH I TUN
PEN-YÜAN SHIH 懇恩詳請題復姓氏以
敦本源事 With reference to the matter of petition for
permission by imperial favor to return to one's original
surname, in order to give due importance to one's origin

If an official in a certain government office desires to
return to his original surname 復姓, he is to petition his
superior, asking the latter to request the Board of Civil
Appointment to memorialize in his behalf. The petition
opens with the above phrase.

"Return to original surname": for example, a given
person's original surname was Li but he had a foster
father by the name of Wang, and (Li's) surname was
changed to Wang. After becoming an official, however, he
wishes to resume the name Li; this can be done only after
it has been memorialized by the Board of Civil Appointment
(for the throne's approval).

214. CH'ING SHENG WU-I CHIH FAN-WEN SHIH 請省無益
之繁文事 With reference to the matter of curtailing
superfluous written communications

Example: in the official correspondence of a government
office there may often be memoranda to various other
government offices that deal with unimportant things; the
administrative staff 司官 of this office then may decide
to petition the chief executives 堂官 to omit such paper
work. The petition opens with the above phrase.

[[13]] Evaluation of officials, I: phrases reporting
good deeds and some specific acts. Nos. 215-252

215. HSING CH'Ü 行取 Special transfer

If among the local magistrates in the provinces there be
any one of exceptional talent and fame, the Board of
Civil Appointment customarily may transfer him to the
capital by written order [to the provincial authorities],
and appoint him to the post of a yü-shih 御史 (provincial

censor) or official of a Board. This was the practice in the K'ang-hsi period, but nowadays is no longer done.

216. HSIEN NENG 賢能 Worthy and competent

(*The following items are phrases of judgment used in the appraisal of achievements). "Worthy" means of virtuous conduct; "competent" means talented.

217. HSÜN LI 循吏 A proper official

One who is honest, incorrupt, and good in his conduct of office is called a "proper official."

218. CHO I 卓異 Outstanding and distinctive

"Outstanding" means having extremely great talents; "distinctive" means being different from others.

[Amended, p. 141:] Once every three years a general appraisal, known as the "great accounting" [see 92], takes place among the provincial officials. Of these the exceptionally talented and capable ones are recommended as being "outstanding and distinctive," and, on imperial instructions, are sent to the Board (of Civil Appointment) and are appointed to higher posts after an audience with the throne.

219. CHING MIN CH'IANG KAN 精敏强幹 Intelligent, efficient, effective, and able

"Intelligent" means to be clear-headed; "efficient," to work with dispatch; "effective," forceful (in what one does); and "able," to be competent.

220. LI-LIEN CHIH TS'AI 歷練之才 A talent which is experienced, and well-versed in the subject matter

Having seen much (of public affairs) constitutes experience, and being well acquainted (with a given subject) is to be well-versed in it.

221. SSU-YING CHIH TS'AI 四應之才 One with well-rounded talent [literally, four-directioned talent]

This indicates that a person's talents are so well-rounded

that he can cope with problems from (all) four directions.

[Amended, p. 141:] This means that a person is endowed with so much talent that he can employ it in any way he pleases to meet the demands of various problems.

222. TS'AI K'AN P'AN-TS'O 材堪盤錯 Ability fit to deal with tortuous and knotty (problems)

There is an ancient saying that "without twisted and knotty wood, the sharpness of an axe cannot be proved." "Twisted and knotty wood" refers to the kind that is bent around, whose grain goes in the wrong directions, and is the most difficult to cut. This is comparable to a task that is difficult to perform. (The over-all meaning of this phrase is that) a given person's talents are fit for dealing with difficult matters.

223. CHU WU TS'UNG-TS'O 諸務叢脞 Everything in a disorderly and useless state

"Disorderly" means confused, without order, and "useless" means ruined and destroyed. This phrase indicates the official (under scrutiny) is incompetent in carrying out his functions.

224. CH'U FAN-CHÜ CHIH JEN 處煩劇之任 Holding a busy and taxing position

"Busy" means there is a large volume of work; "taxing" means the work is demanding. This phrase describes the nature of a given official's post.

225. WU CH'E-CHOU CHIH HUAN 無掣肘之患 No fear of hindrance to his work

When there is hindrance to one's action it is said to be "restraint of the arm," i.e., as when one is prevented from stretching out his hand to reach some thing because his arm has been pulled back, so that he cannot get it. This phrase means a said person has no fear of such hindrance in his work.

226. **CH'ING SHEN CH'IN CHIN** 清慎勤謹 Honest, careful, diligent, and prudent

"Honest" means incorrupt; "careful," not talking or acting unadvisedly 妄 ; "diligent," not indolent; and "prudent," cultivating one's moral conduct.

227. **CHIH-CHENG YÜ-FANG YÜN-K'AN PAO-CHÜ** 治政 有方允堪保舉 A capable administrator quite worthy of recommendation

This means that an official is capable both in governing the people and in administrative work, and is truly worthy of recommendation.

228. **LI-FAN CHIH-CHÜ CHIH TS'AI YU-YÜ FU-CHENG T'I-MIN CHIH HSIN WEI-HSI** 理繁治劇之才有餘敷政 體民之心未細 More than able to take charge of heavy tasks, but not thorough in spreading his adminis-tration and understanding the people

This means that an official has more than enough ability to manage heavy and difficult tasks, but that he lacks complete thoroughness 不能十分細心 in the two things of spreading the benefits of his ministrations to the masses and gaining an understanding of the people's conditions.

229. **HSIU-TSAO T'AI CHAI YEN-CH'A PAO-CHIA** 修造臺寨 嚴查保甲 Repairing and construction of watch towers and strongholds, and strict inspection of [rural] precincts

When there are military activities in a locality, the departmental and district authorities should place it in a state of preparedness by building or repairing the local watch towers 墩台 and private strongholds 寨子 ; further, strict inspection is to be conducted in all the rural precincts so as to prevent the bandits from hiding there.

Towers should be built at intervals of ten li. Below each one are constructed five smoke beacons 烟墩. When an emergency arises a flag is raised on the tower, a cannon is fired, and fire is lighted in the smoke beacons, so that the news can be signaled from place to place.

The officials of bandit-infested areas may also have a
few fortified camps constructed on high ground, and let
the people take refuge in them with their families, bringing
with them foodstuffs, to escape the depredation of the
bandits.

Also, two or three villages may jointly from one chia 甲
[precinct] under a head known as ti-pao 地保 [local
constable], who is charged with keeping track of the
people of the precinct. The presence of bandits (in a
precinct) should be reported to the authorities for proper
punishment.

230. SHIH-HSIN JEN-SHIH 實心任事 Whole-hearted worker

One who does all his work whole-heartedly.

231. HSÜAN-CHIANG SHENG-YÜ SHIH-LIU T'IAO 宣講
聖諭十六條 Exposition of the Sixteen Maxims of the
Sacred Edict

On the first and fifteenth of each month departmental and
district magistrates should gather the local people and read
and expound aloud to them the Sixteen Maxims of the
Sheng-yü kuang-hsün 聖諭廣訓 [Sacred Edict and
Amplifications of the Sixteen Maxims], so that all may
know how to follow the precepts accordingly.

[Amended, p. 142:] Sheng yü kuang hsün: On the first
and fifteenth of each month the hsüeh-kuan 學官 [education-
al officers] of all prefectures, departments, and districts
are required to assemble the (local) gentry and common
people 士庶 at a selected spot and expound to them the
Sacred Edict and Amplifications of the Sixteen Maxims.

The Sixteen Maxims of the Sacred Edict were composed
by the K'ang-hsi Emperor; the Amplifications of the Sixteen
Maxims, the explanatory notes under each article, were
written by the Yung-cheng Emperor.

232. CHÜN-HSÜ K'UNG-CHI TS'ANG-TS'U LI-PAN 軍需孔亟
倉卒立辦 Immediate action in answer to urgent
military needs

When the military forces are in very urgent need for

-39-

provisions and ammunition, (the official mentioned) is able to obtain these expeditiously and send them without delay.

233. CHIEH-LI CHI-KUNG CHI-CHIH I CHEN 竭力急公積滯以振 Exerts effort to expedite government affairs and removes accumulated business

(An official) exerts himself in efficiently restoring to good order all the accumulated government business that has been lagging behind.

234. CH'ENG ERH-CH'IEN-SHIH CHIH LIANG-CHE 誠二千石之良者 Truly a good one among the two thousand shih (officials)

Truly the best official among prefects. In ancient [i.e., Han] times the t'ai-shou 大 [太] 守 was also known as a "two-thousand-shih," because his annual salary was two thousand shih [or tan] of rice; this (post) is the equivalent of the prefect's office at present. [石 as a volume measure (ten tou or pecks) for grain was pronounced shih in ancient times, and tan in later common usage. Cf. my note on the rendering of this term in the "Translator's Notes on General Procedures."]

235. YING CHÜN-HSÜ ERH KUNG-I K'O-CH'IN 應軍需而供億克勤 Diligent in supplying the numerous military needs

An official who is able to supply the multifarious demands of the military forces -- he is indeed diligent.

236. TS'UI FU-K'O ERH SU-PI P'O-CH'ING 催賦科而宿弊頗清 Elimination of some old abuses while collecting taxes

While (an official) is making the usual collection of land-poll taxes 地丁錢粮 from the people he is able to eliminate to some extent long-standing abuses [in tax collection or administration]. [Ti-ting ch'ien-liang: see 416.]

237. MIN LIEN TZ'U K'AI YU [YUN]-K'AN PAO-CHANG I-FANG
敏練慈愷尤 [允] 堪保障一方 Able, experienced, and kindly, worthy to be protector of an area

(An official) is efficient in work and well versed in matters under his charge; furthermore, he is kind by nature and benevolent in the treatment of his subordinates: truly worthy to be [considered] a good official, who can be protector of an area and its people.

238. TS'AI-CH'ING MIN LIEN K'U-HSIN JEN-SHIH 才情敏練 苦心任事 Well talented, experienced, and industrious

(An official) whose talents are not inconsiderable, who is well versed in public affairs, and is also industrious in his work.

239. TAN YA-MEN PU-YEN I-CHIH YÜ-PANG T'ENG I 但衙門 不嚴以致與謗騰矣 But widespread criticism (of him) has arisen because of laxity in the control of (his) office personnel

Although this official has all the above good points, he is unable to exert strict control over his office personnel, so that there have been cases of abusing the people. Consequently there is widespread criticism of him among the public.

240. TZU-HSIN KAI-T'U SHANG K'O-I TS'E-LI 自新改圖尚 可以策勵 Control and exhortation [of his subordinates] are still possible with corrected ways

If the old mistakes are corrected and new and better measures adopted in the conduct [of his office affairs], he can still control and exhort the (subordinate) officials and clerks, so they will not dare mistreat the people [in the future].

241. YING-CHENG CH'IEN-LIANG CH'ÜAN-WAN 應徵錢粮 全完 Complete delivery of the tax quota

A departmental or district magistrate being able to deliver the complete amount of the year's tax grains and money that he should collect from the people.

242. YEN YIN WU-CH'IEN 鹽引無欠 No arrears in salt
distribution

And he has also (effected) the sale of all the salt allotted
to his area without any amount in arrears. [Terms
referring to the salt administration are to be found in
Chapter II, "The Board of Revenue" (Hu-pu 戶部),
1033-1086.]

243. CHIEH-HSIANG WU-SU 解餉無疎 No carelessness in the
dispatch of funds

When funds are being dispatched (by the said official) to
the Board [of Revenue], precautions are taken along the
way, so that there is no loss due to robbery resulting
from (his) carelessness.

244. TU-K'EN HUANG-TI 督墾荒地 To supervise the opening
of unused land

(An official) leading the people in putting unused land
under cultivation and planting it with grain.

245. TSENG-CH'U JEN-TING HU CHIEH T'AO-JEN SHIH-CHI
增出人丁獲解逃人實績　True achievements
in population increase and in the capture and delivery
of fugitives

There is an increase in population in the area under a
departmental or district **magistrate**, and fugitives from the
Eight Banners [t'ao-jen 逃人] are captured and sent to
Peking; these two are true achivements (of the said official).
[T'ao-jen is a legal term that refers specifically to fugitives
from the Eight Banners. In early Ch'ing these persons also
included Chinese slaves who deserted, but generally they
comprised Bannermen of low social status escaping from
their Manchu masters. See KHHT, 57:2b-3b; and Ma Feng-
ch'en, "Manchu-Chinese Social and Economic Conflicts in
Early Ch'ing," tr. E-tu Zen Sun and John DeFrancis, in
Chinese Social History (Washington, 1956), pp. 333-351.]

246. YU-CHIEN I-TZ'U CHI-LU SHIH-TZ'U 有薦一次紀錄
十次 One recommendation and ten recordings of merit

This official has been previously recommended once, and

had his merits recorded ten times [see 33, 37].

247. CHING HSIANG SHEN CHUNG 精詳慎重 Thoughtful, careful, cautious and deliberate

Being clear-minded, careful, and cautious in work, not given to carelessness.

248. SUI-CHIH SUI-CHIEH 隨至隨結 Once undertaken, immediately accomplished

Government business is accomplished with great dispatch and without delay.

249. TS'AN-CHO CH'ING FA 參酌情法 To deliberate (so as to balance) humanity and law

To obtain an equilibrium between (considerations of) humanity and of law through prolonged comparison and deliberation.

250. PU-K'AN YU-AI 不堪有碍 Impermissible and harmful

A harmful and impermissible action. [Naitō notes on p. 147 (in the "Addendum on textual comparisons") that, on the basis of the Manchu version, k'an ought to read shen 甚 . Thus, the above phrase would be pu-shen yu-ai, "not too unsuitable."]

251. TSE-CH'ENG CHIH FA 責成之法 The method of giving (an official) special responsibility

To charge a person with the responsibility of carrying out a specific duty, with a view to obtaining definite results.

252. MI-WU TS'UNG-SHIH 密勿從事 Careful performance

(An official) exerts great effort in performing his public duties.

[Amended, p. 141:] Mi-wu: careful and guarded. (This phrase) means one performs one's official duties in a careful and guarded way.

[[14]] Evaluation of officials, II: phrases reporting
illegal or corrupt deeds. Nos. 253-385

253. PA FA 八法 The eight proscriptions

In the appraisal of officials there are eight things that are
considered the most illegal. These are called the "eight
proscriptions." [During the Chia-ch'ing period the eight
proscriptions were changed to the liu fa 六 法 , the six
proscriptions, which are listed in KHHT as follows:
(1) improper in conduct; (2) tardy, weak, and incompetent;
(3) shifty and hasty; (4) incapable; (5) aged; (6) in ill-health.
These are the general standards used in the scrutiny of
officials. It is specifically stated that officials who are
avaricious or cruel are individually impeached, but that
these characteristics are not included in the six proscriptions. KHHT, 11:4. Cf. note under 261.]

254. T'AN-K'U 貪酷 Avaricious and cruel

"Avaricious" means accepting bribes; "cruel" means
mistreatment of the people.

255. T'AN-LI 貪戾 Avaricious and perverse

To be against human sentiment is to be perverse.

256. T'AN-LIEH 貪劣 Avaricious and inferior

To be degraded and without ability is to be inferior.

257. T'AN-TS'AN 貪殘 Avaricious and oppressive

To be fierce and unkind is to be oppressive.

258. FOU TSAO 浮躁 Shifty and hasty

"Shifty" means to be restless in character; "hasty"
means lacking patience.

259. CH'ING-FOU 輕浮 Flippant and shifty

"Flippant" means to be unrespectable in conduct.

260. PAO-LI 暴戾 Tyrannous and perverse

> To be violent-tempered is tyrannous. For "perverse" see above [255].

261. PU-CHIN 不謹 Improper

> Any action of an official which does not conform to the correct bureaucratic style is termed "improper." (*The above are the eight proscriptions [253].) [Not all of the eight proscriptions are to be found in 254-261, which list only four of the proscriptions in force before the Chia-ch'ing period. The eight are: (1) avarice; (2) cruelty; (3) tardiness and weakness; (4) impropriety in conduct; (5) age; (6) illness; (7) incapability; and (8) shiftiness and hastiness. Thus, 254-257 appear to be different expressions of the same offenses; the same is true of 258 and 259. The rest of the eight proscriptions are in 268, 274, 276. Cf. Wen-hsien t'ung-k'ao, 5:5404.]

262. T'AN-LAN 貪婪 Greedy

> (One who is) avaricious for bribes, and vilely corrupt besides.

263. TSANG KUAN 贓官 Corrupt official

> An official who is not clean-handed.

264. CH'ING KUAN 清官 Honest official

> The opposite of "corrupt official" [263].

265. SHOU TS'AI 受財 Accepting money

> Receiving money [or other valuables] from others [i.e., being bribed].

266. PAO-TSU 苞苴 Wrapped package

> (An official,) having been bribed, does not perform his duties seriously, so that many matters are often badly glossed over. [To receive a] "wrapped package" means to cover up [for some person].

> [Amended, p. 142:] Bribery. In the old days there were some people who paid bribes but feared detection. Therefore

(the bribes) were covered with grass wrappings as a means of concealment. Hence bribery is referred to as receiving a "wrapped package. "

267. KUO-FU 過 付 Transmittance

To pass along the bribe (to another person).

268. TS'AI-LI PU-CHI 才 力 不 及 Incapable

Both the talent and the ability (of an official) are below standard.

269. PU-CHIH 不 職 Unfit for the post

A person's talent is not sufficient for a (specific) post.

270. PU-CH'EN-CHIH 不 稱 職 Unsuitable for the post

Same as the previous item [also cf. 77].

271. PU-HSIAO 不 肖 Unseemly

(An official's) behavior does not conform to the (pattern of) correct conduct of officials; that is, it shows a low-grade, inferior personal character.

272. NI CHIH 溺 職 Disgracing the post

Vile behavior constituting a blemish on the official position; or not being sufficiently endowed with ability to qualify for officialdom.

273. K'UANG KUAN 曠 官 Truant official

(One who) leaves all the duties of an official position unattended and undone.

274. LAO-PING 老 病 Aged and ill

(An official) who is old and in ill health, unable to take up responsibilities.

275. KUAN KUAN 瘝 官 Sick official

An official is in ill health but does not resign from his post, as if making the position ill also. Kuan 瘝 means to be sick.

276. P'I-JUAN 罷(同疲)軟 Tardy and weak

> To be ineffective is weak; to be slow and delaying
> (in action) is tardy.

277. P'I-WAN 罷玩 Tardy and trifling

> For "tardy" see the previous item. "Trifling" means
> to toy with government business.

278. TAI-WAN 怠玩 Indolént and trifling

> Having a lazy and idle character, and trifling with
> government business.

279. SU-HU 疎忽 Careless

> Mistakes or omissions in the conduct of government
> business resulting from lack of care are referred to as
> "careless" (conduct).

280. LAN-TO 懶惰 Lazy and idle

> To love comfort and ease is to be lazy, and to be not
> diligent is to be idle.

281. T'A-JUNG 闒茸 Fuzzy-headed

> Having an unclear mind and a weak will, and being unable
> to exert oneself to meet situations: this is called
> "fuzzy-headed."

282. YÜ-HUAN 迂緩 Obstinate and slow

> To insist on one's own view is to be obstinate; to be
> slow in tempo is to be slow.

283. T'OU-AN 偷安 Loafing

> To seek ease and leisure without regard [or without
> attending] to government business is termed "loafing."

284. PU-CHÜEH SHIH CH'IU 不覺失囚 Not realizing the
prisoner's escape

> An agent charged with bringing a prisoner (to another
> place) is negligent in taking precautions or properly
> guarding him en route, so that the prisoner escapes

without his knowing.

285. SHIH-YÜ CHIEN-TIEN FANG-FAN 失於檢點防範
Negligent in inspection, roll-call, and preventive measures

See the previous item.

"Inscription" means to examine; "roll-call" means to check the prisoners by calling them [individually] by name.

286. MAO MING TAI-T'I 冒名代替 Posing under a false name

To assume the name of another person in order to take a public examination or fill an appointment in the latter's behalf.

287. KUEI-PI 規避 Avoidance of difficulty

Intending to avoid [judgment for] one's misdeeds is called "avoidance of difficulty."

[Amended, p. 142:] In the intentions and actions of an official all the following are termed "avoidance of difficulty": to choose the easy over the difficult, pleasure over hardship, gain over [immediate] disadvantage, and merit over demerit.

288. HSING-CHIH PU-TUAN 行止不端 Unprincipled conduct

Everything that (this person) does is depraved and improper.

289. TAI-MAN WU-SHIH 怠慢悞事 Bungling an affair through indolence

An indolent official is tardy in carrying out his official duties, thus bungling the matter.

290. YEN-YÜ AO-MAN 言語傲慢 Arrogant in speech

(An official's) speech is unreasonably proud and lacking in humility and courtesy, indicating that he is scornful of others.

291. MENG-MEI CHIH-MI 朦昧執迷 Unenlightened and prejudiced, or stupid and bigoted

(An official) is without a clear thought in his head yet stubbornly holds fast to his private opinions; his actions resemble the gropings of a lost person.

292. HSING-CHIH YU-K'UEI 行止有虧 Wanting in moral conduct

(An official's) moral character is not satisfactory, with much that is wanting.

293. YU-CHAN KUAN-CHEN 有玷官箴 A blemish to officialdom

(An official's) unprincipled conduct is a shame to officialdom.

294. KANG-PI HSING-CH'ENG 剛愎性成 By nature un-yielding and self-willed

"Unyielding" means a temperament that is not harmonious; "self-willed" means extremely self-confident and not heeding others' advice. (This phrase) depicts one who is naturally of such a character.

295. LI-YÜ HSÜN-HSIN 利欲薰心 Blinded by desire for gain

(An official) is originally well-intentioned, but he has been corrupted by the attraction of money [and other material gains].

296. HSING T'UNG MU-OU 形同木偶 Resembling a wooden figure

An official is incapable of doing his work, just like a figure made of wood.

297. T'AN-LAN PAI CHIEN 貪婪敗檢 Greed has destroyed one's moral character

Too many instances of greed and graft (perpetrated by this official) have ruined the good points of his usual moral self-discipline.

298. YU-CHAN CH'ING-PAN 有玷清班 A stain on the pure group

The offices of the Han-lin Yüan 翰林院衙門 (Hanlin Academy) are exalted places of high standards, whose members are referred to by outsiders as the "pure group."

If, however, among the members here there are those who are morally depraved, then these (persons) constitute "a stain on the pure group."

299. YU-JU KAO-P'I 有辱皋比　Unworthy of the tiger skin

Kao-p'i means tiger skin. In ancient days noted scholars used to sit on tiger skins while giving lectures, hence an educational officer is referred to nowadays by this term. (This phrase) means that an official having teaching responsibilities in schools should set an example by being morally upright, otherwise he will be unworthy of his position.

[Amended, p. 141:] Kao-p'i: tiger skin, pi 比 pronounced p'i [i.e., "skin"]. In ancient times teachers all used to sit on tiger skins while lecturing. Nowadays this (term) is used to denote the position of a school teacher.

300. YEN-HSI TZU-YU 偃息自由　Freely indulging in leisure

When an official is concerned only with comfort and ease, and willfully lets government business pass unattended, he is said to be "freely indulging in leisure."

301. HU-YING PU-LING 呼應不靈　Not effective in command

When an occasion arises and a superior official is either unable to summon his subordinates as needed, or to have his orders obeyed (by them), then he is described as "not effective in command."

302. SHIH-YÜ CHUEH-CH'A 失于覺察　Neglected to investigate

If in a matter that requires investigation before [action is taken] (an official) neglects so to investigate, he is guilty of an offense.

303. CH'IEN-CH'AI PU-SHEN 簽差不慎　Lacks care in making assignments

When a superior official assigns office runners [to do certain tasks] he should select the persons with care. If tricky and dishonest persons are mistakenly given the assignment, so that corrupt deeds are (later) committed, he is said to "lack care in making assignments."

304. SHIH-CH'A MAO-K'AI 失察冒開 Fraudulent accounts not checked

[Some] office clerks present padded financial accounts with the intention to embezzle. If their superior official does not verify the details carefully, when the fraud is later uncovered he should be punished.

305. CH'ENG SHEN CH'UAN-TS'O 承審舛錯 Erroneous trial of a case placed in one's charge

When (an official), who has been delegated by his superior to try [certain] criminals, does not conduct the trial with careful deliberation, resulting in errors and misjudgments, he is to be handed over to the Board (of Punishment) for severe punishment.

306. PI-NAN CHIU-I 避難就易 To avoid the difficult and choose the easy [cf. 287]

To shun difficult work and prefer loafing [cf. 283] in one's conduct of affairs. Such as, for example, choosing the easier of two tasks for oneself, leaving the more difficult for others to do.

307. FEI-FA HSING-SHIH 非法行事 To take action not according to regulations

In the performance of one's official duties one should abide by the laws 律法. It is considered an offense to act willfully contrary to the established system of government 法度.

308. HSÜ-WEN FAN-YEN 虛文泛言 Empty words and generalities

"Empty words" denotes much verbiage with little substance; "generalities" means to speak broadly in general terms without pointing to a specific issue. Officials should not discuss anything in such a manner.

309. PU-HSING K'AI-PAO 不行開報 Failed to report [the catastrophe]

In case (a certain area) has suffered from flood or

drought, it is the duty of the department or district magistrate having jurisdiction over that area to investigate (the situation) and list the number of persons injured or made homeless, and send the report to his superior (along with a) request for relief. If this action [of the magistrate] is delayed the superior official is by regulation allowed to impeach him by memorial. The charge reads: "At place X, the responsible local official 該管官 has failed to report the number of persons who are victims of the catastrophe."

310. CH'U-JU PU-CH'ANG 出入不常 Irregular visiting

It is an established regulation that, aside from seeing their superiors for government business, the department or district magistrates in the provinces are not allowed frequent visits to their superior officials. Anyone who acts contrary to the regulation and visits his superior's office frequently when no government business is involved should be impeached on the ground that "this official engages in irregular visiting of his superior's office, and it is feared he may be seeking favors or committing other such dishonest acts." [Cf. 340.]

311. T'AN-SHIH PU-SHIH 彈事不實 The impeachment is unfounded

The function of censors is to impeach (any) official whether he be metropolitan or provincial, high or low, and an impeachment is sustained if the charges are based on actual misdeeds. If it is not based on true fact, however, then it will be said that "the impeachment is unfounded." (*The impeaching memorial of a censor is known as "balance document," 彈章 meaning that it acts like the balancing of a scale 彈天平 whereby inequities are remedied.)

312. WANG-NIEH CHIH-SHIH 妄捏摭拾 Fabricating, and collecting hearsay

"Fabricating" means to make up [tales] at will on non-existent matters; "collecting hearsay" means to gather rumors that have been circulating among various people.

Both are dishonest acts that victimize others.

313. **KU-SHENG CHIH-CHIEH** 故生枝節 Deliberately creating complications

Example: when a major affair is about to be concluded a scheming person purposely derives some other matter from it, so as to involve certain people therein. [This process] is like lateral branches growing from the trunk of a tree.

314. **KOU SO LO-CHIH** 鉤索羅織 To hook, search, and entrap

"To hook" 鉤 means to induce or seduce others with talk; "to search" 索 is to look for wrongs where no crime exists; and "to entrap" 羅織 means to lay a trap for others to [fall in and] commit a wrong. All these are crimes in scheming to victimize other persons.

315. **TUNG-SHIH CH'Ü FA** 動事曲法 Habitually unjust in legal judgments

When passing sentence on a criminal the authorities 官府 should always follow the Code [or statutes and precedents] 律例 without partiality or error. If a person who ought to receive heavy punishment is given a light sentence, or one who should receive a light penalty is given a heavy one, then (the official) is "unjust in legal judgments." (The present item) means that he passes unjust sentences very frequently and is very unfair. [Ch'ü fa 曲法 , literally, "twisting of law" or "twisted law."]

316. **HSI KAI WEN-CHÜAN** 洗改文卷 Erasing and alteration of (official) papers

(*The word kai 改 "alteration" is omitted in the Chia-ch'ing edition and in the annotated edition 註本 reads huan 換 "changing" instead.)

To wash off and make changes in the original wording of official communications and records. This is a dishonest act done by clerks.

317. WANG-SHENG I-I 妄生異議 Unreasonable dissent

When the opinion of one or two persons is different from that of all the others, and it is unreasonable as well, then it is termed "unreasonable dissent."

318. MENG-LUNG PAO-CHÜ 朦朧保舉 Recommendation made without clear knowledge

Example: a subordinate official, having accomplished some meritorious act, asks his superior to memorialize a recommendation (in his behalf), and the latter proceeds to recommend him without having first looked into the extent or validity of the merit. This is known as "recommendation made without clear knowledge."

319. KUNG CHIN PU KUO 功僅補過 The merit is only sufficient to offset the demerit

Example: an official who previously was guilty of an offense later achieves some merit, and the latter's extent corresponds to that of the demerit. In this case the two will just cancel each other, and he is not to receive any further rewards.

320. P'IEN-JEN HSI NU 偏任喜怒 Partial treatment (of subordinates), [literally, giving vent to one's likes and dislikes]

A superior official's proper attitude [toward subordinates] should be absolutely fair without the least partiality. If he rewards the favorites and penalizes those whom he dislikes, he is indulging in partisan use of his [personal] likes and dislikes, and is unjust. [Cf. 366.]

321. CHIH ERH PU-CHÜ 知而不舉 Knowingly not reporting (misdeeds)

When a superior official learns of misdeeds on the part of any of his subordinates, he should memorialize an impeachment. When a department or district magistrate finds out the misdeeds committed by clerks and runners, he should report them [to his superiors]. Otherwise (these officials will be) "knowingly not reporting

misdeeds, " and will be considered also guilty when such
are discovered.

322. CHIAO-CHIEH P'ENG-TANG 交結朋黨 Formation of
cliques

An official should consider government business as the
only important thing regardless of personal relations
情面 . If cliques are formed among colleagues, then
the latter are liable to exercise mutual protection.
Therefore, the action [i.e., formation of cliques] is
prohibited.

323. AN-YAO JEN-HSIN 暗邀人心 Clandestinely courting
popularity

(*Yao 邀 "courting" means to "establish, " chieh 結 .)

The proper conduct of an official is to be just and fair
in the carrying out of his duties without regard to others'
opinions. If (an official) disregards the laws of the land
國法 and strives only for popularity, he is said to be
"clandestinely courting popularity. "

324. I-CH'IU CHIN-CH'Ü 以求進取 Angling for advancement
and gain

An official should consider government business as the
only important thing. He who exerts himself to please
his superior as a stepping stone to advancement, or as
a way to attain fame and material gain, is not a good
official.

325. YU-KAN FA-CHI 有干法紀 Violation of laws and
regulations

How can an official be considered not guilty, if he acts
willfully so that the laws of the country are violated,
and the regulations of the government are contradicted?

326. KAN MING FAN I 干名犯義 Contrary to ethics and
justice

The laws of the land 國法 do not permit an official to
act either against the ethical teachings 名教 or in

-55-

contradition to common justice 公義 .

327. CHUNG-T'U TOU-LIU 中途逗留 Delaying en route

When a subordinate official is sent on a mission by his superior, he should be expeditious both in going and returning. Purposely dallying while on the way is called "delaying en route." [...]

328. I-TS'O KUO-SHIH 遺錯過失 Guilty of omission or error

(An official) is considered guilty because of omission or error in carrying out his official duties.

329. WEI-HSIEN, CHAN-HSIEN 違限, 展限 Infraction of the time limit; postponement of the time limit

All matters administered by the Board (s) are to be completed according to time schedules. When (a thing) is not done within the time limit it is considered an infraction of the regulations, and [the officials concerned] are to be punished. If, however, a particular matter is too complicated for completion within the time limit, an extension may be obtained by memorializing the throne.

"Extension" refers to a lengthening (of the limited period). [Cf. 332.]

330. CH'IH-YEN SU-FANG 遲延疎防 Delay; negligent in preventive measures

When a subordinate official, having been ordered by his superior to take charge of a certain matter, fails to report the results after a long period, it is called "delay."

When criminals in the charge of a department or district magistrate break from prison and escape, the said magistrate has committed the offense of being "negligent in preventive measures." [Cf. 285.]

331. CH'IN PU AN-CHIEN 欽部案件 A case referred by the throne to the Board

A case referred by imperial order to the Board for deliberation. [This phrase also refers to cases tried by a local official but rejected by the Board of Punishment.]

332. YÜ-HSIEN PU-CHI I-YUEH 逾限不及一月 Over the time-limit by less than one month

Usually anything done in more than the prescribed time limit is subject to punishment [cf. 329], but (the officials responsible for the delay) may be pardoned if the extra time amounts to less than one month.

333. SHAN-KOU SHU-KUAN 擅勾屬官 Arbitrarily arresting [one's own] subordinate official

If the subordinate of a superior official has been accused at court by others and should undergo trial, then (the superior) should memorialize for removal (of the subordinate) from his post, so that the latter can participate in the trial. If he sends office runners to arrest the subordinate on his own authority without memorializing, then he has "arbitrarily arrested his own subordinate," and is punishable according to regulations.

334. KUNG-SHIH CHI-CH'ENG 公事稽程 Procrastination in government affairs

Prolonged delay in the conduct of government business.

335. FU-YÜ WU-FANG 撫馭無方 Inept in governance

A local official 地方官 having no effective means of caring for and administrating the affairs of the people.

336. SHIH-YÜ FU-I 失於撫義 Contrary to the principles of good administration

A local official not acting according to the principle of caring for the common people.

337. CHI-PIEN LIANG-MIN 激變良民 Goading law-abiding people to revolt

A harsh and tyrannous local official rousing the anger of law-abiding people, thus causing rebellion and riots to take place.

338. LI PEI CHIEN TZ'U 立碑建祠 Establishing tablets [or stone monuments] and construction of shrines

It is considered a grave infraction of the prohibitory

laws for a local official to order the people to set up "merit tablets" 功德碑 and build "life-time shrines" 生祭祠 [i.e., shrines erected to a living person] in his honor.

339. **CHIAO- T'UNG CH'U-JU** 交通出入 Keeping up a relationship

When officials in the provinces make friends with those in high metropolitan positions, carrying on correspondence with them and seeking favors, it is known as "keeping up a relationship."

340. **PEN-TSOU CH'I MEN** 奔走其門 Running to his house

(This means) a subordinate makes frequent visits to the home of his superior official. [Cf. 310.]

341. **LING K'AI PIEN-MEN** 另開便門 Opening of a side-gate

A provincial official opens a small side-gate in his office building, so that his personal followers may have free access [to him] and commit dishonest acts.

342. **I-SHU CHIEN-SUNG** 貽書薦送 Sending letters to make nominations or give presents

(This refers to) such acts as sending letters to a colleague to nominate a personal favorite [for a post], or to give presents [to other officials]. [Cf. 347.]

343. **YU-K'O YU-LING** 遊客優伶 Idlers and actors

[The acts of] an official must be very well-advised. No idle visitors and actors [or opera singers] should be allowed to stay at the official residence, and infraction of this prohibition is severely punished.

344. **K'OU-CHIEN YUEH-LIANG** 扣減月糧 Withholding monthly provisions

An official is not permitted to discount or deduct the slightest amount from the monthly provisions due the clerks and runners serving under him.

345. TI-CHIA MAI-WU 低價買物 Buying goods at low price

> Regulations prohibit all officials from abusing their
> positions to mistreat merchants, and pay low prices for
> high quality goods.

346. K'UEI-TUAN CHIA-CHIH 虧短價值 Short payment of (an agreed) price

> Prices previously agreed upon between government buyers
> and merchants must be paid in full, and should not be
> purposely paid short.

347. K'UEI-SUNG LI-WU 餽送禮物 Sending presents

> Officials of low rank should not send presents to their
> superiors, lest it be an infraction of law [cf. 342].

348. LI-CHIEH WANG-LAI 禮節往來 Exchange of gifts

> Even among officials of the same rank the mutual exchange
> of gifts on festivals is prohibited.

349. CH'ENG-SHUN FENG-YING 承順逢迎 Blind agreement and anticipation [or yessing and guessing]

> A subordinate official should not flatter and agree with
> his superior without regard to the advisability of a
> [proposed] act; nor sould he anticipate by guessing at
> the ideas of his superior so as to fall in with the latter.

350. PAI-SHOU HSING-HO 拜壽行賀 Offering felicitations on birthdays and other occasions

> It is against the regulations for a subordinate official
> to congratulate his superior on the latter's birthday, or
> to celebrate any of the latter's happy occasions.

351. HSING-HUI HAI-MIN 行賄害民 Mistreating the people under the protection of bribes

> A department or district magistrate who bribes his
> superior official and, relying on the latter's protection,
> mistreats the people at will, is said to "mistreat the
> people under the protection of bribes."

352. YIN-YÜAN T'UNG-HUI 夤緣通賄 Bribery through
   intrigue

   An official should not present bribes to his superior in
   the house of the latter's relatives or friends while no
   one is watching. (*Yin 夤 refers to those hours in the
   morning or evening when no one is present to watch.)
   [Yin-yuan 夤緣 means to climb to high places through
   connections with influential persons. The phrase has
   nothing to do with morning or evening. See Tz'u-hai.]

353. T'UNG-HUI CH'I MIEH 通賄起滅 To initiate or suppress
   [a matter] through bribery

   (*"To initiate" means to begin (action on) a matter; "to
   suppress" means to stop (proceedings relating to) a
   matter.)

   A subordinate official should not bribe his superior
   [for sanction] to undertake something that ought not to
   be done, or to shelve a matter that ought to be done.

354. T'AN-TSANG HUAI-FA 貪贓壞法 Greedy and lawbreaking

   [The law] provides penalties for officials who are greedy
   for bribes and violate the laws and regulations of the land

355. YIN-YÜAN TSO-PI 夤緣作弊 To commit misdeeds by
   bribery

   It is a serious offense for an official to present bribes to
   his superior through an intermediary, hoping that (the
   superior) will relax his vigilance, so that the official
   can commit misdeeds at will.

356. I TS'AI YING-CH'IU 以財營求 Seeking [advancment]
   through money

   A subordinate official who seeks to obtain promotion
   by means of bribes is said to be "seeking advancement
   through money."

357. YANG-WAN YING-KAN 夾浼營幹 Seeking [advantages] through an intermediary

If a subordinate official asks a person trusted by his superior to arrange in his behalf for a lucrative assignment, or filling a post, or any other advantageous thing, it is known as "seeking advantages through an intermediary."

358. HUI-LO KUNG-HSING 賄賂公行 Publicly engaging in bribery

Usually the bribing [of a superior official] by a subordinate, and the receiving of the bribe by the superior, are done clandestinely. However, their boldness [may] increase with the passing of time, so that these acts are done openly without fear of publicity. When provincial censors find this out and impeach them, the offense is termed "publicly engaging in bribery."

359. HSÜ-SO CH'ANG-LI 需索常例 Exaction of customary fees

(*"Customary fees" means fixed perquisites.)

In connection with the appointments of persons handled by the Board of Civil Appointment, all the clerks (of the Board) [customarily] demand money payments from the candidates, each post having its fixed amount [to be paid]. [Cf. 362.]

360. T'UNG-O HSIANG-CHI 同惡相濟 Mutual assistance in evil

Two bad officials mutually helping each other to commit evil deeds and oppress the people.

361. CH'IAO-LI MING-SE 巧立名色 Skillfully set up categories

To establish expense items cleverly, so as to exact money payments from the populace. Example: a department or district magistrate, when collecting the land-poll taxes, exacts additional payments (from the taxpayers) under the pretexts of expenses for stationery, or food costs for the office clerks, etc.

362. TA- TIEN SHIH-FEI 打點使費 Making arrangements
for fees for office personnel

(*"Making arrangements" 打點 is another term for
giving bribes.)

[This refers to] such cases as when a candidate for
appointment to an official post gives presents of money
to the office clerks 書辦 in the Board of Civil Appointment,
in the hope that with the latter's help he may be assigned
to a good post. [Cf. 359.]

363. MAI-FANG JEN-CHIANG 賣放人匠 Laborers [or artisans]
absconding through bribery

[This refers to] such cases as when a laborer [or artisan]
on a government construction project, unwilling to continue
his work owing to very oppressive treatment, gives
presents of money to the clerks in charge of the work [crew],
and the latter, after receiving the bribe, let him abscond.

364. T'UNG-T'UNG T'O-FANG 通同脫放 Allowed to abscond by
agreement

If the construction project is an important one [see 363],
and the minor functionary dares not accede on his own to
the request of laborers [or artisans] to abscond, he will
give half of the bribe to the official in charge of the
construction, and by agreement with the latter, allow the
laborers to do so.

365. CHIA KUNG CHI SSU 假公濟私 Working for private
gain under the name of public business

Using public funds to meet one's private expenditures
under the pretext of [attending to] government business.

366. A-HSÜN PU-KUNG 阿徇不公 Unfair sheltering

When a superior official does not act according to the
principle of fairness in his handling of affairs, but
arbitrarily protects his personal favorite(s), it is known
as "unfair sheltering." [Cf. 320.]   (*"Sheltering" 阿
means protection.)

367. SHUO SHIH KUO CH'IEN 説事過錢 To arrange for
favors and bribes

When a clerk in behalf of others clandestinely negotiates
with the local official, asking for special favors and
offering bribes, it is known as "to arrange for favors and
bribes."

368. T'ING-HSÜ TS'AI-WU 聽許財物 Acceding to request
on account of money [promised]

When office clerks, asking for favors, present money
and other things to their superior official, and the latter
accedes to their requests. [T'ing-hsü ts'ai-wu is an
offense specifically provided for in the Ch'ing Code
(Ta-Ch'ing lü-li, ch. 31), the definition of this term
being "If an official has accepted money or other valuables,
even though they have not yet been received.... the penalty
is to be lighter by one degree (than in the case where the
bribe has been actually received)." The interpretation
given in the present item therefore needs to be modified.
Boulais renders the phrase clearly as "Présents promis
mais non encore reçus." See Guy Boulais, S. J.,
Manuel du Code Chinois, Variétés Sinologiques No. 55
(Shanghai, 1924, hereafter Boulais), p. 659.]

369. HO-CHA CH'IU-SO 嚇詐求索 Blackmail

When office clerks and runners threaten criminals [or
prisoners] with dire consequences as a way to extort
money and other things from them. [Cf. 372.]

370. HSÜ-SO LE-K'EN 需索勒掯 Forced exaction

Officials should be expeditious in the handling of affairs.
Sometimes, in order to obtain fees, a matter is purposely
delayed, thus forcing the person(s) concerned to pay
bribes. This is called "forced exaction." (*"Forced"
勒掯 means to compel.)

371. CH'IN-TAO CH'IEN-LIANG 侵盜錢糧 Embezzlement of
tax funds

[This refers to] a department or district magistrate

embezzling and stealing for his private use the land-poll taxes which he [has collected and] ought to deliver to the provincial treasury

372. I-LE K'UNG-HO 抑勒恐嚇 Extortion with threats

Office runners verbally threatening criminals [or prisoners] so as to exact money payments from them [cf. 369.]

373. YIN KUNG K'O-LIEN 因公科歛 Special levy in the name of government project

A department or district magistrate drawing up a prospectus of money payments and asking the people to contribute toward the carrying out of a government project.

374. CH'IN-CH'I NO-I 侵欺挪移 Embezzlement and transference

(*Ch'i 欺 ["cheating"] is given as ai 挨 in the Chia-ch'ing edition, and as ai 捱 in the annotated edition 註本 ; both are erroneous.)

The amounts of money and grain in the treasury and granary controlled by a department or district magistrate are fixed, and (he) should not make unauthorized use thereof. To keep for private use a portion of the funds for (official) expenditures is called "embezzlement." To delay purposely the carrying out of a matter because (the magistrate) wants to avoid spending the necessary sum is called "procrastination 捱." To use money earmarked for one thing to do something else is called "transference." All three are subject to penalties and call for restitution of the funds [by the guilty official]. [I have translated the sentence on 捱 as given in the text, although neither as individual characters nor as a conventional phrase does ch'in-ch'i no-i have the meaning of "procrastination."]

375. CHIH-CH'ENG HSIU-LI 指稱修理 On grounds of making repairs

A department or district magistrate is also punishable if he uses treasury funds without authorization, on the

ground that repairs have had to be made on his office
building.

376. **CHIA-HAO HENG-CHENG** 加耗橫徵 Extra meltage
fees and unreasonable levies

(*Cheng 徵 is given as cheng 征 in the annotated edition
註本 .)

To collect meltage fees in addition to the regular taxes,
and through tyrannous methods to levy extra amounts
beyond the (tax) quota. (*"Money fees" 火耗 : the
amount unavoidably lost when silver fragments are
melted (to be cast) into whole shoes.)

377. **CHAN-HSI PU-FA** 占郤不發 Withholding payment of
appropriations

(*Chan 占 is given as ku 古 in the Chia-ch'ing edition,
and as k'o 尅 in the annotated edition. Both are
erroneous.)

To withhold a certain portion of appropriated funds that
ought to be paid, or to be unwilling to make prompt
payment because (the official) wishes to save the money.

378. **YIN-NI CH'I-LUNG** 隱匿欺朧, Concealment and deception

When a subordinate official conceals from his superior
a case of murder or robbery within his own territory, and
does not report it; or (when reporting it) makes light of
a serious case in an effort to deceive his superior and hide
his own guilt: these [offenses] are called "concealment
and deception. "

379. **HSÜN-P'I NIEH-CHIEH** 徇庇捏結 (To give) unfair
protection by false report of completion [of a case]

A department or district magistrate, charged with the
capture of bandits or the trial of a legal case, is unable
to finish the business after prolonged delay, and is being
severely pressed by the governor-general (and/or) the
governor. Because of favoritism, however, the intendant or
prefect directly above the magistrate, in order to protect

the latter, fraudulently reports that the case has been
completed. [If] later this is uncovered (the superior)
official) will be punished along with the magistrate.

380. A-TSUNG PU-CHÜ 阿縱不舉 To shelter and connive, and
not report [misdeeds]

An intendant or prefect should report to the governor-
general and governor all misdeeds of the department or
district magistrates under his control. If he knows of
misdeeds but because of favoritism lets them pass without
reporting, then he is also to be punished along with (the
offending magistrate) when the matter is discovered.

381. YU-SSU T'I-TIAO 有司, 提調   Authorities concerned;
proctors

Officials charged with the administration of civil affairs
are called the "authorities concerned," meaning they are
concerned with the people.

For such occasions as the provincial or metropolitan
examinations, or the establishment of an institute 舘 to
compile a gazetteer, etc., a special official will be
designated by the superior official to manage all sundry
matters [pertaining to that particular project]. This
person is known as T'i-tiao 提調 (Proctor), and is discharged when the matter at hand is finished. This post is
filled by a prefect or an intendant in the provinces, and in
the capital by a lang-chung 郎中 (department director)
or yuan-wai-lang 員外郎 (assistant department director)
[of one of the Six Boards].

382. CHIEN-LIN, CHU-SHOU 監臨, 主守 Supervising official;
government clerk or keeper, etc.

During the provincial and metropolitan examinations, in
addition to the Chu-ka'o 主考 [Chief examiner] another
high official is appointed to be the Chien 監 (Inspector),
whose duty it is to prevent the candidates' dishonest
practices, and to protect the examination halls. This post
is filled in the capital by the prefect of Shun-t'ien 順天
府尹 , and in the provinces by the governors-general

and governors. [Chien-lin and chu-shou are two categories
of officials only incompletely described in the present
entry. According to the Ch'ing dynasty Code, chien-lin
is a term applicable to any metropolitan or provincial
official who has subordinates under his supervision, and
whose work entails written communications with other
officials. Chu-shou refers to government personnel who
are custodians of government property, e.g., a clerk
in charge of documents, a treasury-keeper in charge of
grain and funds, a jail warden, etc. Ta-Ch'ing lü-li,
5:97.]

[Amended, p. 141:] Chien-lin, Chih kung-chü 監 臨, 知
貢 舉 Inspector; Supervisor of graduates.

During a provincial examination the governor [of the
province] serves as the inspector; but during a metropolitan
examination in the capital this (post) is filled by the
prefect of Shun-t'ien, who then is known as the "Supervisor
of graduates"

383. YA-TU, CHI-NIEN 衙 蠹, 積 年 Office termites and old hands

Bad characters among clerks and runners are known as
"office termites," meaning that they ruin government business in the same way termites ruin things.

"Old hands" are persons well-versed in litigations and
arguments, meaning that with years of experiences behind
them there is nothing (these persons) cannot do.

384. CHIEN-HSÜ HUA-LI 奸 胥 猾 吏 Evil runners and scheming
clerks

[These refer to] evil and bad office runners, and dishonest,
scheming clerks.

385. CHIEN-SHOU [TAO,] CH'ANG-JEN TAO 監 守 [盜], 常 人
盜 Stolen by an official custodian, and stolen by an
ordinary individual

If a person who serves in a yamen but is not an official,
is appointed to guard (government) treasury stores or
other institutions, and he proceeds to steal the things

in his own custody, it is known as "theft by the custodian" and the severity of the punishment is proportionate to the amount stolen. This treatment is accorded to personnel who are not officials themselves. If, however, (the custodian) is a regular official, then the case would be differently considered, and the penalty would be more severe 加等治罪. [The present item refers to two distinct laws in the Criminal Code (Ta-Ch'ing lü-li, Hsing-lü, ch. 23): 1. Chien-shou tao ts'ang k'u ch'ien-liang 監守盜倉庫錢粮, "theft of (public) funds or grain by an official custodian," and 2. Ch'ang-jen tao ts'ang-k'u ch'ien-liang 常人盜倉庫錢粮 "theft of (public) funds or grain by an ordinary individual." The official Ch'ing definition of ch'ang-jen in the present instance is "all persons outside of the officially appointed custodians (of a given treasury, etc.) 不係監守外皆是." See Boulais, pp. 477-479. These two categories of theft are among the six types of illegal gain for which an official might be prosecuted: KHHT, 54:2b.]

[[15]] Some disciplinary acts. Nos. 386-393

386. **WAN-NAN I-JIH KU-JUNG MIN SHANG I-WU CHIH-SHOU** 萬難一日姑容民上 以誤職守 Must not fail in [my] duty by being lenient and allow [a bad official] to govern the people one day longer

In order to live up to their positions all department and district magistrates should be diligent, careful, and honest. Any one who is indolent or greedy should be impeached by the governor-general and governor above (the magistrate) who must under no circumstances allow him to govern the people and thereby fail in their duty as guardians of the land.

387. **CH'EN PU-PI HSIEN YUAN** 臣不避嫌怨 Your minister, not shunning [or fearing] the displeasure and resentment [of others]....

All high officials, such as governors-general or governors,

should be serious in scrutinizing their subordinates, and memorialize impeachments truthfully against the corrupt and unfit ones. The memorials often declare, "Your minister, not fearing the displeasure and resentment of others,"--and proceed to impeach the subordinate according to the facts.

388. CH'I-TE WEI CHIH HSÜN-LIANG CHOU-MU TSAI 豈得
謂之 循良 州牧 哉   How can you be considered a good and proper department magistrate?

(*Chou-mu 州牧 is another term for chih-chou 知州, department magistrate.)

A department magistrate should conduct his office according to the laws and regulations (of the country), and govern the people kindly and benevolently. Then he may be called a good and proper official. If one acts contrary to this, his governor-general and governor will warn him by saying: "In your conduct of such-and-such an affair you did not conform to the rules and regulations, and also in another affair your actions were unkind; how can you be considered a good and proper department magistrate?"

389. LAO-PING-CHE HSIU-CHIH 老病者休致 The aged and sick (official) should be retired

If a department or district magistrate is aged or in ill-health, his governor-general and governor should memorialize the fact so that he can be retired from his post.

390. T'AN-K'U-CHE KO-CHIH T'I-WEN 貪酷者革職提問
The avaricious and hard-hearted (official) should be dismissed from office and summoned for questioning

If a department or district magistrate is avaricious for bribes and harsh in his treatment of the people, his governor-general and governor are to memorialize an impeachment, dismiss the said magistrate from his post, and have him brought to the provincial capital for questioning.

391. P'I-JUAN WU-NENG CHI SU HSING PU-CHIN-CHE CHÜ
     KO-CHIH 罷軟無能及素行不謹者俱革職

> All tardy and weak, incompetent, and habitually improper
> (officials) should be dismissed from office

> (*"Tardy and weak" etc., are phrases used in the scrutiny
> of officials, see above.) [See 261, 276.]

> If any department or district magistrate is found to fit
> such descriptions, he should be dismissed from his post.

392. FOU-TSAO CH'IEN-LU TS'AI-LI PU-CHI-CHE CHIANG-CHI
     TIAO WAI-YUNG 浮躁淺露才力不及者降級
     調外用 Shifty and hasty, shallow, and incapable
     (officials) should be lowered in rank and transferred to
     the provinces

> If any metropolitan official is found to fit such descriptions
> [see 258, 268] he is to be impeached by his superior,
> lowered in rank by one, two, or three classes, and trans-
> ferred to fill a minor post in the provinces.

393. KU PU-KAN A-HAO ERH P'I I-JEN, I PU-KAN SHEN-WE
     ERH HSIEN I-JEN 固不敢阿好而庇一人，亦
     不敢深文而陷一人 While [I] dare not protect
     anyone out of partiality, [I] also dare not victimize
     anyone through insinuation

> (*"Insinuation" 深文 : to pronounce a phrase of evaluation
> full of implications 深刻的考語.)

> When a superior official undertakes to impeach his
> subordinate(s), it should be done justly. While he must
> not unfairly protect those whom he favors, he also must
> not use insinuation to victimize those whom he dislikes.

> Here the wording "dare not" and so on is a phrase
> traditionally employed in the memorial written by a superior
> official to impeach his subordinate(s). "Insinuation" means
> to [attempt to] establish wrong where it does not exist, such
> as saying, "Although there is no actual evidence of X's
> abusing the people, yet investigations have indicated that
> his intentions are probably not good."

[[16]] Terms concerning official documents. Nos. 394-415

394. WEN-P'ING 文憑 Certificate

Before a provincial official goes to his post he is given
a certificate by the Board of Civil Appointment which,
upon arrival in the province, he will present to the
governor-general and governor for examination. [Cf. 49.]

395. CHA-FU 劄付 Directive

When an official is assigned by his superior to carry out
a mission, he is given a written order called a "directive."

396. P'IN-CHI K'AO 品級考 Rank and class reference [file]

The record books at the Board of Civil Appointment
containing data on the rank and class of all officials, high
and low, metropolitan and provincial, and the records of
(their) advancements, recordings of merit, etc., to be
used for reference purposes, are called the "rank and
class reference file."

397. T'ANG-CHA 堂劄 Ministerial directive

The (written) instruction given by a chief executive of the
Boards to his subordinate(s), who has been assigned to
carry out a mission, is known as "ministerial directive."

398. WEI-P'AI 委牌 Assignment tablet

When a governor-general or governor assigns a [sub-
ordinate] official to carry out a mission, the latter is
customarily given an instruction or directive [cf. 395].
Then the text of the instruction is written on a wooden
tablet and hung at the gate of the office so that all may
know of it. This is called an "assignment tablet."

399. TI-CH'AO 邸抄 Grand Secretariat transcripts

An official residence is a ti 邸 ; here the word refers to the
Grand Secretariat 內閣 .

This term denotes the copies of imperial edicts made in the
[offices of the] Grand Secretariat. [Entries 399, 400, 401

-71-

describe the different facets of Ching-pao 京報, known to
Westerners as the Peking Gazette.   It involved a process
whereby Court news and official documents, which have
been passed by the authorities for promulgation, are made
available to the reading public.   There are two sources from
which such information might be obtained: the Grand
Secretariat (399), and the Office of the Six Sections (400).
At these offices the news and documents--including edicts
and the texts of memorials--are copied every day by agents
of the Peking Gazette printing offices, which are private
concerns authorized by the government to engage in the publication of these papers for general circulation for a profit.
The printed copies of the Ching-pao are delivered to sub-
scribers in the Peking area; they are also sent to the
provinces for the information of the local authorities.   On
the basis of the speed and fullness of coverage, Ching-pao
is classified into several editions, each fetching a different
price accordingly.   From mid-nineteenth century on,
selections from its contents began to get translated into
English, and appeared in Hongkong newspapers as well as
in the North China Herald.

An account of the procedures concerning the publication of
Ching-pao is given in three brief sections preceding the
chapter on the Board of Civil Appointment in the Naitō
editions of the present book (pp. 1-3); for background,
cf. Lin Yutang, A History of the Press and Public Opinion
in China (Chicago University Press, 1936), pp. 14-16,
77-78. Oda, Shinkoku gyōsei hō p. 40, also contains an
account of the Peking Gazette and its relations to provincial
couriers; based partly on an article by W. F. Mayers, this
version indicates that the printing offices are an adjunct
of the courier service.]

400. K'O-CH'AO 科抄 Section transcripts

Copies of imperial edicts made in the Liu-k'o ya-men
六科衙門 (Offices of the Six Sections) (in the
Chi-shih-chung ya-men 給事中衙門 [Office for the
Scrutiny of Metropolitan Officials]). (B. 210B)

401. WAI-CH'AO 外抄 Printing Office transcripts [literally, outside copies]

> Copies of imperial edicts and of memorials made in Ching-pao fang 京報房 ("Peking Gazette" Printing Office, B. 435C) outside [the Palace] are known by the general term "Printing Office transcripts."

402. T'ANG-PAO 塘報 Military post courier reports

> Official title [sic] of the military officers attached to the provincial courier services in the capital [cf. 198]. Sent by the provincial (governments) to be stationed in Peking, and to transmit official correspondence, (these officers) are controlled by the Board of War. (They) make copies of imperial edicts and despatch them to their respective provinces. (These documents) are called T'ang-pao [Military post courier reports].

403. KUNG-WEN 公文 Official correspondence

> A general term for correspondence dealing with government business.

404. NIEN-TAN 粘單 Enclosed sheet

> For reference purposes, correspondence from another office relative to the matter at hand is copied on a separate sheet of paper, and pasted to the end of the present official letter.

405. NIEN-CH'AO I-CHIH 粘抄一紙 Enclosure: one copy

> All official letters that contain enclosed sheets are (each) marked at the end: "Enclosure: one copy."

406. CH'UANG-KAO 創稿 Original draft

> The general term for the rough draft of official correspondence and memorials is "original draft."

407. HUI-T'I 彙題 Memorialized collectively

> Unimportant matters need not be memorialized individually, but can be collectively memorialized when several items have accumulated.

408. HUI-T'I 會題 Joint memorial

> (*Hui 會 "joint" is given as hui 彙 "collective" in the Manchu-Chinese editions.)

> Matters pertaining to two or three provinces in common should be jointly memorialized by the governors-general and governors of these provinces. [Naitō notes in his "Explanations on style" (fan-li 凡例), p. 1, that the Ch'ien-lung and Chia-ch'ing editions are referred to to together as the Manchu-Chinese editions 滿漢本.]

409. I-TZU SHIH 移咨事 With reference to the matter under discussion

> This is the opening phrase of despatches written between (government) offices of equal rank.

410. TZU-WEN NEI 咨文內 According to the despatch

> This refers to the matter stated in a despatch (between offices of equal rank).

411. FU-TU 伏讀 Humbly read

> If a governor-general or governor receives an edict containing instructions as to the conduct of some affair, when he later memorializes in reply he must state: "Your minister, having humbly read the imperial edicts," etc.

412. P'ENG-TU CHIH HSIA 捧讀之下 After respectfully reading [the edict]

> Or, in the same circumstances as the previous case [411], the memorial in reply (to an imperial order) may state: "Your minister received the imperial edict on such-and-such a day, and after respectfully reading it is filled with immeasurable admiration and gratitude," etc.

413. PEN NEI NIEN-CH'U YU CHOU-WEN 本內粘處有縐紋 There are creases in the memorial where [the pages are] pasted together

> When a memorial is too lengthy and must (have extra pages) pasted on, the spots where the pages join together should be smooth and correctly placed. It is considered

to be gross disrespect [to the throne] if "there are creases in the memorial where the pages are pasted together."

414. **KUA PU** 刮補 Scraping and mending

Miswritten words in a memorial may be scraped off with a knife, and (the spot) mended with fresh paper, on which (the word is) written anew.

415. **KUAN-CHIEN** 管見 Very limited view

(This phrase is used) by officials when speaking to the Emperor, denoting that their own views are very limited, as if (they are) looking at the world through a tube.
[This phrase may also be used by a subordinate official when speaking to his superior.]

CHAPTER II

THE BOARD OF REVENUE

[[1]] Categories of taxes and fees. Nos. 416-475

416. TI-TING CH'IEN-LIANG 地丁錢糧 Land-poll tax funds

> Taxes on land and the [adult male] population are collected
> by the local officials every year in accordance with
> statutory provisions, in order to supply the government
> granaries and treasuries.

> [Amended, p. 142:] Ti-ting 地 丁 , land-poll tax(es).
> Originally the usage was to have the local officials assess
> and collect the land and poll taxes (separately) from the
> people. During the K'ang-hsi period[1662-1722], however,
> Emperor Sheng-tsu manifested special grace by incorpor -
> ating the poll tax into the land tax, the former thenceforth
> never to be increased. This has been the practice ever
> since. [This was the measure taken in 1711 (K'ang-hsi
> 50). Until then the ti-shui 地 税 , land tax, and the ting-fu
> 丁 賦 , poll tax on male adults, had been separately
> collected, the latter being reassessed on the basis of new
> census [i.e., registration] figures once every five years.
> In 1711 the poll tax was "frozen" at the amount levied in that
> year, so that subsequent increases in population, while
> evident in the registration records, would not cause a
> corresponding rise in the people's tax obligations. In 1723
> (Yung-cheng 1) the poll tax was merged into the land tax for
> purposes of easier administration, and the combined levy
> was collected, and administered, as a single item under the
> name ti-ting 地 丁 , which I render here as land-poll tax.
> In substance the ti-ting represented a reassessed land tax,
> and more than ever before the land became the major source
> of the government's revenue. See Hsiao I-shan 蕭 一 山 ,
> Ch'ing-tai t'ung-shih 清代通史 (A general history of the
> Ch'ing dynasty; Shanghai, 1932, hereafter CTTS), I,
> 664-665.]

417. CHENG-HSIANG CH'IEN-LIANG 正項錢糧 Principal tax funds

The two taxes collected in a department or district on land and adult male population (respectively) are known as the "principal taxes." Other levies are known by the general term "miscellaneous taxes." [Cf. 418, 455.] [Ti-ting liang hsiang 地丁兩項: This clearly refers to the pre-1711 practice whereby the land and male adult taxes were separately collected. See 416.]

418. TSA-HSIANG CH'IEN-LIANG 雜項錢糧 Miscellaneous tax funds

In a department or district, the sums besides the land-poll tax levied by the officials, such as the taxes on local products, cattle, horses, and other livestock, are known by the general term "miscellaneous taxes." [Cf. 417, 455.]

419. CHIEH NAN CH'IEN-LIANG 解南錢糧 Tax funds for delivery to the South

The tax funds appropriated and dispatched from the treasury of the Board (of Revenue) to such offices as the Imperial Manufacturies (Chih-tsao 織造) in Chiang-nan and other provinces, for procurement of things used at Court.

The Imperial Manufacturies have their own treasury funds, but sometimes (additional money) has to be transferred from the Board treasury or from a provincial treasury (fan-k'u 藩庫). [Cf. 420.]

420. HSIEH-CHI CH'IEN-LIANG 協濟錢糧 Tax funds for assistance [of other offices]

Tax funds being appropriated and dispatched from the provincial treasury to help make up deficits in such government offices as the Imperial Manufacturies (Chih-tsao).

421. HSIEH-CHI PING-HSIANG 協濟兵餉 Funds to assist in military provisions

When the cost of supplying the army in a province, where there is military activity, becomes too large for the

-77-

financial resources of the province, then money is sent
by other provinces as help, and is termed "funds to
assist in military provisions." [Cf. 518.]

422. YA-I KUNG-SHIH 衙役工食 Office runners' food and
wage costs

The food costs and wages received by runners of the
government offices.

423. FENG KUNG YIN-LIANG 俸工銀兩 Salaries and wages

Officials' stipends and salaries and runners' food and
wage costs are known generally as "salaries and wages."

424. WEI-I KUNG-SHIH 未役工食 Off-duty wages

To those laborers (owing labor service) 工役人等
who have been summoned by the government but who have
no work to do in off-duty periods 平日未作工之時
wages are also paid for their subsistence.

425. KUNG TS'AO CH'OU-FEN 供漕抽分 Tithe for tribute
grain

In the provinces of Kiangsu and others, one-tenth of the
income from [all] local passengers and freight shipping
[duties] each year is taken to be used as transportation
fees for tribute grain boats. These (duties) are called
"shipping dues" 船鈔.

426. CH'UAN-CH'AO HSIEN-YÜ 船鈔羨餘 Surplus from
shipping dues

Of the shipping dues collected each year, the amount left
over after payment of the transportation fees for tribute
grain boats is termed "surplus from shipping dues."
"Surplus" means an excess amount.

427. LIANG-T'OU SHUI-YIN 樑頭稅銀 Boat beam tax

Local authorities collect a certain amount of shipping
dues from the lead boat of a group (*a fleet) of freight
boats passing through the [Grand] Canal. This is known
as "boat beam tax," colloquially called "boat prow money"
船頭錢.

428. HUANG-K'UAI TING YIN 黄快丁銀 Poll-tax money of the Yellow Speeders

Among the grain transport boats, some are government (-operated), and others are privately (operated), each having their own classification. There is a group of boats known as the Yellow Speeders, whose operators must pay a tax on their adult (crew) members every year. (*The government-operated boats are owned by the government, the crew members all belonging to the Military status (Chün-chi 軍籍). The privately operated boats are rented from the people [by the government]. [These government transport workers were drawn from the military agriculturists who cultivate government land. See Harold C. Hinton, The Grain Tribute System of China (1845-1911) (Harvard University, Center for East Asian Studies, 1956), p. 11. KHHT, 17:1, explains that the chün-hu 軍戶 "military status households" comprised mainly such agriculturists, plus convicts sentenced to this status and their descendents.]

429. YING TSENG TSU-YIN 應增租銀 (Tax(es) due for increase

Any of the government's taxes of which an increase should be considered is termed "tax(es) due for increase."

430. WU-MI SHIH-YIN 五米十銀 Five-rice and ten-silver

On the best grade of land in Kiangsu and other provinces, taxes are collected every year in both rice and silver, the rate per ch'ing (*one ch'ing equals one hundred mou) being five hu 斛 of rice and ten taels of silver.

[One hu 斛 contains five pecks 斗 , or is equal to half a tan 石 . It was a unit of measure much used by the Ch'ing government in its handling of grain, and the official dimensions of a hu are specified in the Hui-tien. See Wu Ch'eng-lo 吳承洛 , Chang-kuo tu-liang-heng shih 中國度量衡史 (A history of Chinese weights and measures; Shanghai, 1937), pp. 269, 293.]

431. **WU-CHENG SHUI-YIN** 無徵稅銀 Non-collectable taxes

   [This refers to] remote and impoverished regions, where
   no miscellaneous taxes [see 418] can be collected .

432. **TS'AI-T'ING FU-YIN** 裁停夫銀 Crew wages eliminated
   or stopped

   Wages due to be paid to any category of crew members
   of grain transport boats, and to the boat-pullers, that
   have to be eliminated [from the pay-roll] or be temporarily stopped on account of shortages in the treasury.

433. **CH'ÜEH-KUAN FENG-YIN** 缺官俸銀 Salary funds
   during vacancy of an official post

   When the former incumbent of a post has already left
   but a successor has not yet been appointed, the salary
   funds for this post are to revert to the government and
   be stored in the [local] treasury. This is known as
   "salary funds during vacancy of an official post. "

434. **LIU-SHENG K'U-YIN** 六升庫銀 Six-pint money in
   treasury

   Of the rice allotment to troops, six pints 升 are withheld
   from each tan, converted. into silver and stored in the
   [government] treasury. Once a year the accumulated
   money is given to each soldier in a lump sum, to be
   used for the repair of uniforms and weapons.

435. **CHAO-TAN TAO FEI** 照單道費 Circuit license fee

   (Any person) engaging in a business for which a government license or permit (chih-chao-tan 執照單) must
   be obtained should go to the office of the intendant (taotai)
   in charge, and pay the required fees. This is called
   "license fee" 照單費 .

436. **SHUI-CH'ENG TAO FEI** 水程道費 Circuit waterways fee

   All operators of boats plying the waterways must also
   obtain permits from the intendant's office, and pay the
   required fee.

437. **P'ENG-CH'ANG YIN-LIANG** 蓬廠銀兩 Money for pavilions and sheds

The Board of Revenue customarily pays the cost of erecting mat pavilions and sheds, such as the public examination pavilions 考棚 [cf. 1323], and sheds for relief gruel stations 施粥廠 .

438. **P'ENG TA TSU-YIN** 蓬搭租銀 Rent for pavilions and sheds

Where no government land is available for the erection of pavilions and/or sheds, money must be appropriated to rent land from the people for this purpose.

439. **YUNG-LU HSIANG-YIN** 鎔爐餉銀 Provisions [for Peking] in remelted silver

(*<u>Yung</u> 鎔 "melt" is given as <u>t'ieh</u> 鐵 "iron" in the Manchu-Chinese edition.)

Silver fragments and copper cash collected in the land-poll tax, salt gabelle, and the like should all be commuted into silver by the offices of the Financial Commissioner of the respective provinces, melted and recast into shoes or smaller ingots, before being sent as provisions to Peking.

440. **CHUANG-FU KUNG-CHIA** 壯夫工價 Able-bodied laborers' wages

For such services as repairing city walls or river conservancy, the official in charge 承辦官 should recruit able-bodied laborers to carry out the work. [Their wages] are appropriated by the Board (of Revenue) and are called "able-bodied laborers' wages. "

441. **LING YIN CHIEH-FEI** 領引解費 Expense for transmittance of (salt) certificates

The sale of government salt is undertaken by merchants, each of whom operates within his own demarcated territory, which is recognized in government-issued certificates called "salt certificates" 鹽引 . Such certificates are printed by the Board (of Revenue), and agents are sent by the provincial governors-general and governors to the capital to obtain them and bring them back to the province for distribution [or sale] to the merchants. Expenses incurred in these proceedings are called "expenses for transmittance of salt certificates."

442. TING-KUNG [sic] HSÜ-SHUI 定弓虛稅 Dated incomplete tax payments

(*The Chia-ch'ing and annotated editions misprint kung 弓 "bow" as jih 日 "date.") [Here the editor's note is in error. The context shows that jih 日 is the correct word.]

Any tax that cannot be completely paid at once may be recorded first in the books, and paid up later at a fixed date.

443. K'AI YIN CHIH-CHIA 開引紙價 Cost of paper for (salt) certificates

The cost of paper for making salt certificates is to be obtained [from the Board of Revenue treasury].

444. LO-TI-SHUI YIN 落地稅銀 Duty (paid) for unloading goods

When a load of merchandise reaches a place, duty must be paid as soon as it is unloaded. This is known as "duty (paid) for unloading goods."

445. HSING-LIANG 行糧 Field rations

Food rations given to soldiers in the field during a military campaign.

446. YÜEH-LIANG 月糧 Monthly rations

Food rations that should be paid to soldiers every month.

447. T'UN-LIANG 屯糧 Military agriculturists' rations

Food rations received by persons of military status who cultivate the land of the military agricultural settlements

448. TO-LIANG 墮糧 Dropped rations

"Dropped" means to be in disuse. Food rations belonging

to soldiers dropped from the rolls should revert to the government.

In meaning (this item) parallels "salary funds during vacancy of an official post." [Cf. 433.]

449. T'IAO-PIEN [HSIANG-YIN] 條邊[餉銀] Willow Palisades frontier [provisions]

The Willow Palisades are in Feng-t'ien province, and mark the borderline between Liao-yang, the [Manchurian] Mongols, and Korea. Garrison forces are stationed at the passes [along the Palisades]. Provision for these forces is paid separately by the Board (of Revenue), which renders accounts of it [to the throne]. This is called "Willow Palisades frontier provisions." [Under Manchu policy the Willow Palisades demarcated tribal territories of the Manchurian Mongols from the Liao-tung region, where Chinese agriculture had penetrated. Owen Lattimore, The Mongols of Manchuria (New York, 1934), pp. 45-46, and the map captioned "Manchuria."]

450. LIAO-PIEN 遼邊 Liao [-tung] frontier

(*Pien 邊 "frontier" is given as t'iao 条 "(Willow) branches" in the Manchu-Chinese editions.)

Same as above [449].

451. SHUI-LIANG 稅糧 Taxes [literally, tax-grain]

The tax on adult [male population] and the land tax that should be paid by the people.

452. SHUI-YIN 稅銀 Tax money

A general term for any kind of tax collected.

453. KUAN-SHUI 關稅 Customs duties

The duties levied at all the maritime and inland customs stations.

454. HANG-SHUI 行稅 Business tax

The taxes paid by all trades and businesses.

455. CHENG-SHUI 正税 Principal taxes

The land-poll tax and customs duties are called "principal taxes;" all others are "miscellaneous taxes." [Cf. 417.]

456. TSA-SHUI 雜税 Miscellaneous taxes

See above [455; cf. 418].

457. LAO-SHUI 老税 Old taxes

Taxes instituted in times past with fixed quotas.

458. HUO-SHUI 活税 Non-quota taxes

Newly added taxes without fixed quota, such as likin and the like.

459. TSU-SHUI 租税 Tax on rentals

The tax that should be paid [by the proprietor] out of receipts of rentals for house or land.

460. PAO-SHUI 包税 Contract tax

Taxes the payments whereof have been contracted by a village head [li-chang 里長] or a business (guild).

[Amended, p. 142:] Taxes that used to be contracted by either a village head or a business (guild) to collect and pay (to the government), but nowadays their payments are sometimes contracted by the [individual] gentry or merchant.

461. FU-SHUI 埠税 Wharf tax

A tax is paid to the government on all privately owned wharf space along waterfronts, such as river landings and piers. This is called "wharf tax."

462. YA-SHUI 牙税 Broker's tax

One who sells merchandise for another person is a broker, who must also obtain a (government) permit and pay a tax called "broker's tax."

463. TIEN-SHUI 典税 Pawn-broker's tax

The tax paid by those who engage in the business of

pawnshops. [This is presumably the same as tang-shui
當 稅 , lised in KHHT, 18:1, under "Miscellaneous
taxes."]

464. MO-SHUI 磨 稅 Milling tax

In provinces like Szechwan most of the people mill their
rice, wheat, and other grain in water mills 水 磨 , which
are located on public rivers. Each mill constituted a
milling area, which must pay (the government) a certain
sum in taxes [for the use of the water power].

465. CHENG-KUNG 正 供 State's supply

Rice destined for government granaries is called "state's
supply."

466. TSU-YIN 租 銀 Rent money

[For example], the money paid for the rent of government
land or buildings.

467. TSU-CHIA 租 價 Rental

Same as above [466].

468. KUNG-SHIH 工 食 Food Cost

The cost of food for laborers.

469. K'OU-YIN 扣 銀 Money withheld

Funds that should be withheld, and payment stopped thereof,
are called "money withheld."

470. TSENG-YIN 贈 銀 Grant money

To grant is to give help. "Grant money" refers to money
that should be paid as aid [to some government office].

471. K'OU-LI 扣 利 Interest from a loan is deducted (from the
principal)

Interest is increment (of money). When government funds
are loaned at interest to [private] merchants, the monthly
interest earnings are deducted in advance [from the sum
to be lent].

472. LING-YIN 廩銀 Government stipendiaries' silver

The government stipendiaries' [ling-sheng 廩生] rice stipends are commuted into silver and thus paid to them. [Cf. 1281.]

473. HUA-YIN 花銀 Earnings of money

"Earnings" refer to interests; hence (this item) means interest money.

474. SHAN-HSIEN 簽羨 Surplus from boat repairs

Shan 簽 means to repair boats; surplus means excess amount. (This item refers to) funds left over from appropriations for boat repairs.

475. SHUI-K'O 水課 Water levies

"Levies" mean taxation. (This item refers to) taxation that should be instituted on water [or marine?] resources.

[[2]] Money or silver in administration
      A. Administrative expenses. Nos. 476-487

476. CHING-FEI YIN 經費銀 Administrative expenditures fund

Ching 經 means regular . All government offices regularly receive an annual appropriation for the miscellaneous office expenses, and this is called "administrative expenditures fund."

477. FENG-HSIN YIN 俸薪銀 Stipend and salary fund

The annual remuneration received by an official is called stipend; in addition he is paid a monthly sum which is called salary.

478. HSIN-HUNG YIN 心紅銀 Red ink fund

"Red ink" is the ink pad for seals. (This item refers to) the money spent every year by a government office on ink for seals.

479. CHIH-CHANG YIN 紙張銀 Paper fund

Money spent by a government office on paper for the conduct of official business.

480. CHIN-HUA YIN 金花銀 Gold-flower silver

Candidates who have newly won the degree of provincial graduate or metropolitan graduate are customarily given gold flowers (by the Emperor) to decorate their caps. Such gifts are converted into silver and paid (to the graduates) by the Board of Rites. [Cf. 1348, 1349.] [Chin-hua yin 金花銀 is a term that was passed on from the Ming dynasty, when it denoted top-grade silver paid into the Palace treasury that was used primarily for official salary payments. Since the term then was descriptive of a grade of silver, "gold-patterned" would seem to be a more suitzble rendering, such as, for example, in Lien-sheng Yang, Money and Credit in China: A Short History (Harvard University Press, 1952, hereafter Yang), 5.21; and in Liang Fang-chung, The Single-Whip Method of Taxation in China, tr. Wang Yü-ch'üan (Harvard University, Center for East Asian Studies, 1956), p. 50. But in the more direct context of the present item, "gold-flower" is clearer. There is a discussion on chin-hua yin in the Ming dynasty, including a quotation from the present item, in Shimizu Taiji 清水泰次, Chugoku kinsei shakai keisai shi 中國近世社會經濟史 (Social and economic history of early modern China; Tokyo, 1950), pp. 91-100.]

481. CH'A-KUO FEI 茶菓費 Tea and cake fund

(*The Manchu-Chinese edition gives ch'a-kuo yin 茶菓銀 "tea and cake silver.")

Tea and cakes used in government offices are customarily covered by official appropriations; also known as "refreshments fund" 點心費.

482. P'U-TIEN YIN 舖墊銀 Pad and cushion fund

Such items as bed mattresses, table cloths, chair cushions, etc., are generally termed "pads and cushions" and are bought with officially appropriated funds.

483. SSU-CHIA YIN 絲價銀 Silk price silver

Silk due to be paid to the government [as a part of taxation in kind] is commuted into payment in silver.

484. CHIH-SHU YIN 紙贖銀 Silver for redemption of deed papers

Merchants, who deliver the deed papers of their property to the government as security for loans from public funds, will redeem these papers with money at the designated time.

485. HSIAO-CHIEN YIN 小建銀 Small month fund

All customs duties are collected on the basis of thirty days to the month, without regard to whether the month is actually large [i.e., thirty days] or small [i.e., twenty-nine days], but delivery of the (collected duties) is made on the basis of twenty-nine days to the month, and (this sum) is called "small month fund." The duties collected on the thirtieth day of the large month are retained [at the customs station] for administrative expenses; this is known as "extra-day collection" 建曠.

486. CHIEH-K'UANG YIN 截曠銀 Retained extra-day fund

"Retain" means to keep. That is, keeping the duties collected on the thirtieth day of a large month to be used for administrative expenses.

487. LU-FEI YIN 路費銀 Travel fund

The travel expenses given officials being sent on missions.

[Amended, p. 142:] The money needed by officials sent out on government business for such expenses as bearers, horses, boats and carriages, etc.

[[2]] (continued)
B. Silver (I). Nos. 488-499

488. TI-CHU YIN 滴珠銀 Bead silver

The small round nuggets (of silver) melted and cast in

government furnaces are known as "beads"; the larger pieces are called "ingots" 錁子 or "shoes" 元寶.

489. CH'E-CHU YIN 車珠銀 Little cart silver

Small square nuggets (of silver) are called "little carts" because of their resemblance to the latter in shape; larger pieces are called "square trench" 方槽.

490. HUO-HAO YIN 火耗銀 Meltage fee

When silver fragments are melted, a certain percentage is unavoidably wasted. According to statutes an additional sum of Tls. 0.02 or 0.03 per tael [of taxes] is levied when (the taxes) are collected, so as to replace the wasted silver. This is called "meltage fee."

491. CHIA-HAO YIN 加耗銀 Extra silver for melting

See above [490).

492. CH'ING-CHI YIN 輕齎銀 Easy delivery silver

[...] When grain tribute is diverted 截送 [from its original destination, Peking] to the provinces, it is often converted into silver, because the latter is less bulky and easier to deliver. [Ch'ing-chi 輕齎, according to a nineteenth century authority, was one of several kinds of extra wastage fees accompanying the collection of grain tribute. It was levied in terms of rice but always collected in silver, and was used for the transportation costs of grain tribute destined for the metropolitan granaries. SCYC (1890 ed.), 4:5.]

493. TS'AO-CHIEH YIN 漕截銀 Diverted grain tribute silver

When grain tribute destined for the capital is diverted, converted into silver, and sent to another province.

494. JUN-HAO YIN 閏耗銀 Intercalary meltage fee

The meltage fee for an intercalary month.

495. T'IEH-CHIEH YIN 貼截銀 Diverted supplementary fund

To supplement means to help meet what is necessary. When funds marked for delivery to the capital are diverted (elsewhere) to help defray the cost of some important government undertaking, it is known as "diverted supplementary fund."

496. T'I-CHIANG YIN 提江銀 Dyke fund

(*T'i 提 reads ti 堤 in the annotated edition.)

Each year an official appropriation should be obtained for the maintenance and repairing of flood-control embankments built at river estuaries. (This money) is called "dyke fund."

497. LIANG-CH'IEN YIN 糧簽銀 Fund from land-poll taxes

[...] (This item refers to) the appropriation of money from land-poll tax payments to be used for office expenses.

498. YU-CHA YIN 由閘銀 Canal passage fund

The duties paid by freight boats passing government collecting posts [kuan-cha 官閘] on the Grand Canal are called "Canal passage tax" 過閘稅.

499. T'AN-HSI YIN 燂洗銀 Hot-Wash fund

[At the end of the transport season] empty grain transport boats are anchored in their original ports, repaired and washed with hot water, and made ready for use in the following year. The cost involved in this operation is called "hot-wash fund."

[[2]] (continued)
  C. Tax funds being processed: including quota, collection, transfer, and delivery. Nos. 500-528

500. MEN-T'AN YIN 門攤銀 Door-to-door allotted tax

[...] This item means taxes are levied on the people by (official agents) allotting the amounts from door to door.

501. SHIH-CHENG YIN 實徵銀 (Tax) money actually collected

The money actually obtained each year from the land-poll tax and customs duties, aside from that which is short

of quota, is known as "tax money actually collected. "
[Ch'u pu-tsu-o chih wai 除不足額之外 : the
presence of this phrase here is questionable, as usually
all the money actually collected, whether it is over or
short of the quota, was referred to as shih-cheng yin.]

502. YING-CHENG YIN 應徵銀 Budgeted tax collection

The fixed amount of land-poll tax and customs duties
that should be collected each year. However, (the
actual collection) is often short of quota.

503. O-CHENG YIN 額徵銀 Tax quota

Same as above [502]. However, "quota" refers to fixed
amounts of long standing, whereas "budgeted tax collection"
may also include amounts set up by new regulations.

504. CH'I-CHENG YIN 起徵銀 Taxes initially collected

The amount of land-poll tax and customs duties collected
at the beginning.

505. TAI-CHENG YIN 帶徵銀 Taxes collected in installments

When the tax quota cannot be realized in full within the
year, it may be completed by making partial collections
through a number of years.

506. WAI-P'AI YIN 外派銀 Extra assessment

The extra sum that is assessed and collected from the
people in addition to the regular (tax) quota

507. O-PIEN YIN 額編銀 Taxes allotted by quota

[...] This means to allot the annual (tax) quota to all
the different localities. [Cf. 626, O-pien 額編, which
shows a different interpretation.]

508. T'AN-SA YIN 攤洒銀 Divided allotment of taxes

[...] The amount (of taxes) that should be collected is
divided among all the localities and so collected.

509. TUAN-P'AI YIN 短派銀 Short allotment

In making the tax allotments, the places whose loads

are too light may have their allotments increased.

510. CHING-SHOU YIN 經手銀 Money handled by ...

The money that is handled and spent by a certain person.

511. PEN-SE YIN 本色銀 Permanently commuted. tribute
rice silver

Se refers to the quality of rice. Of the tribute rice,
a portion is to be collected in kind, and another portion
in silver that has been commuted from rice according to
the latter's quality. This category of commuted payment
is termed "permanently commuted tribute rice silver."
[This term, as well as the next one (512), is translated
in accordance with the interpretation given here rather
than literally; cf. Hinton, The Grain Tribute System
of China (1845-1911), p. 9. Under che-cheng 折徵 ,
"commuted payment" in KHHT, 22:1b, no such terms
as pen-se yin and che-se yin 折色銀 (512) are found.
Usually pen-se means "in kind" and che se "in commutation" or "commuted to money payments."] [The text
here reads: tz'u-hsiang che- chia chih pen-se yin 此
項折價之本色銀. It appears to be a misprint for
tz'u-hsiang che-chia chih yin wei-chih pen-se yin 此項
折價之銀謂之本色銀.]

512. CHE-SE YIN 折色銀 Temporarily commuted tribute rice
silver

When the full amount of rice in kind (i.e., tribute rice)
cannot be realized, the balance is to be collected in silver
that has been commuted (from the uncollectable rice).
[See first note under 511.]

513. KAI-CHE YIN 改折銀 Revised commutation price silver

When the price of commutation [of rice into silver] is
changed either upwrad or downward, it is known as "revised
commutation price."

514. TZU-LI YIN 籽粒銀 Seed fund

When unused land is being put under cultivation by the
people, the government should furnish the seeds, which

are converted into money and then distributed. This
is called the "seed fund." [Tzu-li yin may be subject to
two interpretations: (a) The cost of seeds and grain
rations lent by local officials to the victims of a natural
disaster; the present text approximates this interpretation.
KHHT, 19:5b. (b) One of the categories of taxable, private-
ly-owned land was known as hao-ts'ao tzu-li ti 蒿草籽
粒地 , barren land that was "overgrown, yielding little
grain." Tzu-li yin thus could refer to the tax money derived
from this type of land, CTTS, II, 338. Cf. 677.]

515. PIEN-CHIA YIN 變價銀 Property sales proceeds

Useless government property is sold and the money so
obtained is paid into the government treasury.

516. CH'I-CHIEH YIN 起解銀 Dispatched funds

Funds that are dispatched from the provinces to be
delivered to the capital.

517. PO-HSIEH YIN 撥協銀 Subsidy funds

[...] When a locality [a province?] is short of funds,
other places will help by transferring some of their
money to it.

518. HSIEH-CHIEH YIN 協解銀 Funds dispatched for assistance

The money that has been dispatched to help [the government
of] another province. [KHHT, 19:4, gives the following
explanation for hsieh-hsiang 協餉 : "funds transferred
to assist a neighboring province." Cf. 421, hsieh-chi
ping-hsiang 協濟兵餉 .]

519. TA-FANG YIN 搭放銀 Money for mixed payment

"Mix" means to put together. For example, if rice is
insufficient [for troops' provisions], money may be paid
to the soldiers along with (the rice), and this is called
"money for mixed payment." [Cf. 655.]

520. TS'OU-CHIH YIN 凑支銀 Money assembled for payment

"Assembled" means to make up the shortage, as when
funds are insufficient for a given item of expenditure,

the deficient amount is taken from that earmarked for other items so as to make up the total sum and complete the payment.

521. TIEN-FA YIN 墊發銀 Payment with advanced money

[...] When (the proper appropriation for) a certain item has not yet been received, payment for it is made by temporarily borrowing the money earmarked for some other item. [Cf. 532, 656.]

522. T'OU-CHIH YIN 透支銀 Overdrawn money

This means to take money clandestinely to enrich one's own pocket. [This interpretation is erroneous. See amendment to 654.]

523. MAO-CHIH YIN 冒支銀 Money taken under false pretense

[...] This means to take money for oneself by posing as official personnel 辦公之人 , or under the pretense of (needing it for) government business.

524. MAO-LING YIN 冒領銀 Money obtained under false name

To obtain funds from the treasury of the Board (of Revenue) by assuming another (person's) name. [Cf. 640.]

525. TSOU-HSIAO YIN 奏銷銀 Money reported on official account

At the completion of a government mission the expenses incurred are reported in an account rendered to the Board, where it is settled.

526. CHAO-CHI (-KEI) YIN 找給銀 Reimbursed money

[...] When the money originally given for the conduct of an official business proves insufficient, it is reported to the Board, which is requested to reimburse the amount. [Cf. 652.]

527. WEI-WAN YIN 未完銀 Incomplete tax payments

The part of the land-poll tax, customs duties, etc., that has not been paid and is lagging in arrears. [The scope of the present item appears to be restricted to officials who are delinquent in forwarding tax funds to the higher offices, and does not include the common taxpayer unable to meet tax obligations. For the latter see 531, min-ch'ien yin 民欠銀 .]

528. WAN-PAN YIN 完半銀 Half-complete tax payments

Payment has been half completed on funds [receipts from taxes] that are due.

[[2]] (continued)
        D. Deficits and delinquencies. Nos. 529-542

529. K'UEI-K'UNG YIN 虧空銀 Deficit sum

[...] When the store in a treasury is short of the proper amount, [because] the money has been used by the official in charge, it is called a "deficit. "

530. PU-FU YIN 不敷銀 Insufficient funds

(To have) insufficient money, as when funds are not enough for government administration, or when one cannot deliver the proper amount of official funds.

531. MIN-CH'IEN YIN 民欠銀 Money owed by the people

The money owed (the government) by the common people, who are not able to pay the full amounts of their land-poll and other taxes.

532. NO-I YIN 挪移銀 Shifted funds

When funds that should be used for item A are shifted to pay for item B, they are called "shifted funds. " [Cf. 521, 642.]

533. CH'IN-SHIH YIN 侵蝕銀 Embezzled funds

To embezzle is to steal, to misappropriate for selfish use. (This item) means putting to personal use the government funds under one's charge.

534. JU-CHI YIN 入己銀 Pocketed funds

Government funds being embezzled and put into one's own pockets.

535. WU-TI YIN 無抵銀 Unrestitutable (amount of) funds

Nothing being available to be paid as restitution for deficits in government funds.

536. P'EI-T'OU YIN 賠頭銀 Funds to be restored

[...] Those parts of government funds for which restoration should be made.

537. PAO-P'EI YIN 包賠銀 Funds restored by guarantor

To restore (certain) government funds in behalf of another person.

538. TAI-NA YIN 代納銀 Funds paid for another person

To pay money [to the government] in behalf of another person.

539. CHUI-P'EI YIN 追賠銀 Funds restored later

If deficits have occurred in the money previously handled (by an official), such sums should be restored (to the government) later when the fact is uncovered.

540. PU-CHUI YIN 補追銀 Funds recovered later

Same meaning as above [539].

541. P'EI-TIEN YIN 賠墊銀 Funds repaid [?]

If deficits have occurred in the money previously handled.... (* The rest of the text is missing in the original edition.)

542. CHIU-CH'IEN YIN 舊欠銀 Old arrears in taxes

The amount of arrears in land-poll tax, customs duties, etc., that has accumulated through the years.

[[2]] (continued)
E. Bookkeeping terms. Nos. 543-587

543. CH'IEN-PO YIN 欠撥銀 Funds not yet issued

Of the total amount of money that should be disbursed,

a certain sum has already been issued, and another sum has not yet been issued.

544. HOU-K'OU YIN 候扣銀 Funds to be deducted

When funds are to be issued, the sum that should be deducted and retained 扣留 is to be so handled in the correct amount.

545. FANG-CH'IEN YIN 防欠銀 Reserve fund

A sum is set aside beforehand as a precautionary measure against possible insufficiency of the appropriation for expenditures.

546. KUNG-TING YIN 供丁銀 Labor service fund

The money paid by the people as commutation for government labor service is called "labor service fund."

547. HUO-MIEN YIN 寬免銀 Remitted taxes

[...] Payment of (tax) money owed by the people is remitted by imperial favor.

548. T'U-T'IEN YIN 塗田銀 Marshland tax

The land tax 租銀 to be paid on marshy lowlands that have been newly placed under cultivation.

549. SHUI-CH'I YIN 稅契銀 Property deeds tax

A tax, (assessed) in accordance with the price (of the property), is paid on deeds concluding the purchase of land or house, and an official seal should be affixed.

550. LU-K'O YIN 蘆課銀 Reed land tax

The annual tax that should be paid on shoals or sandbars 沙洲 where reeds are grown is called "reed land tax."

551. YEN-K'O YIN 鹽課銀 Salt gabelle

Tax on salt.

552. SSU-CHU YIN 四柱銀 Funds [recorded] in four columns

(*Chu 柱 "column" is given as ch'uan 傳 "transmit"

in the Manchu-Chinese edition.)

Government treasury funds are recorded under four headings, which are: "balance forwarded" (chiu-kuan 舊管), "new receipts" (hsin-shou 新收), "present balance" (hsien-ts'un 現存), and "expenditures" (k'ai-chih 開支). These are known as "funds recorded in four columns." ["All financial reports must be rendered in the form of the four-columned book, that is, first, 'balance forwarded' 舊管 ; second, 'new receipts' 新收 ; third, 'expenditures' (k'ai-ch'u 開除); and fourth, 'present balance' (shih-tsai 實在)." KHHT, 19:4.]

553. CHIH-HSIAO YIN 支銷銀 Expended funds

Money that has already been spent.

554. TS'UN-LIU YIN 存留銀 Balance on hand

Money that is left and kept.

555. CHIEH-LIU YIN 截留銀 Funds diverted and retained

Funds designated for some other place are diverted [from their destination] and retained here to meet urgent needs.

556. I-CHIA YIN 溢價銀 Procurement surplus

If the money appropriated for official procurements exceeds the cost of the things purchased (the surplus) should be returned (to the government) forthwith.

557. I-O YIN 溢額銀 Quota overflow

When the customs duties flourish, and the amount of duties collected exceeds the quota. [Here the customs serve as illustration only; "quota overflow" may be applied to any tax levy, and is not restricted to customs collections.]

558. CH'ÜEH-O YIN 缺額銀 Quota deficiency

The sum of money (by which collection) falls short of the amount fixed by the quota.

559. CHENG JUN YIN 正閏銀 Funds for the regular and the intercalary months

Money that is to be issued (by the government) in the regular months and the intercalary months.

560. TS'UN-K'U YIN 存庫銀 Treasury-retained funds

Government tax funds that are retained in the local treasury, except for the amount delivered to Peking.

561. TS'UN-SHENG YIN 存剩銀 Retained excess funds

Excess money left after expenditures is kept in the [local] treasury.

562. TUNG-FANG CH'IEN-PEN YIN 動放錢本銀 Issuance of coinage cost funds

Tung is to expend; fang, to issue; ch'ien-pen, the cost for minting coins. To issue money from [the Board of Revenue] treasury to the government mints to defray the cost of coinage.

563. CHIEN-JANG K'O-CHENG YIN 減讓科徵銀 Reduction of taxation

[...] To reduce by a small percentage the amount of taxes that should be collected according to statute.

564. CH'IEN-CH'UAN KUNG-CHÜ YIN 淺船貢具銀 Funds for grounded tribute boats

"Tribute" refers to tribute goods destined for the Palace. When boats transporting them are grounded (en route), money must be issued for hiring boat-puller in order to expedite progress.

565. KUNG-YING PU-FU YIN 供應不敷銀 Inadequate appropriation for supplies

When the appropriated sum is not sufficient to pay for the supplies for government offices.

566. TS'UI-CHENG PU-TE YIN 催徵不得銀 Unobtainable arrears

When (an official) is unable to obtain, after repeated

efforts, the tax arrears owed by the people.

567. K'OU-LIU CHENG-HSIANG YIN 扣留正項銀 Funds retained from the principal taxes

A certain amount is deducted and retained from the principal tax funds to be delivered to Peking, in order to meet urgent (local) needs.

568. TS'UN-LIU PEI-CHIH YIN 存留備支銀 Emergency fund

(The sum) kept in the treasury, to be used when the occasion demands.

569. HUAI-KUAN SSU-SHUI YIN 淮關四稅銀 Huai (-an) customs four-quarter dues

Huai means Huai-an Prefecture in Kiangsu; "four-quarter," the entire year. This item refers to the amount that should be collected annually at the Huai-an customs station.

570. YEN-K'O CH'E-CHU YIN 鹽課車珠銀 "Little cart" silver from the salt gabelle

Money collected in the salt gabelle is cast into "little cart" ingots [489] and delivered to Peking.

571. SSU-YÜEH WAN-PAN YIN 四月完半銀 Tax half-paid in the fourth month

The people must pay half of the land-poll tax in the fourth month each year. This is the so-called "busy first season tax" 上忙錢粮. [KHHT, 18:3b, gives the schedule of tax payments as follows: "collection is begun in mid-spring, and stopped in mid-summer. [Interlinear note:] (by the fourth month half of the tax is paid, and in the fifth month collection is stopped, which is known as 'stopping for the farmer's busy season. ') It is resumed in mid-autumn, and completed in mid-winter. "]

572. TI-MA KUNG-LIAO CH'IEN-LIANG 遞馬工料錢粮 Wage and fodder fund

Money for couriers' food costs and horse fodder at military post stations (i-chan 驛站).

573. K'ANG-CHIAO FU-I CH'IEN-LIANG 扛轎夫役錢糧
Fund for chair-bearers

(Money for) food costs of corvée laborers serving as
chair-bearers.

574. T'UNG-JUNG PO-HSIEH CHAN YIN 通融撥協站銀
Fund for cooperative assistance of a station

To "cooperate" means to help by transferring (one's
funds). For example, if this [military post] station is
strategically located and has large contingents of
laborers at service, so that its official appropriations
prove insufficient, funds can be transferred hither from
another place [station?] to help.

575. HSING CHE TS'AO-CHIEH YIN 行折漕截銀 Diverted
grain tribute dispatched in silver

Grain tribute diverted to help another area is converted
into silver for the sake of convenience, and thus
dispatched.

576. FENG-HSIN CHING-FEI YIN 俸薪經費銀 Funds for
stipends, salaries, and administrative expenses

See above [476, 477].

577. TS'AI-CHIEN FU-LI I-CHAN YIN 裁減復立驛站銀
Funds for reactivated military post stations

(*Li 立 "establish" is given as erh 二 "two" in the
Manchu-Chinese edition.)

When a previously abolished military post station is
reactivated, the necessary funds are also to be allotted
to it.

578. SHAO-CHE WU-FAN ERH-MI CHIA YIN 少折五飯
二米價銀 Reduced and commuted station laboers' pay

The established reward for military post station laborers
consists of five bowls of cooked rice per day and two pecks
斗 of uncooked rice per month, known as "five bowls
and two pecks. " These are all somewhat reduced and
paid in commutation.

579. LI-CHANG KUNG-YING FU MA CH'IEN-LIANG 里長供
應夫馬錢糧 Funds from the village head for
laborers and horses

Money needed for the laborers [and couriers?] and
horses (at military post stations) is provided by the
village heads [li-chang 里長], who levy it from the
people.

580. TS'AI-TING CHIEN-T'IEN CHENG-SHOU TSU-YIN 裁丁
減田徵收租銀 Reduction in land-poll tax

Reductions made in the land-poll tax according to
imperial order.

581. CH'ING-HSIAO TI-CHU CHIA-HAO YIN 傾銷滴珠加
耗銀 Meltage fee for bead silver

[...] When silver fragments are melted and recast
into bead silver there is an unavoidable wastage in the
melting process. Therefore an extra T1s. 0.01 or
0.02 per tael [of taxes] are collected to replace it.

582. YEN-CH'ENG HAI HSIEN WU-CHENG YIN 鹽埕海陷
無徵銀 Eroded salt flats tax remission

Salt flats are the level beaches along the seashore where
salt is made by evaporation. When the flats are eroded
by the sea the tax (on such land) should be remitted.

583. LIN-CH'ING CHA HSIEH-TSAI CHIH-CHIA SHUI-YIN
臨清閘卸載紙價稅銀 Paper duties on unloading
at Lin-ch'ing customs post

Lin-ch'ing Department in Shantung is an important center
of North-South communications. Upon reaching here
freight boats from the south will unload twenty to thirty
per cent of their merchandise of paper, which is then
distributed and sold in various parts of Shantung. The
unloading duties that should be paid are computed on the
basis of the price of the paper.

584. KUANG-CHI-CH'IAO CHIU-O YEN-TS'AI YIN 廣濟橋
舊額鹽菜銀 Kuang-chi Bridge salted vegetable
fee (paid) according to old regulation

Kuang-chi Bridge spans the Grand Canal at T'ung-chou.
Here grain transport boats are unloaded and (the tribute
grain) is transferred to the granaries. According to old
regulations, a few fen 分 or candareens (of silver)
of salted vegetable fees in addition to their wages are paid
each of the laborers serving as grain carriers.

585. K'EN-FU YEN-CH'ENG WANG-HANG TU-CH'UAN TENG-
HSIANG YIN-LIANG 墾復鹽埕網桁渡船等
項銀兩 Reinstitution of taxes on salt flats, fish weirs,
ferries, etc.

"Salt flats" are salt fields; "fish weirs," banks along which
fish are caught; "ferries," boats that transport passengers
back and forth. When salt flats, etc., are inundated by the
sea, taxation should be stopped, but later when these places
are restored to their former state the taxes are also
reinstituted.

586. SHIH-CHENG, CH'ING-CHI, HSING-YÜEH, JUN-HAO, PEN
CHE TENG-HSIANG YIN-LIANG 實徵, 輕齎, 行月, 閏
耗, 本折, 等項銀兩 Funds, including taxes actually
collected, easy delivery (silver), field provisions, intercalary meltage fee, (taxes) in kind and in commutation

"Taxes actually collected" refer to the actual amount of rice
and silver received [cf. 501]; "easy delivery," grain tribute converted into silver [cf. 492]; "field provisions,"
funds spent (for troops) on the march [cf. 445]; "intercalary meltage fee," expenditure incidental to an intercalary month [cf. 494]; and "in kind and in commutation"
are rice and silver respectively.

587. SUI-TS'AO CH'IEN-LIANG, SHIH-CHENG, CH'ING-CHI,
CHE-HSI, PEN CHE, HSING-LIANG, JUN-HAO, TENG-
HSIANG YIN-LIANG 隨漕錢糧 實徵, 輕齎折
蓆, 本折, 行糧, 閏耗, 等項銀兩 Funds, including grain
tribute surcharges, taxes actually collected, easy delivery
silver, mat conversion (silver), in kind and in commutation,
field rations, intercalary meltage fee

[Grain tribute surcharges] are the miscellaneous fees collected along with the regular rice tribute; "taxes actually collected," see [586]; "easy delivery silver," [ibid.];"mat conversion silver" is the cost of mats, used to construct rice bins, commuted into silver; "in kind and in commutation," see [586]; "field rations" are the same as "field provisions" [586]; "intercalary meltage fee," also see [586].

[[2]] (continued)
F. Silver (II). Nos. 588-598

588. PU FA 部法 Regulations of the Board

Rules and regulations established by the Board (of Revenue) with regard to specifications in the weight and fineness of silver are termed "regulations of the Board."

589. T'IEN-P'ING 天平 Balance

The scale for weighing silver.

590. CHENG-TING 整錠 Whole ingots

All uncut (silver) ingots regardless of size, from shoes to bead silver [see 488], are called "whole ingots." The ones that have been cut are called "fragments" [san-sui 散碎].

591. SAN-SUI 散碎 Fragment silver

See above [590].

592. CH'ING-HSIAO 傾銷 Remelting

Melting fragment silver and casting it [again] into whole ingots are termed "remelting."

593. TI-CHU 滴珠 Bead (silver)

See above [488].

594. YIN-HSIAO 銀鞘 Silver sheath

A "silver sheath" is a length of wood that has been split

[vertically] and a cavity hollowed out inside. After silver shoes are placed in the cavity the two halves of the wood are brought together and bound with iron strips. One sheath encloses ten shoes; that is five hundred taels.

595. YIN-KUEI 銀櫃 Silver chest

For the purpose of tax collection a "silver chest" is placed in the office or [every] prefectural, departmental, or district government. According to statute, the people in paying taxes should seal their money and themselves drop it into the chest.

596. T'AN-TUI 彈兌 Adjusting the balance

To weigh silver. In doing this both ends of the balance must be made to hang evenly, hence it is called "adjusting the balance."

597. HSIAO-FENG 小封 Small envelopes

In addition to the principal taxes, the people must also pay other levies such as meltage fees and miscellaneous taxes. The latter items are paid enclosed in "small envelopes."

Along with the small envelopes a few candareens (of silver) are wrapped in a small packet and paid as fees for office personnel [shih-fei 使費]. This is called "companion packet" [sui-pao 隨包].

598. SUI-PAO 隨包 Companion packet

See above [597].

[[3]] The handling of tax funds (I): collection, arrears, mismanagement, assessment. Nos. 599-644

599. CHING-SHOU 經手 Personally in charge

The official who is in charge and handles the collection of taxes. [Ching-shou 經手 simply means to take charge of a matter personally, and is not limited to handling tax funds. The latter is properly expressed by the next item, 600.]

600. CHING-CHENG 經徵 Personally in charge of (tax) collection

Same as above [599].

601. TZU-LI 自理 Administered personally

When an incumbent official himself administers the tax matters of his office without deputizing others, it is known to be "administered personally."

602. HSIEN-CHENG 現徵 Present collection

Taxes collected at present.

603. CHIEH-CHENG 接徵 Continuing collection

Continued collection of taxes from now on.

604. YA-CHENG 壓徵 Advance collection

"Ya" is beforehand. When taxes due in the following month are collected in advance in the present month, it is known as "advance collection."

605. TAI-CHENG 代徵 To collect (taxes) in place of...

(*Tai 代 "in behalf of" is given as tai 帶 "bring along" in the annotated edition.)

[...] When an official, who had been in charge of the tax collection, has for some cause had to leave the job before its completion, and his successor takes charge in his place.

606. O-CHENG 額徵 Quota

The fixed amount (of taxes) that should be collected. [See 503]. [Annual quotas established for all the major taxes, including customs levies, constituted the core of the system of taxation. While they were not always met in the actual collections--and occasionally the latter might exceed the quota, as sometimes happened with the customs duties--they nevertheless provided a goal or a norm to be aimed at, and a basis on which to plan the government's fiscal administration. The quotas were to be fulfilled in kind as well as in money. The Hui-tien gives the following as the sum total of quota taxes (exclusive of customs) due each year from the entire country as of 1899: silver, Tls. 31,184,042+; cash, **123,600+** strings; grain (in kind and in commutation, and including a variety of beans), 3,624,532+ tan; hay, 5,262,800+ bunches and 14,902,000+ catties. KHHT, 8:1,2.]

607. CH'ANG-CHENG 長徵 Longstanding quota

[...] The tax quota that has had a long history.

608. CH'ENG-TS'UI 承催 (To serve as an) expediter

To undertake the work of expediting tax collection.

609. TU-TS'UI 督催 Supervision of tax collection

To direct subordinates in achieving the expeditious collection of taxes. This is the job of prefects and department magistrates.

610. CH'IH-YEN 遲延 Delayed (tax collection)

When an expediter is unable to accomplish his task of collecting the taxes within the set time limit, he should be held responsible for the delay in collection.

611. PU-LI 不力 Negligent

[E.g.] Being negligent in expediting tax collection with the result of being at fault for delay.

612. I-WAN 已完 Sum already paid

The sum (in tax funds) that has already been paid.

613. NO-TIEN 挪墊 Shifted sum

A sum is shifted from another category to make up for the amount that has not yet been collected under a given category, so that the latter can be dispatched to Peking [within the time limit].

614. T'O-CH'IEN 拖欠 Prolonged arrears

[...] Taxes that for long periods have been in arrears and not forwarded [by a local office].

615. CH'ÜEH-CHIH 缺支 Short balance

[...] (An official) using tax funds without authorization,

with the result of shortages in the regular tax quotas.

616. CH'IN-SHIH 侵蝕 Embezzle; misappropriate

To put public funds to one's private use [cf. 533].

617. CH'IN-FEI 侵肥 Embezzle; misappropriate

Taking public funds to line one's own pockets.

618. CH'IN-YÜ 侵漁 Embezzle; misappropriate

This also means to encroach and seize, like a fisherman's catching fish.

619. WU-TI 無抵 Unrestitutable (funds)

To use up tax funds [for private purposes] without being able to make restitutions [cf.535].

620. P'ENG-FEN 烹分 Cook-and-share

[Two or more officials] dividing the public funds [and privately taking possession thereof], like cooking a mess of meat and then sharing in eating it. [烹分 may be an error for the common expression p'eng-fen 朋, "shared among accomplices."]

621. WEI-WAN 未完 Unpaid sum

The amount (of tax money) which has not yet been completely paid.

622. WEI-CH'IEN 尾欠 End sums owed

Small sums owed (the government) are known as "end sums owed."

623. SHENG-K'O 陞科 Rated for taxation

[...] When unused land is first opened and rented to the people for cultivation 民人佃種 (land) taxes are exempt during the first three years. After the third year the land is (considered as) "matured" 成熟, and becomes incorporated in the tax registers [cheng-shou ts'e 徵收冊]. This process is known as "rated for taxation." [The number of years in which newly cultivated (or recultivated) land was exempt from taxation varied from time to time. At the beginning of Ch'ing statutory provisions called for three years, but during the K'ang-hsi reign a number of changes were made, and from 1679 to the end of that reign the tax-exempt period was fixed at six years. (Item 1000--liu-nien sheng-k'o 六年陞科 "taxable in six years"--seems to be a reference to the practice prevailing in this period). In 1723 (Yung-cheng I) the paddy fields [shui t'ien 水田] were con-sidered separately from the dry fields [han t'ien 旱田], the former being still allowed six years of tax exemption while the latter were given ten years. The same rule was in effect in the nineteenth century. KHHT, 19:5a-b; CTTS, II, 423-424.]

624. HSIN-SHENG 新陞 Newly rated

Land that has recently been rated for taxation.

625. SHENG-TSENG 陞增 Gradual rate increase

Taxes on newly rated land are collected at a half rate [as compared with ordinary land], but the amount is increased every year. This is known as "gradual rate increase. "

626. O-PIEN 額編 Classified by quota

Newly rated taxable land is entered into the land-poll tax books 地丁冊 according to its tax quota.

627. CHO-P'AI 酌派 Proportional allocation

When the people are asked to contribute money for some (government) undertaking, the allocation (for payment) should be made in proportion to (each family's) ability to pay.

628. T'AN-P'AI 攤派 Divide and allocate

To divide means to partition equally. The total amount of contributions is divided equally into so many parts among the people, who are then told to pay the amount allocated.

629. TUAN-P'AI 短派 Reduced allocation

To assess [a person or an area] less than the amount

that usually should be allocated, owing either to the person's impecuniousness, or to the poverty of the region.

630. K'O-P'AI 科派 To tax by allocation

Tax being allocated according to fixed rates [sic].

631. CH'IN-LOU 侵漏 Embezzle and steal

To embezzle and steal public funds.

632. FEI-SA 飛洒 To scatter [one's misappropriations]

This means to divide and distribute [the guilt], [e.g.] dividing the embezzled amount and recording it under various expense items, thus (seeking to conceal the theft by) rendering a fraudulent account.

633. K'O-LO 剋落 To squeeze

To squeeze public funds and put them into one's own purse.

634. YING-SHE 影射 To delude

To mistake one thing for another, --like the yü-turtle 蜮 shooting at shadows.

635. CH'IN-K'O 侵剋 To embezzle and squeeze

The embezzlement and squeezing (of government funds).

636. K'O-LIEN 科歛 Tax allocation and collection

[...] To allocate and collect taxes according to fixed regulations.

637. JU-CHI 入己 To pocket (government funds)

See above [534].

638. P'ENG-FEI 烹肥 "Cooking fine meat"

See above [620].

639. FOU-MAO 浮冒 Fraud

Fou 浮 means non-existent. To fabricate non-existent

items (of expenditure) so as to steal government funds.

640. MAO-LING 冒領 To obtain under false name

To act under false pretenses so as to obtain government funds with which to enrich oneself [cf. 524].

641. CH'IN-CH'I 侵欺 Embezzling and cheating

To embezzle public funds on some pretext, thereby cheating the imperial government 朝廷.

642. NO-I 挪移 To shift [funds]

See above [532; also cf. 613].

643. K'UEI-K'UNG 虧空 Deficit

The abuse of having deficiencies and shortages (in treasury funds), to be short of quota [cf. 529].

644. SHOU CHIAO 收繳 Collect and deliver

To collect the taxes and deliver them to the (government) treasury.

[[4]] The handling of tax funds (II): payments, transfer, delivery, and retention. Nos. 645-690

645. KUO-FU 過付 Fund handler; to handle

[...] The person who personally handles and delivers the funds.

646. CH'U NA 出納 Outlay and income

The disbursement and receipt of funds.

647. PO-PU 撥補 Transfer for replenishment

To transfer funds.

To transfer money under item A in order to fill the deficiency under item B.

648. HSIEH-PO 協撥 Transfer for assistance

"Assistance" means help. To transfer money in order

to help [another agency]. [Cf. 517, po-hsieh 撥協.]

649. CHO-PO 酌撥 Transfer at discretion

To transfer money of which the amount has been carefully considered.

650. P'O-I 裒益 To maintain balance

(*P'o 裒 is given erroneously as chung 衷 in both the Manchu-Chinese and the annotated editions.)

Chung 衷 means harmonious; i 益, surplus, is (short for) "deficit or surplus." The public funds should show a harmonious balance between deficit and surplus, and the abuse of imbalance must not be allowed to appear. [The present text, however, also gives chung. P'o appears to be the correct word, because the term p'o-i 裒益 is an abbreviation of the saying p'o-to i-kua 裒多益寡 , "to subtract from that which is numerous and add to that which is few," that is, to maintain an even balance of things.]

651. PAN-CH'OU 辨抽 To draw for payment

[...] To draw a small amount from the money marked for one item in order to pay for the expenses of another.

652. CHAO-CHI(KEI) 找給 Reimburse

When the previously appropriated funds are not enough (for the intended purpose), the short amount is reimbursed (to the spending office). [Cf. 526.]

653. NO-TS'O 挪撮 Shift and assemble

Assemble means to put together. To draw money from different categories in order to [have the necessary amount to] accomplish a matter.

654. T'OU-CHIH 透支 Overdraw

See above [522].

[Amended, p. 142:] "Over" is to go beyond. This item means that an official has spent more than his quota of government funds.

655. TA-FANG 搭放 To issue mixed payment

"Mix" means to allocate and put together. For example, if there is not enough silver, then copper cash or rice can be allocated to make up the correct amount [of pay] and issued to the troops. [Cf. 519.]

656. TIEN-FA 墊發 To pay with advanced money

When (an item of expenditure) should be paid out of a certain fund, but the latter has not yet been received, then the sum may be temporarily advanced from another fund so that the payment can be made. [Cf. 521.]

657. CH'I-CHIEH 起解 To dispatch and deliver [funds]

The funds that are sent from a province to be delivered to the Board of Revenue.

658. YA CHIEH 押解 Escort of delivery

To escort is to oversee. This refers (to the official) who is in charge of the delivery of government funds [to Peking].

659. CH'ANG CHIEH 長解 Through delivery

When (funds) are accompanied by government runners from the province of origin all the way to Peking, it is known as "through delivery." When the accompanying personnel is changed at every post station, it is called "short-distance delivery."

660. TUAN CHIEH 短解 Short-distance delivery

See above [659].

661. HUI CHIEH 彙解 Joint delivery

When several items of (government) funds are put together and dispatched and delivered in one lot, it is called "joint delivery."

662. FU CHIEH 附解 Appended delivery

Odd sums are appended to the principal funds and delivered together to the Board (of Revenue).

663. HSIEH CHIEH 協解 Delivery of subsidy

> To dispatch and deliver the subsidy funds [see 517] to the place where they should be transferred.

664. KANG CHIEH 槓解 Delivery in lot

> A shipment is termed a "lot." This refers to sending all the funds to be delivered in one shipment.

665. TIEN CHIEH 墊解 Delivery made on advanced money

> This occurs when the funds due for dispatch and delivery [to the capital] have not yet been fully collected, and the delivery is made with funds advanced from elsewhere.

666. TSOU-HSIAO 奏銷 To render financial account

> To report to the throne the sums that have already been spent, thus accounting for them.

667. T'I-LIU 題留 [Funds] retained by memorializing

> [...] To memorialize for the retention of funds that should be delivered to Peking, in order to meet provincial needs.

668. TS'UN-LIU 存留 Retained [funds]

> Funds that are [regularly] kept in the province for local use.

669. CHIEH LIU 截留 [Funds] retained through diversion

> Funds for delivery to Peking are stopped en route and diverted to another place instead.

670. CHIEN-TS'UN 減存 To keep the deducted sum

> (*Ts'un 存 "keep" is given as liu 留 "retain" in the annotated edition.)

> Of the funds that should be delivered (to Peking), half [半 , sic for pu 部 "a part"?] is deducted therefrom and kept in the province.

671. LIU-TI 留抵 [Funds] retained as substitute payment

> To retain funds that should be delivered (to Peking) in

order to meet necessary expenses in some other matter.

672. LIU-TI 流扺 Short-term transfer substitute [funds]

"Short-term transfer" means temporary. This means to retain a certain sum temporarily as substitute for another sum.

673. LIU-CHIEH 流借 Short-term transfer loan

To borrow temporarily.

674. TIEN-P'EI 墊賠 To restore with advanced (funds)

The money that should be restored [to the government by an official] has not been fully paid, and the restitution is completed with money advanced from elsewhere.

675. P'EI-LEI 賠累 Losses resulting from making restitutions

The sums that should be restored are so great that, as a result, losses are suffered [by the one making the restitution].

676. K'ANG LIANG 抗糧 Resistance to taxation

To resist is to oppose. People opposing the government at tax collecting time and refusing to pay their taxes.

677. PU-NA TZU-LI 不納籽粒 Paying not one grain

(People) refusing to pay even one single grain (in taxes). [Tzu-li may also be a shortened form of tzu-li yin; cf. 514].

678. PAO-P'EI 包賠 To restore in whole

To pool all the funds that ought to be restored [to the government] and pay as a whole. [Cf. 537, which gives a different interpretation of pao-p'ei yin 包賠銀.]

679. PAO HUANG 包荒 To contract for unused land

To contract for payment of taxes on unused land 荒田.

680. SHU NA 輸納 Payment and delivery

[...] The people paying their taxes and delivering them to the government.

681. LO NA 樂納 Happy payment

> The people pay their taxes happily; this refers to times of prosperity.

682. PAO-LAN 包攬 To contract or be in sole charge (as tax middleman); to monopolize

> [...] The gentry or village head of a village whose special interest it is [e. g.] to contract for tax payments of the [common] people. [Cf. 1658 pao-lan tzu-sung 包攬詞訟.]

683. HUO-MIEN 豁免 Tax remission

> Payment on tax arrears owed by the people are exempted by special favor of the throne.

684. CHIN-SHOU CHIN-CHIEH 儘收儘解 Complete collection and total delivery

> "Complete, total," mean "to the utmost." This means to exert one's utmost in collecting the taxes, and to deliver to the government the entire sum so collected.

> [Amended, p. 142:] "Complete, total" mean "entirety." This means that no limit is set up [as tax quota], but that the entire sum that is possible to collect should be delivered.

685. YU-CHENG WU-CHIEH 有徵無解 (Tax) collected but not delivered

> Although taxes are collected, they have not been delivered to the provincial capital. This is a misdeed of the department and district officials.

686. TAI-TSUI CHENG-SHOU 帶罪徵收 To collect (taxes) bearing record of a misdeed

> When a department or district magistrate is negligent in the collection of taxes, his superior will enter this misdeed in the records, but will charge him to continue to collect taxes while bearing this record of his misdeed.

687. CHU-HSIAO K'AI-FU 註銷開復 Cancellation and restoration

When an official bearing the record of a misdeed has achieved merit in tax collection, the misdeed is struck off the books, and he is restored to his former position

688. T'UNG-JUNG PO-CHI (-KEI) 通融撥給 To issue (funds) by special arrangement

[...] This means when funds are not sufficient for the amount to be issued, some special arrangement is resorted to so as to make up the necessary sum.

689. CH'ENG-CHUI I-NIEN HSIEN-MAN 承追一年限滿
One-year limit is ended for the collection of arrears
The one-year limit for (an official's) collection of tax arrears is now ended, and his merit or demerit will be

decided according to the percentage of the arrears that he has been able to collect.

690. WEI-WAN PU-CHI I-FEN I-SHANG I SHIH-FEN WEI-LÜ
未完不及一分以上以十分為率 Remaining
unpaid arrears are less than one part out of a total of ten

The time limit of one year for (an official) to collect tax arrears is now at an end, and the punishment of the official is decided in [reverse] proportion to the amount in arrears he has been able to collect. When (the remaining arrears) are less than one-tenth (of the total), he is to be punished with one-tenth [the severity], and so on up to the tenth part, with penalties graded accordingly.

[Amended, p. 142:] In collecting taxes each year the department and district magistrates divide the quota into ten [equal] parts as a basis for computation. If over nine-tenths have been collected and the arrears amount to less than one-tenth of the total (the magistrate) will not be considered as guilty of a major offense.

[[5]] The grain tribute system
      A. Categories and descriptions of tribute rice
        and grain. Nos. 691-731

691. MI WEI TAO-MI KU WEI TSA-LIANG 米為稻米穀為雜糧 "Rice" refers to [paddy?] rice; "grain" to miscellaneous grain

These are called "rice and grain." (*According to the Manchu-Chinese editions the proper heading for this item should be "Rice and grain.")

[Amended, p. 143:] MI KU 米穀 Rice and grain

Of the [rice] collected by the local department or district authorities, the husked is called "rice," and the unhusked is called "grain."

TSA-LIANG 雜糧 Miscellaneous grain

Beans, wheat, etc. are known as "miscellaneous grain."

692. TS'ANG-CH'U 倉儲 Granary stores

Grain stored in the granaries.

693. P'ING MI 平米 Level rice

When rice is level with the top of the bin it is said to be "level rice." [Cf. 751.]

694. CHIEN MI 尖米 Heaping rice

When excess rice is heaped over the top of the bin it is said to be "heaping rice."

695. CHENG MI 正米 Principal rice

The original amount of rice that should be paid as the principal tribute rice.

696. FU MI 副米 Rice surcharge

The amount of rice that is to be paid in addition to the principal tribute rice, for the purpose of making up for wastage incurred in the latter, is known as "rice surcharge."

697. YÜ MI 餘米 Extra rice

Besides the rice surcharge [696], a certain amount of "extra rice" is also levied, to be used as transportation fee for the grain tribute.

698. HUO MI 火米 Heated rice

(Tribute) rice that has become wet with water but has been baked dry again.

699. TS'AO MI 糙米 Unpolished rice

Rice of a coarse, unpolished quality.

700. TSENG MI 贈米 Subsidy rice

"Subsidy" means adding to help. (This rice) is retained to help pay any expenditure for which the [appropriated] funds are insufficient.

701. NAN MI 南米 Southern rice

A general term for tribute grain from the southern provinces. [Cf. 713.]

702. FU MI 撫米 Governor's rice

(The rice) that is collected and dispatched under the sole direction of the provincial governor and is not under the jurisdiction of the Ts'ao-yun tsung tu 漕運總督 (Director general of grain transport).

703. CH'IU LIANG 秋糧 Autumn grain; autumn tax

The tribute grain that is collected in the autumn.
[Ch'iu-liang is also generally used to designate the second portion of the land-poll tax that is collected in the autumn, in contrast to the first part paid in the fourth month which is traditionally termed hsia shui 夏稅 or "summer tax." Cf. 571. The system of collecting the taxes in two semi-annual installments dates from the liang-shui 兩稅 in the T'ang dynasty.]

704. WAN T'IEN 晚田 Late fields

Fields wherein the late variety of rice is planted.

705. K'OU-LIANG 口糧 Food rations

The monthly food rations allotted to each laborer in service.

706. PING MI 兵米 Army rice

The rice that is issued to soldiers as food.

707. FENG MI 俸米 Stipend rice

The rice that is paid to officials as their annual stipends.

708. HSÜEH TSU 學租 School [land] rent

The rent collected from government school lands that is used as tuition fees [for government scholars]. [Hsüeh-t'ien 學田 "School land" constituted a separate category of government land in the fiscal system, and was distinct from the ordinary privately owned agricultural land which yielded the land-poll tax. Some of the categories of land are described in [922-958]. See the classification of land in CTTS, II, 336-339.]

[Amended, p. 142:] Rent from government school lands is collected by the schools to meet their expenses.

709. HSI KU 息穀 Interest grain

[...] When government grain is loaned to the people, it is to be repaid with interest at the autumn harvest and thus returned to the (government) treasury.

710. PA CH'IEN 壩欠 Dam construction costs

(*Pa 壩 "dam" is unrecognizable in the Chia-ch'ing edition; it looks like lei 壘, which the annotated edition often follows.)

When the water in the Grand Canal is too low for navigation, dams are built to accumulate enough water to allow the [grain] boats to pass along. The construction costs are taken from the tribute rice, and the deficit amount thus incurred in the rice is termed "dam construction costs."

711. CH'IAO CH'IEN 橋欠 Bridge costs

> The costs for building pontoon bridges in order to transfer [tribute] rice ashore. [The parallelism in terms suggests that the bridge costs are also paid out of the tribute rice, as is the case with the dam construction costs in [710].]

712. SHU-HAO MI 鼠耗米 Mice wastage rice

> The amount of rice lost due to mice and vermin. [Cf. 757.]

713. TS'AO-LIANG 漕糧 Tribute grain

> A general term for rice transported (to the capital) from the South. [This interpretation is at variance with actual usage. Ts'ao-liang is the general term that includes not only tribute rice from the southern provinces, but also rice, wheat, millet, and beans from Honan, Shantung, and Fengtien.]

714. CHUANG-PAN SHANG- PAI 舂辦上白 Polished top white (rice)

> Top-quality white rice that has been polished with a hand pestle.

715. TS'U-O SUI-MI 粗惡碎米 Coarse, low-grade, fragmented rice

> (*The Manchu-Chinese editions read ts'u sui o mi 粗碎惡米 , "coarse, fragmented, low-grade rice.")

> Rice that is coarse and unpolished, fragmented and not whole-kernel.

716. HSIN-SHOU K'O-CH'ENG 新收課程 Scheduled levy just collected; newly collected taxes

> [...] The scheduled amount of [e.g.] tribute grain that has been newly collected.

717. TA-FANG PING MI 搭放兵米 Mixed rations for troops

> Rice somewhat coarse in quality is not used to pay official

salaries, but is distributed among the troops as a part of their rations.

718. CHENG-KUNG TAO-MI 正供稻米 Court rice

Top-grade rice for the use of the Court.

719. CH'U-T'IAO FEI MI 除挑廢米 Discarded waste rice

Moldy, spoiled and useless rice that is to be picked out and discarded.

720. KU-P'IN K'OU-LIANG 孤貧口糧 Poor relief rations

Homeless and poor people without support, who are admitted into public relief homes [yang-chi yuan 養濟院], are each given a monthly food ration.

721. CHENG SSU ERH HAO 正四二耗 Four-principal and two-wastage [tribute rice]

For every four parts of the tribute rice collected, a wastage amounting to two parts is also levied. [This would make the ratio of principal to wastage rice 2:1, a proportion most closely approached, and exceeded, in the collection of pai-liang 白糧 or "white rice," the special obligation of Kiangsu and Chekiang. In late Ch'ing the amounts due from these provinces in principal and wastage-plus-extra rice, respectively, were: Kiangsu, 69,025 tan and over 38,653 tan, and Chekiang, 29,975 tan and over 26,527 tan. Both these amounts were exclusive of the grain transport fees payable in money that also accompanied the collection of rice. For the general tribute rice or grain the wastage [ts'ao-hao 漕耗] did not appear to be as high as that for white rice. Here the statutory ratio of principal to wastage usually ranged from 2.5:1 to 5.8:1; these figures also do not include grain transport and other fees that were regularly levied in money. See KHHT, 22:1b-2.]

722. CHÜAN-CHI CHIEN KU 捐積監穀 Grain contributed for [membership in] the National College of Letters, and accumulation [of the grain]

In famine years contributions are accepted (by the

government), and in return for their grain contributions the rich people are given the title of Kuo-tzu-chien Sheng 國子監生 (Collegian of the National College of Letters). The grain so received is accumulated and used for relief of the poor.

[Amended, p. 142:] In years of famine rich persons are permitted to contribute grain (to the government) in return for Collegianships in the National College of Letters, and the grain is used for relief of the famine victims. Although contributions for this purpose were without precedent in the past, (it is now done) according to the principle of grain contribution in ancient times. Consequently purchase of office has come to be termed "contribution of grain."

723. CH'ING-YAO PAI-CHI MI 青腰白臍米 Green-waist white-navel rice

The appearance of (a kind of) rice, which has a white-specked band of green around the middle (of the kernel).

724. MAI CH'IAO PAI-CHE MI 麥蕎白折米 Wheat and buckwheat commuted into white rice

The wheat and buckwheat that the people of the southern provinces have to pay as taxes are commuted into white rice and then paid.

725. MIN-T'UN LIEN-JUN MI 民屯連閏米 Agricultural colonizers' rice, including intercalary months

(This refers to) the total amount of rice paid by [civilian] agirucltural colonizers who cultivate government land, including the (amounts due in) intercalary months. [That is, instead of a uniform annual amount due from the colonizers, the total amount collected from them in some years may consist of thirteen monthly portions.]

726. CH'IEN-CHI(-KEI) TI-CHUI MI 欠給抵追米 Substitute payment for arrears in rice

Rice owed by the people in arrears may be paid with other things as substitute, and the collection of the latter should be strictly enforced.

727. TSENG-T'IEH P'AN-CHIAO MI 贈貼盤腳米 Extra
rice for transport cost

[...] A few additional percent of rice [per <u>tan</u>] are
collected aside from the principal amount, to help defray
the cost of [tribute grain] transportation.

728. SHU-T'IEN SHENG-K'O CHENG MI 熟田陞科正米
Principal (tribute) rice from rated matured land

When a piece of land is "matured," the regular amount
of tribute rice is levied therefrom according to statute.
[Cf. 623.]

729. PAI-HSI CHING NO CHENG HAO MI 白細粳糯正耗
米 Principal and wastage [portions] of fine, white non-
glutinous and glutinous rice

This refers to the whitest and finest grades among the
two categories of rice, the non-glutinous and the glutinous.
(This fine rice) is specially collected according to statute,
and is also classified into principal and wastage rice.

730. SHIH CHENG CHENG-CHANG TSENG PING LU-K'O KUEI-
TS'AO MI 實徵正丈增垃蘆課歸漕米
Tribute rice derived from actual taxes on measured
reed land of increased or merged acreage

When the acreage of reed land [see 550, 958] is measured,
certain increases or mergers may develop. The [land]
tax actually collected from such acreage is to be paid under
the heading of tribute rice.

731. HSIAO-HU CH'I-LING MI 小戶畸零米 Odd amounts
of rice from small households

Poor and small households do not pay much [tribute] rice
save for odd amounts.

[Amended, p. 142:] The odd amounts of rice paid by poor
and small households which do not reach any sizable amount.

[[5]] (continued)
     B.   Measuring, handling, and storing of rice and grain.
     Nos. 732-791

732. HU TAN TOU SHENG 斛石斗升 The hu, tan, peck and
      pint

     (These are) instruments for measuring rice; also units
     for calculating [the volume of rice or grain].

733. KO SHAO CH'AO TS'UO 合勺抄撮 One-tenth, one-
      hundredth, one-thousandth of a pint, and one pinch

     Small amounts [in the above sequence] in the measurement
     of rice.

734. TS'AI-MAI 採買 [Government] purchase

     [...] [For example:] Tribute rice due the government
     may be commuted and paid in money according to the
     (market) price, and the government (uses this sum) to
     purchase the rice and deliver it (to the capital).

735. HAO-PAN FU-CH'UAN MI 耗辦夫船米 Rice for transport
      boat labor cost

     Labor cost for the repairing and hiring of (grain transport)
     boats should be defrayed out of the principal part of the
     tribute rice.

736. CHAO-LI CHUN CH'U CHE-HAO 照例准除折耗
      Wastage (rice) as allowed by statute

     The wastage rice levied in addition to the principal
     tribute rice that is (statutorily) permitted. [Cf. 721 and
     footnote.]

737. MA KAN 馬乾 Horse fodder

     Feed for horses.

738. TS'AO I-SU 草一束 One bunch of hay

     A bundle of hay.

739. **T'IEN YÜ** 天庾 Imperial granaries

[...] Imperial granaries are [public] granaries and storage places belonging to the government.

740. **SHE-TS'ANG** 社倉 [Village] public granaries

Government-established granaries for storage of grain in a village or town are called "public granaries." [A nineteenth-century authority describes she-ts'ang 社倉 (literally, "community granaries") as the granaries established in villages, while those in towns were termed i-ts'ang 義倉 (literally, "charity granaries"). They were government-supervised institutions theoretically under the management and control of the local people. Grain stored in them was loaned to the people in bad times, usually to be repaid with interest. For a fuller account see SCYC, 4:29b-34.]

741. **CHIN TOU** 金斗 Metal pecks

[...; character explanation is incorrect.] New-fashioned pecks and tan that differ from the old measuring instruments.

[Amended, p. 142:] Because (measuring instruments made of) wood deteriorate rapidly and cannot give accurate measurements or rice, the Board (of Revenue) has cast [standard] packs of iron, which are distributed (to government offices) for use. "Metal" [literally, "gold"] is a euphemism for iron.

742. **CHIN TAN** 金石 Metal tan

See above [741].

743. **SHIH TOU** 市斗 Market peck

The peck used in the market for trading (in grain).

744. **KUAN-TUNG TOU** 關東斗 Manchurian peck

The peck used in the Three Eastern Provinces [Manchuria].

745. **TS'ANG HU** 倉斛 Granary hu

The hu [i.e., five pecks or half of a tan] used at government granaries in measuring their receipts and outlays (of grain).

The various measures mentioned above [741-745] are all different in size.

746. PU-K'AN SHUI-SHIH HSIAO TS'AO 不堪水濕小草 Unusable, damp, and thin hay

The hay is thin in size, damp with water, and cannot be used as horse feed.

747. HU-FU 斛夫 Hu handler

The laborer who handles the hu to measure the rice [at government granaries].

748. TAO HU 倒斛 Tipping the hu

To pour out the rice in the hu.

749. TA-TANG 打攩 Level off

To fill a hu with rice, then pass a wooden board over the top so that it becomes level, is called "leveling off."

750. CHIEN-LIANG 尖量 Heaping measure

When rice is heaped over the top of the hu it is called "heaping measure" [cf. 694].

751. P'ING-LIANG 平量 Level measure

(When rice) is level with the top of the hu, it is called "level measure." [Cf. 693.]

752. NA HU 納戶 [Tribute grain] payer; also, taxpayer

Households that pay the tribute grain.

753. LUNG HU 礱戶 [Tribute grain] payment monopolizer

(*Lung 礱 "millstone" is given erroneously as lung 壟 "monopolizer" in the annotated edition.) [The annotated edition is correct.]

Lung 壟 [literally, "mound"] means to monopolize to contract for the entire amount. This refers to the large households that contract for payment of the tribute grain.

754. T'UN MI 囤米 Placing rice in the bins

(*T'un 囤 "bin" is given as chün 囷 "a round bin" in the Manchu-Chinese editions.)

To store rice in mat bins to await measuring and storage is called "placing rice in the bins."

755. SHANG TS'ANG 上倉 Mounting the granary

To put rice in the granaries for storage is called "mounting the granary."

756. CHIN AO 進廒 Entering the store-rooms

[The placing of grain in] the separate rooms into which the space in a granary is divided is known as "entering the store-rooms."

757. SHU-HAO 鼠耗 Mice wastage

(Rice) that has been eaten and damaged by insects and mice. [Cf. 712.]

758. HUNG HSIU 紅朽 Red and rotten

Spoiled rice having become red in color and rotted.

759. I-LAN 浥爛 Damp and rotten

Rice rotting as a result of having become wet with water.

760. MEI-SHIH 霉溼 Mildewed

Rice becoming discolored as a result of exposure to dampness.

761. CHENG SHAI 蒸,晒 Steamed and sun-dried

Damp rice getting steamed and then dried in the sun.

762. SHAI YANG 晒颺 Sunning and winnowing

To screen rice with a bamboo screen, winnow off the chaff, and then dry it in the sun.

763. SHAI YANG 篩颺 Screening and winnowing

See above [762].

764. KUAN- CHI(-KEI) 關給 To issue; to distribute

> To supervise the distribution [or issuance] of rice.

765. P'AN-CH'A 盤查 Checking and examining

> To check and examine [e. g.] both the incoming and outgoing rice.

766. CH'UO TAI 戳袋 Stamping the bags

> To stamp the rice bags with a seal.

767. CHAN TUI 占堆 To draw lots for (rice) piles

> When soldiers receive their rice rations, they are to draw lots for the particular rice pile from which each person is to take his share.

768. CHIH TS'ANG CHIH T'UN 指倉指囤 Designation of a granary or bin

> (*T'un 囤 is given as chün 囷 in the Manchu-Chinese editions.)

> A particular bin is designated for several soldiers, or a particular granary is designated for some hundreds or a thousand of them, where they may obtain their rice rations.

769. LIU-NAN 留難 Raising obstacles

> Runners attached to granaries refusing to issue the rice in their attempt to obtain bribes by making delays and raising obstacles.

770. TIAO-TENG 刁蹬 Knavish obstruction

> [...] This refers to soldiers knavishly refusing to accept the rice (issued to them) on the pretext that it is bad rice.

771. CH'OU HU 籌斛 Mark off the hu

> Each hu (of rice, etc.) measured is marked off with a wooden tally as a way to record the number of hu done.

772. CHI-CHU 積貯 To store

> To keep.

773. CHIH-HSIAO 支銷 To expend

    To pay out.

774. TOU-CHI 斗級 Measurer

    The government runner in charge of measuring [the rice, grain, etc.].

775. HSIAO-CHIAO 小腳 [Grain] porters

    The laborers in service who transport the grain with shoulder poles and bags.

776. PEN-SE 本色 In kind

    See above [511].

777. CHE-SE 折色 In commutation

    See above [512].

778. KAI-CHE 改折 Revised commutation

    See above [513].

779. HSIEN-YÜ 羨餘 Surplus

    Rice in excess [of the quota].

780. TSENG-HAO 增耗 Added wastage

    Additional amount in wastage rice.

781. CHIA HSI 加息 Increase of interest

    To increase the interest.

782. I YIN 易銀 Exchange for silver

    To exchange rice for silver.

783. SHIH-CHIA 時價 Current price

    The current market price.

784. SHIH-CHIA 市價 Market price

    Same as above [783]. (*All the above items [772-784] refer to rice.)

785. P'ING-T'IAO 平糶 Sale of government grain at low price

   When the price of rice is high on the market, rice is
   sold from government granaries so as to lower the
   market price. [For this item and 787, 788, there is a
   helpful account of the operation of this system in the Ch'ing
   period in **SCYC**, 4:34-40.]

786. SHE-LI MING-SE 設立名色 Establishing categories

   The issuance and receipt of rice is recorded under
   various headings that have been set up (such as) the
   ones shown above [i.e., 776, etc.].

787. CH'U-CH'EN I-HSIN 出陳易新 To sell the old in
   exchange for new (rice)

   Old rice stored in the granaries is sold, and is replaced
   with new supplies of rice.

788. TS'UN-CH'I T'IAO-SAN 存七糶三 Store seven parts
   and sell three

   Seven-tenths of the rice [in a government granary] are
   kept in storage while three-tenths are sold. [This was
   the proportion of the grain usually sold from government
   granaries in a normal year; the aim was to make room
   for fresh grain that would replace the old in storage.]

789. NIEN-FEN TS'ANG-K'OU 年分倉口 The date and the
   name of the granary

   The name and month in which rice was stored, and the
   name of the granary concerned.

790. CH'AN-HO SHIH-HUI YAO-MI [sic] 攙和石灰藥米
   Adulterated with lime and chemicals

   (*Mi 米 "rice" is an error for shui 水 "liquid.")

   (This is) an offense committed by granary runners, who
   increase the bulk of the rice by mixing it with lime,
   or soaking it in chemical solutions, causing it to expand.
   [...]

791. LING-HSING T'IAO-MAI PU-HSÜ CHENG-T'UN SHOU-CHU
零星糶賣不許整囤收貯 (The rice) is to be sold retail and hoarding whole bins is prohibited

(*T'un 囤 is given as chün 囷 in the Manchu-Chinese editions.)

Rice merchants should keep a constant supply of rice from their warehouses on the retail market, and are not allowed to hoard it without selling, because they may thus make rice scarce, raise the price, and thereby cause the people to suffer.

[[5]] (continued)
C. The tribute grain in transit. Nos. 792-837

792. TSUNG-PU 總部 General director [of grain transport)

The Director-general of Grain Transport 漕運總督 himself.

793. HSIEH-PU 協部 Provincial headquarters [of grain transport]

The governor of the province concerned.

794. YÜN-KUAN 運官 Transport officials

Officials who supervise the transportation of tribute grain.

795. CH'I-TING 旗丁 Bannermen

Membership in the crews of [government] grain transport boats is hereditary. The men are given land and rations similar to the treatment of the soldiers of the Eight Banners, hence they are called "Bannermen." Each boat is identified by a "Banner number" 旗號.

796. CH'I-CHIA 旗甲 Banner chief

"Chief" is "head". Some one hundred Bannermen are organized into a unit [chia 甲] under the control of a chief.

797. CH'UAN-T'OU WU-CHANG 船頭伍長 Captain of the lead boat, and company head

Captain of the lead boat is that of the first transport boat (in a fleet); a wu-chang 伍長 [company head] is placed above the Banner chiefs [796] to oversee the proceedings.

798. CHIEN-TUI T'ING 監兌廳 Supervisory bureau of (grain) delivery, [or (Tribute grain) receiving station]

The yamen that supervises the delivery of the tribute rice to the government.

799. PU YÜN 部運 Supervision of grain transport

Pu 部 means to supervise the subordinates [sic?]. This item means to supervise the management of matters pertaining to grain transport.

800. KAI-TUI 改兌 Deflected transport

The tribute rice that should be delivered might, when the time arrives, be changed into payments in silver, etc. [This interpretation is erroneous. Kai-tui 改兌 and cheng-tui 正兌 are the two main categories in which tribute grain was sent to the metropolitan area: the latter, "direct transport," was the grain or rice sent directly to granaries located in Peking, while the grain under kai-tui or "deflected transport" was sent for storage in granaries at T'ung-chou. Each of these categories had its own quota of grain to be delivered, and both were long-established terms in the grain transport system. See KHHT, 22:1.]

801. CHAO-TUI 找兌 Making up [deficiency in] delivery

This means to fulfill the entire (scheduled) amount of the delivery (of tribute grain) of which a certain portion was previously deficient.

802. TUI-LIU 兌留 Delivery [of rice for] retention

The delivery and receipt of rice to be retained in the province.

803. TUI-HSING 兌行 Delivery [of rice to be sent] in transit

The delivery and receipt of rice to be transported.

804. TUI-YÜN 兌運 Delivery [of rice for] transport

The delivery and receipt of rice to be transported to Peking.

805. CH'I-YÜN 起運 To commence transport

When delivery of the rice has been completed, the journey to transport it is begun. (*Words probably erroneous.)

806. LING-YÜN 領運 (Official) in charge of transport

The official who heads the (grain) transport convoy.

807. YA-YÜN 押運 (Grain) transport escort officials

The officials who escort a grain transport convoy.

808. CH'IEN-YÜN 僉運 Assignment for transport

The assignment of various officials to grain transport duties.

809. HSIEH-YÜN 協運 Assisting transport

Officials who assist in the transportation of (tribute) grain.

810. TSUNG-YÜN 總運 Combined transport

The tribute grain from several shipments being transported together to the capital.

811. FU-YÜN 附運 Appended transport

The tribute grain of another category being sent along with the present shipment.

812. TA-YÜN 搭運 Distributed transport

To place the grain to be transported under various headings.

[Amended, p. 142:] To distribute [a shipment of?] tribute rice for transportation [with other units ?].

813. CHIA-TAI 夾帶 Merchandise allowance

The merchandise carried in transport boats which is to be sold in the capital is called "merchandise allowance."

814. PO WAN 剝挽 To lighten and haul

To "lighten" means to reduce, and to "haul" means to pull. When a heavy (grain) boat is stranded in shallow water, the load of grain is reduced and the progress of the boat is continued by pulling.

815. P'AN-PO 盤剝 To transfer

This means to remove. [E.g.] the heavy cargo of rice from a large boat is removed and distributed onto smaller vessels.

816. PO-CH'UAN 剝船 Lighter (s)

A small boat that carries the cargo taken out [from a larger boat].

817. LIANG-CH'UAN 糧船 Grain boat(s)

A general term for boats used in grain transport.

818. KUNG-CHÜ 貢具 Tribute equipment

The necessary equipment in a tribute [grain?] boat.

819. PANG-CH'UAN 幫船 A fleet

Some scores of boats joining together in a group is called "a fleet."

820. K'AI PANG 開幫 Departure of the fleet

The grain boats leaving on their voyage in fleets.

821. T'OU PANG 頭幫 Head fleet

The first fleet.

822. WEI PANG 尾幫 Tail fleet

The last fleet.

823. HUI K'UNG 回空 Return of empty boats

The empty boats which, having transported the grain to the capital and discharged it, are now returning to the south.

824. HUI TZ'U 回次 Return to location

[...] The empty boats should return to their original places and moor in port, to be used again for the next year's journey.

825. KO-CH'IEN 擱浅 Stranded

When a heavily laden boat gets into shallow water and is unable to proceed further.

826. TUNG-TSU 凍阻 Iced in

When (the grain boats) are frozen in the ice of the Pei-ho and unable to return south.

827. SHEN-LOU 滲漏 Leakage

When a boat is damaged and the river water leaks in.

828. TSAO FENG 遭風 Encountering storm

The boats encountering a storm en route.

829. P'IAO-MO 漂沒 Missing after shipwreck

[The effects and/or men aboard a wrecked boat] have disappeared in the waves.

830. LIANG CH'UAN HSIANG-TI 兩船相抵 Collision of two boats

Two boats colliding and damaging each other.

831. FU TZ'U LING-TUI 赴次領兌 To receive (grain) delivery at the [proper] location

Grain boats are to proceed to the place where the rice is delivered, there to load up and start on the transport voyage.

832. SHUI-TZ'U CHE KAN 水次折乾 Commutation into dry value in port

"Dry value" refers to money. The rice that should be received for transport is commuted into silver payment at the port (of loading).

833. KUAN SHOU KUAN TUI 官收官兌 Collected and delivered by officials

The officials collect (the tribute rice) and personally see to its delivery into the transport boats.

834. LI SHOU KUAN YÜN 吏收官運 Collected by clerks and transported by officials

Government clerks collect and deliver (the tribute rice), which is transported under the supervision of officials.

835. I ERH SAN YÜN 一二三運 The first, second, and third transport shipments

Each year the southern grain tribute sent to Peking is dispatched in three [successive] shipments, which are termed (respectively) the first, second, and third transport shipments.

836. CHOU LU HSIEN-CHIEH 舳艫啣接 Stern to bow [or, stern touching bow]

"Stern" and "bow" refer to boats, and "to" [or "touching"] indicates continuous without break. This means the boats [are so numerous that they] pass to and fro without a break.

[Amended, p. 142:] "Touching" refers to the grain boats proceeding with one following another, stern to bow.

837. TSAI-HOU KAN-PANG CH'UAN 在後趕幫船 Straggler boat

A boat that is slow and left behind speeds up to rejoin the main fleet.

[[6]] Rural officials. Nos. 838–845

838. YÜ-CHANG 圩長 Village headman

In southern provinces a large village is called a yü.
The present term refers to the chief head of a village.

839. CH'IU-CHANG 坵長 Village headman

[Ch'iu] also denotes a large village; the term varies in different provinces. [In some places it denotes a subdivision of a large village.]

840. CH'Ü-CHANG 區長 Section head

The head of a ch'ü 區 [section] in the rural areas 鄉中.

841. TI-FANG 地方 Local constable

The policeman in a rural area.

842. TSUNG-CHIA 總甲 Village administrator

In large villages and towns 村鎮 the area [of each] is divided into several chia 甲 [precinct], [each consisting of] some scores or a hundred households. Each precinct is again subdivided into a number of p'ai 排 [tithing] and hsiang 鄉 [hamlet]. Overseeing the tithing is the p'ai-chia 排甲 [tithing head], and controlling the hamlet is the hsiang-yüeh 鄉約 [hamlet controller]. There are also li-chang 里長 [village heads] who are in charge of exhorting (the people) to be law-abiding. All are under the jurisdiction of the tsung-chia 總甲 [village administrator], who is an official appointed by the department or district government.

843. P'AI-CHIA 排甲 Tithing head

See above [842].

844. HSIANG-YÜEH 鄉約 Hamlet controller

See above [842].

845. LI-CHANG 里長 Village head

See above [842].

[[7]] Labor force. Nos. 846-848

846. TIEN-HU 佃戶 Tenant farmer

One who owns no land, but rents and cultivates land belonging to a wealthy family, is called a "tenant farmer."

847. TS'UI[sic]-KUNG 催工 Hired labor; or wage laborer

(*Ts'ui 催 "to urge" is erroneously given as yung 傭 "wage-hire" in the annotated edition.) [The correct word is ku 催 .]

A laborer who is paid a monthly wage.

848. TING-CH'AI 丁差 A service

(*Ting 丁 "male adult" reads i 一 "one, a, " in the Chia-ch'ing and annotated editions.)

When the people are ordered by the local authorities to contribute money or materials to some government project, the assignment of duties is known as "assignment of service" 派差 , and each individual item is called "a service" 差 .

[[8]] Population
  A. Concerning some ethnic minorities. Nos. 849-864

849. SHA MIN 沙民 Sandbar population

The people who cultivate and live on the sandbars off the sea coast of Kwangtung and Fukien provinces are known as the "sandbar population. "

850. I PA 彝把 Chief(s) of the I people

The I people on the [southwestern] Yünnan border have chiefs whom they refer to as pa把; in other words, these are I chiefs, and they are differentiated [among themselves] as first chief(s) or second chief(s)

851. HAN PA 漢把 Chief(s) of the Chinese

The Chinese living along the Yünnan border also use this term [i.e., pa or chief] in referring to their own chiefs.

852. YAO-MAN 傜蠻 Yao barbarians

The aborigines of the mountains in Kwangsi are called Yao barbarians.

853. YAO T'UNG 傜童 Yao boy

(*T'ung 童 "boy" should be written as 僮 or 獞 .)

The son of a Yao barbarian. [If the character 僮 chuang, the name of another minority group in Hunan and Kwangsi, rather than 童 "boy" is intended here, then the interpretation should be amended to read: "The Yao and Chuang peoples. "]

854. FAN-I 番夷 Fan barbarians

The frontier barbarians in Szechwan and Kansu provinces are called Fan barbarians.

855. MIAO-TZU 苗子 The Miao people

Aborigines of the mountains in Kweichow.

856. LO-LO 玀玀 Lolo

A kind of aboriginal people.

857. NA-TA 哪達 Na-ta

(*Ta 達 is given as 噠 in the Manchu-Chinese editions.)

Same as above [856]. Both the Lolo and the Na-ta tribes are ruled by the tribal authorities 土司 of Yünnan province.

858. T'U-SSU 土司 Tribal authorities

[These are] the high chiefs of the aborigines in the provinces of Szechwan, Kwangsi, Yünnan and Kweichow, whose offices are hereditary. Known as tribal prefect, tribal department magistrate, tribal district magistrate, etc., they are referred to as "tribal authorities" in general.

[Cf. 203-208 under the Board of Civil Appointment.]

859. T'U-SHE 土舍 Tribal leader(s)

The (tribal) leaders who carry out the administration of the tribal authorities.

[Cf. 208.]

860. T'U-MU 土目 Tribal head

The head man [or men] among the tribal barbarians.

861. SHE-PA 舍把 Chief leader

The chief of the tribal leaders.

862. PA-SHE T'U-FAN 八舍土番 The Eight Leaders of the tribal people

In Yünnan the most powerful tribal authorities comprise eight families, such as the Lungs, the Ch'ens and so on. They are known as the "Eight Leaders of the tribal people."

863. WAI-FAN SE-MU JEN TENG 外番色目人等 People of various foreign origins

[...] (This phrase) refers to people who belong to some categories of foreign barbarians, but who are not members of the races in China.

864. HUI-CHIAO CHUNG JEN 回教中人 Moslems

People who follow the Islamic religion.

[[8]] (continued)
   B. Census statuses and administration. Nos. 865-886

865. T'U-MIN 土民 Native people

The people who are natives of the locality. Those from other places temporarily residing [here] 流寓 are termed "temporary residents" 客民.

866. P'ING-MIN 平民 Common people

Full civilians.

867. HUA-MIN 花民 Lower classes [or castes]

People of low [official census] statuses. Hua 花 means miscellaneous.

868. LIU-YÜ 流寓 Temporary residence

See above [865].

869. CHUANG-TING 壯丁 Able-bodied men

Men of the common people in their prime of life.

870. T'UN-TING 屯 丁 Agricultural settlers

   Men who are agricultural settlers and live by cultivating government land.

871. CHENG-TING 正 丁 Men of the family

   The originally [registered] male adults of a family.

872. HU-TING 戸 丁 Men of the clan, [men of the household]

   The male adults in an entire clan. [Hu-ting is possibly a reference to all male adults in a household, including servants, apprentices, and others besides the men of the family. Cf. CTTS, II, 471, on the pao-chia system.]

873. LI-TING 力 丁 Labor-service men

   Male adults owing labor service to the government.

874. CHÜN-TING 軍 丁 Military-service men

   Male adults who should serve as soldiers.

875. YÜ-TING 餘 丁 Extra-quota men

   Aside from those who owe military service, all other male adults [in a family] are termed "extra-quota men."

876. HSIEN-TING 閑 丁 Non-quota men

   Same as above [875].

877. CH'ENG-TING 成 丁 Adult male

   When a youngster reaches twenty years in age he becomes known as an "adult male."

878. SHE-TING 舎 丁 House men

   The sons of family slaves.

879. PIEN-SHEN MIN-TING 編審民丁 Recording of census

   A census of the households and their male members is taken once every three years by the local officials among the people, and the mature and able-bodied men are recorded in the government files. This is known as "recording of census."

880. FU-HUI TING-K'OU 復回丁口 Returned men and women

People who had fled and scattered during a military or natural catastrophe have returned to their original homes.

881. LING-HU JEN 另戶人 Men of an individual household

[Members of] an independent household that belongs to no clan.

882. K'AI-TANG JEN 開檔人 Off-the-record men

Men whose names have been stricken from the [census] records and are no longer listed in the files [cf. 879].

883. KUAN-CHUANG PO-SHIH-K'U 管庄撥什庫 Treasurer of an [imperial] estate

Po-shih-k'u is a Manchu term equivalent to "treasurer" in Chinese, and refers to the man among the [Banner?] troops who is in charge of accounts. (This item) refers to the treasurer in charge of [the finances of] an imperial estate.

884. T'UN PO-SHIH-K'U 屯撥什庫 Treasurer of an agricultural settlement

The treasurer in charge of [financial] matters at an agricultural settlement.

885. CHÜN-SAN AN-CHIA HSIEN-TING 軍三安家閑丁 Non-quota men to look after affairs of a three-soldier family

When three men from a family are already doing military service, then the rest of the men [or extra-quota men, cf. 875] are not assigned any labor duties, but are allowed to look after their family affairs. They are known as "non-quota men to look after the affairs of a three-soldier family."

886. CHAO-FU MIN-TING CH'I-FEN LING 招復民丁七分零 Over-seven-tenths of the men have been recalled

Over seven-tenths of the men who had fled [because of some catastrophe in the locality] have now been called back [by the authorities] and have returned to their occupations.

-143-

[[9]] Relief administration. Nos. 887-920

887. YANG-CHI-YÜAN 養濟院 Public Relief Home(s)

Government-established institutions where the indigent may stay and receive relief.

888. KU-P'IN TIEN-LIEN 孤貧顛連 Solitary, indigent, homeless wanderers

Persons who are without family, impoverished, and shifting from place to place.

889. YIN-SHIH P'ING-MIN 殷實平民 Substantial people

People who are well-to-do and law-abiding.

890. SHIH JU HSÜAN-CH'ING 室如懸磬 House resembling an empty shell

Having absolutely no possessions in one's house.

891. P'IN-NAN HSIA HU 貧難下戶 Indigent, low-class household

An impoverished low-class family that finds it difficult to subsist.

892. YING-SHE CH'AI-I 影射差役 Evasion of labor duty

To avoid government labor service on some pretext.

893. FANG FU CH'AI P'IN 放富差貧 Letting off the wealthy and assigning duty to the poor

Government runners, having accepted bribes, let the wealthy people off [without labor duty] and assign the labor duties only to poor families.

894. T'O-LOU HU-K'OU 脫漏戶口 Missing census counts

When taking the census (an official) makes incomplete counts and recordings, so that the number of persons and households recorded are not complete.

895. HU-YU CHIH-CHAO 戶由執照 License for change of residence

The background and reasons for [a family's] change of residence are told to the authorities [of the new locality], who will issue a license to the applicants, and also officially record them as having become local residents. This refers to a change in one's official, permanent place of residence where one is native 籍貫 , e.g., moving from one district to another.]

896. **T'AO-HU CHOU-CHIH WEN-TS'E** 逃戶週知文冊
List of refugee households

To record in a book [the names of] all persons and households who have fled the local area, so that [the authorities] may know the situation at a glance.

897. **CH'IUNG-K'UN WU-I** 窮困無倚 Impoverished and without support

Persons who are poor, in dire circumstances, and have no one to support them.

898. **CHIU-SHIH HU-K'OU** 就食糊口 To earn a subsistence by going to another place

(A man) unable to find a livelihood in his native place hires himself out as a wage laborer.

899. **KUA-MIEN CHIU-HSING** 鵠面鳩形 Haggard and emaciated

Shivering with hunger and cold.

[Amended, p. 143:] Starving and cold people, whose faces are haggard and bodies emaciated.

900. **AO-AO TAI PU** 嗷嗷待哺 Wailing and waiting for sustenance

(Starving people) crying aloud as they beg for food.

[Amended, p. 143:] Ao-ao 嗷嗷 "[sound of] wailing" originated in the sentence in the Book of Poetry, "the sorrowful wailing of the bird," here used to describe the weeping of hungry people. "Waiting for sustenance" means that these people are unable to support themselves, but must wait for others to provide food--colloquially termed "being fed."

901. JEN-HSIN HUANG-HUANG 人心惶惶 The people are alarmed

"Alarmed" means agitated; the people have become agitated and nervous.

902. HUANG-HUANG WU-TS'O 惶惶無措 Alarmed and nervous

Same as above [901].

903. JEN-MIN LIU-LI 人民流離 The people are scattered

The people have fled and scattered during wartime.

904. TO-FANG CHAO-FU 多方招撫 To recall and pacify (the people) through many ways

"Through many ways" means to devise the way. Local authorities devising ways to call back the displaced persons who had fled, so that they will return to their native place and be cared for. [See also 880, 886.]

[Cf. 905, 907, 911. 912, 913, 920. The calling together of famine refugees as a means of maintaining some stability in the economy was an important function of the local officials during times of disaster.

In late Ch'ing there were twelve officially stipulated measures in relief administration that included, among other things, the extermination of locust larvae, remission of taxes, promotion of the sale of rice, and public works programs. One of the measures was the "calling together of displaced persons" (chi liu-wang 集流亡), which aimed at preventing the local people from leaving their homes as well as inducing those who had already fled to return. See KHHT, 19:5-6.]

905. CH'ÜAN-YÜ CHAO-LAI 勸諭招徠 Urging (people) to encourage the coming (of displaced persons)

Local authorities urging the gentry and the wealthy citizens to contribute money as a means of encouraging the displaced persons [i.e., refugees from a famine or war] to settle in this locality.

906. AI-HUNG FU-CHI 哀鴻甫集　The victims are just flocking here

"The victims" refers to starving, weeping people.　The famine victims are beginning to gather.

907. CHIEN YU CH'I-SE 漸有起色　Gradually reviving

With the people gathering [to settle here], the locality is showing signs of revival.

908. JIH SHEN I-JIH, NIEN FU I-NIEN 日甚一日，年復一年 [Worsening] from day to day, and from year to year

Both phrases mean that a locality continues to decline day by day and year after year, without a sign of revival.

[Appendix to 908　(p. 142):] Liu-wang wei fu 流亡未復. not yet recovered from loss of population.

This means that, at the end of a famine or war, [a locality] has not yet recovered from the loss of its population which had fled or scattered.

909. MIEN-LI CHÜAN-CHEN 勉力捐賑　To exert oneself in contributing to relief

To exert oneself in making the largest possible money contribution for relief of the poor.　[Cf. 722.]

910. CHU-CHOU CHEN-CHIU 煮粥賑救　To save (the poor) by donating gruel

To donate rice for cooking into gruel, which is daily distributed to the poor, thus saving their lives.

911. FU-CHI FU-YEH 附籍復業　Establishing residence and restoring occupation

To let people from elsewhere establish their residence in this locality, so that they may resume their former occupations.

912. HU-K'OU JIH FAN 戶口日繁　Steady increase in population

As more displaced persons gather [at a locality] day

-147-

after day, the population [literally, households and men] has also steadily increased and flourished.

913. HO-CH'U FU-CH'A CHIH MIN 荷鋤負鍤之民
Persons laden with hoes and spades

Displaced persons who carry with them agricultural implements, and come to work on uncultivated land to earn a living.

914. SUI-K'U LI-CHIEH CHIH CH'IUNG-MIN 髓枯力竭之窮民 Bone-poor and exhausted people

People who are extremely impoverished and daily becoming more emaciated.

915. WU-YEH YU-SHOU LAI-LI PU-MING CHIH JEN 無業遊手來歷不明之人 Persons without occupation or clearly-known past

Vagrants who have never had regular occupations, but have wandered all over the country, and whose origins are not known.

916. HUO NO-I JIH-SHIH SHAN CHÜ-CHIA CHIH CH'IN-TS'UI 或那移日食殫舉家之勤瘁 (People who) exhaust their entire family's labor yet (only) eat haphazardly

To "eat haphazardly" means being unable to eat regular daily meals; "exhaust" means to use up. This item means the hard labor of an entire family cannot earn enough food for its members.

917. HUO CHIEH-TAI NIU-CHUNG CHIEH CHUNG-NIEN CHIH PING-TI 或借貸牛種竭終年之胼胝 (People who obtain) oxen and seeds on borrowed money, and work hard all year

(These people) go into debt in order to buy their oxen and seed grain, and work so hard on the land all year long that thick callouses have developed on their hands and feet.

918. AI-K'AN LIU-MIN MING-CHI NAN NÜ TA HSIAO TING-K'OU 挨勘流民名籍男女大小丁口 House-to-house

census of the displaced persons as to their names, native place, sex, age, and number of male adults

To make a house-to-house inspection of the displaced persons' families and the number of individuals, and to enter [the data] in the [government] records.

919. P'AI-MEN FEN-PI SHIH-CHIA PIEN-WEI I-CHIA HU-HSIANG PAO-SHIH 排門粉壁十家編為一甲互相保識 To be written on the white walls; organize each ten families into a tithing [in which all members] must mutually guarantee and know each other

Each ten families are organized into a tithing [chia 甲] (within which) the families are to guarantee each other's past history. The names and occupations of the men in each family are to be written in whitewash on the walls, so that the information can be known at a glance.

920. CHAO-CHI LIU-I 招集流移 Calling together the displaced persons

To call together people who are displaced or have moved away, so that they can cultivate the land.

[[10]] The land
    A. Types of land.   Nos. 921- 980

921. T'IEN-TI 田地 The land

The general term for fields and land. [In North China, ti designates dry fields, while t'ien refers to paddy fields. E.g., KHHT, 17:3.]

922. FEI T'IEN 肥田 Fertile land

Land whose soil is rich [or productive].

923. CHI T'IEN 瘠田 Poor land

Land whose soil is thin and bad.

924. SHAN T'IEN 山田 Mountain land

Land in the mountains.

925. HU T'IEN 湖田 Lake land

    Sandy land along the shores of lakes.

926. YÜ T'IEN 淤田 Alluvial land

    The land composed of silted soil, that is exposed when a river changes its course.

927. T'U T'IEN 塗田 Mud land

    Muddy land near a body of water.

928. KUAN T'IEN 官田 Government land

    Land owned by the government.

929. MIN T'IEN 民田 Private land

    Land privately owned by the people.

930. TSU T'IEN 租田 Rented land

    Land that has been rented for cultivation.

931. K'O T'IEN 科田 Taxable land

    Land that has been rated for taxation.

932. T'UN T'IEN 屯田 Agricultural-settlement land

    Land cultivated by troops [i.e., military agriculturists].

933. CHÜN T'IEN 軍田 Military land

    Land allotted by the government to the army for cultivation and pasturage.

934. HUNG T'IEN 弘田 Extended land

    Land [the borders of which] have been extended.

935. YÜ T'IEN 餘田 Surplus land

    The land in excess of that for which a principal use [has been designated].

936. KUNG T'IEN 功田 Merit-award land

    The landed estate awarded by the Emperor to a meritorious official.

937. K'O T'IEN 客田 Guest-resident's land

Land bought by a temporary resident. [See 865, 954.]

938. KUAN T'IEN 馆田 Post station land

Land of which the rent is used to defray the expense of the military post stations.

939. MIAO T'IEN 苗田 Miao land

Land in the provinces of Yunnan and Kweichow that is the property of the Miao people.

940. TING-KUNG T'IEN 定弓田 Bow-measured land

Land the measurements of which are ascertained in terms of the bow 弓 . [One kung or "bow" equals five ch'ih (Chinese foot) in length: KHHT, 17:3.]

941. ERH-TOU T'IEN 二斗田 Two-peck land

Land whose annual tax assessment is two pecks per mou; that is, top-grade land.

942. CHI-CHUANG T'IEN 寄莊田 Land under a manager

Land that has been turned into the hands of a tenant [-manager], who collects the rents for (the owner). [Chi-chuang t'ien may be alternatively rendered as "absentee-owned land," since it describes the land in a given district owned by a resident of another. Hu-pu tso-li (1851 ed.), 9:7b. This might have partly been the fact on which the interpretation given in the present entry is based.]

943. TSA-LIANG T'IEN 雜糧田 Miscellaneous grain land

Land that can be used to raise no rice but only other cereals.

944. CHÜAN-CHU T'IEN 捐助田 Contributed land

Land that has been donated by wealthy persons to help defray government expenses.

945. HSÜEH CHI T'IEN 學祭田 School and shrine lands

Land belonging to the [government] schools, or to ancestral shrines, and temples.

-151-

946. SHUI-HSIANG T'IEN 水鄉田 Well-watered land

Land in the southern provinces that is situated near water supplies, and is suitable for the cultivation of rice.

947. CH'UNG-TSU T'IEN 重租田 Sub-rented land

Land that was first rented to A, and A in turn rents it to B to cultivate.

948. MO-KUAN T'IEN 没官田 Confiscated land

Land that has been confiscated by the government.

949. SHU TI 熟地 Mature land

Land that has matured through cultivation.

950. HUANG TI 荒地 Unused land

Deserted, overgrown land that has not been cultivated.

951. LU TI 鹵地 Brine land [or, salt land]

Land from which [or where] salt is produced.

952. CH'IEN SHA 遷沙 Shifting sands

Land on sandbars off the sea coast. Sometimes, when it is shifted by wind and tide, it is called "shifting sands."

953. T'U-CHU TI 土著地 Native owned land

Land owned by natives of the locality.

954. LIU-YÜ TI 流寓地 Temporary-resident owned land

Land owned by one who is a temporary resident (in the locality). [Cf. 937.]

955. HSING-LIANG TI 行糧地 Field rations land

Land that produces rations for troops on active service.

956. CH'I-SHA TI 棄沙地 Sandy wastes

Sandy land that is useless and has gone to waste.

957. CHI T'IEN 籍田 Mapped land

Land which has been marked off with dykes and paths.

[Amended, p. 143:] Land that has been charted on maps.
[籍田 also denoted the fields which the Emperor himself
ploughed in annual Spring rites. CTTS, II, 338.]

958. LU T'IEN 蘆田 Reed land

Land where reeds are planted.

959. SHUI-TZ'U 水次 Waterfront

Areas along the river.

960. SHAN-CH'ANG 山廠 Mountain areas

Areas in the mountain.

961. HU-PO 湖泊 Lakes

Islands [sic?] in a lake.

962. CH'A YUAN 茶園 Tea orchard

An orchard where tea is planted.

963. LU TANG 蘆蕩 Reedy islet

An islet where reeds grow.

964. HO-T'AN TI 河灘地 River sand-bank land

Land on sand-banks in the river.

965. KO-MO [TI] 割沒[地] Partitioned and confiscated [land]

Land that has been apportioned to the government.

966. TS'AO-T'A TI 草塌地 Grass-grown land

Land overgrown with wild grass.

967. T'OU-CH'UNG CH'I-TI 投充旗地 Banner land from
Chinese adherents

The land presented by the [Chinese] people to the Eight
Banners, to be owned by the latter and used as their
public land. [The question of t'ou-ch'ung or Chinese
adherents of the Manchu Banners was one that came up
frequently in the early years of Ch'ing dynasty, and it
generated social and economic problems in a situation
already tense. Ma Feng-ch'en briefly discusses it in

his article on "Manchu-Chinese Social and Economic Conflicts in Early Ch'ing," <u>Shih-huo</u>, IV, nos. 6, 8, 9.]

968. T'AN-T'A T'IEN-TI 坍塌田地 Eroded land

Land on river banks that has been washed away by water.

969. T'AN-CHIANG T'IEN-TI 坍江田地 River-eroded land

Land that has been eroded and fallen into the river.

970. PAN-HUANG T'IEN-TI 版荒田地 Unregistered land

Unused land of which the ownership has not been registered.

971. K'EN-KUO T'IEN-TI 墾過田地 Cultivated land

Land that has been put under cultivation.

972. MA-CH'ANG YÜ TI 馬廠餘地 Surplus land of imperial horse pastures

The excess land in imperial pasturages. [Horse pasturage was an important matter to the Manchus, who at the beginning of their rule had set aside certain amounts of land for this purpose, which were known as <u>mu-ch'ang</u> 牧塲 or imperial pasturages. With the decline in the number of horses in later years, the excess land of the pasturages was often put under cultivation. See the account given in SCYC, 4:55-56.]

973. CH'IAO-CH'ÜEH PU-MAO 磽确不毛 Stony and barren [land]

Gravel and stone-covered land [or, desert] where not a blade of grass will grow.

974. TI TUO HUANG-WU 地多荒蕪 The land is largely unused and overgrown

The land has largely gone to waste and is not cultivated.

975. HAI-T'AN YÜ-SHA TI 海灘淤沙地 Sandy alluvial land on the coast

Land that has been formed along the sea coast by silting from the flow of sandy water.

976. HUANG T'IEN CH'ENG-SHU TI 荒田成熟地 Land
matured from unused land

The land was formerly unused, but has become mature
land after having been put under cultivation.

977. MIN-FU KENG-MING T'IEN-TI 民賦更名田地
Private, taxable, changed-ownership land

Taxable land privately owned by the people is being sold,
and thus entails a change in the owner's name. [Keng-ming
t'ien 更名田 , "changed-ownership land", was a classification of land dating from the beginning of Ch'ing. It
comprised land confiscated by the Manchus from the former
Ming feudatories and was added to the ordinary agricultural taxable land to be privately owned by the people:
KHIIT, 17.0. The interpretation given here may be a later
derivation of the term.]

978. TIAO-TS'AN CHI-PO CHIH TI 凋殘瘠薄之地
Devastated, poor land

A war-devastated area of sparse population, where the soil
has become poor through prolonged lack of cultivation.

979. TS'UNG-CHEN MAO-TS'AO CHIH CH'Ü 叢榛茂草之
區 Area of flourishing brambles and grass

(A place) where brambles and thorny bushes abundantly
grow and wild grass flourishes; this describes the appearance
of an uncultivated waste area.

980. TS'UNG-CHING TIEH-CHI CHIH TI 叢荊疊棘之地
A place of abundant brambles and thorns

Same as above [979].

[[10]] (continued)
B. Taxation, measurement, and other agricultural
matters. Nos. 981-1015

981. SHIH PEI-TSAI T'IEN ERH-CHIA LING 實被災田二
甲零 The land of two precincts or more has been actually
ruined

To check on the actual acreage of land that has been ruined by the catastrophe [.....? Sentence appears incomplete.]

982. CHAO SHANG CHUNG HSIA TSE CH'I-K'O 照上中下則起科 [Land taxes are to be] assessed according to the high, medium or low rating of the land

To check the quality of the land, classifying it into the three grades of high, medium, or low, and then assess the taxes according to statute.

983. K'EN-KUO MIN-FU KENG-MING T'IEN-TI, CHI KUEI-PING T'UN-T'IEN 墾過民賦更名田地及歸併屯田 Cultivated taxable changed-ownership land, and merged agricultural settlement land [or merged tax-value land]

(*T'un 屯 "agricultural settlement" is given erroneously as chih 直 "value" in the Chia-ch'ing and annotated editions.)

Land that has been put under cultivation, on which taxes are paid by the people and of which the ownership has changed [cf. 977]; and, two separate lots of land the assessed tax values of which have been merged into one single item. [This interpretation conforms not to the present heading but to that given in the Chia-ch'ing and annotated editions, which Naitō considers erroneous.]

984. K'EN-KUO CHUNG HSIA TZ'U SAN-TSE T'UN T'IEN 墾過中下次三則屯田 Cultivated agricultural settlement land of medium, low, or secondary quality

Cultivated land in military agricultural settlements is also classified into three categories.

985. YU-CHU CHUNG YU ERH-WEI KO CHIU-HUANG YÜ T'UN-T'IEN 有主中右二衛各舊荒餘屯田 Agricultural settlement land derived from surplus uncultivated land owned by the Central and Right Wing Garrisons

The Central and Right Wing Garrisons designate military camps. This item refers to the surplus uncultivated land owned by these two army camps that is turned into military agricultural settlement land [i.e., placed under cultivation by the troops].

986. HSIA-TSE KO CHIU-HUANG T'UN-YÜ KUNG SHUI WU-PAI MU 下則各舊荒屯餘共稅五百畝
Taxes from five hundred <u>mou</u> of low-grade formerly uncultivated land, and from agricultural settlement land derived from surplus

There are five hundred <u>mou</u> of taxable land consisting of low-grade, formerly uncultivated land, and the surplus land that has been put under cultivation by agricultural settlers.

987. FU-CHIEN NAI HAI-YA CH'IH-LU CHIH HSIANG, CH'AO-SHIH MEI-CHENG CHIH TI 福建乃海涯斥滷之鄉潮濕霉蒸之地 Fukien is a seaboard area that has briny soil and a damp, steamy [climate]

Fukien, situated on the sea coast, has soil that is often saturated with salt water, and a climate which is damp, warm, and steamy, where things are easily spoiled.

988. SHAN T'IEN TS'O-LO CH'I-CH'Ü, SHUI HSIANG YÜ-HUI CH'Ü-CHE 山田錯落崎嶇, 水鄉迂迴曲折
Mountain land on rugged terrain, and water land with twists and turns

Mountain land that lies on uneven ground, and twisting, turning, fragmented land near the water.

989. CH'ING-CHANG 清丈 Surveying

To measure the acreage of land and to clarify its boundaries.

990. CHANG-LIANG 丈量 Measurement

Same as above [989].

991. CHANG-CH'U 丈出 Result of measuring

The figures resulting from the measurement (of land).

992. CHANG-TSENG 丈增 Measured increase

The increase of acreage that shows up in a measuring of land.

993. T'ING-LIU 停留 A halt [in measuring the land]

    To delay the measuring for the time being.

994. K'AI-K'EN 開墾 To place under cultivation

    To open up unused land and let the people cultivate it.

995. CH'ÜAN-K'EN 勸墾 Exhortation to cultivation

    To exhort the people to cultivate unused land.

996. FU-YEH 復業 Return to [one's] occupation

    The refugees have returned to their former occupations.

997. LO-YEH 樂業 Happy in [one's] occupation

    People living in security and happily pursuing their respective occupations: the sign of prosperous and peaceful times.

998. NIU-CHUNG 牛種 Calf [or calves]

    Young cattle [or ox, buffalo, etc.].

999. TZU-LI 籽粒 Seed grain

    Seeds for planting the fields. [Cf. 514, 677.]

1000. LIU-NIEN SHENG-K'O 六年陞科 [Land to be] taxable in six years

    When unused land is put under cultivation it is not taxed until after the sixth year. [This seemingly contradicts 623, which states that tax exemption for newly opened land was in effect for three years. See the note under 623.]

1001. JEN-T'U TSO-KUNG 任土作貢 Tribute of local products

    To present to the government the things that are produced in the locality.

1002. YIN-CHAN LIANG-T'IEN 隱占糧田 Concealed possession of taxable land

    People concealing their possession of land on which taxes should be paid; that is, being unwilling to pay the taxes due the government.

1003. NIEH-K'EN PAO-KUAN 捏墾報官 False report to government of opening land for cultivation

(*The word kuan 官 "government" is missing from the Manchu-Chinese editions.)

Making false reports of having put unused land under cultivation, so as to receive government funds for calves and seed grain.

1004. I-CH'IU HUAN-TUAN 移垃換叚 Removing field paths and changing demarcations

To alter the demarcations on the farmers' field paths with the intention to encroach [on the land].

1005. CH'IN-CHAN T'IEN-TI 侵占田地 Encroaching on the land

To devise ways to encroach and occupy the land that belongs to others.

1006. **T'IEN-CHIEH HSIANG-LIEN** 田界相連 Adjacent fields

The borders of the fields touch each other.

1007. HU-SHUI KUAN-T'IEN 戽水灌田 Irrigating the fields by baling up water

To bale up water with a swing bucket [lun-tou 輪斗 ; same as hu-tou 戽斗 ?] and irrigate the fields with it.

1008. HUANG-CH'IEN 荒歉 Poor harvest

In a bad year, when the harvest of all grains is scanty.

1009. HEI-TAN HUANG-TAN 黑丹黃丹 Black blight, yellow blight

If black or yellow blemishes appear on the rice just before ripening, the grain will rot. [The disease] is commonly called "black blight" or "yellow blight."

1010. TA-SHUI CH'UNG-NI 大水沖溺 Inundated by flood

Flood waters from the river destroying houses and fields and drowning people.

1011. HAN-PA WEI NÜEH 旱魃為虐 Disaster wrought by the drought demon

"Drought" is a catastrophe resulting from lack of water.
(This phrase) originated in the Book of Poetry.

[Amended, p. 143:] This phrase originated in the Book
of Poetry. The superstitious people of antiquity believed
that droughts were caused by the malicious doings of
demons, and in later times the phrase has been traditionally
used [to indicate a drought].

1012. PING-PAO TA-SHANG T'IEN-HO 氷電打傷田禾
Hail has damaged field crops

The crops in the fields are damaged by a hail storm.

1013. CH'ENG-TSAI PU-CH'ENG-TSAI 成災不成災
In a state of disaster; not in a state of disaster

During a flood or drought, [an area] is said to have
reached a "state of disaster" if the crops have suffered
damage, and to be "not in a state of disaster" if they have
not.

1014. HSIEN I HUANG-NAN CHI TSAO SHUI-TSAI 先罹蝗
蝻繼遭水災 Having first suffered from locusts, later
is hit by flood

[An area] first is plagued by locusts, and then is hit by
a flood.

1015. TUNG-TSO CHI-SHIH CH'IU-CH'ENG WU-WANG 東作
旣失秋成無望 Having missed Spring planting, the
Autumn harvest is hopeless

(*Tung 東 "East" is given erroneously as ch'un 春
"spring" in the annotated edition.)

Since planting was missed in the Spring because of
drought, what could one expect of the Autumn harvest?

[[11]] Some conventional phrases. Nos. 1016-1032

1016. K'AN-KUAN YIN-CHIEH 勘官印結 Inspecting official's
sealed statement

The official who inspects a disaster [or famine] area should present to his superior a statement with his seal affixed to it, as a means to guarantee the correctness [of the report].

1017. LI-CHIEH NAN-CHIH 力竭難支 Exhausted and difficult to carry on

(One is) exerting one's utmost efforts to carry on, but (the matter) is very difficult to manage. [Sic ?]

1018. WU-TS'UNG CHUI-PU 無從追捕 There is no way to track down and capture [a criminal]

An offender of the law has fled, his destination is not known, and it is not possible to track down and capture him.

1019. KUEI-HSIAO CHIH FA 歸銷之法 The procedure of (debt) cancellation

The procedures of paying back the indebted sum of money and closing the account.

1020. I-TSU YUAN-O 以足原額 In order to fulfill the original quota

In order to make up the entire sum originally set in the quota.

1021. WU P'IEN-K'U CHIH T'AN 無偏枯之嘆 Without the complaint of unequal treatment

"Unequal" means unfair. When (an official) is fair and just in his work of inspecting the famine and distributing relief material, the people then will not feel they are given discriminatory treatment.

1022. CHUAN-YEN CHIH CHIEN 轉眼之間 In the twinkling of an eye

Very quickly, in a little while.

1023. I CHUAN-I CHIEN 一轉移間 In changing [the procedures of a matter]

To carry out a matter by shifting or changing (the procedures), as such changes are mutually beneficial.

1024. **HSIANG-CH'Ü PU-YUAN** 相去不遠 Not far from

Approximately, almost.

1025. **PU-SHEN YU-AI** 不甚有碍 Not inconvenient

There are no inconveniences involved [in doing a thing].

1026. **SHENG SO-TANG SHENG** 生所當生 To create that which ought to be created

To create means to add; that is, in the conduct of public affairs, that which should be added must be added. [The common usage for this phrase is <u>hsing so-tang hsing</u> 興所當興 .]

1027. **KO SO-TANG KO** 革所當革 To remove that which ought to be removed

To remove means to eliminate; that is, whatever should be eliminated must be eliminated.

1028. **CH'ING HUANG PU-CHIEH CHIH HOU** 青黃不接之候 The season of pre-harvest food shortages

The period before the new grain is harvested while the old grain is nearly finished, when the people do not have enough food to tide over the period.

1029. **KENG-CHIU YÜ-SAN CHIH KU** 耕九餘三之穀 Three years' surplus grain out of nine years of cultivation

After nine years spent in hard work tilling the soil, the people must have surplus grain enough for three years.

[Amended, p. 142:] <u>Keng chiu yü san</u> 耕九餘三 , "Three years' surplus out of nine years of cultivation": According to the <u>Book of Rites</u> 禮記, "after three years of cultivation there will be [extra] food for one year, and after nine years of cultivation there will be extra food for three years." That is to say, [that much grain] is accumulated out of the surplus, as a means of providing against famines.

1030. **LI I-FA CHI-YU I-PI** 立一法即有一弊 Each new law [or regulation, system] established means a way opened to a new abuse

A new law [or regulation, system] established in government administration will certainly benefit [some things], but it also is sure to lead to a new abuse.

1031. TZU-WU CHIEH-TZ'U NO-PI CHIH PI 自無借此挪彼之弊 The abuse of [spending money] under improper pretenses will naturally not occur

To shift and exchange [items of expenditure] in government business, using the funds expressly obtained for one thing to pay for another: if preventive measures are strictly enforced, then of course this abuse cannot occur.

1032. PU-WU I-CHIA CHIU-I CHIH YÜ 不無移甲就乙之虞 It is feared (the practice of) doing A in the name of B might not be avoidable

The abuse of shifting [the funds for?] item A to take care of item B is probably not to be unexpected.

[[12]] The salt administration. Nos. 1033-1086

1033. YEN FA 鹽法 Salt laws

Regulations pertaining to the salt administration are termed "salt laws" in general.

1034. YEN YIN 鹽引 Salt certificates

These are the permit tickets for the sale of salt. Each certificate [allows the sale of] a definite amount [i.e., a specific number of catties of salt] and the area of sale is also designated. It is similar to the travel permits 路引 for travellers. The (salt) certificates are made [printed?] at the Board of Revenue, and the entire lot [for a season] is issued to the head salt merchants 盐務總商, who receive it after paying the taxes. This procedure is known as "turning over to the shippers" 歸綱 [1039], the "shippers" being the merchant chiefs 大總. (The certificates) are then distributed among the individual salt merchants, who will obtain their salt at the salt factories and then sell it. This is called the "dispersal of certificates"

拆引 [See 1035, 1038]. [There are two technical interpretations of the word yin 引 as applied to the administration of salt. One, as indicated in the present item, refers to the actual permit paper required of salt merchants; that is, a "certificate", as I have rendered it here. The other denotes the standard weight catties of salt officially prescribed for each certificate, an amount that varied from time to time and also in different localities. When used in this context I shall render yin as "certified unit." Some sample data relating to the areas of sale, numbers of units certified, and the amount of salt revenue realized in the 1840's are to be found conveniently in SCYC, 5:33ff. For a description of the system of salt production and distribution in the Ch'ing period see Ho Ping-ti, "The Salt Merchants of Yang-chou: A Study of Commercial Capitalism in 18th Century China," Harvard Journal of Asiatic Studies, 17.1 and 2:130-168 (June 1954). In a number of cases I have adopted Mr. Ho's renderings of the special terms.]

1035. TS'O SHU 醝書 Salt Affairs Manual

Book of regulations on salt affairs, such as [the rules governing] the dispersal of certificates [see 1034].

1036. TS'AN YIN 殘引 Excess certificates

Of the certificates that were received (by the head salt merchants) from the Board of Revenue, the ones left over after distribution are termed "excess certificates," and should be returned to the government.

1037. YIN T'ING 引艇 Certificate delivery boats

Small boats that deliver the salt certificates to their various destinations.

1038. CH'E YIN 拆引 Dispersal of certificates; or, distributed certificates

The salt certificates that have been distributed by the head merchants to the individual salt merchants. [Cf. 1034.]

1039. KUEI KANG 歸綱 Turning over to the shippers

The issuance of the salt certificates in an entire lot [to the head merchants]. [Cf. 1034.]

1040. SHANG-KANG 商綱 Head merchant(s)

The ones overseeing all salt merchants.

[Amended, p. 143:] The supervisers of salt merchants, also known as head merchants 總商.

1041. TSAO-HU 竈戶 Salt-maker's household

A family engaged in making salt is called a "salt-maker's household."

1042. TSAO-TING 竈丁 Salt worker

The man who makes salt.

1043. YEN-CH'ANG 鹽場 Salt factory

Where salt [production] is supervised. It is headed by an official with the title of [yen-ch'ang] ta-shih [鹽場] 大使 (salt receiver B. 835A).

1044. T'ING-FANG 埠房 Storage place

The building in which the salt is stored.

1045. YEN-CH'ENG 鹽埕 Salt flat

The flat land where salt is produced by sun evaporation.

1046. YEN-LOU 鹽漏 Salt screen

The instrument used to purify the salt [brine]. It is made of iron and is commonly called a "strainer."

1047. CH'IH-CHIH 掣摯 Spot inspection

[...] To pick a bag of salt at random and inspect it.

[Cf. p. 143, Ch'ih-yen 掣驗 :] To prevent the salt merchants from clandestinely selling more than their legal limits of salt, [inspection] stations are established where officials are assigned to inspect the salt merchants' wares by picking out bags at random at unspecified times and weighing them. These officials are titled <u>Ch'ih-yen</u> <u>wei-yüan</u> 掣驗委員 [Inspection station deputies].

1048. CHIANG CH'IH 江掣 Yangtze consignment

[The products of] the salt factories of the Liang-Huai region are classified into (two categories): South of the Yangtze River, and North of the Yangtze River. That which is consigned by lot [see 1049] to the south is called "Yangtze consignment," and that which is consigned to the north, "Huai consignment" 淮掣

1049. CH'IH YEN 掣鹽 Consigning of salt

The consignment of finished salt at a given factory to the individual salt merchant(s) is determined by the drawing of lots. The government has established the <u>chien-ch'ih t'ung-chih</u> 監掣同知 (inspector of salt distribution, B. 835A) to be in charge. [In B. 835A the first character is misprinted as <u>yen</u> 塩.]

1050. CH'ENG-P'AN 秤盤 Weight check

"To check" means to examine. To weigh the bags of salt on big scales in order to see whether they are of the correct [or standard] weight.

1051. YING-CH'IH 應掣 To be consigned

The salt that should be made into consignments by lot.

1052. K'O YEN 客鹽 Market salt

The salt that is offered for sale by salt merchants.

1053. HAO-LU YEN 耗滷鹽 Brine wastage salt

(*<u>Lu</u> 滷 "brine" is given erroneously as <u>hai</u> 海 "sea" in the Chia-ch'ing and annotated editions.)

The amount of salt wastage per <u>tan</u> that results from the processes of sun evaporation and cleaning, after the salt is made from boiling sea water. [Cf. 1079.]

1054. HSING-YEN PAN-K'O 行鹽辦課 Issuance of salt (certificates) and collection of the (salt) revenue

The issuance of the salt certificates [as a means to] collect the revenue for the government. [Cf. 1080.]

1055. SUI-O YIN-YEN 歲額引鹽 Annual salt quota

The fixed annual quota of (legal) salt permitted to be sold by the issuance of certificates.

1056. CHAO-NA CH'ENG KANG 找納呈綱 Report to head merchants on insufficiency or surplus [in certificates]

If the salt certificates issued to the merchants are short of the quota, the number lacking should be made up to them; if there are more than the quota, the surplus should be returned to the government. All these matters are to be reported to, and handled by, the head salt merchants [kang-tsung 綱總,, same as tsung-shang 總商 ?].

1057. K'EN-FU YEN-CHE 墾復鹽折 Restoring salt reduction

A former area for the sale of salt is later abandoned; the number [of certified units of salt sold in the area] should also be reduced to the original amount. [There seems to be some omission in the text.]

1058. CHIEH-CHIAO T'UI YIN 截角退引 A clipped and returned certificate

An unused salt certificate that is given back [to the government] should have one of its corners cut off before being returned.

1059. LING-KEI YU-T'IEH 另給由帖 Additional (salt) license

Besides receiving the salt certificates, merchants who sell salt are given another permit paper called a "license."

1060. T'AO TA CHIH YIN 套搭之引 Retransacted or complementary certificates

A certificate issued to one merchant is turned over to another, or [the certified units allowed each merchant] are combined and sold jointly.

1061. T'AN-SHA CH'I-TSAO 攤沙起竈 Setting up a saltern

To level the sandy land by the sea and build a saltern

in order to make salt.

1062. MIN CHIEH TAN-SHIH 民皆淡食 The people eating unsalted food

In remote regions, to which government salt is not allotted, it is difficult to obtain salt for eating.

[Cf. p. 142, Min huan tan-shih 民患淡食 :] "The people suffering from unsalted food." This means that excessively high taxes [on salt] have raised the price of salt beyond the (purchasing) power of the people, so that they suffer from eating unsalted food. It is the view of the health experts that a person will fall ill if his diet lacks salt, hence the word "suffer."

1063. TS'O-K'U JU HSI 鹺庫如洗 The salt treasury is cleaned out

The treasury of the salt administration is empty.

1064. CHUNG-YEN LAI-LI 中鹽來歷 Background of the designation of salt sales

The specific areas where the certified units of salt [are to be sold] are all decided upon beforehand, a procedure known as "designation of salt sales." "Background" refers to the past history (of the procedure).

1065. CHOU-SUI O-PAN 週歲額辦 Annual quota

The quota of the salt certificates received and handled by the salt merchants each year.

1066. K'UEI-TUI K'O-CH'ENG 虧兌課程 Deficits in the salt revenue

Amounts that are short in the salt revenue paid to the government.

1067. YEN-T'U SSU-FAN 鹽徒私販 Salt smuggling

There are hoodlums who, paying no taxes, illegally transport and sell salt in different places. This is strictly prohibited by statute.

1068. CHIEN-T'IAO PEI-FU, I-MI TU-JIH 肩挑背負易米度日 Small amounts (of salt) sold to obtain daily rice

Although the smuggling of salt is strictly forbidden by statute, the latter does not forbid the sale of small amounts of illegal salt by the poor people.

[Amended, p. 143:] Statutes call for the capture and suppression of salt smugglers who engage in this business on a large scale, using convoys to transport their salt. But as for (the salt) that can be carried on a man's shoulders or back, the amount is insignificant, and the sale of such salt is not statutorily prohibited.

1069. TIEN-CHU WO TUN 店主窩頓 Concealed and stored by inn keepers

[...] The owners of inns clandestinely keeping and hiding illegal salt for smugglers.

1070. WO-TS'ANG CHI-TUN 窩藏寄頓 Concealing and storing

Same as above [1069].

1071. TSU-HUAI YEN FA 阻壞鹽法 Disrupting the salt laws

Benefits of the salt laws being sabotaged and destroyed by the (salt) smugglers.

1072. T'ING-TS'ANG CHIH JEN 停藏之人 Concealer

One who stores and hides illegal salt.

1073. SHANG-KUNG 上供 Tribute for the throne

Things presented as tribute to the Emperor.

1074. FANG-WU 方物 Local products

Things that are produced or manufactured in the locality itself.

1075. T'U-I 土宜 Native products

Same as above [1074].

1076. PIEH-CHING FAN CHIEH HUO-MAI 別境犯界貨賣 [Salt] from another area is sold in violation of the borders

Specific areas are marked out for the sale of government salt, and salt that has been designated for one area is not allowed to be sold in another. Any merchant acting contrary to this rule is said to have "violated the borders."

1077. YEN-CHENG LI YU K'AO-CH'ENG 鹽政例有考成 Statute calls for inspection of achievements in the management of salt affairs

There is a provision in the Statutes and Regulations of the Salt Administration [Yen-wu lü li 鹽務律例] that calls for the[periodic] inspection of the achievements of officials in charge of salt factories.

1078. TANG-TS'AO PU-SHENG TSAO K'U KUNG-CHIEN 蕩草不生竈苦供煎 Salt makers are distressed by the lack of reeds for fuel

When there is only a scanty supply of reeds at the seashore, the salt makers will lack fuel for making salt.

1079. MEI YIN CHO-TAI HAO-LU YEN ERH-SHIH CHIN 每引酌帶耗滷鹽二十觔 Twenty catties of brine wastage salt are carried in each certified unit

Loss of salt is expected because of rainy or hot weather, when the bagged salt will dissolve into brine. Twenty catties of brine wastage salt therefore are carried in each certified unit in addition to the regular amount, in order to replace the loss. [Cf. 1053].

1080. HSING-YEN PAN-K'O I-TSU YÜAN-O 行鹽辦課以足原額 To issue salt (certificates) and collect the revenue to fulfill the original [salt gabelle] quota

If the original quota of the salt gabelle cannot be realized, [additional] salt certificates are to be issued

for (other) areas as a means of obtaining the desired
revenue and making up the deficiency. [Cf. 1054.]
[Word inserted by Naitō.]

1081. FEN-KUAN CH'ENG-CH'IH I-TU CH'Ü-PI 分關秤製
以杜趨避 Weight checks at the toll houses to prevent
theft

Salt being transported by salt merchants is checked for
weight at all the toll houses [customs stations] to see
whether it conforms [to the standard weight], and to
prevent theft [by the merchants.--i.e., stealing government salt to sell for private profit].

1082. KEI-KUO YIN-MU TU-TS'UI KO-SHU 給過引目督
催各屬 Urging subordinates to expedite the payment
of salt revenue

After salt certificates have been issued to the merchants,
the subordinate officials are asked [by the official in
charge] to urge the merchants, each according to the
number of certificates he has received, to sell their
salt quickly and pay their taxes promptly.

1083. TS'AN YIN CHUI-PIEN, SSU-FAN SHU-YÜAN 殘引追
變私販贖錢 Excess certificates are converted into
money; salt smugglers' redemption fund

"Redemption fund" is the money with which a criminal
buys his own freedom. If, out of the certified units (of
salt) issued to the salt merchants, there are any unsold
excess portions, these are to be retrieved, converted
into money according to their worth, and be used for the
redemption of the smugglers.

[Amended, p. 143:] Excess certified units of salt that
have not been sold by the salt merchants are to be returned
(to the government) and their value converted into money;
the smuggler illegally selling salt who has been captured
must pay a fine to redeem his offense. These refer to
two different things and should not be confused as one.

1084. CHIEH-SHENG CHING-FEI CH'ING-CH'U CHI-YÜ 節省
經費清出積餘 To economize office spending, and

set aside the savings and surplus funds

Office expenditures of the salt administration should be economized; the savings accumulated through the years should be sought out, item by item, and be used for other needs.

1085. TS'AI-CHIEN HSIN-HUNG CHIH-CHANG KUNG-FEI CHEN-
CHI CH'IUNG TSAO 裁減心紅紙張公費賑
濟窮竈 To reduce the costs of seal ink, paper, and office expenses for relief of impoverished salt makers

When salt makers are too impoverished to make salt, the expenses for seal ink, paper supplies, and other office expenditures in the salt administration should be temporarily reduced; the amount thus saved will be used for the relief of the salt makers.

1086. CHAO-FU CH'IEN-I FU-YEH HSIN-TSENG CHUANG-TING
招撫遷移復業新增壯丁 To recall and rehabilitate [the salt makers who had] moved away, and to add new men to the job

Those salt makers who had moved away and scattered are to be called back, restored in their old occupation, and be given good care and rewards. At the same time new, able-bodied men are added [or recruited] to help them in their work.

[[13]] Other economic activities
A. Trade. Nos. 1087-1097

1087. KUAN-SHANG 官商 Government merchant(s)

Merchants operating with government permission, such as the salt merchants.

1088. FU-T'OU 埠頭 Wharf

The place where freight [or trading] boats are anchored, commonly called a pier 碼頭.

1089. CHING-CHI 經紀 Agent; manager

The man who personally handles [or manages] a business concern.

1090. YA-HANG 牙行 Broker

The person who brings together the two parties to a business deal and acts as guarantor.

1091. YA-PAO 牙保 Broker-guarantor

Same as above [1090].

1092. PO-SHANG 舶商 Maritime [or boat] merchant

A merchant who transports his goods by boat and conducts his business via waterways.

1093. K'ANG-T'OU 埕頭 Crew chief

The head of sailors [of a boat crew].

1094. HSIEH-CHIA 歇家 Hostel

A house where merchants and their goods can stop over.

1095. TANG-TS'AO 當槽 Waiter(s)

The men who wait on the merchant patrons at an inn.

1096. LIANG-P'ING CHIAO-I 兩平交易 Mutually fair transaction

A [business] transaction that is fair and just to both parties, commonly known as a "fair deal."

1097. HSING-FAN CH'U-CHIN 興販出津 Large-scale export of goods

To transport goods on a large scale, cross customs barriers and sell them at another place.

[[13]] (continued)
  B. Coinage. Nos. 1098-1107

1098. CH'IEN FA 錢法 Coinage laws

The statutes and regulations pertaining to the coinage office 鑄錢局. Also, affairs of the coinage office.

1099.　CHIH-CH'IEN 制錢 Standard cash, one-cash coin

The copper cash that is officially minted according to regulations laid down by the government. [In general usage chih-ch'ien is rendered simply as "copper cash" in English.　E.g., Yang, 4:16.]

1100.　SSU-CHU CH'IEN 私鑄錢 Illegal coins

Coins minted illegally by counterfeiters who have set up their own casting furnaces.

1101.　CHANG-CHU 掌鑄 Overseer of coinage

The official in charge of the minting of coins.

1102.　SHE-CHÜ CHU-CH'IEN 設局鑄錢 To establish a mint for coinage

To set up a mint for the casting of coins.

1103.　CH'IEN-FAN CH'ING CHENG 錢範清正 Coin molds are clear and fine

The "molds" are used for casting (the coins); "clear and fine" refer to the inscriptions that have been engraved clearly and properly into them.

1104.　LUAN-SHA 亂沙 Sand-cooling

When taken out of the molds (the coins) are spread in sand to harden. This is known as "sand-cooling."

1105.　TA SHA 打沙 Rubbing off the sand

After they have hardened in the sand, the coins are rubbed free of the sand grains that have adhered to them, and then are polished until shiny. These (processes) are called "rubbing off the sand" and "polishing" respectively.

1106.　MO CH'IEN 磨錢 Polishing the coins

See above [1105].

1107. K'AN HUO 看火 Watching the furnace

To watch and check on the furnace temperature while the copper is being melted for coinage.

[[13]]   (continued)
C.   Tea, etc. Nos. 1108-1113

1108. CH'A FA 茶法 Tea laws

The regulations pertaining to the government's collection of taxes on tea.

1109. CH'A YIN 茶引 Tea certificates

In Szechwan province and some others [e.g., Yunnan], tea merchants who transport and sell tea to the aborigines must operate within their respective designated areas; they also have to pay taxes and receive certificates, as is the case with the sale of salt. This rule, however, does not apply to the rest of the country.

1110. CHIA CH'A 假茶 Falsified tea

Low-grade tea that is passed off [and sold] as of good quality.

1111. YA CH'A 芽茶 Bud tea

The tender buds of tea leaves; that is, top grade tea.

1112. HSING-CH'A TI-FANG 行茶地方 Areas for the sale of tea

The delimited territories where tea is sold.

1113. LU-CHENG 蘆政 Reed land tax administration

Matters concerning the collection of the reed land tax [see 550] in Kiangsu and Chekiang are known as "reed tax administration."

[[14]] Publications; types of official documents.
Nos. 1114-1154

1114. FU-I CH'ÜAN-SHU 賦役全書 The Complete Book of
Land Tax and Labor Service

The book that gives general data on the land-poll taxes
in all the provinces.

1115. HSIN PIEN CH'ÜAN-SHU 新編全書 The Complete
Book (of Land Tax and Labor Service), Revised

Because of the frequent changes that take place in
taxation (the Fu-i ch'üan-shu) is revised periodically once
in a few decades.

1116. T'UNG-HSING TSE-LI 通行則例 Prevalent regulations
and precedents

The regulations and precedents of the Board of Revenue
that are uniformly observed in all the provinces.

1117. K'AO-CH'ENG TSOU-TS'E 考成奏冊 Volume of
memorials on the appraisal of achievements

Each year the provincial officials are checked for their
achievements in tax collection, and the results (of the
inspection) are assembled into one volume of memorials
for reporting to the throne.

1118. SSU-CHU CH'ING-TS'E 四柱清冊 Four-columned
account book

In the government granaries and treasuries of the departments and districts, the four-columned account book
is used to facilitate the transfer of the office [to any new
appointee]. The four headings are: balance forwarded,
new receipts, present balance, and expenditures. [Cf.
552.]

1119. HUNG-PU CH'IH-TS'E 紅簿赤冊 Red books

[Official] record books that have been marked in
vermilion by the superior official.

1120. HSÜN-HUAN PU 循環簿 Circulating record book

The record book that is passed from one person in charge to another by monthly rotation.

1121. I-CHIH YU-TAN 易知由單 Memorandum bearing a résumé

The history of an item of government business is briefly summarized, so that the superior official could learn it easily.

1122. CH'UAN-T'OU HAO-P'IAO 船頭號票 Boat license

The permit for government boats.

1123. HUNG-P'I CHAO-P'IAO 紅批照票 Red-noted license

A license paper that has been noted for approval by the superior official in vermilion.

1124. CH'IN-T'IEN HUNG-TAN 親填紅單 Personally dated red paper

(*The word tan 單 "paper" is missing in the Chia-ch'ing and annotated editions.)

An official document on the cover of which the date, penned in vermilion, has been written in personally by the official.

1125. TIEN-MAI SHUI-CH'I 典買稅契 Taxed deed papers for mortgage or purchase (of property)

A tax is to be paid on the deed paper concluding the mortgage or purchase of landed property, and the official seal is to be affixed thereon by the authorities.

1126. YÜ-LIN TS'E 魚鱗冊 Fish-scale books; land record books

The general record books on the people's land holdings, [the entries being] arranged in the order of the sizes of the holdings.

1127. HUA-MING TS'E 花名冊 Labor service roster

Names of [persons owing] labor service are listed and assembled into volumes.

1128. CHIH-CHAO 執照, Receipt; certificate; permit

> The certifying paper given after one has received such things as silver or official documents. Also, the certificate that proves (a person's) appointment to an official post.

1129. TSE-LI 則例 Regulations and precedents

> The general term for the laws and precedents obtaining in all government offices. [More specifically, tse-li in the present context probably refers to the Hu-pu tse-li 戶部則例 "Regulations and Precedents of the Board of Revenue." See 1116.]

1130. K'O-TSE 科則 Rules and regulations

> Rules for the conduct of public affairs.

1131. TS'AO-TAN 漕單 Grain transport notice

> The paper listing the amounts of tribute grain that have been issued for transport.

1132. PANG-T'IEH 幫帖 Fleet pass; fleet license

> The official permit issued to a fleet of boats.

1133. PU-TAN 部單 Board notices

> The certifying papers issued by the Board of Revenue to the various bureaus and offices.

1134. CH'ÜAN-TAN 全單 Complete statement

> A final statement on the entire amount of government funds that comprise various items.

1135. SHUI-CH'ENG 水程 Waterways schedule

> The [official) time-table specifying the schedule of grain transport [boats] on the waterways.

1136. HUNG-HSIEN 紅限 Time limit [written] in red

> Time limits [or the effective dates] of all government certificates are written in vermilion by the official concerned.

1137. HSIEN-P'IAO 限票 Time-table; time ticket

A ticket showing the time limits allowed (a man) who has been sent on a journey on government business.

1138. CH'UAN-P'IAO 串票 Receipt for land tax

The certifying document given by the authorities to the common taxpayers, who have paid their land-poll taxes.

1139. LING-CHUANG 領狀 Statement of receipt

An official who serves as the receiver of government funds should personally write out a statement of receipt as proof of the transaction [or for the record].

1140. SHOU-WEN 收文 Receipt for documents

The receipt of correspondence from the provinces to the Board of Revenue is acknowledged by issuing these papers in return.

1141. TS'ANG-SHOU 倉收 Granary receipt

The receipts issued by the government granaries which have taken in rice.

1142. SHIH-SHOU 實收 Treasury receipt

The receipts issued by government treasuries that have taken in silver. [Shih 實 "actual" here seems to be a misprint for k'u 庫 "treasury," and I have translated accordingly.]

1143. P'I-HUI 批迴 Notation in reply

The view of the superior official is written down at the end of an official document as a way to notify his subordinates.

1144. HUNG-TAN 紅單 Red receipt

A receipt written in vermilion ink.

1145. KUAN-T'IEH 官帖 Government license

The permits issued by the Board of Revenue to the business establishments allowing them to operate.

1146. YA-T'IEH 牙帖 Broker's license

The permits issued to brokerage companies.

1147. SHUI-T'IEH 税帖 [Business] tax receipts

Receipts certifying the payment of the [business] taxes.

1148. CH'I-WEI 契尾 Attachment to the deed

The official certificate that is attached to the end of
a deed paper for land or house.

1149. LIANG-TAN 糧單 Grain invoice

The paper showing the amounts of tribute grain delivered
and received [at government receiving points].

1150. P'I-T'IEH 批帖 Annotated license

Any certificate that bears at its end notations by the
official.

1151. CHIEH-CH'I 借契 Loan contract

The document containing the agreement reached for a
loan of money.

1152. T'UNG-KUAN 通關 Circular

An official document that is sent to circulate everywhere
to notify (the local authorities).

1153. TSUNG-CH'E WEI-SHU 總撤尾數 General financial
account

The books and files giving an account of the general
amounts [of money, or grain, etc.] involved.

1154. HUI-SHU 彙數 Collective account

A number of accounts that have been assembled together.

[[15]] Fiscal administration: acts and descriptive phrases. Nos. 1155-1199b

1155. CHIU-KUAN 舊管 Balance forwarded

The funds previously left (in the account).

1156. HSIN-SHOU 新收 New receipts

Funds recently received.

1157. K'AI-CH'U 開除 Expenditures

Funds expended.

1158. SHIH-TSAI [sic] 實在 Present balance

The actual balance left at present. [Tsai 在 is a misprint for ts'un 存 .]

1159. HO-SUAN 核算 To check and compute

To check into all items of expenditure and compute them carefully preparatory to submitting a financial account.

1160. HSIAO-SUAN 銷算 Compute for report

See above [1159],

1161. TSOU-HSIAO 奏銷 Submitting an account or financial report to the throne

To render to the throne a financial account.

1162. HO-HSIAO 核銷 To compute and give account

See above [1159, 1160].

1163. HO-CHIEN 核減 To check for reduction

When the figures are too high in a financial report, the Board (of Revenue) will order the official to reduce the sum by recalculating it.

1164. FU-HO 覆核 To compute again

To check and calculate (a sum) again.

1165. CHIEH-SHENG 節省　To economize

　　　To be economical in office expenses in order to reduce unnecessary spending.

1166. FU-SHIH 覆實　To recalculate the real sum

　　　To work out the sums again according to true figures.

1167. FEN-TENG 分登　Separate entries

　　　To enter each item clearly and separately in the records.

1168. KUA-HAO 掛號 Register

　　　To write into the records the serial number (of each item).

1169. KUA-P'I 掛批 Referred to in notation

　　　[A given item] has been enumerated in the notation to a document written by the higher official.

1170. KUA-FA 掛發 Registered for issuance

　　　The item of government money that has been registered in the records is to be issued on the same day.

1171. P'I-HSING 批行 Authorized to act; an authorized act

　　　[A government act] that has been authorized by the superior official.

1172. HUI-TS'E 彙册 Collective (record) books

　　　Record books containing the general data.

1173. TSUAN-TSAO 攢造 To compile data

　　　To put all the records together into a general record book 總册.

1174. SHU-HUI 書會 Written notice

　　　To notify others by a written message.

1175. TUO-K'AI 多開 Overstating the expenses

　　　The sum spent is too high.

1176. SHAO-K'AI 少開 Understating the expenses

　　　The sum spent falls short [of estimates].

1177. CH'UNG-K'AI 重開 Repeated entry of expenses

Repetitious statements on the same items of expenses.

1178. LOU-K'AI 漏開 Unrecorded expenses

An expended sum is left out [in a financial statement].

1179. KUEI-CHI 詭寄 [Spending] under false pretext

To spend [public funds] carelessly under the false name of government business.

[Amended, p. 142:] An avaricious official, having embezzled government funds and fearing exposure, pads the embezzled sum into the items of public expenditures, and hopes thus to escape detection.

1180. CHIEN-MING 簡明 Concise

Brief and clear.

1181. TS'AN-CH'A 參差 Inconsistent

A self-contradictory (statement).

1182. KUA TUO TS'O-CHU 寡多錯注 Miswriting the small and large sums

Making mistakes by writing down the large and small sums incorrectly.

1183. SHIH-CH'A MAO-K'AI 失察冒開 Fraudulent accounts not checked

A superior failing to check into the fraudulent statement of expenditures prepared by his subordinate. [Cf. 304.]

1184. CH'U-MING WEI-CHIH CHIH SHU 除明未支之數 Deduction of the unexpended sums

To compute clearly those amounts in an item [of public funds] that have not been spent, and deduct them from the total sum.

1185. K'UNG-YA WEN-P'IAO 空押文票 A signed certificate without the seal

A certificate or deed paper bearing only signatures, without the official seal.

1186. SHE-LI MING-SE 設立名色 Setting up categories

To set up various categories under which taxes are collected, such as the "one-percent levy" 抽厘 , etc.

1187. CHU-I FEN-HSI 逐一分晰 Distinction of each item

To distinguish clearly each individual item of the expenditures.

1188. CHU-I TENG-TA PAO PU 逐一登答報部 Recording and explanation of each item for report to the Board

To enter into a record book each of the expended items separately, with explanations, in order to submit the report to the Board of Revenue.

1189. TSOU-HSIAO AN-NEI PU PO KO-K'UAN 奏銷案内 部駁各款 Items in the report rejected by the Board

Those items in a financial report that have been rejected by the Board of Revenue, which refuses to permit these expenditures.

1190. TSUN-CHIH CHU-CHIEN TENG SHIH 遵旨逐件等事 With reference to the following matters under inquiry by the throne:

Matters that the throne had inquired about in an imperial order are now reported upon in detail one by one.

1191. KUNG-CH'EN SSU-K'UAN TENG SHIH 恭陳四款等事 Respectfully reporting on the four matters:

The contents of the "four matters" are not specified here; they are generally matters relating to the improvement of government revenue that are being respectfully reported to the Emperor.

1192. KUAN-FANG LIANG-HU TENG SHIH 關防糧斛等事 With reference to the checking of grain measures:

The hu or five-peck measure used in receiving the grain tribute suffers from a variety in size, an abuse that is to be prevented with some device.

1193. SAN SHANG K'EN-HUANG WEI-CHIN TENG SHIH 三 上
墾荒未盡等事 A third memorial on the unfinished
report on the opening of unused land:

A single memorial cannot finish the report on such a
matter as putting unused land under cultivation, therefore
three memorials are presented on the subject.

1194. KUAN-SHUI HSI LI-TS'AI CHIH YAO-SHIH 關稅係
理財之要事 Customs duties are an important factor
in fiscal administration

The duties levied at the customs stations constitute an
important item in the government's fiscal administration.

1195. HAO-MU SHIH-HSIANG WEI-NAN TENG SHIH 蒿目時餉
維難等事 With reference to the unbearable
difficulty in securing the current provisions

"Unbearable" means too painful to look at; that is, it is
very difficult to secure military provisions at this time.

[Cf. p. 142, Ch'ou k'uan wei-nan 籌款維難 :] "Very
difficult to secure funds:"--Government funds are insufficient and it is very difficult to get the required amount.

1196. PING-HSIANG CHIH CH'ÜEH-O JIH SHEN TENG SHIH 兵餉
之缺額日甚等事 With reference to the increasing
shortages in military provisions

Shortages in the quota of military provisions are becoming
more pronounced by the day.

1197. K'EN-HUANG CHI FENG YÜ-CHIH TENG SHIH 墾荒既
奉俞旨等事 With reference to the fact that an edict
has approved the opening of unused land

The placing of unused land under cultivation has already
been approved by the throne in an edict.

1198. HSIEH-CHI PEN-K'O T'UNG-JUNG TENG SHIH 協濟
本可通融等事 With reference to the fact that military
assistance funds can be arranged

The matter of sending funds to assist in the military
provisions [of a neighboring province] is usually arranged
for mutual benefit. [Cf. 421.]

1199. CH'ING SHIH TSAO-PAO PING-MA CH'IEN-LIANG I-PIEN
CHI-HO SHIH 請式造報兵馬錢糧以便稽核
事 Requesting [you] to compile the military and tax data
according to form, so as to facilitate auditing

To request the high officials in the provinces to submit
to the Board (of Revenue) reports, in the usual forms,
on the figures relating to the troops, horses, and land-
poll taxes in their respective provinces, in order that
(the Board) might audit them.

1199a. YU-CHU CHIH K'UAN 有著之款 Dependable funds

Funds that have a definite source and can be relied upon
for use. [Entries 1199a and 1199b are two items found
in the "Amendments" of the Naitō edition; they are
appended here as a logical spot for their inclusion.]

1199b. WU-CHU CHIH K'UAN 無著之款 Undependable funds

Funds that have no definite source, and cannot be relied
upon for use. [See note under 1199a.]

CHAPTER III

THE BOARD OF RITES

[[1]] Sacrificial and state ceremonies. Nos. 1200-1253

1200. TA SSU 大祀 Great Sacrifices

The rituals of grand sacrifices 大祭之禮 , to be used only for the highest deities, [such as at] the Temple of Heaven and the Temple of Earth. It is said, for example, "conduct the great sacrifice to Heaven at the Round Altar" 圜丘 , and "conduct the great sacrifice to Earth at the Square Pond" 方澤.

1201. CHUNG SSU 中祀 Superior sacrifices

[Rites] that are below great sacrivices are all called superior sacrifices, such as that at the Altar of Earth and Grain 社稷壇 , the Altar of the Planet Jupiter 太歲 , and the temples of Confucius and of Kuan-ti. [A different classification of sacrificial rites actually prevailed: Ta ssu 大祀 , chung ssu 中祀 , and ch'ün ssu or hsiao ssu 羣祀,小祀 Earth and Grain belonged to the first category, which also included the offerings at the imperial ancestral temple [1202]. The temple of Kuan Yü (Kuan-ti) 關羽 falls within the middle category of chung ssu as stated in the present item, and not within the third category of ch'ün ssu as given by B. 572. My rendering of She chi t'an differs from Brunnert's version. See KHHT, 35:1-2b.]

1202. MIAO HSIANG 廟享 Offerings at the [imperial ancestral] temple

The Great Temple 大 (太) 廟 is the ancestral temple of the Emperor. "Offering " means presenting the sacrifice. This phrase refers to the sacrifices at the imperial ancestral temple.

1203. CH'IU-T'AN 丘壇 Raised altar

An "altar" does not display the image of any divinity. It
is a mound built of earth, on which an altar is set up
bearing the sacrificial offerings, [the worshipper] making
obeisance to open space: such is called a "raised altar."
In general, [a shrine] is known as an "altar" if divine
images and tablets are not displayed, and as a "temple"
if they are. This is the difference between an altar and
a temple.

1204. CHIH-CHAI 致齋 Major fast

To show reverence by carrying out the rites of fasting
[see 1205-1207].

1205. CHAI CHIEH 齋戒 Fasting and purification

"Fasting" means to alter one's diet, and "purification"
means to avoid unclean things. Before performing sacrifices to a deity these must be observed for three days as
evidence of one's sincerity and reverence.

1206. SAN CHAI 散齋 Minor fast

"Major fast" is observed for a Great Sacrifice, while
"minor fast" is observed for a Superior Sacrifice [see
1200, 1201]. For the major fast the Emperor should stay
for three days in the Fasting Hall 齋宮 within the premises
of the altar before performing the sacrifice; for the minor
fast he need only keep fast while staying in his own palace
apartments, and go forth (to the altar) to perform the
sacrifice at the designated time.

1207. CHIH CHAI YÜ NEI 致齋於内 Observing the major
fast in the palace

The fasting prior to a Great Sacrifice should be kept by
staying within the altar premises; but, if ill health or
some other important matter prevents him from so doing,
the Emperor may observe it in his own palace apartments.
It is then termed "observing the major fast in the palace."

1208. P'EI-CHI 陪祭 (To serve as) associates in sacrifice

Princes and high ministers who accompany the Emperor in performing the sacrificial rites beside him are called "associates in sacrifice."

1209. P'EI-SSU 陪祀 (To serve as) associates in worship

Officials below the ranks of the high ministers who are not entitled to accompany (the Emperor) on the altar, but can only make obeisance [at their respective stations] below it, are called "associates in worship."

1210. CHU-CHI 助祭 (To serve as) sacrificial assistants

The administrative officers 司員 of the Board of Rites have the job of assisting with the procedures of a sacrifice, such as attending to kindling the incense, presenting the libation cup and the food offerings.

1211. CHI-I 祭儀 Sacrificial offerings; sacrificial ceremonies

The things presented as offerings at a sacrifice.

1212. CHI-WEN 祭文 Sacrificial ode or prayer

The ode read aloud at a sacrifice.

1213. HSIANG-CHIEN 饗薦 Food offering

Food presented as sacrificial offering.

1214. AN-I 案衣 Altar drape

The long table on which sacrificial offerings are placed is [first] covered with yellow figured silk 黃綾; it is similar to the tablecloth of the Western nations 西洋.

1215. YÜAN-HSIAO 元霄 First night of full moon

The fifteenth day of the first month is the festival of the first full moon [...]

[Cf. 1220.]

1216. CH'U-HSI 除夕 New Year's Eve

The thirtieth day of the twelfth month is New Year's Eve. [...]

1217. HUAN-CH'IU 圜丘 Round Altar

> For sacrifices at the Altar of Heaven an earthen mound is built, round in shape after [the shape of] heaven; there the sacrifices are held. It is known as the "Round Altar."

1218. FANG-TSE 方澤 Square Pond

> For sacrifices at the Altar of Earth, a square pond is dug and filled with water, where the sacrifices are performed. It is known as the "Square Pond."

1219. YÜAN-TAN LING-CHIEH 元旦令節 Fair festival of New Year's Day

> The first day of the first month is New Year's Day. "Fair festival" means joyous festival.

1220. TENG-CHIEH 燈節 Lantern festival

> The thirteenth to the seventeenth day of the first month is the lantern festival. Originally it lasted only for three days, but two more days were added during the Sung dynasty to symbolize "a plentiful harvest of the five grains."

1221. WAN-SHOU SHENG-CHIEH 萬壽聖節 Ten-thousand-years imperial birthdays

> The birthdays of the Empress Dowager and the Emperor are referred to as "ten-thousand-years imperial birthdays."

> [Amended, p. 143:] The birthdays of the Retired Emperor, the Empress Dowager, and the Emperor are all termed ten-thousand-years imperial birthdays.

1222. CH'IEN-CH'IU LING-CHIEH 千秋令節 One-thousand-years imperial birthdays

> The birthdays of the Empress and heir apparent are referred to as "one-thousand-years imperial birthdays." In ancient times this term could also be applied to the noble princes, but the current practice (in this respect) is not known. [Text reads chin pu-hsiang 今不詳 .

Hsiang is probably a misprint for hsü 許 ; i.e.,
"nowadays this is not allowed."]

1223. **CH'ING-HO PIAO CHIEN** 慶賀表箋 Congratulatory
memorials and messages

That which is presented to the Empress Dowager or
Emperor is called a memorial; to the Empress or heir
apparent, a message. Both contain congratulations.

1224. **CHÜ TIEN LI-CH'ENG** 鉅典禮成 Completion of a
grand ceremony

At the conclusion of the ceremonies celebrating an
important occasion, the Emperor should assume
honorific titles and grant favors to all officials.

1225. **CH'ING SHANG TSUN-HAO** 請上尊號 Petition for
assumption of honorific titles [by the Emperor and
others]

"Honorific titles" are euphemious [or auspicious]
designations--such as Tz'u hsi tuan yu 慈禧端佑
[kindly, gentle, dignified, blessed] and so on-- which
the high ministers petition the Retired Emperor, the
Empress Dowager, or the Emperor to assume. [Such
a petition] may or may not be assented to.

Further, in the case of the Retired Emperor and the
Emperor, these designations are called honorific titles
尊號 ; of the Empress Dowager, special titles 徽號.
All such titles given after death are termed posthumous
honors 尊謚.

1226. **CHÜ-SHOU CHIA-O** 舉手加額 The forehead salute

In ancient times people express gladness [and gratitude]
by putting both hands together and raising them to the level
of the forehead. Nowadays only the phrase remains, for
no one actually salutes like this.

1227. **TA-HSING HUANG-T'AI-HOU TSUN-SHIH** 大行皇太后
尊謚 Posthumous honors of the late Empress Dowager

Ta-hsing means having departed without return; that is,
dead. Before posthumous honors can be definitely

fixed after the passing of the Empress Dowager or the Emperor, each is referred to as "the late."

[Amended, p. 143:] Ta-hsing 大行 : After his death an Emperor is referred to as ta-hsing. There are two ancient interpretations of "the late Emperor": one is that he has departed without return; the other, that it is a temporary term of reference (to be used) until his posthumous honors can be fixed, (the words ta-hsing) meaning "great and comprehensive virtuous conduct." For the former interpretation hsing is pronounced in the second tone as in "going away," and for the latter interpretation, in the fourth tone, as in "virtue." Since both these interpretations are acceptable, it is best to keep them both.

1228.   CH'U CHI 初祭 First sacrifice

On the first seventh day after the Emperor's death, libational and sacrifical rites are performed, which are called "first sacrifice."

1229.   TA CHI 大祭 Grand Sacrifice

The seventh seventh day after the Emperor's death is known as the "ultimate seventh" 終七 . On this day the rites of the Grand Sacrifice should be performed.

1230.   CH'I TIEN 啟奠 Removal libation

When an Emperor's coffin is to be moved to another place, the rites of libation should be performed before the removal begins; this is called the "removal libation."

1231.   CH'AO-CHIN 朝覲 An audience [with the Emperor]

In ancient times when the feudal princes presented themselves to see the king it was called an "audience." Nowadays the governors-general of the provinces.... (*The rest is missing in the original text.)

1232.   CH'AO-KUNG 朝貢 An audience and presentation of tribute

When [emissaries of] such tributary countries as Mongolia come to see the Emperor and present their native products, it is known as "an audience and presentation of tribute."

1233. LI-WU 禮物 Gifts; presents

Social intercourse among government officials may entail the exchange of gifts, which are either public or private in character. Public gifts are not prohibited, while private presents are. [Cf. 347, 348.]

1234. TZ'U YEN 賜宴 Court banquets; banquets granted by the Emperor

When [emissaries from] tributary nations arrive for an audience and the presentation of tributes, a banquet is given for them in the palace. Banquets are given for the princes and high ministers on occasions of national celebration, such as the ten-thousand-years birthdays [see 1221] and New Year's Day, and they are given also for the candidates who have newly attained the degree of chü-jen 舉人 (provincial graduate) or chin-shih 進士 (metropolitan graduate).

1235. HSIANG YIN-CHIU LI 鄉飲酒禮 Country wine feast

The country wine feast is an ancient ceremony that in some cases has survived to the present day. At the appropriate times of the year the local officials invite those of the locality who are venerable in age and sound in reputation, and feast them in the public halls. This is done as a gesture of respect for the old.

1236. JU-FA CHUANG-FENG 如法裝封 Packed and sealed according to regulations

All tribute articles and memorials must be packed in cases and sealed and stamped according to statutory provisions, and then sent to the capital for presentation [to the throne].

1237. P'IN-CH'ANG YÜ SHAN 品嘗御膳 Tasting of the Emperor's food

[...] Before any food is served to the Emperor, the official in charge must first taste it as a precaution.

1238. CH'ENG-YÜ FU-YÜ WU 乘輿服御物 Imperial wardrobe and articles of daily use

Ch'eng-yü denotes the Emperor. This phrase refers to the clothing and things used by him. [...]

[Amended, p. 143:] Ch'eng-yü denotes the imperial carriage. Because of his most exalted position, the Emperor cannot be treated disrespectfully [by direct reference], hence he is referred to through his carriage. This is comparable to addressing an ordinary person as ko-hsia 閣下 [literally, your abode]. "Wardrobe" and "articles of daily use" are the things used by the Emperor.

1239. LU-PU TA-CHIA 鹵簿大駕 Full regalia and grand equipage

The ceremonial insignia, pennants, banners, and imperial carriage, which are not used by the Emperor in his ordinary travels, but are brought out only on the occasions of great sacrifices or great ceremonies; colloquially known as "the full set of equipments" 全副執事.

1240. CHIH-CHIN CH'AO I 織金朝衣 Audience robe of gold brocade

A robe worn at a great audience, with patterns woven in gold thread. It is different from the [more common] dragon robes and jackets.

1241. SHIH-WU CH'AO-HO 失誤朝賀 Missing a congratulatory audience

On festivals and days of important ceremonies all officials are to present their felicitations to the Emperor at an audience. Any person who misses and is absent from it is penalized according to statute.

1242. P'AN SHU HSING-SHA 判署刑殺 Sentencing and authorizing of capital punishment

"Sentencing" is to decide [on the judgment]; shu is to execute as well as to write out [the sentence]. Officials sitting at criminal or manslaughter cases should not pass sentences on them during periods of [the Emperor's] fasts or celebrations; that is, they are to refrain from criminal judgment. [Text reads shu pan-yeh yu hsieh-yeh 署辦

也 又 寫 也. In the present context the character shu actually means "to sign," i.e., to authorize capital punishment.]

1243. TIAO-SANG WEN-CHI 弔喪問疾 Condoling the bereaved; visiting the sick

Officials selected to participate [with the Emperor] in the sacrifices in the altars and temples should not go to the homes of friends and relatives to condole a death or visit sick persons.

1244. LI-TAI LING-CH'IN 歷代陵寢 Imperial mausolea of past dynasties

The mausolea of former dynasties, such as the Thirteen Mausolea [of the Ming]. Sacrifices are performed there at appropriate times of the year, by officials sent from the Board of Rites.

1245. PAN TSANG-CHIA YIN 半葬價銀 Half the burial cost

High officials, officers, and soldiers who have died in action, are customarily given burial costs after their deaths, the amounts being fixed at rates proportionate to the rank of the deceased. The full sum given is called "full burial cost"; half the sum, "half burial cost."

1246. CHUNG-CH'EN LIEH-SHIH 忠臣烈士 Loyal ministers, and patriots

To be loyal to the sovereign is "loyal"; one who is loyal to friends is a lieh-shih.

[Amended, p. 143:] "Loyal" and "patriotic" mean to be faithful and righteous. These terms refer to loyal and patriotic officials in general; the distinction between loyalty to the sovereign and that to friends does not enter in.

1247. KU-SHENG HSIEN-HSIEN 古聖先賢 Ancient sages and past worthies

(*Ku 古 "ancient" is given as hsien "past" in the Manchu-Chinese editions.)

The sages were such persons as the Three Sovereigns, the Five Emperors, the Duke of Chou, and Confucius. The worthies were people like [the disciples of Confucius] Yen Hui and Min Tzu-ch'ien [and the philosophers] Ch'eng Hao, Ch'eng I, and Chu Hsi 顏 閔 程 朱 .

[Amended, p. 143:] These terms refer to the sages of ancient times and the worthies of past ages. They are also general terms, and do not specify any individual in particular.

1248. HSIAO-TZU SHUN-SUN 孝子 順孫 Filial son, submissive grandson

A [good] son is described as "filial"; a grandson, "submissive. "

1249. I-FU CHIEH-FU 義 夫 節 婦 Faithful husband, chaste wife

[A widower] who does not remarry is called a "faithful husband"; [a widow] who does not remarry is called a "chaste wife. "

1250. LIEH-FU 烈 婦 Virtuous woman

[A woman who] commits suicide after her husband's death, or dies struggling against violence, is called a "virtuous woman. "

1251. LIEH-NÜ 烈 女 Virtuous girl

Same as above [1250], but one who is unmarried.

(*Sacrifices should be performed for all the above categories of people [1246-1251].)

1252. CHING-PIAO 旌表 Public commendation

Ching means to praise, and piao means to publicize. The Board of Rites customarily memorializes for "public commendations" for persons who were loyal, faithful, chaste, or virtuous.

1253. CHIEN FANG 建坊 To erect an honorary arch

In cases where public commendation is in order, money

should be granted for the erection of honorary arches in the places (where the honored) lived. The arches might be built of either stone or wood. They were known as memorial columns 華表 in ancient times.

[[2]] Astronomy and eclipses. Nos. 1254-1266

1254. T'IEN-WEN 天文 Astronomy

"Astronomy" is the general term for knowledge concerning the heavenly bodies and astrology.

1255. CHENG CH'U-K'O 正初刻 On the hour, and a quarter....

These words are used to indicate the time of a solar or lunar eclipse. For example, (an eclipse) starting at the first quarter past the meridian of the wu [午正初刻 i.e., 12:15 P.M.], or at the second quarter past the tzu [子初二刻 i.e., 11:30 P.M.] hour, etc.

1256. SHIH-K'UEI 始虧 First contact

The first appearance, as a narrow band, of the shadow in an eclipse of the sun or the moon is known as "first contact."

1257. CH'U-SHIH 初食 Beginning of eclipse

The same as first contact; the terms are interchangeable.

1258. SHIH-SHEN 食甚 Maximum phase of an eclipse

The farthest point reached by the shadow is called the "maximum phase of an eclipse."

1259. FU-YUAN 復圓 Return to fullness

When the sun or moon has recovered its original fullness at the end of an eclipse, it is known as "return to fullness."

1260. CHAN-HOU 占候 Calculating and predicting

The art of the Ch'in-t'ien chien 欽天監 (Imperial Board of Astronomy) in forecasting the dates of eclipses and the changes in constellational positions is known as "calculating and predicting."

1261.   SHIH-SHEN JIH CH'AN HUANG-TAO HSING-CHI-KUNG
ERH-SHIH FEN 食甚日纏黄道星紀宮二十
分 Maximum phase (occurring) when sun is at 20°
in Capricornus on the ecliptic

[...] This phrase means that the maximum phase of an
eclipse of the sun occurs at a point where the sun has
reached the twentieth degree in Capricornus along the
ecliptic.

1262.   JIH JU TI-P'ING WEI FU-KUANG 日入地平未復光
Light is not restored at sunset

That is to say, the sun in eclipse has not yet returned
to fullness as it sets for the night.

1263.   WU WEI ERH-SHIH-PA SUO 五緯二十八宿
The five planets and twenty-eight zodiacal constellations

The five planets are: Venus, Jupiter, Mercury, Mars,
and Saturn.

The twenty-eight zodiacal constellations are: Spica,
Virgo, Libra, Scorpio, Antares, Sagittarius, Aquarius,
Equuleus, Pegasus, Andromeda, Pisces, Aries, Musea
Borealis, Pleiades, Hyades, Taurus, Orion, Gemini,
Cancer, Hydra, Crater, Corvus. [These names, showing
the constellations from which the determinant stars of the
Chinese zodiacal constellations were drawn as in 1800,
are given in the table in R.H. Mathews, A Chinese-English
Dictionary (Cambridge, Mass., 1950), p. 1177.]

1264.   JIH YUEH CH'UNG-LUN ERH SHIH 日月重輪珥食
Eclipse of the sun or the moon with double-halo, or
with crescent(s)

[During an eclipse], when one or two rings of light appear
outside the [shadow] disc of the sun or moon, it is known
as the "double-halo"; when one or two small spots of light
show on the left and/or right side, it is called a "single
crescent" or a "pair of crescents." [...] [It is not quite
clear whether the term ch'ung-lun 重輪 refers to the halo
around the eclipsed sun, or whether it also includes the
spectacle presented by an annular eclipse of the sun.]

1265. T'UI-PU TS'E-YEN CHIH SHU CHAN HSIU-CHIU
推步測驗之書占休咎 Books on astrology and
estimation are for predicting luck or misfortune

[...] This phrase means that the said books teach
the techniques of predicting good fortune or misfortune
in the future.

1266. T'U-HSIANG CH'AN-WEI CHIH SHU CHAN CHIH-LUAN
圖象讖緯之書占治亂　　Books written in
pictorial signs, and those on prophecy and divinations
are for predicting peace or disturbance

[...] Books of this kind, such as T'ui-pei t'u 推背
圖 , can be used to predict peace or disturbance in
the empire.　They are prohibited, and their contents are
excluded from reference in the public examination essays.

[[3]] Seals. Nos. 1267-1271

1267. YIN-MO 印模 Seal molds

The molds used for casting seals. They are made of lead
and are colloquially called yin-mo-tzu or "seal presses."
The seals of all government offices--metropolitan and
provincial, high and low--are cast and distributed by the
Chu-yin Chü 鑄印局 (Office of Seal Casting) in the Board
of Rites. The seals of high officials are cast in silver,
those of middle and lower ranks, in bronze: all are
inscribed in both Manchu and Chinese in the seal script
篆文.

It is considered more honorable for civil officials to have
oblong seals, and for military officials to have square
seals.

1268. CHU HUAN 鑄換 Casting and replacing [seals]

When the characters inscribed on the seals of any government office have become blurred through long use, [the
official concerned] should ask the Board of Rites to replace
them with newly cast ones. The old seals are to be
destroyed.

1269. YIN-CHIAO WEI T'A 印角微塌 Corner of seal slightly
worn off

A seal that has been used for many years, or lost and
recovered, showing damage at its corner(s).

1270. K'ANG-TZU WU-SHIH HAO YIN-HSIN 康字五十號
印信 Seal no. K'ang - 50

At casting, [official] seals are serialized by following
the word order of the Ch'ien tzu wen 千字文 [Primer
of one thousand characters], and (each seal) is given a
number, which is recorded in the files along with the
date (of casting). The serial number [such as given in
the present item] then is engraved in the back of the
seal to facilitate future checking.

1271. CHUAN-WEN MO-HU TZU-HUA MO PIEN 篆文模糊
字畫莫辨 The engraved characters on a seal are
blurred, the strokes illegible

This phrase describes the appearance of old, worn-out
seals mentioned above [1268].

[[4]] Public examinations
A. Degrees; the administration and procedures of
examinations. Nos. 1272-1326

1272. I-CHIA TZ'U CHIN-SHIH CHI-TI 一甲賜進士及第
The degree of First Class Metropolitan Graduate is
granted to [successful candidates of] the first rank

The kung-shih 貢士 presented scholars who have successfully passed the metropolitan examination are given the
palace examination, out of which the successful candidates
fall into three rank-groups. The first rank consists of
three places, i.e., chuang-yuan, pang-yen, and t'an-hua
狀元，榜眼，探花 on whom is conferred the degree of
First Class Metropolitan Graduate. They are appointed
to posts in the Hanlin Academy 翰林院.

[Amended, p. 143:] First rank: The presented scholars

who, having successfully passed the metropolitan examination, are given the palace examination and divided into three rank-groups. The first rank consists of three places; of these the highest is entitled chuang-yuan, the second pang-yen, and the third t'an-hua. The first is appointed to the position of a Hsiu-chuan 修撰 (Compiler of the First Class) in the Hanlin Academy, and the second and third to those of Pien-hsiu 編修 (Compilers of the Second Class) in the Hanlin Academy.

1273. ERH-CHIA TZ'U CHIN-SHIH CH'U-SHEN 二甲賜進士 出身 The degree of Second Class Metropolitan Graduate is granted to [successful candidates of] the second rank

There is no fixed number of places for the second rank The candidate winning the highest places is known as ch'uan-lu 傳臚, while all (who pass the examination) receive the degree of Second Class Metropolitan Graduate. They are either designated Shu-chi-shih 庶吉士 (Bachelors) and sent to the Department of Study in the Hanlin Academy, or dispersed among the Six Boards as apprentice Chu-shih 主事 (Second Class Secretaries of the Boards, B. 292).

[Amended, p. 144:] Second and third ranks: The highest-placed candidate of the second rank is called ch'uan-lu. Those below him receive various appointments, in the order of their attainments, to posts such as Second Class Secretaries of the Boards, Chung-shu 中書 [Clerical secretaries of the Grand Secretariat], district magistrates, education directors, etc. [See also 1275.]

1274. HSIANG-SHIH WAI-LIEN WU-SO KUAN 鄉試外簾五 所官 Officials of the Five Bureaus of the outer section at provincial examinations

Administrators at the [provincial] examination hall are classified into inner and outer sections. The latter is located without the second gate and consists of five separate bureaus: the Bureau for Sealing 彌封所, the Bureau for Receiving the Papers 受卷所, the Bureau of Copying 謄錄所, the Bureau of Proofreading 對讀

所 , and the Bureau of Supplies 供給所.

For details (on these offices) see below [1300-1304].

[Amended, p. 144:] The inner and outer section officials
at a provincial examination: Administrative officials at
a provincial examination are classified into inner and
outer sections. Those of the inner section are in charge
of reading and grading the examination papers, while those
of the outer section have charge of such matters as sealing
the papers, proofreading, and so on.

1275. SAN-CHIA TZ'U T'UNG-CHIN-SHIH CH'U-SHEN 三甲賜
同進士出身 The degree of Third Class Metropolitan
Graduate is granted to [successful candidates of] the
third rank

The third rank-group (of metropolitan graduates) also
contains no fixed number of places. All who are in this
group receive the degree of Third Class Metropolitan
Graduate, and are appointed to the posts of district magistrates, education directors, etc. [Cf. amendment to 1273.]

1276. SAN CH'ANG T'I-KO 三場體格 Literary forms for the
three sittings [or parts] of an examination

In the provincial and metropolitan examinations, the first
sitting consists of three essays on the Four Books 四書 ;
the second, five essays on the Five Classics 五經 ; and the
third [or last] sitting, two discourses on the formulation of
policies 策論 . Each [type of writing] has its own form
to be followed, such as word limit, alignment of the lines,
characters to be avoided, etc.

[Amended, p. 144:] The three sittings: In the past the first
sitting of the provincial and metropolitan examinations
called for three essays on the Four Books, and one poem of
the five-character eight-rhyme style, the second sitting,
five essays on the Five Classics of the Book of Poetry,
Book of History, Book of Changes, Book of Rites, and the
Spring and Autumn Annals; the third sitting, five discourses
on the formulation of policies.

1277. CHING-SHU CH'I I 經書七義 The seven purports of the Classics

This term refers to the <u>Book of Poetry</u>, <u>Book of History</u>, <u>Book of Changes</u>, <u>Book of Rites</u>, and the tree Commentaries of the <u>Spring and Autumn Annals</u> [i.e., the Kung-yang, Ku-liang, and Tso Commentaries]. Together these constitute seven purports that are used as examination themes.

1278. KU CHING TIAO-HUAN 孤經調換 Variations on [a theme from] one single Classic

There were scholars in the past who studied especially one of the Five Classics. [In the second sitting of an examination] such a scholar would give up the essays on all other Classics, and write five essays with varying interpretations on only one of the themes. Known as "variations on a theme from one single Classic," this practice has been discontinued.

1279. HUI-SHIH CHÜ-JEN 會試舉人 Metropolitan examination candidates; provincial graduates at the metropolitan examination

The provincial graduates who are due to take the metropolitan examination.

1280. PA-KUNG 拔貢 Imperial student by special selection

There are five types of imperial students: by imperial favor 恩 ; by special selection 拔 ; of the supplementary list 副 ; by virtue of noteworthy accomplishments 優 ; and by seniority 歲 . Those who are granted the title by special imperial favor are known as imperial students by imperial favor; those selected from among the licentiates 秀才 on account of their literary ability are called imperial students by special selection; aged government stipendiaries 廩生 permitted to become imperial students are called imperial students by seniority; those whose names appear on the supplementary list of successful candidates 副榜 at the provincial examination and are permitted to become imperial students are termed imperial students of the supplementary list;

and when licentiates of reliable character are chosen to
be imperial students, they are known as imperial students
on account of noteworthy accomplishments. [These
classifications and explanations differ from B. 629A.
Cf. KHHT, 32:4, 33:1. My rendering of the terms are
adapted from Chang Chung-li, The Chinese Gentry
(Seattle, 1955, hereafter Chang, Gentry), pp. 27-29
and passim.]

1280a. FU-SHENG 附生 Secondary government student; a
licentiate

[Amended, p. 144:] (Among those who have achieved the
degree), the ones of better literary ability who receive
a government stipend are the regular government students
正生員 [cf. 1281], whereas those who do not receive
it are known as secondary government students 附生 .
"Secondary" signifies to follow along, as in a secondary
position. [B. 629A gives fu-sheng 附生 as "licentiate
of the first 1   followed by tseng-sheng 增生
"licentiate of the second class, " which does not appear
in the present chapter. In the Hui-tien the latter is given
as tseng-kuang-sheng 增廣生 and is placed ahead of
fu-sheng. Each locality in the country, down to the
districts where there were government academies, had
its quota of licentiateships of all types to fill at every
examination. KHHT, 31:3b-5.]

1281. LING-SHAN-SHENG 廩膳生 Government stipendiary

An outstanding licentiate receives a monthly rice allowance,
and is known as a "government stipendiary. "

Nowadays (all) licentiates are called "government
students" 生員 .

1282. FU CHIAO-SHOU 府教授 Prefectural Director of Schools

The education official for a prefecture. [Every Director
of Schools in a prefecture, department, or district was
assisted by a Hsün-tao 訓導 (Sub-director of Schools)
with the exception of Shun-t'ien prefecture, where two-
directors were present, one Chinese and the other Manchu.
KHHT, 31:16.]

1283. CHOU HSÜEH-CHENG 州學正 Departmental Director of Schools

The education official for a department.

1284. HSIEN CHIAO-YÜ 縣教諭 District Director of Schools

The education official for a district.

1285. LI-SHENG 禮生 Master of Ceremonies

During worship at the Confucian temple, or at shrines of the sages, the official who sings out the procedures of the ceremony such as "rise," "kneel," "bow," etc., is known as the "Master of Ceremonies." The Tsan-li-lang 贊禮郎 (Ceremonial Ushers, B.382B) are the officials [who fulfill the same duties] at the Emperor's sacrifices.

1286. CHAI-FU 齋夫 Studio attendant

The laborer on duty at the study of an education official is called a "studio attendant."

1287. HUO-FU 火夫 Cook

The servant who cooks tea and meals.

1288. CHUN-KUNG, SUI-KUNG 準貢, 歲貢 Selected to become imperial student, imperial student by seniority

See above [1280].

1289. T'IEN-SHE TAO HSIEN AN-I CHIH-SHIH KUNG-SHIH 填 [添] 設道縣挨衣執事工食 Extra wages for the valets and runners attending the intendant and district magistrate

[...] An-i 挨衣 literally means a tablecloth, now used to denote the servants who personally wait upon the official; chih-shih 執事 are the runners who precede the sedan chair of an intendant or district magistrate bearing the latter's insignia or beating a gong, etc. During a provincial examination the intendant and district magistrates would all move into the examination halls and thence conduct their affairs, and the attendants who accompany them should be given additional wages.

1290. CHIH KUNG-CHÜ KUAN 知貢舉官　Selectors of provincial graduates

This term refers to the chu-k'ao 主考 (examiner), both principal and deputy, at a provincial examination. In the provinces they are designated as ta chu-k'ao 大主考 [grand examiner], whereas at the triennial examination in Shun-t'ien prefecture they are called chih kung-chü 知貢舉 [selectors of provincial graduates]. [This interpretation differs from that given in 382.]

1291. TA CHU-K''AO 大主考　Grand examiner

The principal examiner [at a provincial examination].

1292. FU CHU-K'AO 副主考　Deputy examiner

The secondary examiner [at a provincial examination].

1293. NEW WAI LIEN KUAN 内外簾官　Inner and outer section officials

See above [1274].

1294. T'I-TIAO 提調 (To serve as) proctor

The official in charge of the sundry matters at the examination hall; the post is filled by an intendant or a prefect. [Cf. 381].

1295. CHIEN-LIN 監臨 (To serve as) inspector

The official having general supervision over the examination hall; the post is filled by the governor-general or the governor. [Cf. 382.]

1296. CHIEN-SHIH 監試 (To serve as) supervisor of examination

The official who checks on malpractices during an examination; this post is filled by an intendant, a prefect, or a provincial censor 御史.

1297. T'UNG-K'AO KUAN 同考官　Associate examiners

Officials who assist the principal and deputy examiners in grading the examination papers.

1298. FANG-K'AO 房考 Examiners-in-rooms

    This term refers to associate examiners [1297].
According to statute, eighteen such persons are appointed
to serve [at one examination], each of whom is lodged
in a separate room where he reads and grades the
examination papers allotted to him. Hence the present
appellation.

1299. HSÜN-SHIH KUAN 巡視官 Guard officer

    According to statute, a military officer is assigned to
police the area around the examination hall with soldiers,
in order to prevent the candidates from communicating
[with persons outside: cf. 1333].

1300. KUNG-CHI(KEI) SO 供給所 Bureau of Supplies

    (*So 所 "bureau" is given as kuan 官 "official" in the
Manchu-Chinese editions.)

    All types of supplies needed in the examination hall,
such as food stuffs, tea, water, lamps and fuel, and so
on, are under the charge of specially appointed officials
who function in the Bureau of Supplies. This is one of
the Five Bureaus.

    [For 1300-1304 cf. 1274.]

1301. MI-FENG SO 彌封所 Bureau for Sealing

    The candidates' names are all written on the covers of
their own examination papers. These should be turned
over by the Bureau for Receiving Papers [1302) to the
Bureau for Sealing, where the names are covered and
sealed with paper, and stamped with an (official) seal.
The seal is not broken until after the paper has been
judged to have passed the examination, when the list of
the successful candidates is to be written out. This is
done to prevent [possible] favoritism on the part of the
examiners, who might be relatives or friends of some of
the candidates.

1302. SHOU-CHÜAN SO 受卷所 Bureau for Receiving Papers

When the essays have been composed, the candidate writes them into the examination papers and submits them to the Bureau for Receiving Papers.

1303. T'ENG-LU SO 謄錄所 Bureau of Copying

From the Bureau for Receiving Papers (the examination papers are) sent to the Bureau of Copying, where a vermilion copy of each paper is made. This copy is presented to the examiner instead of the original paper. It is done to prevent [possible] malpractices arising out of the handwriting [of the individual candidates].

1304. TUI-TU SO 對讀所 Bureau of Proofreading

After the copy of a paper has been completed, it is sent to the Bureau of Proofreading, where it is proofread against the original to insure that every single word is correct. It is then taken by the Shou-chüan Kuan 收卷官 [Examination-paper conveyor] for presentation to the examiner.

1305. T'ENG-LU SHU-SHOU 謄錄書手 Copyist

Scribes who do the writing in the Bureau of Copying.

1306. PIN-HSING 賓興 Gathering of scholarly guests

The provincial examination is also known as a "gathering of scholarly guests." Derived from the sentence in the Book of Poetry, "Honored guests are here with us" 我有嘉賓 , it implies that all candidates are guests invited by the state, and is a gesture of respect toward men of letters. [The phrase pin-hsing is derived from the Rites of Chou 周禮 , meaning "to raise the virtuous and entertain them at banquets." Government students who intended to take part in the provincial examinations were, in many localities, entertained by the local authorities and given travelling expenses. See Chang, Gentry, p. 41.]

1307. HUI-SHIH 會試 Metropolitan examination

The examination taken by provincial graduates in order to achieve the degree of metropolitan graduates.

1308. TIEN-SHIH 殿試 Palace examination

> After passing the metropolitan examination the candidates are known as <u>kung-shih</u> 貢士 [presented scholars]. (They then present themselves) at the palace examination in Pao-ho Tien 保和殿 [Hall of Continuing Harmony] in the presence of the Emperor, after which they are classified into, or given the titles of, the three classes of metropolitan graduates [cf. 1272, 1273, 1275].

1309. LU K'O 錄科 Eligible for the examination

> Before the provincial examination takes place the licentiates are subjected to a preliminary test by the education officers [of the province]. The names of those who show facility in writing are made into a list and sent to the examination hall. These persons are known as being "eligible for the examination."

1310. K'O-CHÜ 科舉 Public examinations; public examination system

> (One who is due to take the examination for the degree of provincial graduate.

> [Amended, p. 144:] A general term for [the system of] examinations through the various regular stages.

1311. K'O-K'AO 科考 Second examinations

> Same as above [1310]. [See note under 1312.]

1312. SUI-K'AO 歲考 First examinations

> Each year the licentiates and government stipendiaries are given a test by the education officers, to distinguish the good from the poor (student) and determine the awards and penalties. This is known as the "first examinations." [Each year the government students 生員 of every province were tested by the provincial Director of Studies 學政. The examinations were given on a three-year rotating basis in the following order: "first examinations" 歲考 in the first year;

"second examinations" 科考 in the second, and
"provincial examinations" 鄉試 in the third. Thus
each type of test in the series took place once every
three years. KHHT, 32:1-2.]

1313. KUNG-YUAN 貢院 Examination compound

The examination hall.

[Amended, p. 144:] The places where provincial and
metropolitan examinations are held.

1314. LUNG-MEN 龍門 The dragon gate

The main gate of an examination hall.

1315. TAO-K'AO, YÜAN-K'AO 道考,院考 Circuit
examination; chancellor's examination

A t'ung-sheng 童生 [student) wishing to take the
examination for the degree of government student should
first be tested by [the authorities of] his own prefecture
and district. This is followed by an examination by the
circuit intendant (Taotai), which is followed by a further
examination by the Literary Chancellor 學院 (that is,
the Hsüeh-cheng, 學政 provincial Director of Studies).
The candidate becomes a secondary government student
附生 after passing all these examinations. [Cf. 1280A.]

1316. HAO-FANG 號房 Examination cells

These are built within the examination hall, consisting
of several thousands of small cubicles that are numbered
serially according to the word order of the Primer of One
Thousand Characters 千字文 , like "heaven," "earth,"
"black," "yellow," and so on. [Each candidate was
assigned to one of these cubicles and stayed there for the
duration of the examination.]

1317. K'O-CHIA 科甲 Advanced degrees

A provincial graduate taking the examination for the
degree of metropolitan graduate is known as achieving
an advanced degree.

[Amended, p. 144:] A general term referring to all those
who have achieved the degrees of provincial or metropolitan graduates.

1318. HSIEN-SHU 賢書 The book of worthies

Passing the examination and becoming a provincial
graduate is known as "entering the book of worthies";
that is, one's name is among the worthies to be recommended
[for public service].

1319. CH'AI HAO 拆號 Unsealing the examination papers

When the examination papers have been read, those that
pass will be unsealed on a designated date in the order
of their [serial] numbers. The (authors') names (thus
revealed) are written into the list of successful candidates.
This is called "unsealing the examination papers. "

1320. T'IEN PANG 填榜 Writing the list of successful candidates

See above [1319, and 1301].

1321. CHIEH-HSIAO 揭曉 Publication of the list

The list of successful candidates is hung up on a high
spot, in order that it may be known to the public [cf.
1322].

1322. CH'U PANG 出榜 Issuing the list

The same as publication of the list [1321].

1323. P'ENG-KUEI 棚規 Cost [or fee] for examination pavilions

(*P'eng 棚 "pavilion" is given as pang 榜 "list of names"
in the Manchu-Chinese editions.)

When the Director of Studies of a province proceeds to
give examinations in the prefectures, departments, and
districts under his jurisdiction, mat pavilions are erected
in places where no examination halls exist, in order to
house the examination cells. Known as "examination pavilions, " their costs are defrayed by the prefectural and
district [governments] and are called "costs (or fee) for
examination pavilions. "

[Amended, p. 144:] The place where the primary examinations 小考 [for the degree of licentiate or government student] are held is termed hsüeh-yuan 學院 [academy], also known as "examination pavilions" because the tests are held in separate pavilions. "Fee" refers to the regular fees paid by the prefectural, departmental, and district authorities to the Director of Studies. Since the latter conducts the examinations in the pavilions, [this payment] hence is known as "cost, or fee, for examination pavilions."

1324. CHUNG-SHIH CHU MO CHUAN 中式硃墨卷 Vermilion and ink examination papers of passing candidates

The "ink examination papers" are the originals written by the candidate himself, while the "vermilion examination papers" are the copies made in vermilion ink in the Bureau of Copying [see 1303]. After passing the examination the two versions are compared to see if all the words and sentences are the same. This is done to prevent the malpractice of getting the papers illegally changed. [Cf. 1326].

1325. T'I-MING LU 題名錄 Passing names list

When the list of successful candidates 榜 is published after a provincial or metropolitan examination, many bookstores print the names in the order of their places on the list and sell the printed copies, which are called "passing names list."

1326. MO-K'AN, MO-TUI 磨勘, 磨對 Thorough checking; thorough comparison

An examination essay that has passed the test will be subjected to a check as to its phraseology and syntax, to see if any prohibitions have been violated; this is known as "thorough checking." Also, the ink and vermilion copies [of a paper] are compared for possible discrepancies between the two; this is known as "thorough comparison" [Cf. 1324].

[[4]] (continued)
B. Discipline and reward. Nos. 1327-1351

1327. I (YEH) PO (PAI) 曳 白 Presenting a white paper

(When a candidate) is unable to compose an essay or to write even a single word, but must submit a blank paper to the examiner, it is known as "presenting a white paper, " colloquially called chiao pai-chüan-tzu, "handing in a blank. "

1328. YÜEH FU 越 幅 Skipping a page

To skip a [double] page accidentally when writing an examination paper, so that the writing is not found on consecutive pages, is known as "skipping a page. '"

1329. YU MO WU 油 墨 污 Oil or ink stain

When writing the examination paper the candidate has carelessly upset his lamp or ink-stone, thereby staining the paper.

1330. KUAN-CHIEH 關 節 Seeking connection

[...]

To ask someone to seek favor and offer bribes, so as to reach an understanding with the examiner who is asked to pass (the candidate). In other words, to seek personal favor.

1331. CHIA-TAI 夾 帶 Smuggling test material

To enter the examination hall with ready-written essays hidden in one's clothes or other effects, in the hope that one might luckily pass by copying (these smuggled essays), is known as "smuggling test material. "

1332. HUAI-TAI 懷 帶 Carrying test material

Same as above [1331].

1333. CH'UAN-TI 傳 遞 Communicating with others

To ask a friend to compose the examination essays and

-213-

clandestinely sent them [to the candidate], who then
submits them as his own work. [Cf. 1299.]

1334. TING MING 頂名 Assuming one's name

To ask a friend to sit at the examinations in one's behalf
under one's own name is called "assuming one's name."

1335. MAO CHI 冒籍 Fraudulent claims to a native place

To take part in the examinations by falsely claiming
to be the native of a place; such as, for example, persons
from other provinces claiming to be natives of [the metropolitan prefecture of] Shun-t'ien.

1336. T'IEH-CH'U 貼出 Public expulsion

According to statute, any (candidate) guilty of [one or
more of] the above malpractices [1327-1335] is to have
his name and case written in blue ink and publicly displayed
outside the examination hall gate. He is expelled and
barred from taking the examinations, and is known as
having been "publicly expelled."

1337. FA K'O 罰科 Penalty of exclusion from examinations

If in the course of thorough checking [1326] infractions
of rules are discovered in a paper that has already passed
the metropolitan examinations, (its author) is to be
penalized by exclusion from one or two turns of the
palace examination [i.e., for three or six years].

[Amended, p. 144:] If in the course of thorough checking
infractions of rules are found in the papers written by
a provincial or metropolitan graduate who has already
passed the examination, the degree is to be withdrawn
from the author if the offense is of a major nature. If
it is minor, then the penalty of exclusion from examinations is invoked. [Under this] a provincial graduate is
barred from the metropolitan examination, and a metropolitan graduate is barred from the palace examination;
the number of turns during which he is to be excluded de-
pends on the seriousness of the offense.

1338. WEN-LI YU T'UNG LIEH-WEI I-TENG 文 理 優 通 列 為 一 等 First class: showing literary excellence and logic

Candidates who have passed the provincial examination are given an honors test [fu shih 覆 試], after which they are classified into three groups. Those who show superior literary excellence and logic should be placed in the first class.

1339. MING T'UNG 明 通 Lucid and logical

[One whose] style is lucid and whose argumentations are logical and informed.

1340. P'ING T'UNG 平 通 Even and logical

[Writing that is] even-paced, logical and informed.

1341. YU-TS'U 有 疵 Blemished

There are shortcomings in the essay.

1342. HUANG-NIU 荒 謬 Fantastic and absurd

The essay contains fantastic and absurd statements.

1343. PU-T'UNG 不 通 Not perspicuous

The style of writing is not perspicuous.

1344. TS'U-MENG NIU-LEI 疵 蒙 謬 累、 Full of errors and absurdities

[...] These are all undesirable characteristics in writing.

1345. KUNG-CHÜ FEI CH'I JEN 貢 舉 非 其 人 Unsuitably passed [or selected]

The scholars passed by the examiners are all of bad quality. [Cf. 1290 for chih kung-chü kuan 知 貢 舉 官 .]

1346. KUNG-T'UNG CHIU-TING 公 同 鬮 定 Jointly decided by lot

When the number of passing candidates is short [of the quota], the examination officials will jointly draw lots

and thus select one person from among those who have
not passed, in order to fill the place.

1347. EN-JUNG YEN 恩榮宴 Banquet of Bestowed Glory

The banquet given at the Board of Rites in honor of the
new metropolitan graduates is called "Banquet of Bestowed
Glory," while that given at the prefectural office for the
new provincial graduates is called "Banquet of Auspicious
Omen" 鹿鳴宴 [literally, Deerneigh Banquet. Cf. 1348].

1348. JU-LIEN LU-MING YEN PEI-P'AN TUAN-P'I HUA HUNG
TENG HSIANG 入簾鹿鳴宴盃盤緞疋花紅
等項 Such expenditures as silver service, ornaments
and silks [given to] the examination officials attending
the Banquet of Auspicious Omen

"Examination officials" is the general term denoting all
the examiners, associate examiners, and inner and outer
section officials [at a provincial examination. See 1274,
1291, 1292, 1298]. At the conclusion of an examination
they are all entitled to attend the Banquet of Auspicious
Omen [1347], where they are customarily presented with
silver cups and plates, gold flowers, brocades, etc.
However, rather than receiving these things in kind, they
are given their prices in money.

1349. HSIN-CHUNG CHÜ-JEN HUA HUNG 新中舉人花紅
Ornaments and silks for the new provincial graduates

New provincial graduates should be given gold flowers
and colored silks.

1350. K'AN-K'O HSIANG-SHIH LU HSIA-MA SHANG-MA YEN
CH'A-HUA CHI KEI PIAO-LI TENG HSIANG 刊刻
鄉試錄下馬上馬宴插花及結表裏等項
Such expenditures as for printing the provincial examination
list, welcome and farewell banquets, ornaments and dry
goods

"Provincial examination list" is the name list of the
provincial graduates who have passed the examination;
"welcome and farewell banquets" [literally, "dismounting

and mounting banquets"] are those given by the local
officials for the provincial Director of Studies upon the
latter's arrival at, and departure from, the prefectures,
departments, and districts which he visits to hold
examinations; ("ornaments and dry goods") refer to the
gold flowers used as personal ornaments and clothing
material given to the new provincial graduates [cf. 1349].
*[The shang-ma-yen 上馬宴 is described in the Hui-tien
as a banquet given for the chief examiner, the associate
examiners, the proctors, inspectors, and other officials,
on the day when they began their temporary sojourn in the
examination hall for the provincial examinations. This
banquet was given in all the provincial capitals except
the metropolitan prefecture of Shun-t'ien.   KHHT, 33:3b.]

1351. HSIU-LI KUNG-YUAN CHENG-TSAO IISI-SHE CHI P'U-TIEN
KUNG-KEI(-CHI) 修理貢院整造蓆舍及舖墊
供給. [Expenditures for the] repair of examination
halls, maintenance and erection of mat sheds, and
furnishings and supplies

Any damage in the buildings of the examination hall should
be repaired in the year when examinations are to be held;
"mat sheds" are the examination pavilions mentioned above
[1323]; "furnishings" are the necessary things needed in the
buildings; and "supplies," the food and drink used in the
halls.

CHAPTER IV

THE BOARD OF WAR

[[1]] The military officialdom
     A. Phrases describing meritorious officers.
     Nos. 1352-1393

1352. CHIANG-TS'AI 將材 Having the ability to be a general;
or, cut out to be a commander

This means that a given person's ability is suitable
for generalship.

1353. T'UNG-HSIA 統轄 In command of

To have over-all charge [militarily] of a certain post
is termed "in command of. "

1354. CHEN HSIEH 鎮協 Brigade and regimental [commander]

The chief military officer is called brigade commander,
and the deputy officer, regimental commander. [In
the old Army of the Green Standard, the forces in a
province, under the general command of a t'i-tu 提督
(commander-in-chief), were divided into chen-piao 鎮
標 or brigade commands, which were in turn subdivided
into hsieh-piao 協標 or regimental commands (cf. B. 749).
The relationship between chen and hsieh was hence
superior-subordinate rather than chief-deputy, as is
stated here.]

1355. T'U PIEN 土弁 Tribal petty officers

Low-ranking military officers of the local tribal
administration.

[The term t'u-pien is not a general designation, but refers
to particular tribal military officers of a specific number
who were under the control of the governors-general of
Shensi-Kansu, Szechwan, and Yunnan-Kweichow, and the
governor of Kweichow. Their ranks ranged from that of

Tu-ssu 都司 (First Captain) to Wai-wei 外委 [Sergeant (?)]. KHHT, 45:5b.]

1356. WU-CHIH CHUAN-HSÜN 武職專汛 A post district under exclusive military control

A military post district 汛地 under the exclusive jurisdiction of military authorities, where no civil administration functions. [See 1524.]

1357. WU-CHIH CHIEN-HSIA 武職兼轄 Mixed military control

A place originally under civil administration, but where military authority can also exert control.

1358. CH'ING-NIEN CH'ANG-CHI 青年長技 Youthful and skillful

[One who is] young in years and possessed of great skills [in the use of weapons].

1359. TS'AI CHI YU-CH'ANG 材技優長 Excellent ability and skill

This means that [a given man] is good in respect of both generalship and military skills.

1360. KUO-KAN YUNG-WANG 果敢勇往 Resolute and courageous

Being spirited and shrewd, unafraid and courageous, one who goes forward and never retreats.

1361. YÜN K'AN PAO-CHANG 允堪保障 Capable of serving as the defender

[An officer] is truly able to defend the territory, and protect it from enemy forces.

1362. CHENG-CH'IH YING-WU 整飭營伍 Putting the camp in order

To maintain and put in good order the camp [or barracks] and the troops.

1363. HO-CHI PING MIN 和輯兵民 Bringing about harmony between troops and civilians

1364. HSÜN-LIEN SHIH-TSU 訓練士卒 Training of soldiers

To teach and drill the soldiers.

1365. T'UAN-LIEN HUO-CH'I 團練火器 Practice of firearms

To let the troops practice the use of guns, cannon, and other such firearms.

1366. SHU-HSI FENG-T'U 熟悉風土 Familiar with local customs

To know and understand the local environment, the people and their customs.

1367. SHU-AN TI-LI 熟諳地理 Well-versed in the geography [of the locality]

Having full knowledge of the geography of a given locality.

1368. SHAN CH'IH YING-WU 善飭營伍 Able in administering the camp

[An officer who is] able in administering and maintaining order in the camp and among the troops.

1369. LAO-CH'ENG LIEN-TA 老成練達 Experienced and competent

When coping with a problem [this man] is poised, resourceful, experienced and competent.

1370. MOU YUNG CHIEN-YU 謀勇兼優 A good strategist and brave

Being more than capable both in military planning and in courage.

1371. CHÜN JUNG SHU-LIEN 軍戎熟練 Well-versed in field and garrison duties

[One who is] well-versed in the techniques of an army on the march as well as of garrison duties.

1372. TS'AI YUNG CHIEN-YU 才勇兼優 Talented and brave

Being both highly talented and courageous.

1373. CH'Ü SHIH CH'IN-CH'Ü 趨事勤劬 Diligent in work

Being industrious and hardworking in doing a job.

1374. NIEN LI CHING CHUANG 年力精壯 In the prime of life and full of vital force

In age only.... (*The rest is missing in the original text.)

1375. HSÜN-LIEN P'O CH'IN 訓練頗勤 Quite diligent in training

Being very diligent in teaching and drilling [the troops].

1376. KUNG-SHAN YU CH'AO-TSE(TSEI) CHIH KUNG 攻山有剿賊之功 [One is] credited with fighting the rebels in the attack on (their) mountain

Having the achievement of killing rebels [literally, "bandits"] during a drive against their mountain strong-holds. [Tsei 賊 "bandits" will be rendered as "rebels" throughout this chapter whenever it appears that the word designates an armed anti-government force. The Ch'ing Criminal Code classifies treason and rebellion against the state as the two leading crimes within the category of "Banditry" 盜賊 . KHHT, 53:3b.]

1377. CHI-PU WU T'AO-PU CHIH HUAN 緝捕無逃逋之患 There is no worry of [rebels] escaping while being hunted

No one will escape from [the given official's] hunt for rebels; there is no question of future disturbances being created by the latter.

1378. FEN-YUNG TENG-SHAN SHE-FA CHI TSE(TSEI) 奮勇登山設法緝賊 Bravely to ascend the mountain and devise ways to capture the rebels

To scale the mountain courageously and devise ways to capture the rebels.

1379. CHI NENG JU-CH'I TS'AO-LIEN KENG SHIH HU-SUNG WU-YÜ 既能如期操練更使護送無虞 [One who] can train the troops on schedule, and also perform escort duties without mishap

To be able to train the soldiers according to schedule, while the high officials passing through, as well as the funds being dispatched to Peking, are all duly escorted [by troops under the given officer's command] without mishap.

1380. CHENG-LIEN YING-WU I-SHIH TS'AO-YEN 整練營伍以時操演 Keeping the camp in good order and drilling on schedule

To commit to memory all the [work] pertaining to the maintenance and administration of military camps and troops, and also to be able to drill the soldiers at the required times.

1381. HU-HSIANG FANG-HAI CHÜN CH'ENG PU-LAN 護餉防海均稱不懶 Not indolent in the protection of funds and in the defense of the coast

With regard to the protection of military provisions and the defense of the sea coast [a given officer] may be considered as not indolent.

1382. TS'ENG YÜ CH'AO-NI LI YU CHAN-KUNG 曾于勦逆立有戰功 Has record of merit in the campaign against rebels

[An officer] has accomplished meritorious achievements in the fighting against rebel bandits.

1383. SUI FA-FENG ERH-TZ'U NAN-YEN CH'I CH'ANG 雖罰俸二次難掩其長 His strong points cannot be obscured in spite of two forfeitures of salaries

Although on account of some minor offense [an officer] has been penalized with forfeitures of salaries [see 126], his strong points still cannot be thus obliterated.

1384. CHUNG PU-YEN CH'I SO-CH'ANG 終不掩其所長 Cannot hide his strong points

Same as above [1383].

1385. K'AN-YING TZ'U JEN 堪膺此任 Able to bear this responsibility

Being able to assume this position of great responsibility.

1386. K'AN-JEN TZ'U CHIH 堪任此職 Able to take this post

Same as above [1385].

1387. TE-SHOU CHIH-PI CHIH HSIAO 得收指臂之效
Getting effective cooperation

A superior official finding a given subordinate very
cooperative in carrying out his orders, producing
results just as effectively as do a man's fingers that are
being motivated by his arm.

1388. YÜN-CH'ENG JEN TI HSIANG-I 允稱人地相宜
The man and the locality are mutually suitable

The man and the locality may be said to be suited to each
other, when a certain individual is appointed to a certain
post.

1389. YU TU PING-CH'E 遊都並掣 Appointable to the post
of either Major or First Captain

To be appointed by drawing lots to the vacant post either
of a Yu-chi 遊擊 (Major) or of a Tu-ssu 都司 (First
Captain). This is because a given individual has been
recommended [twice?], therefore can be appointed to
[either one of?] two different posts.

1390. HSIEN-CH'ÜEH HSIANG-TANG 銜缺相當 Corresponding
posts

(An official's) original post is equal in rank to the one to
which he is transferred; thus (the transfer) does not
involve a promotion in rank. [Same as 27.]

1391. I MOU-JEN PU-YUNG 以某人補用 Let X fill the post

This sentence indicates the designation of a certain
person to fill a particular post.

1392. CHAO WEN-MING ERH HSI SHOU-SHIH 朝聞命而夕
受事 Receives the order in the morning and assumes the
duties in the evening

Having received the imperial orders in the morning,
(an official) is ready to take over the seal and assume
his duties by evening.

This is but a figurative way of saying "without delay";
the words "morning" and "evening" must not be under-
stood too literally.

1393. YAO-TI YING-WU YU-LAI I 要地營伍有賴矣
[A man] to be relied upon in strategic places

Truly a reliable man in the military camps [or to be in
charge of the forces] at any strategic spot.

[[1]] (continued)
    B. Some administrative terms. Nos. 1394-1406

1394. HO TANG K'UNG-TAO FANG-PIEN YING I CH'OU-MIU
河當孔道防弁應宜綢繆 Precautionary
defense measures should be kept up by troops who guard
the river beside [or intersecting?] an artery of
communications

A river running alongside a major highway is of the utmost
[strategic] importance. Armed forces guarding it should
take all precautions during normal periods, so that confusion may be avoided when an emergency arises.

1395. CH'IH-LING YEN CHIA FANG-FAN PU-TI TSAI-SSU
飭令嚴加防範不啻再四 Having repeatedly
ordered [the troops] to be strictly on guard

Orders have been repeatedly issued to the troops that they
should be strictly on guard over the area.

1396. WU CH'EN CHIEN-CHÜ CHI I CHÜ-HSING 武臣荐舉
亟宜舉行 The recommendation of military personnel
should be carried out expeditiously

The high metropolitan and provincial officials should
quickly carry out the recommendation, on the basis of
facts, of good military officers whom they know [or know
about]. [The text here reads only hao wu 好武; it

-224-

apparently should be <u>hao</u> <u>wu-kuan</u> 好武官 .]

1397. TZU CH'EN 自陳 Self-presentation; or to memorialize concerning oneself

To memorialize the Emperor clearly on one's own merits and demerits.

1398. K'AO-HSÜAN CHÜN-CHENG 考選軍政 Inspection of military personnel

To carry out the inspection of military personnel by testing [the officers'] mounted archery and dismounted archery, so as to select the suitable persons for [further] appointments. [The inspection of military personnel 軍政 took place once every five years and was designed to parallel the triennial appraisal of achievements among the civil officials [see 86, 91, 92). KIIIT, 15:1.]

1399. PIEN-CHIANG 邊疆 Frontiers

The areas bordering on foreign lands.

1400. YEN-CHIANG 嚴疆 Frontiers important for defense

The frontiers that should be carefully guarded and garrisoned.

1401. FU-LI 腹裏 The interior

This means China Proper.

1402. AI-K'OU 隘口 Narrow pass

The narrowest and most strategically situated pass.

1403. HAI-CHIANG 海疆 Coastal frontier

The frontier along the sea coast.

1404. YÜAN-PIEN KUAN SAI 緣邊關塞 Frontier passes and forts

All passes [and forts?] along the frontier; a general term of reference to the frontiers.

1405. PIN-HAI YAO HSÜN 濱海要汛 Strategic coastal military district

The most important military post district(s) on the coast.

1406. YEN-HAI K'OU-TZU 沿海口子 Coastal ports

A general term for the shores and ports along the sea coast.

[[1]]   (continued)
C. Phrases describing acts of demerit.
Nos. 1407-1421

1407. SHOU-PEI PU SHE 守備不設 No defense is prepared

No measure has been taken to set up defense and security systems.

1408. TI-PEI PU YEN 隄備不嚴 Security measures are lax

Defense preparations and security measures have been [carried out] carelessly instead of strictly.

1409. CHÜN-SHIH PU CH'ÜAN 軍士不全 Incomplete troop (rolls); or, troops short of quota

The number of soldiers under the command [of a given officer] is short of the required quota; this is a matter for impeachment and punishment.

1410. TIAO-TU KUAI FANG 調度乖方 Actions contrary to regulations

All the acts [of a given officer] in the deployment and use of troops are not done according to military regulations [or the laws of the Board of War?].

1411. HSÜN TIEN PU-YEN 巡點不嚴 Lax in inspection and roll-call

Such matters as the inspection [of troops] and roll-call are not strictly checked [by a given officer], thus giving rise to abuses.

1412. YU-SHIH CH'IEN-SU 有失鈐束 Remiss in control [of troops]

[An officer] is not strict in the control of his troops, resulting in the occurrence of disturbances.

1413. SHIH-YÜ P'AN-CHIEH 失于盤詰 Remiss in interrogating

Being negligent in examining and interrogating, thus allowing spies to slip through.

1414. SHIH-WU CHÜN-CHI 失誤軍機 Missing a military opportunity

Having failed to take a good opportunity to attack the rebels.

1415. MAO-MING TAI-T'I 冒名代替 To be present under an assumed name

To let a person take another's place under the latter's name owing either to shortage in the quota of soldiers, or to his absence at the time of roll-call.

1416. CHUNG-CHUNG HSÜ-SO 種種需索 All kinds of exactions

(*In the Manchu-Chinese editions this entry is given as tzu- chu pi so 錙銖必索 , "exactions down to the last cent.")

Troops passing through an area making demands on the local officials for all sorts of supplies.

1417. PU-NIEN HO-KO 不念荷戈 Unmindful of the spear-bearers

Army officers who think only of their own comfort and are unmindful of the soldiers who, weapons in hand, have to work on patrol duty.

1418. WEI-CHIN HSIA-HAI 違禁下海 Illegally putting out to sea

In the past the law of the land prohibited the people of China to go overseas on their own. Violation of this restriction was heavily punished according to statute. [The Board of War was in charge of the restrictive measures over the fishing and commercial enterprises of the coastal population, as well as the regulations with regard to the size and types of ships to be used, contraband, etc. KHHT, 49:3b.]

1419. YÜEH-CH'U CHIEH-SHIH 越出界石 To overstep [or extend beyond] the boundary markers

At places where foreign countries adjoin Chinese territory--such as in the cases of Annam, Siam, and Russia--stone markers are erected to indicate the boundary lines. These boundaries are mutually inviolable.

1420. MAO-TU YÜEH-TU 冒度越度 To go across [Shanhaikuan, or a pass] fraudulently, or circuitously

To cross beyond the [Shanhaikuan] Pass either by assuming another person's name, or by taking a roundabout route.

1421. SSU-TU KUAN-CHIN 私度關津 Clandestinely [or illegally] passing customs stations

To pass a customs station without declaring oneself, either in regard to one's travels, or to the weapons and contraband in one's possession, with the intention of smuggling or illegally passing through.

[[2]] The actions and fortunes of war: intelligence, army administration, the battlefield. Nos. 1422-1547

1422. CHI-MI TA-SHIH 機密大事 An important, top secret matter

(*Chi-mi 機密 "top secret" is given as chün-chi 軍機 "military" in the annotated edition.)
A matter of high military secrecy and importance.

1423. CHÜN-CHI CHUNG-WU 軍機重務 Important military matter

Same as above [1422].

1424. FEI-PAO SHENG-HSI 飛報聲息 Swiftly report
[literally, "make a flying report of"] the intelligence

To report swiftly to one's own camp news of the enemy.

1425. FEI-PAO CHŪN-CH'ING 飛報軍情 Swiftly report
the military situation

To report immediately any news of the military situation
that one has gathered.

1426. HUI-CHŪN JIH-CH'I 會軍日期 Date for joining forces

Two separate contingents of troops joining together on a
designated date. This refers to elements of the forces
on one side only, and does not include enemy troops.

1427. SUI-CHENG KUNG-CHI (-KEI) 隨征供給 Field supplies

The provisioning of all kinds of supplies to go along
with the army camps. Nowadays known as the liang-t'ai
糧台 (commissary).

1428. CHŪN-HSÜ K'UNG-CHI 軍需孔亟 Urgent military needs

Things needed in the army camps of which the supply must
not be delayed even for a moment--such as foodstuffs,
weapons, gun powder, and so on.

1429. TAO TSE(TSEI) LIANG-HSIEH 擣賊兩脇 Assault on
the rebels' two flanks

To divide the troops into two parts and charge into
rebel force from two sides.

1430. HUANG-HUANG WU-TS'O 惶惶無措 In nervous confusion

To attack the enemy when he is off guard, [so that] he is
startled and confused and knows not what to do.

1431. SSU-TI PU-T'UI 死敵不退 Fight to the death without
retreat

Although the rebel forces are fierce, the government
troops still fight with all their might and do not yield
the slightest ground.

1432. TA-SSU CH'ANG-CHÜEH 大肆猖獗 On the rampage

The rebel troops are showing signs of becoming fierce and are gaining advantages.

1433. TSE(TSEI)-SHIH PU-TI 賊勢不敵 The rebels are weakening

The rebels are weakening against the [strength of the] government troops.

1434. I-KU K'O P'O 一鼓可破 To shatter the enemy at one stroke [literally, "with one round of the drum-beat"]

To beat the drums to urge on the battle and encourage the soldiers, so as to crush the rebel troops at one stroke.

[Amended, p. 144:] I ku 一鼓 : this originates from the phrase i ku tso ch'i 一鼓作氣 "drawing strength from the first round of the drum beat" in the Tso Chronicles 左傳.

1435. T'OU-FU CHIH TSE (TSEI) 投撫之賊 Rebels who have surrendered

The rebels who have surrendered either voluntarily or in response to [the government's] call.

1436. HSIAO-CHÜ PU-SAN 嘯聚不散 Mobbing together without let up

Rebels calling together the members of their group, congregating and refusing to disperse.

1437. CH'UNG-CH'IH TZU-MAN 充斥滋蔓 A full and spreading [force]

The ranks of the rebel troops are full, and their power is spreading over many areas.

1438. SHIH CH'U PU-TS'E 事出不測 Unexpected occurrence

An unexpected [or unforeseen] catastrophe has suddenly occurred.

1439. LI YU CHAN-KUNG 立有戰功 Having won merit in battle

This individual had accomplished meritorious achievements in battles in the past.

1440. HENG-CH'UNG I-WANG CH'IEN-LAI 橫衝一往前來
Charging forward from the flank

To go forward either by charging from the side or by starting on the side.

1441. SHENG-SHIH LIEN-LO HU-HSI HSIANG-T'UNG 聲勢連絡呼吸相通 Field communications are well connected, and [the units] mutually informed

The units of the government forces are so well deployed that the action and condition of each is known to the other, and each unit remains informed of the news of the others.

1442. CHIEN CHUNG-PING KU-YUNG HSIN-HUANG K'OU-TUN 見眾兵鼓勇心慌口遁 Fleeing in noisy confusion at sight of the soldiers' charge

The rebels, seeing that the government troops are bravely charging forward, become nervous and shout to each other to "get out of here fast."

1443. JO-FEI T'IEN YEN CH'ENG-CH'IN LIU-TU PU-CHIH HO-SO TI-CHIH 若非天厭成擒流毒不知何所底止 Had Heaven not turned against him, making possible his capture, it would have been hard to foretell where this evil could have been halted

This rebel leader is very capable. Had Heaven not rejected him and helped the government forces to capture him at an early stage, it would be difficult to say when his tyranny over the people could have been brought to an end.

1444. SHIH-KUAN YING-PING CHUNG-WU 事關營兵重務
An important matter concerning the armed forces

An important, urgent matter concerning the armed forces in camp [or concerning the administration of the troops].

1445. WU-T'U MAO-LAN I-CHI 武途冒濫已極 Improper promotion of the military personnel is at the utmost point

Among the military officers the practice of falsely assuming merits and reporting victories, so as to get recommendation on these untrue bases, has become so prevalent that it is unbearable [literally, "has reached the extremity"].

1446. TSUNG-FANG CHÜN-JEN HSIEH-I 縱放軍人歇役 Letting soldiers go off duty at will

To be lax and lenient, allowing the soldiers to stay off the service [as they wish].

1447. TAI-FENG CH'AI-TS'AO 帶俸差操 On training mission with salary

To dispatch a military officer, to be stationed in some other place and in charge of troop training. Although this officer has been relieved of his original post, nevertheless his salary is not stopped and he continues to receive [the original?] salary.

1448. CHUI-PEN CHU-PEI 追奔逐北 To pursue [or in pursuit of] the defeated

To pursue the rebels who have fled and capture those who have been defeated.

1449. SHEN-MING CHÜN-YÜEH 申明軍約 Proclamation of military rules

To proclaim to the troops the rules and regulations of the camp, in order that they may know them.

1450. KUAN TS'AO KUAN-YUAN 管操官員 Drill officer

The officer in charge of the drilling of the soldiers.

1451. CHING-PI 警蹕 Security guard

[Units] in charge of patrolling and security are known as the "security guard."

1452. CHING-PEI YEN-MI 警備嚴密 Strict security measures

All measures relating to police and security are carried out strictly and carefully.

1453. LUN-TS'AO KUAN-CHÜN 輪操官軍 Training the government troops by rotation

To train the government forces by taking turns at it.

1454. HAI-FEN WEI CHING 海氛未靖 Coastal disturbances not yet pacified

The pirates along the sea coast have not yet been subdued.

1455. TANG-CHIH HSÜN-LO 當直巡邏 On patrol duty

To be responsible, by daily rotation, for the patrolling and policing duties.

1456. HAO-LING SEN-YEN 號令森嚴 The orders are inviolable and strict

All the orders issued [by a given officer] are clear and to be strictly observed.

1457. MA I PU CHIU 馬一步九 One cavalryman to nine infantrymen

The work done by one cavalryman is equal to that of nine infantry soldiers.

1458. CHEN-SHOU FANG-SHOU 鎮守防守 To garrison, to defend

To be in charge of a force either for garrison duty, or for defense.

1459. KUAN-FANG T'I TU 關防提督 Guarding and commanding

To be on guard for defense, and to command and lead [the troops].

1460. T'IEH-FANG 貼防 Auxiliary defense; to assist in defense

To help in defense work.

1461. FANG–FAN 防範 To guard against

To guard and defend.

1462. HAN-YÜ 捍禦 To resist with arms

This means to fight against the enemy.

1463. T'AN-YA 彈壓 To suppress

This means to subjugate and control.

1464. YÜ-WU 禦侮 To resist aggression

To fight against foreign invaders.

1465. CHING-LÜEH 經略 To plan and administer

This means the administration [of a given matter] is somewhat settled [sic].

1466. FU-WEI 撫慰 To pacify and comfort

To call together and sooth those who have surrendered.

1467. T'UAN-LIEN 團練 Training of militia

To call together able-bodied men and train them into [armed] units.

1468. TIEN-SHIH 點視 Inspection by roll call

To muster the troops and inspect their physical fitness by calling the roll.

1469. TIEN-HSÜAN 點選 Selection by roll call

To call the roll and select the soldiers.

1470. CH'IEN-P'AI 僉派 Assignment

This means to select and assign [men] to troop duty.

1471. CHIH-JIH 值日 On day duty

To be on duty for service by daily rotation.

1472. CHIH-SU 值宿 On night duty

To be on duty for night service by nightly rotation.

1473. CH'OU-TS'AI 抽裁 Apportioned reduction

To withdraw a certain percentage from the main body of troops as the portion to be reduced.

1474. KAI-CHENG 改正 Correction(s)

Any error in the [management of] army affairs should be corrected forthwith.

1475. SU-WEI 宿衛 Night guard

The soldiers on guard duty at night.

1476. SHOU-WEI 守衛 Guards; to guard

Soldiers who guard and protect [the camp, etc.].

1477. TIAO-PO 調撥 Transfer

To transfer troops to some other place, either for combat or for garrison duty.

1478. T'I-PO 提撥 Apportioned transfer

To withdraw a certain number from the main body of troops as the portion to be transferred elsewhere.

1479. CH'AO FU 勦撫 To extirpate and to pacify

[There are two ways] to deal with rebels: either to exterminate them, or to pacify them.

1480. CH'AO-MIEH 勦滅 To exterminate

To kill and destroy every last one of the rebels.

1481. YUAN—CH'AO 援勦 To aid in extirpation

Sending soldiers to reinforce our troops in their extermination campaign against the rebels.

1482. AO-CHAN 鏖戰 To battle fiercely

To fight a raging battle to the death without let-up.

1483. YAO-CHI 邀擊 Intercept and attack

To cut off the rebels' way of escape and attack them.

1484. YEN-HSI 掩襲 Surprise attack

(*Hsi 襲 "attack" is given as hsi 息 "rest" in the annotated edition.)

An unexpected attack; to attack when the rebels are not prepared for it.

1485. HUO-CHO 活捉 To capture alive

To capture the rebel(s) alive.

1486. CH'IEN-FENG 前鋒 Vanguard

The troops who make the first charge in the forefront.

1487. P'ING-FAN 屏藩 Screen

Troop units that are deployed around [the main force] to serve as a protective screen.

1488. SUI-CHENG 隨征 Advance with the army

Persons who advance with the main body of the troops.

1489. NEI-YING 內應. Infiltration

To infiltrate into the enemy's lines and, at the proper moment, respond to [the attack of] our own force.

1490. HSIEH-YING 協應. To assist infiltration

To help in matters pertaining to infiltration. [Sic]

1491. TS'E-YING 策應. Reinforcement

The troops sent to reinforce the main body of the army after a battle are known as "reinforcements."

1492. TA-SHENG 大勝 Major victory

To score a very big victory in battle.

1493. CHUI-KAN 追趕 To pursue

To press after the rebels while [our] victory is fresh.

1494. LU-LIANG 擄掠 Plundering; pillage

Rebels and soldiers who flout discipline willfully, taking men, women, and valuables from among the populace.

1495. CH'AO-CH'IANG 抄搶 Robbery

Rebels and bad soldiers breaking into the people's houses and robbing the latter of valuables.

1496. KU LEI 固壘 Strengthening of the base

To strongly fortify the military base.

1497. FU KU 負固 Trusting on the strength [of the base]

Relying on the strength of the base and refusing to surrender.

[Amended, p. 144:] Relying on their strong position in terrain, [the enemy] refuse to surrender.

1498. CHÜ HSIEN 據險 Entrenched in a strategic spot

Relying on their possession of a dangerous and strategic spot, [the enemy] refuse to surrender.

1499. CHAN CHIEH 展界 To extend the border

To expand the territory and extend its borderline.

1500. MI-CHO 密捉 Secret capture

To capture a rebel secretly and grill him as to the [enemy's] positions.

1501. TUAN-HOU 斷後 Rear guard

When the army withdraws, a unit consisting of crack troops is assigned to protect its rear columns, so as to prevent the enemy from pursuing it.

1502. TANG-P'ING 蕩平 Eliminating [the rebels]

To eliminate [literally, "sweep clean"] the rebels entirely and bring peace to the region.

1503. CHAO-FU 招撫 To call for surrender, to pacify

To call upon the rank-and-file of the rebels to surrender, and to pacify those who do.

1504. T'OU-CH'ENG 投誠 To surrender one's allegiance

Coming forward to surrender in good faith.

1505. FAN-CHENG 反正 To return to the right path

Those who were rebels at first regretting their error and coming to surrender to the government forces, thus to return to the right path.

1506. HSÜN-NAN 殉難 To die for the country

To die at the hands of the rebels, thus serving the country with the utmost loyalty.

1507. CHIN-CH'UANG 金瘡 Battle-wound abcess [literally, "metal-caused abcess"]

A sword wound inflicted in battle which, after prolonged (infection), develops into an abcess.

1508. P'ING HSI 屏息 In breathless quiet

To stop all noises and silently await [the enemy].

1509. MIEH CHI 滅跡 To destroy all traces

To wipe out all traces or trails so that others will not be able to find them.

1510. CH'IH-CH'Ü 馳驅 To gallop

To [urge? whip?] the horse and go (fast). [The word preceding "horse" is missing in the text.]

1511. CHÜN-HSÜN 逡巡 To shrink back

To hang back and be reluctant to go forward.

1512. CH'ANG-LUAN 猖亂 Creating violence

The rebel forces are ferocious and creating disturbances in the area.

1513. PA-HU 跋扈 To tyrannize; tyrannous

To be strong, violent, and not amenable to reason.

1514. PING HUANG 兵荒 Ravages of war

To have experienced the disasters wrought by war.

1515. K'OU TS'AN 寇殘 Devastated by rebels

The area has been devastated and ruined by the rebels.

1516. SHA HSIEH 歃血 Blood oath; to take a blood oath

(*Sha 歃 "to sip" is given as ch'a 插 "to stick" in the Manchu-Chinese editions.)

Before rebels launch their revolts, animals are killed whose blood is smeared by every person around his mouth, and then an oath is taken.

1517. TIAO PI 掉臂 With folded arms

To disregard [a situation] with arms hanging--that is, being unwilling to give succor.

1518. CHIEN-HSI 奸細 Spy

Undercover agent sent by the enemy to find out military information.

1519. CHIEH-YIN 捷音 News of victory

Report on a victory.

1520. SU-YÜ 疎虞 Careless mistake

Mishap resulting from carelessness.

1521. HUI-FU 恢復 To recover; to reconquer

To plan to take back the territory seized by the enemy.

1522. KUEI WU 歸伍 To return to one's own unit

Retreating soldiers rejoining their respective battalions 營 and companies 隊 is known as "to return to one's own unit."

1523. CH'UAN-HSÜAN 傳宣 Heralds

Officers whose job it is to pass along the orders of the day.

1524. HSÜN-TI 汛地 Military district

The post under the jurisdiction of a Green Standard officer is known as a "military district." [Hsün-ti is the term used to designate the area under the jurisdiction of a Pa-tsung 把總 (Sub-lieutenant), who commands a ssu 司 (squad). B. 752f.]

1525. PIAO-YING 標營 Regimental staff

Officers subordinate to a high officer of the Green Standard Army are known as the "regimental staff."

1526. YING-SHAO 營哨 Battallion patrols [?]

[Interpretation is missing from this item.]

1527. T'ANG-PING 塘兵 Military courier station messenger-soldiers

[A post] smaller than a military district [1524] is a military courier station 塘, and one smaller than that is a military courier sub-station 鋪. Here (at the courier station) only about a dozen soldiers are stationed, whose jobs are to forward government dispatches and keep watch at night; they are not sufficient for use in combat. [T'ang 塘 and p'u 鋪 are two of the six categories of courier stations described in the Hui-tien of late Ch'ing: t'ang were set up for the transmission of military correspondence between Peking, Kansu, and further on to Sinkiang, while p'u were the numerous post stations in the provinces of China Proper that served to connect Peking with the provincial capitals, the prefectures, and down to the districts. KHHT, 51:1.]

1528. P'U-PING 鋪兵 Courier sub-station messenger-soldiers

See above [1527].

1529. MA-PING 馬兵 Cavalrymen

All soldiers in the Green Standard cavalry units are called "cavalrymen."

1530. PU-PING 步兵 Infantrymen

Soldiers in the infantry units of the same [i.e., the Green Standard Army].

1531. CHIH-PING 制兵 Regular troops

The troops in the Green Standard Army for whom regular quotas are set up are known as the "regular troops." This does not include the milita [or braves]

1532. HUO-PING 火兵 Mess soldiers [literally, "fire soldiers"]

Soldiers who prepare and cook the food are called "mess soldiers"--they are not "fire-fighting" soldiers.

1533. HU-PING 護兵 Escorts; guards

Soldiers who escort a convoy of materiel and provisions.

1534. CHIN PING 勁兵 Crack troops

The strongest, best soldiers.

1535. CHING-JUI CHIH PING 精銳之兵 Sharp [or picked] troops

Soldiers who are well-trained, brave, and effective.

1536. PO-PING 撥兵 A shift of soldiers

Soldiers guarding a pass or station take turns in shifts to stay on duty.

1537. KUAN-TUI 管隊 Company commander

The minor head of a company

1538. LEI PING 羸兵 Weak soldiers

Weak and ineffective soldiers.

1539. TSO T'ANG 坐塘 Stationed at a courier station

Soldiers left on guard at a local military courier station.

1540. LIAO-WANG 瞭望 Look-out

To watch the enemy's movements from a high elevation.

1541. KUAN PAO 關堡 Pass and fort

The naturally dangerous mountain terrain being used as a frontier gateway is called a pass; a stronghold, built in a dangerous [or strategic] mountain spot with troops stationed therein, is known as a fort.

1542. TUN-T'AI 墩臺 Signal mounds; watch towers

Beside the main highways one high mound is built in every ten li, on which a signal beacon is placed and guarded by soldiers. When an emergency arises the beacons are lighted [one after another], thus spreading the warning.

1543. CHAO-T'AN YEH PU-SHOU 爪探夜不收 Intelligence agents rest not at night

Persons who hunt abroad for military information throughout the night.

Such people are like the claws and teeth of an army, therefore are dubbed "claw spies."

1544. CHIA-P'AO YEH PU-SHOU 架砲夜不收 Artillery crews rest not at night

Soldiers who man the cannons day and night.

1545. WANG-KAO HSÜN-SHAO CHIH JEN 望高巡哨之人 Look-outs and patrols

Those who watch [the enemy camp] from a high place, and who patrol various places in order to seek information concerning the rebels' force.

1546. CH'ANG-CH'UAN SHOU-SHAO 常川守哨 Constant patrol

Those who regularly and unceasingly patrol the vicinity of the military post areas or the military courier stations, so as to gather information about the rebels' situation.

1547. SAN-T'ING CHÜN-SHAO 三停軍哨 Three-tenths of the force

Three-tenths of the units of the entire army. Here the word shao 哨 denotes "units" 隊.

[[3]] Equipment and weapons. Nos. 1548-1563

1548. WANG-MING CH'I P'AI 王命旗牌 Imperial command flags and plaques

The provincial governors and governors-general are each given four gold-lacquered plaques and four small flags of yellow silk, each bearing the words "by Imperial command." In the event of an urgent military situation, when there is no time to wait for instructions from the throne, these flags and plaques are used to authenticate the orders [given by the governor or governor-general] as though they were issued upon direct command from the Emperor.

1549. PA-MIEN KAN 八面桿 The eight staffs

See above [1548]. Four flags and four plaques make eight [items that are mounted on] staffs or poles.

1550. LING-CH'I LING-CHIEN 令旗令箭 Command flags, command arrows

All provincial governors and governors-general as well as high-ranking army commanders are given flags and arrows each bearing the word "command." These are used as proof of authority when ordering the transfer [or deployment] of troops.

1551. LU-CHIAO P'ANG-P'AI 鹿角傍牌 Cavalry traps, side barricades

"Cavalry traps" [literally, "deer antlers"] are made of wood, constructed in such a fashion as to resemble the antlers of deer. They are usually placed in the front of the battle field or the camp to prevent the enemy cavalry from charging in. "Side barricades" are built by lashing wood together, and they are placed on the sides of the camp or the battle field to ward off flanking charges by the enemy cavalry. [In common usage p'ang-p'ai meant "shield(s)."]

1552. YÜN-T'I P'AI PA 雲梯牌鈀 Scaling ladder [literally, "cloud ladder"], shield, and scaling hook

Wooden ladders, built in various forms, are used in scaling city walls; they are called "cloud ladders" on account of the heights they can reach. A "shield" is made of bamboo, wood, or rattan, and is held in the hand to ward off sword blows and arrows. A "scaling hook" consists of a wooden handle tipped with a five-pronged iron hook; it is also used in scaling city walls.

1553. KUNG-NU YAO-CHIEN 弓弩藥箭 Cross-bow, poisoned arrow

A cross-bow releases several arrows at one shot; the arrows that are poison-tipped will inflict fatal wounds.

1554. TA-TAO CH'ANG-CH'IANG 大刀長槍 Broad sword, long spear

Long-handled broad swords and long-handled spears are effective weapons on the battlefield. They were widely used in the old days, but with the prevalence of firearms nowadays these are no longer in use.

1555. MAI-SUI LIU-HSING 麥穗流星 Three-headed flail [literally, "wheat tassel"], iron ball [literally, "meteor"]

The "three-headed flail," commonly called "three-piece stick," consists of three sturdy short sticks tied together with an iron chain. The "iron ball" is a round ball made of iron and attached to a silken cord. Both are weapons used in olden times.

1556. HAO-TAI HUO-T'UNG 號帶火筒 Command streamer, flare gun

A "command streamer" is a long strip of cloth, tied to the top of a pole and used to direct the soldiers. A "flare gun" is a rocket.

[Cf. 1562.]

1557. CHANG-FANG LO-KUO 帳房鑼鍋 Tent, cauldron

The cloth huts in which the troops are quartered are known as "tents." A "cauldron" is made of copper. Shaped like a cooking pot, it is used to prepare food during the day, and at night it serves as the gong sounded by the night patrol. This was known as tiao-tou 刁斗 in ancient times.

1558. HUNG-I NIAO-CH'IANG 紅衣鳥槍 Red-coat's musket

"Red-coat" (hung-i) is a corruption of the term "red (-haired) barbarian" (hung-i 紅夷). In the old days the Dutch were called "red barbarians," or "red-haired." [The muskets] are so called because firearms were introduced into the East by the Dutch.

1559. P'ANG-AO MIEN-CHIA 胖襖棉甲 Fat [or padded] jacket, floss vest

A short jacket very thickly padded with cotton wool gives a fat appearance, therefore is called a "fat jacket." A lined short jacket, filled with silk floss and finely stapled with thread, is called a floss vest. These are both worn [by soldiers] in battle as protection against spear thrusts and arrows.

1560. P'I T'IEH K'UEI-CHIA 皮鐵盔甲 Leather or iron helmet and armor

Helmets and armor in the old days were made of either cow [or water buffalo?] hide or iron. [The iron ones] were fashioned of iron plates strung together.

1561. TU CH'I 纛旗 Marshal's banner

The large flag of the commander-in-chief is called "marshal's banner."

1562. KAO-CHAO CH'I 高招旗 Direction pennant

This is the field command pennant, tied to a long pole and used to direct soldiers [in action].

[Cf. 1556].

1563. TSA-SE CH'I 雜色旗 Multi-colored flag

A five-colored flag, raised when [different units?] have congregated together.

[[4]] The military post system. Nos. 1564-1602

1564. YU-FU 郵符 Postal credentials

The identifying certificate(s) carried by an official or soldier on the road. They are issued by the Board of War . [The exact meanings of the terms in 1564, 1565, 1567, and 1570 are to be found in the Hui-tien. There are three sorts of yu-fu or "postal credentials" issued by the

Board of War: (1) The k'an-ho or "tallies," used by
officials travelling on the post road; (2) the huo-p'ai
or "express tags," used by soldiers and government
messengers 兵 役 ; and (3) the ping-p'ai or "troop
tags," used by soldiers passing through an area on
escort duty. All three types of credentials entitle the
holders to obtain supplies and transportation facilities
at the stations. The huo-p'iao or "express warrant," on
the other hand, serves a different purpose. It is a
certificate showing the time schedule that must be observed
in the transmission of a government document via the
post road, done by relay from station to station. The
express warrant is attached to the document itself and is
an entirely different thing from the huo-p'ai. KHHT,
51:2-3; cf. John K. Fairbank and Ssu-yü Teng, "On the
Transmission of Ch'ing Documents," in Ch'ing Administration: Three Studies (Cambridge, Mass., 1960),
pp. 7, 9.]

1565. HUO-P'AI HUO-P'IAO 火牌火票 Express tag, express
ticket
When an official or soldiers travelling via the post road
arrive at a station, the local authorities will immediately
dispatch a written notice to the local officials at the next
station, so that (the latter) can make the necessary preparations. The written notice is called "express warrant"
to emphasize the need for haste--as in a fire. "Express
tag" is another term for express warrant [sic; see note
under 1564].

1566. LIANG-TAN 糧單 Provisions list

[This is the document] submitted by a commanding
officer to his superior, which contains an itemized list
of the food and allowances paid every month to the
soldiers under his command.

1567. K'AN-HO 勘合 Tallies

When an official or soldiers travelling via the post road
arrive at a station they must show the local officials the
certifying documents [or identifying certificates, see

1564] issued by the Board of War; when these are examined and found to be in good order the things [needed] will be supplied. Such certifying documents are called "tallies." [See note under 1564.]

1568. TI-PAO 邸報 TI-CH'AO 邸抄 The Peking Gazette

These are both references to the Peking Gazette

1569. LIEN-MING T'ANG-PAO 聯名塘報 Jointly signed courier report

When an urgent issue arises the officers [heading] several military post stations and post districts [1524] will jointly sign a report to their superior officer(s).

1570. PING-P'AI 兵牌 Troop tag

The tag [of identification] carried by each soldier. [See note under 1564.]

1571. K'OU-LIANG 口糧 Rations

LIN-CHI 廩給 Stipend

Monthly pay for the soldiers and monthly pay for the officers, respectively.

These two terms are used   the armed forces.

1572. KUNG-SO 公所 Office; public hall

Place where public affairs are conducted.

1573. TSOU-CHIAO 奏繳 To memorialize an account and return [funds]

To memorialize on the unexpended military funds and return the sum to the government.

1574. TSOU-HSIAO 奏銷 To submit a final account to the throne

To memorialize on the funds received and expended, and close the matter.

1575. TIEN-YUNG-KUO 墊用過 [Funds] advanced

When the funds for a certain undertaking have not yet been received, sums are advanced from another item so as to carry out the matter in question. Later when reporting to the Board [the official in charge] will state: "funds had been advanced for this undertaking to such-and-such an amount."

1576. HAO-SHU 號數 Serial number

The serial numbers attached to military uniforms, weapons, and so forth.

1577. I-TI 驛遞 Via the (military) post

To dispatch government documents, memorials and reports through the (military) post system. [Cf. 1593.]

1578. MA-CHAN 馬站 Horse post

To send the government documents speedily on by riders at every post station.

In the South where boats are used on waterways it is known as water post 水站.

1579. MA-T'OU 馬頭 Chief groom

The head of grooms (at a military post station).

1580. MA-FU 馬夫 Grooms

The men who have charge of the horses at a (military) post station. [This differs from 1578, where the term ma-fu is used in the sense of "riders."]

1581. CHAN-FU 站夫 Post station men

Laborers serving at the (military) post stations.

1582. I-FU 驛夫 Post station men

Same as above [1581].

1583. CH'ANG-FU 長夫 Permanent labor; long-term labor

Laborers employed for long periods.

1584. TUAN-FU 短夫 Temporary labor; short-term labor

Laborers employed for a temporary period only.

1585. CH'ANG CHIEH 長解 Long haul; long escort duty

    This is when the men escorting the dispatch of military provisions [or funds] are engaged in the original locality and are not changed en route. [Cf. 659.]

1586. TUAN CHIEH 短解 Short haul; short escort duty

    When (the men escorting the funds) are changed [at stations] en route. [Cf. 659.]

1587. KUAN-CHIEH 管解 Dispatch overseer

    The officer who is in charge of the dispatch of military funds.

1588. HU-SUNG 護送 Escorts; guards

    Low-ranking officers with soldiers are sent to escort the military funds in transit through the locality.

1589. KANG CHIEH 槓解 Send by pole-bearers

    Things such as guns and other weapons are sent [from one place to another] by being borne by laborers using cross-bar poles.

1590. TI-HUI 遞回 Extradition

    To send back to his native district, by way of the proper post stations, one who creates trouble in a different part of the country.

1591. CH'IEN-CH'Ü PING-FU 僉取兵夫 Assignment to army duty

    Men serving their labor duties as soldiers are assigned by their local officials, after the latter have received notices [asking for men] from the commanding officers.

1592. CH'IEN-TAO MA-T'OU 僉到馬頭 The assigned chief grooms

    Men who have been assigned by the local officials to serve as chief grooms [1579].

1593. YU I CH'UAN-TI 由驛傳遞 To send through the (military) post

To send government documents, memorials and reports through the (military) post system. [Cf. 1577.]

1594. FENG PU PIEN-CHI 奉部編給 Issued by the Board

The [identifying] characters and numbers on such things as weapons are serialized by the Board of War and issued to the commanding officers for implementation. [The text reads tsun-feng erh hsing 遵奉而行 : not clear in this context.]

1595. CH'AI-SHIH LO-I 差使絡繹 Unending need for service

In strategically located departments and districts there is always a continuous need to provide carts and horses for officials and couriers on the road, as well as to fulfill many other requests.

1596. CH'EN-NI KUNG-WEN 沈匿公文 Loss or concealment of government document

To lose or [purposely] conceal a government document and not deliver it to its destination.

1597. KUNG-SHIH CHI-CH'ENG 公事稽程 To delay government business

To take longer than the time limit set for a government business.

1598. MO-TS'A FENG-T'AO 磨擦封套 Rubbing the envelope

The envelope containing a government document is rubbed and damaged en route.

1599. JU-FA CHUANG-FENG 如法裝封 Packaged and sealed according to regulation

Government documents, memorials and reports, etc., have been placed in envelopes and sealed according to regulation.

1600. TZU-PEI AN MA 自備鞍馬 With one's own horse and saddle

To be equipped with one's own horse and saddle, and not use those provided by the military post stations. [Cf. 1608.]

1601. CH'ING CH'I CHIEN TS'UNG 輕騎減從 To travel light with reduced retinue

To pack the horses lightly, and travel with a reduced entourage.

1602. CH'IH-I CHIU-TAO 馳驛就道 To travel via the post road

To go on a journey and travel by following the post stations.

[[5]] The management of horses.   Nos. 1603-1636

1603. MA CHENG 馬政 Horse administration; the management of horses

The general term for matters pertaining to horses.

1604. I MA 驛馬 (Military) post horses

Horses provided by the (military) post stations.

1605. **CHAN MA** 站馬 Station horses

Same as above [1604].

1606. **CHAN MA** 戰馬 War horses

Horses to be used in combat.

1607. KUAN MA 官馬 Government horses

Horses issued by the government.

1608. TZU MA 自馬 Private horses

Horses provided by individuals themselves.   [Cf. 1600.]

1609. CH'I-TS'AO 騎操 Cavalry drill

(*The word ma 馬 "horse" follows ch'i-ts'ao in the Ch'ien-lung edition, but is missing in the Chia-ch'ing edition.)

The drilling of cavalry troops.

1610. HSIEH-CHI MA 協濟馬 Auxiliary horses

Horses outside the regular quota, to be used as [additional] help.

1611. TAN MA 單馬 Extra horses

[Horses] especially provided.

1612. CHENG MA 正馬 Regular horses

Horses provided in the regular quota.

1613. HUO MA 伙馬 Stable-mate horses

(*Huo 伙 [literally] "group" is given as huo 火 "fire" in the Manchu-Chinese editions.)

Horses being prepared to serve at the same place.

1614. CHUNG MA 中馬 Selected horses

Horses that have been selected [to serve]. [The meaning of the character 中 here is highly ambiguous without a more clearly defined frame of reference. In addition to "selected," it might also mean "suitable," "mediocre," or possibly even "to obtain by exchange" (see note under 1635). The translation is here rendered according to the interpretation given in the present item.]

1615. CHIEN-HSÜAN K'AN CHUNG 揀選堪中 Selected and found suitable

Same as above [1614]. This phrase applies to horses only.

1616. CH'A MA 茶馬 Tea-exchange horses

In the frontier areas of Szechwan and Kansu, trade is conducted whereby Chinese tea is exchanged for the horses of the barbarians. [Such trading is] generally termed the "tea and horse market" 茶馬市 . [Cf. 1635.]

1617. FU MA 夫馬 Pack horses

Horses used exclusively as beasts of burden for transporting goods; they are comparable to the bearers [or carriers] among human beings.

1618. MA KAN 馬乾 Horse fodder

Hay and beans for feeding horses.

1619. MA CHIA 馬價 The price of horses

All horses issued by the government to the soldiers are evaluated for price. In case one becomes lost its price is to be paid by the soldier [who took charge of it].

1620. P'ENG YIN 棚銀 Stable [construction] costs

(*P'eng 棚 "stable" is given as p'eng 朋 "companion" in the Manchu-Chinese editions.)

The money for building a horse stable. This is a matter that occurs in the government pasturages.

1621. P'ENG CHUANG YIN 棚椿銀 Stake costs

(*Same as in 1620.)

The sum spent in erecting hitching stakes in the horse stables.

1622. P'ENG-K'UNG YIN 棚控銀 Stabling fee

(*Same as in 1620.]

If a soldier's horse is tethered in a government stable, the stabling fee is deducted each month from the money allotted for the horse's fodder. [K'ung 控 is probably a misprint for shuan 拴 "to tether."]

1623. P'EI-CHUANG YIN 賠椿銀 Indemnity for damaged stake

If a soldier's horse damages the stake in a government stable, the indemnity for it is also to be deducted from the (money for the) fodder.

1624. T'IAO-MA YIN 條馬銀 Appropriations for horses

The money for [the maintenance of?] horses at (military) post stations.

The significance here of the word t'iao 條 is not clear; the interpretation has been made on the basis of the Manchu text.

1625. CHIEN-K'UANG YIN 違曠銀 Extra-day revenue

All appropriations for horse fodder are computed on the basis of thirty days to the month, and a certain amount is issued every month. In case of a small month [i.e., with only twenty-nine days], the unused portion to which the [theoretical thirtieth] day is entitled will be diverted, to be used as administration costs.

1626. TS'AO CHA YIN 槽鍘銀 Trough and [hay-] cutting costs

The wages needed for making horse feed troughs and for cutting hay.

1627. TZU MU TAO-PI 孳牧倒斃 Death of breeding or pastured horse

Death of breeding or pastured horses owing to disease. This refers to the pasturages beyond the Great Wall (K'ou-wai 口外].

1628. TAO MA TS'AI-K'UANG YIN 倒馬裁曠銀 Unused fodder cost of a dead horse

During the interval between the death of an old army horse and the issuing of a new one, the costs of the unused daily [fodder] are [deducted from the soldier's allowance] and returned to the government.

[Cf. 1631.]

1629. I-CHAN CHIEH-CHIH YIN 驛站借支銀 Post station advanced sum

When in providing horses a (military post) station finds itself in need of funds, a request may be addressed to the Board of War to advance it a certain sum, which is to be deducted later from the regular appropriations.

1630. TI MA PIEN-CHIA YIN 底馬變價銀 Cash value of poor-quality horse

When a soldier's horse is sick or of low quality, he is permitted to sell it, and to use the proceeds, plus a little additional sum supplied by his own regiment, to buy a good horse.

1631. KUAN-PING MA-P'I CH'ÜEH-K'UANG YIN 官兵馬匹
缺曠銀 Unused fodder cost

After the death of an army horse and before the purchase
of a new one, the fodder cost that had already been received
for this interval should be returned to the government.
[Cf. 1628.]

1632. I-CHAN SHIH-CHENG HSIEH-CHI CH'IEN-LIANG 驛站
實徵協濟錢糧 Levy for assistance of the post
stations

The actual amount of the revenue needed for the operation
of the (military) post stations is inspected each year by the
local officials, and collected from the people to meet
the needs.

1633. P'I-CHANG PIEN-CHIA YIN-LIANG 皮張變價銀兩
Money from the sale of hides

The Imperial Pasturages... (*The rest is missing
in the original text.)

1634. TING-PU HSIEH-HSIANG MA-FU 頂補協餉馬夫
To fill the places of subsidiary grooms

"Subsidiary grooms" 協餉馬夫 are non-existent
grooms who are allotted provisions each month, such sums
then being returned to the government and used to assist
[military post stations?]. However, their places will be
filled by actual persons in case military duties turn out to
be heavy and numerous, and/or there is a shortage of
grooms in service.

1635. I MA CHUNG-NA CHIH CH'A 以馬中納支茶
To deliver horses in exchange for tea

Each year the barbarians beyond the borders of Szechwan
and Kansu deliver a certain number of horses to the
frontier officials (of China), in return for which they
receive certain amounts of tea. All these [transactions]
are regulated by the statutes on frontier markets. [See
1616; also cf. 1109.]

Note: the words chung-na 中納 are probably erroneous. Translated on the basis of the Manchu text they should read chiao-na 交納 [to deliver]. [The correctness of this note is questionable. The term chung-na (or simply chung) is most likely a direct derivation from the Ming system of salt exchange, k'ai-chung 開中 or chung yen 中鹽 , i.e., in return for much-needed grain delivered to frontier areas, salt merchants were paid by the government in salt certificates entitling them to sell certain amounts of government salt. The frontier barter trade in horses and tea dealt likewise with government-supervised merchandise (tea) and government-needed goods (horses), therefore paralleled the salt exchange in concept. Chung-na or chung hence may be broadly translated as "exchange." The term chung ma 中馬 (cf. 1614), "to obtain horses by exchange," was used to indicate just such a procedure; e.g., SCYC, 5:64, "On tea certificates."]

1636. CHIA-CH'ENG PU JU-FA 駕乘不如法 Driving and riding contrary to regulations

A person acts contrary to the prescribed techniques in driving a carriage or riding a horse.

[[6]] Military examinations. Nos. 1637-1646

1637. AN-CH'A PING-TING 安插兵丁 Settling soldiers

To assign newly arrived troops to suitable quarters.

1638. TS'UN-HSIEH SAN-KO YÜEH 存恤三個月 Three-month posthumous support

The regular pay of a recently died soldier is issued to his family for three months. This is called "posthumous support."

1639. K'AO-SHIH WU-CHÜ 考試武舉 To take the provincial military examinations

To achieve the degree of provincial graduate in the provincial military examinations.

1640.   MIEN YÜEH YIN-CHI 面月印記 Moon-branded face

Horses used in testing [the candidates'] mounted archery in the military examinations are all inspected by the Board of War, and are branded on the face with a half-moon brand.   This is known as "moon-branded face(s). "

1641.   MA PU CHIEN 馬步箭 Mounted and dismounted archery

Mounted and dismounted archery are tested in both the inspection of military personnel [1398] and the military examinations, as a means to ascertain the skills [of the officers and candidates, respectively].

1642.   TO SHIH 掇石 Stone lifting

[The candidate] is asked to lift a large stone in the provincial and metropolitan military examinations as a way to test his strength.

1643.   WU TAO 舞刀 Sword play

He is also asked to wield a broad sword 大刀 as a way to test his skill and courage.

1644.   TSO TS'E-LUN 作策論 Writing a discourse on policy

As a way to test his ability to do strategic planning, he is also given a theme on which to write a discourse on policy.

1645.   NIEN MAO 年貌 Age and visage

CHI-KUAN 籍貫 Native district

MING-HSING 名姓 Name

These three items are inspected by the Board of War during the provincial and metropolitan military examinations; that is, a candidate is noted as to his age, physical appearance, his native place, and his surname and given name. These are rechecked after he has successfully passed the examinations. Should any discrepancy be discovered the candidate will be ordered forthwith to withdraw.

1646. TING-T'I 頂替 Using false identity

> If anyone is found to be taking the examinations by assuming the name of another person, the case will be investigated immediately, and suitable measures taken.

CHAPTER V

[[1]] Initiating a lawsuit.   Nos. 1647-1673

1647. YÜAN-KAO 原告 Plaintiff

The person who initiates a law suit.

1648. PEI-KAO 被告 Defendant

The person who is the object of a law suit.

1649. KAN-CHENG 干證 Witness

The person who testifies concerning (a given case).

1650. LIANG-TSAO 兩造 Both parties

Both the plaintiff's and the defendant's sides.

1651. SHOU-KAO 首告 Accuser

The person who goes before the authorities and lodges a charge aginst the acts of another.

1652. CHIEH-KAO 訐告 Disrespectfully preferring charges against

A subordinate accusing his superior official, or a subject accusing his own local officials: when persons of an inferior station rise against those who are higher, it is termed a "disrespectful act. "

1653. T'OU-SHOU 投首 Turning oneself in

To inform the authorities voluntarily of the things that oneself has done.

1654. PAO-KAO 抱告 To bring a suit in behalf of another person; to bring a suit by proxy

[A man's case] being sent to court by his relations or family retainers.

-259-

1655. TIAO SUNG 刁訟 Cunning litigant

One who is aggressive and skilled in litigation.

1656. WU-KAO 誣告 False accusation; groundless accusation

To accuse someone with a trumped-up charge is called
"false accusation."

1657. TING MING TAI-KAO 頂名代告 To accuse under
assumed name

To enter an accusation [at court] in another person's
behalf by assuming [the latter's] name.

1658. PAO-LAN TZ'U-SUNG 包攬詞訟 In sole charge of
litigation

To take complete charge of a person's case during the
law suit, such as is done by the litigation counsellors
[sung-shih 訟師], etc.

1659. CH'OU P'AN 仇扳 To draw in owing to personal enmity

To draw in means to involve.

To involve an innocent party in a law suit because of one's
own enmity toward him.

1660. CHIA-CH'OU NA-SUNG 挾仇拿送 Arrested owing to
personal enmity

Because of the enmity between himself and government
runners, an innocent person is arrested on some excuse
and sent before the authorities.

1661. FEI-YÜAN CHIA-HAI 飛寃篤害 To bring untrue charges
and frame [the innocent]

To pin the blame [for a crime] unjustly on an innocent
person, and to invent false testimony to ruin him.

1662. CHIAO-SO HSIEN-HAI 教唆陷害 Instigating disaster
[for others]

To encourage and instruct [someone] so that he will bring
about trouble for others.

1663. PO-CHI WU-KU 波及無辜 Innocent bystander being drawn into [a legal dispute]

To accuse an innocent person of a trumped-up charge in order to incriminate him.

1664. WU CH'ING WEI CHUNG 誣輕為重 Imposing a heavy [sentence] for a minor [crime]

To pass a heavy sentence on one guilty of a minor crime by adding false charges to his case.

1665. WU LIANG WEI TAO 誣良為盜 To charge a good citizen with robbery

To falsely accuse a law-abiding person of being a robber.

[Cf. 1792.]

1666. CHU-LIEN SHOU-LEI 株連受累 Being implicated in trouble

To implicate means to involve. This phrase means that one is involved in the affairs of others and is therefore entangled in the troubles of the litigation.

1667. YIN-JEN LIEN-LEI 因人受累 Being implicated by others

Same as above [1666].

1668. HSIEN-TSAI YÜAN-TSO 現在緣坐 Presently convicted for a cause

To be convicted of a crime.

1669. KOU-SUNG PU-HSI 構訟不息 Endlessly engaged in litigation

[...] To be a party to a law suit for some cause, and the case continues for a long time without termination.

1670. SHEN-SU YÜAN-WANG 申訴冤枉 Pleading for [redress of] grievance

To tell the official [or magistrate] the injustices [one has suffered] so that he may redress the wrong.

1671. CHIAO-SU YÜAN-CH'Ü 叫訴寃曲 Crying for [redress of] grievance

To cry out [to an official] and plead for justice.

1672. YÜEH-SUNG CHIA-TENG 越訟加等 [Penalty] increased for by-passing in litigation

When a law suit is not brought before the local officials, but instead is laid directly before the governor-general or governor, it is known as "by-passing in litigation, " for which the penalty is doubly severe.

[Amended, p. 144:] Yüeh-k'ung 越控 "to by-pass in submitting a plaint. "

To by-pass in submitting a plaint means that when a law suit arises the people [concerned], instead of bringing it before their local department or district magistrates, send it directly to the office of the prefect, the intendant, the two provincial commissioners, or the governor-general or governor. It is contrary [to regulations] to by-pass the proper order of procedures.

1673. PIEN-LI SHENG-SHIH 辨理省釋 To release after investigation

"To investigate" is to examine; "to release, " to free. When a person's innocence has been clearly established after investigation, he is allowed to go free.

[[2]] Trial, interrogation, evidence, sentencing, and other court procedures. Nos. 1674-1722

1674. TZU-JEN PU-WEI 自認不諱 Self-confessed without equivocation

To equivocate is to conceal. [This phrase means] a person has confessed to his own crime with nothing concealed or held back.

1675. CHIEN-KUNG PU-I 堅供不移 Unchangeable testimony

The prisoner insists on the truth of his testimony and will not change it in the least.

1676. FU SHOU TZU-CHAO 俛首自招 Confessing with bowed head

The prisoner admitting his guilt with lowered head.

1677. CH'ING-YUAN TI-CH'ANG 情願抵償 Willing to forfeit; willing to pay the penalty

A person confesses to killing another, and is willing to pay with his own life.

1678. SHANG CHENG CHÜ-CH'ÜEH 傷證俱確 Full evidence of both the wound and witness(es)

Both the body wound and eyewitness(es) are unmistakable and reliable, and there is not doubt in this case.

1679. FAN-TSUI TAI-TUI 犯罪待對 The criminal awaiting confrontation

The criminal waiting to face the person in confrontation. [Cf. 1692.]

1680. JEN CH'I HSIAO-HSIAO 任其嘵嘵 To permit wrangling

"To wrangle" is to argue beyond reason. This phrase indicates that [a magistrate] ought not to permit a prisoner to engage in unreasonable disputations.

1681. CH'IAO-KUNG HUANG-KUNG 巧供謊供 Evasive testimony, false testimony

A testimony that skillfully aims at evasion, and one that consists of lies.

1682. TSANG CHENG MING-CH'ÜEH 贓證明確 Loot and witness are clear and indisputable

Both the loot of a robbery and eyewitness accounts are clear and according to fact.

1683. TSANG CHING CHU JEN 贓經主認. Loot identified by owner

Things looted by robbers are identified [or claimed] by the owner.

1684. CH'I JEN TSANG-WU 起認贓物 Retrieve and identify stolen goods

"To retrieve" means to obtain. That is, to get the stolen articles at the robbers' nest, and call the owner to identify [or claim] them.

1685. CH'U CHAO KUNG-T'U YU-I CHI YU CHIH-SHIH 初招供吐游移繼又支飾 To be uncertain in [his] first confession, later to prevaricate as well

(*Chih 支 is omitted in the Chia-ch'ing edition; in the annotated edition it is given as kuei 詭 "cunning.")

In his confession made for the first time a prisoner makes tentative and uncertain statements; this is followed later by cunning and dishonest testimony.

1686. CH'IU SHEN 秋審 Autumn Assizes (or Trials)

Cases involving major crimes in the provinces are immediately tried and sentenced [locally]; this is known as je shen 熱審. All other cases [i.e., those involving the death penalty where the condemned have been imprisoned to await execution] are referred to the Board of Punishments [after being tried in the provinces], which will deliberate and memorialize on each case, and then pass sentence. These trials are held in the autumn of each year and are known as the "Autumn Assizes (Trials)." [See note under 1688.]

1687. CH'AO SHEN 朝審 Court Assizes (or Trials)

All cases tried and sentenced at the Autumn Assizes [1686] are reported to the throne by the Board of Punishments. [The Emperor] will designate high ministers to deliberate on them once more at Court 朝中 , known as the "Court Assizes (Trials)." [Ch'ao shen refers to cases involving the death penalty tried in Peking by the Board of Punishments, not the review of cases by Court Officials. Actually, all cases of both the Autumn and the Court Assizes (or Trials) were reviewed by high metropolitan officials before the final sentence was passed. Ch'ing-shih kao (Draft history of

Ch'ing, hereafter CSK), "Book of Justice and Law" 刑法志, 155:2-3b; CTTS, I, 543.]

1688. JE SHEN 熱審 Summer Assizes (or Trials)

See under "Autumn Assizes" [1686]. [Je shen, literally, "hot trials," were trials that were held in the summer between early June and the first part of August. The purpose of je shen was to reduce the penalty given to criminals. It was not a term describing on-the-spot trials, as interpreted in 1686. See CSK, "Book of Justice and Law," 155:4b; CTTS, I, 543, 544.]

1689. HSÜ HSING 恤刑 Lenient in the use of punishments

At times special consideration is called for in regard to the use of punishments, such as in the case of old, sick, or female criminals, and in extremely cold or hot weather.

1690. NUNG MANG 農忙 Busy agricultural seasons

Department and district magistrates should suspend all cases of litigation during the periods of sowing and harvesting, known as the "busy agricultural seasons."

1691. NUNG HSI 農隙 Slack agricultural seasons

The periods when farm work slackens.

1692. CHIH-SHEN 質審 Confrontation

The two parties to a law suit confronting and questioning each other [during the trial].

[Cf. 1679.]

1693. YEN SHEN 嚴審 Severe interrogation

To interrogate with the aid of harsh torture.

1694. CHIA HSÜN 夾訊 To interrogate with pressing sticks

[Using] the "three-foot wood" 三尺木 , commonly called "pressing sticks" 夾棍 , which is the most cruel of torture tools. It is used to exact evidence from major criminals.

Punishments

1695. LI SHEN 歷審 Successive interrogation

Having been successively examined and interrogated many times.

1696. CHIEN SHEN 檢審 To inspect and interrogate

To inspect the corpse and/or injuries, and interrogate the prisoner.

1697. SHEN KUNG 審供 To interrogate for evidence

To interrogate the prisoner and to record his testimony.

1698. CHÜ YÜ 鞫獄 To judge a case

[...] This means to examine and judge a case.

1699. PIEN-LI 辨理 To investigate and try

To discriminate between [the evidence? witnesses?] and examine a case.

1700. YÜAN-SHE 援赦 Amnesty granted in conformity with precedent

To conform means to follow. Whenever an amnesty is proclaimed in the country by special favor of the Emperor, [criminals] will have their penalties reduced or completely reprieved according to precedent.

1701. SHE-CH'IEN 赦前 Pre-amnesty

[A man] whose crime was committed before the amnesty will receive the pardon.

1702. SHE-HOU 赦後 Post-amnesty

[A man] whose crime is committed after the amnesty is not allowed to receive the pardon.

1703. HUAN CHÜEH 緩決 Execution suspended; suspension of execution

The execution of a criminal, who has been given the death sentence, is temporarily postponed.

1704. CH'ING-CHEN 情真 Proven guilty

The guilt of a crime is proven to be true, with no miscarriage of justice

1705. K'O-CHING 可矜 Pitiable [case]

The facts of the crime deserve pity.

1706. K'O-I 可疑 Doubtful [case]

The facts of the crime give ground for doubt.

1707. CHING I YU- TZ'U 矜疑有詞 May be considered as pitiable [and/or] doubtful

There is reason for considering (a given case) as pitiable [1705] or doubtful [1706].

1708. CH'ENG-CHAO 成招 Confession obtained

[A prisoner) has made a confession in his testimony.

1709. CHAO CHIEH 招解 Transfer of confessed [prisoner]

To transfer to a superior official a prisoner who has confessed, to be re-examined [by the higher official].

1710. CH'ÜAN CHAO 全招 Complete confession

To give all the facts in a confession.

1711. CHAO NEI 招內 In the confession

In the statement(s) containing the confession.

1712. K'AN-YÜ 看語 Tentative verdict

The tentative judgment at the conclusion of a trial.

1713. CH'ÜAN CHAO FANG-TS'E 全招方冊 Transcript of complete confessions [or testimony]

The volumes in which are recorded the complete testimonies of prisoners.

1714. CH'ING TSUI LÜEH-CHIEH 情罪略節 Résumé of the facts of the case

A general summary of the facts of the crime in the case.

1715. SHIH-FAN YÜAN-YU 事犯緣由 Background of the crime

The roots and circumstances of a crime are discussed and recorded in the volume [of transcripts; 1713].

1716. LÜEH-CHIEH YÜAN-YU 略節緣由 Outline of the background of the case

A concise outline of the background of the case.

1717. CHUNG FAN LÜEH-CHIEH CHAO-TS'E 重犯略節招册 Summarized transcipt of confessions of major criminals

Confessions of those guilty of major crimes are gathered into a volume and sent to the Board (of Punishments) for deliberation.

1718. FEN-PIEH CH'ING-CHEN HUAN-CHÜEH K'O-CHING K'O-I SAN TENG 分別情真緩決可矜可疑三等 [Cases] to be divided into three classes: [1] proven guilty, [2] suspension of execution, and [3] pitiable and doubtful

All cases tried at the Autumn Assizes [1686] fall into one of three categories. The first is "proven guilty" [1704]; these cases involve major crimes and (the criminals) should be executed. The second is "suspended (or suspension of) execution" [1703]; here the crimes are less serious in nature, and the [death?] sentence is suspended to await an amnesty. The third is "pitiable and doubtful" [1705, 1706], including cases of which the facts are either pitiable or doubtful; these should not be sentenced until they have been re-examined in detail. [Sic. When a case is classified into the suspended category, either the penalty is reduced, or the case is re-examined. See CSK, "Book of Justice and Law," 155:2b.]

1719. SAN FU-TSOU 三覆奏 Thrice to reconsider and memorialize

[As an indication of] the value our government attaches to human life, [after a criminal's name has been crossed off by the Emperor; cf. 1721] the Board of Punishments is required to deliberate and memorialize on a case three times before [the criminal] is executed.

1720. LIANG-I CHÜ-TSOU 兩議具奏 To memorialize on the two alternatives

Whether [the penalty for a crime] be light or heavy is decided by the throne following the presentation of a memorial, in which each alternative is illustrated with a precedent.

1721. YÜ-PI KOU-CH'U 御筆勾除 Crossed off with the imperial brush

When a name in the list of criminals is crossed off by the Emperor, that person is to be executed forthwith.

1722. CHIEN-TENG FA-LO 減等發落 To be disposed of with reduced [penalty]

[A criminal] is to be sentenced to [a penalty] lessened by one or two degrees from that provided in the Criminal Code 刑律.

[[3]] The penalties: various degrees and their implementation. Nos. 1723-1795

1723. CHUNG CHANG 重杖 Heavy flogging

From ten to eighty blows in the penalty of flogging is called "heavy flogging."

1724. CH'IH WU-SHIH 笞五十 [Sentenced to] fifty lashes

"Lashing" and "flogging" [literally, to beat with a bamboo stick and a staff, respectively] are ancient ways of punishment of which only the names remain today. Nowadays they are both replaced by the use of split bamboo 竹片, while in the army the beating is done with a horse whip. [Chang 杖 "flogging" refers to beating sixty to one hundred blows with a heavy piece of split bamboo; ch'ih 笞 "lashing" to ten to fifty blows with the use of a lighter piece of the same material. In time, however, the heavy

bamboo became the standard equipment. When a prisoner
is sentenced to so many lashes, the sentence is carried
out by commuting at the rate of ten lashes to four blows
at flogging. In no. 1732, however, the term chang is used in
its original sense, i.e., "staff.") KHHT, 53:1b.]

1725. CHIA-HAO I-KO YÜEH 枷號一個月 To wear the cangue
for one month

The "cangue" is a wooden board affixed around [the
prisoner's] head. [Sic. Should be neck.] The duration of
this penalty may vary from one to two months.

1726. MAN-CHANG 滿杖 Full score of flogging

The limit for flogging is one hundred blows, known as
the "full score of flogging."

1727. CHÜEH-FA 決罰 To convict and punish

To give the verdict and apply the penalty.

1728. TI-CHÜEH 的決 Substantive penalty

"Substantive" means actual. At times such penalties as
lashing and flogging may be reprieved upon the payment of
money; those for which no reprieve is permitted are known
as "substantive penalties."

1729. PU-YING CHUNG LI 不應重例 Statutes of major wrongful
acts

Aside from such crimes as homicide, etc., all other
crimes that are difficult to categorize are collectively
termed "wrongful acts" 不應.. These are classified
into major and minor wrongful acts 不應重, 不應.
輕.

1730. PU-YING CHUNG CHANG 不應重杖 Flogging for a major
wrongful act

To sentence a criminal to be flogged according to the
statutes of major wrongful acts.

1731. CHANG CHING YÜN-I 杖儆允宜 Warning suitably
applied through flogging

It is highly correct to administer a warning for the future by sentencing (a criminal) to be flogged.

1732. YING CHANG I-PAI CHE SSU-SHIH PAN 應杖一百折四十板 One hundred blows of flogging commuted to forty strikes of the bamboo

Flogging with a staff was an ancient penalty that is no longer used nowadays. Any criminal sentenced to one hundred blows of flogging is to receive instead forty blows of the split bamboo.

1733. TZ'U-TZU 剌字 Tattoo

The word "robbery" or "homicide" is tattooed on the face of a criminal found guilty of either of these crimes. Those [convicted] of lesser crimes are tattooed on their arms. [Cf. 1782.]

1734. MAN-T'U 滿徒 Full term in temporary banishment

A convict is sentenced to temporary banishment 徒 and sent to a department or district several hundred li away to serve at hard labor for one, or two, or not exceeding three years. The last is called the "full term in temporary banishment."

1735. PAI CHAN 擺站 Penal service at post stations

A convict serving temporary banishment is sent to do hard labor at a military post station. This is known as "penal service at post stations."

1736. TSA-FAN SSU-TSUI 雜犯死罪 Secondary criminals rating the death penalty

A man convicted of homicide should pay with his own life; he is a true criminal 正 [真 ; see 1738] 犯 , whose death penalth can in no way be mitigated. One who incurs the death penalty on account of some other crime, however, is known as a "secondary criminal rating the death penalty," whose sentence may be mitigated after due consideration of the circums tances [of his crime].

1737. CHANG-LIU CHUN T'U 杖流准徒 Permanent banishment and flogging commuted to temporary banishment

"Permanent banishment" means to exile a convict to a place more than two or three thousand li away. The circumstances of each convict who incurs the penalty of permanent banishment and flogging must be investigated; in the event of a pitiable case [1705, 1718] the sentence may be commuted to temporary banishment. [Flogging is usually given to a convict who is sentenced to either temporary or permanent banishment, and constitutes a part of his punishment. Similarly, wearing of the cangue also accompanies the penalty of flogging, when the case at hand involves a serious crime. KHHT, 53:1b.]

1738. CH'U CHEN-FAN SSU-TSUI WAI 除真犯死罪外 Aside from the true criminals rating the death penalty

This is a reference to the secondary criminals rating the death penalty [see 1736].

1739. AN LÜ CHAN-P'EI 按律站配 To banish to post stations according to the Code

To sentence criminals to temporary banishment according to the Criminal Code 刑律 , and send them to do hard labor at various military post stations.

1740. PI-CHAO MOU LI 比照某例 According to certain precedents

The crime being tried is not covered by written law, and judgment must be made on the basis of precedents.

1741. CHIEN-TENG T'U CH'ENG 減等徒懲 Lessening [of penalty] for correction [of the criminal]

After due consideration a heavy sentence is reduced to some extent, [the resultant penalty] to serve only as a corrective measure.

1742. CHI CH'IN WAN-CHÜ 給親完聚 Returned to family for reunion

Women criminals being released in the custody of their

kin after trial, so that the family may be reunited.

1743. PING TSANG CHIH-TSUI 併贓治罪 Punished for the
total sum of loot

"Loot," to various amounts, denotes the plunder of a
robber as well as the bribes received by an official.
[Individual items] are to be added together and the
penalty [for the robber or the official] should then be decided
on the basis of the total sum.

1744. TSO-TSANG CHIH-TSUI 坐贓治罪 Punished for pecuniary
malfeasance

To be penalized on account of having received bribes.
[Tso-tsang is one of six types of financial offenses
for which a guilty official might be prosecuted. It refers to
ill-gotten gains that do not properly fall under the headings
of bribery or theft--such as collecting extra money from the
people, in the name of taxation, for the official's own benefit. Ta-Ch'ing lü-li, 31:19; cf. KHHT, 54:2b.]

1745. CHI-MO JU-KUAN 籍没入官 Confiscation of property

To confiscate [a criminal's] property and put it in the
government treasury.

1746. TZU-SHOU MIEN TSUI 自首免罪 Penalty waived of
one who turns himself in

When a person guilty of a minor crime turns himself in
to the authorities, he may be exempted from punishment.

1747. FA PIEN-WAI WEI MIN 發邊外為民 To be exiled
beyond the Wall as civilians

Manchus who have committed crimes are sent north of the
Passes beyond the Great Wall, with the status of ordinary
civilians [i.e., reduced from bannerman status].

1748. YÜAN HSÜ NAN-K'UAN 遠戍難寬 No clemency for the
sentence of remote garrison duty

To serve as garrison in a remote place: that is, permanent
banishment in military duty 充軍. A given criminal should

be sentenced to remote garrison duty and it is not possible to grant clemency in his case.

1749. T'OU-HUANG CHIH TSUI 投荒之罪 The penalty of exile in wilderness

To send a criminal to live among the people of the wilderness; i.e., exile beyond the Wall.

1750. NA SHU CH'IU-FAN 納贖囚犯 To redeem a prisoner through payment of money

(*Shu 贖 "redeem" is given as chih 紙 "paper" in the Manchu-Chinese editions.)

Imprisoned convicts are redeemed with the payment of money.

1751. AN-CHIH 安置 To settle; to place

To settle the convicts who [have arrived to] serve their terms in permanent or limited banishment, and assign them to their work.

1752. CHÜN-TSUI LIU-TSUI 軍罪流罪 Convicts serving military sentence, and convicts serving the sentence of permanent banishment

Convicts sentenced to military service are given soldiers' duties, while those sentenced to permanent banishment will serve under the orders of the department or district [i.e., civil] authorities.

1753. PIEN-YÜAN CH'UNG-HSÜ 邊遠充戍 To serve remote garrison duty

To be exiled to a distant frontier area and serve as garrison soldier.

1754. CH'UNG-CHING 充警 To serve police duty

A convict sentenced to serve as policeman [or watchman].

1755. YÜAN LIU 遠流 Distant permanent banishment

To banish permanently to a remote place.

1756. MAN-LIU 滿流 Full distance of permanent banishment

The limit to the penalty of transportation is three thousand li, known as the "full distance of permanent banishment."

1757. T'IEH TUAN 貼斷 Verdict to assist in paying damages

A verdict ordering [a defendant] to help pay damages [to the plaintiff] and so conclude the case.

1758. YÜAN-YU 原宥 Pardon

Imprisoned convicts are redeemed with the payment of money. (*The interpretation of this entry is the same as that of "To redeem a prisoner through payment of money" [1750]; it is probably erroneous.)

1759. T'AO SHOU 絢首 Strangulation

To twist a rope around [a criminal's] neck until he is dead; that is, the death penalty of strangulation.

1760. CHAN TSUI 斬罪 Decapitation

The death penalty of beheading.

1761. CHIEH TSUI LING-CH'IH 磔罪凌遲 The penalty of small cuts, slow slicing

The death penalty of dying by small cuts, commonly called "slicing" 剮罪.

1762. LU SHIH 戮尸 Beheading of a corpse

If a prisoner guilty of a major crime dies before he is executed, his corpse should be beheaded.

1763. PING-CHAN PU-WANG 駢斬不枉 Not unjust to behead the group

There is no injustice in beheading the many members of the same group, as each of them has shared in [or is guilty of] committing a major crime.

1764. TAI T'IEH-SO SAN-T'IAO 帶鐵鎖三条 Wearing three iron chains

A prisoner who is guilty of a major crime is to wear three iron chains: one at the neck, one at the wrists, and one at the ankles.

1765. CHAO-LI T'U-CHÜEH SHU-K'O PI-KU 照例徒決
庶可薮辜 The offense would be compensated by [the
criminal's being] sentenced to banishment according to
statute

To sentence a criminal to permanent or limited banishment
according to statute, so that he gets the just deserts
for his crime.

1766. CHIA-LIU CHUN-T'U PU-WANG 加流准徒不枉
Not unjust to commute permanent banishment plus exile
into limited banishment

A man originally sentenced to permanent banishment is
granted a commutation into limited banishment; this is
done fairly and without injustice. [Text chia-i liu-tsui
加以流罪 is a misinterpretation of chia-liu , which
means adding to the original permanent banishment of
three thousand li the sentence of exile 充軍 --i.e., an
increase in distance of two thousand to four thousand li.
See CSK, 155:2.]

1767. FA YEN-CHANG CH'UNG-CHÜN 發烟瘴充軍
Be exiled to serve military duty in a malarious area

To exile [a convict] to some malarious area, as in
Kwangtung, Kwangsi, and Yunnan, there to serve
military duty.

1768. FA PIEH-TI CHI-PIEN WEI CH'UNG-CHÜN 發別地
極邊衛充軍 Be exiled to the remotest frontier
garrison to serve military duty

To exile a convict to the very farthest frontier garrison
station, there to serve military duty.

1769. LÜ CHIAO CH'ING-TSUI YÜN-HSIEH 律絞情罪允
協 The crime befits the penalty of strangulation as
prescribed by the Code

The facts of the crime are found to fit exactly the provision
in the (Criminal) Code calling for the penalty of death by
strangulation.

1770. AN LÜ CHIAO-TI PAI-HUI HSI-TZ'U 按律絞抵百喙美辭 Strangling is prescribed by the Code and a hundred voices will protest to no avail

[The criminal] has been sentenced to death by strangling according to provisions in the (Criminal) Code, and nothing can be accomplished by protests even though voiced by many persons.

1771. CHIEN-HOU CH'IU-HOU CH'U-CHÜEH CHÜN-WU WANG TSUNG 監候秋後處決均無枉縱 To be jailed and await judgment in the autumn, without injustice or undue leniency

[A criminal] is to be imprisoned until he is brought to trial at the Autumn Assizes, when he will be sentenced. Thus there can be no danger either of injustice or undue leniency [in his case].

1772. I CH'IANG-TAO LI LUN PU-FEN SHOU TS'UNG CHÜ-CHAN 以強盜例論不分首從俱斬 To be decapitated as robbers regardless of the distinction between ringleaders and followers

To convict [the criminals] of robbery, of whom ringleaders and followers alike should be sentenced to death by decapitation.

1773. YING CHAO PU-WANG-FA CHIH TSUI ERH YÜAN-I TSO-TSANG CHIH T'IAO 應照不枉法之罪而援以生贓之條 [To be convicted] on the basis of no injustice in the administration of law while having committed pecuniary malfeasance

An official has committed financial misdeeds but has not caused injustice in the administration of law in the process; he should therefore be [prosecuted and] sentenced according to the article [in the Code] pertaining to pecuniary malfeasance [cf. 1744] without causing injustice in the administration of law.

1774. CHAO TU-PO CHIH HSIN-LI 照賭博之新例 [To be convicted] according to the new statues on gambling

A man who has violated the prohibition against gambling should be [prosecuted and] sentenced according to the new statutes and regulations on gambling.

1775. TSAI YÜAN-FAN CHIH CH'U HSIU-SHOU SHIH-CHUNG 在原犯之處梟首示眾　　Beheading and exhibition at the scene of the crime

Robbers and the like should be beheaded at the scene of their crime, then have their severed heads raised on high poles for public exhibition.

1776. LI-CHÜEH CHENG-FA 立決正法　To be immediately executed for conformation with the law

To be decapitated forthwith so as to conform to the law of the land.

1777. NAN-KUAN FA-CH'ANG 南關法場 The South Gate execution grounds

Execution grounds are usually located outside the South Gate [of a town].

1778. YA FU SHIH-TS'AO 押赴市曹　Proceeding to the market place under guard

The "market place" refers to the big thoroughfare [of a town]. This means a condemned criminal is being escorted through the streets to be executed.

1779. CHÜEH-KUO JIH-CH'I 決過日期　Date of execution

The Board (of Punishments) should be notified on the day when the death sentence has been carried out.

1780. CHIEN-CHAN KUAN 監斬官 Inspectors of executions

The officials who supervise the carrying out of executions.

1781. T'ING-HSING JIH-CH'I 停刑日期 Days of suspension of executions

Executions should be withheld on days such as big national celebrations or sacrifices, or on New Year's day and other festivals.

1782. YU HSIAO PI-PO SHANG TZ'U-TZU 右小臂膊上 刺字 Tattooed on the right forearm

Convicts guilty of major crimes are tattooed on the face; of lesser crimes, on the arm. [Cf. 1733.]

1783. TSANG-FA K'U 贓罰庫 Treasury of Loot and Fines

All confiscated loot and property and money paid [to the government] as fines or redemption fees are stored in this treasury.

1784. TSANG-FA YIN-LIANG 贓罰銀兩 Money from loot and fines

Money from [confiscated] loot and from fines and redemption fees.

1785. TZU-LI SHU-HUAN 自理贖鍰 Self-financed redemption fee

Redemption fee being paid by the convict himself.

1786. TSANG-PIEN YIN-LIANG 贓變銀兩 Money derived from [confiscated] loot or bribes

Money realized from [confiscated] loot or bribes 贓款 that have been converted into silver.

1787. PIEN-CH'AN P'EI-PU 變產賠補 To pay the indemnity by sale of property

A criminal owing the government money will sell his own property, and use the proceeds to pay the debt. [Cf. 1791.]

1788. WAN-FA CHA-TSANG 玩法詐贓 Disregarding the law and exacting bribes

An official who disregards the laws of the country and extorts bribes from the people.

1789. WU-CHU JU-KUAN CHIH TSANG 無主入官之贓 Confiscated ownerless loot

Stolen or plundered articles that have not been claimed by their owners should be confiscated by the government.

1790. CH'IN TSANG 欽贓 Bribes [or loot] confiscated by imperial order

Bribe [or loot] money confiscated by the government upon imperial command.

1791. CHIA-CH'AN CHIN-CHÜEH 家產盡絶 Property entirely spent

The criminal's property is entirely spent, and there is nothing left to sell for paying the government. [Cf. 1787.]

1792. WU-TAO CH'A-TSANG 誣盜插贓 Falsely to accuse (others) of robbery and plant evidence

To falsely accuse a law-abiding person as a robber by placing some other people's belongings in his home, and maintaining that these are stolen goods. This practice is also termed "planting of loot."

1793. K'O-LIU TAO-TSANG 尅留盜贓 Illegal retention of loot

Government runners, when carrying out the order to confiscate the loot of robbers, clandestinely keep [a certain amount] by not turning it in to the authorities.

1794. HUN-JEN MAN-TSANG 混認瞞贓 Fraudulent claim on stolen goods

A person falsely claiming ownership of things that do not really belong to him, in an effort to obtain them among the loot.

1795. MAI-WU TS'AI-TSANG 買物栽贓 Planting of loot through purchase of merchandise

Robbers and thieves using stolen money to buy things, aiming to plant the loot on the store [or storekeeper, who will then be in possession of a part of the stolen money].

[[4]] The tools and personnel for rounding up criminals. Nos. 1796-1857

1796. TA-CH'ING LÜ 大清律 The Code of the Ch'ing Dynasty

The complete test of the Code [or Laws] of the Ch'ing

Dynasty 大清律例.

1797. LÜ-LI 律例 The Code

Same as above [1796].

[Amended, p. 144:] The original laws constitute the lü while those that are added later are the li. [Modern scholars have generally accepted the rendering of Lü-li as the Code, which is defined as "the codification of statutes 律 and precedents" 例 by Ch'ien Tuan-sheng in his The Government and Politics of China (Cambridge, Mass., 1950), p. 41.]

1798. MING-LI 名例 General laws

The name [or title] by which a statute is known [sic].

1799. TSE-LI 則例 Regulations and precedents

The rules and regulations derived from a precedent.

1800. SAN-CH'IH 三尺 The three-foot [sticks]

The use in punishment of the "three-foot sticks," commonly known as the "pressing sticks." It is the harshest of all punishments [cf. 1694, 1809].

1801. HUI-TIEN 會典 The Institutes (of the Ch'ing Dynasty)

The complete text of The Institutes of the Ch'ing Dynasty 大清會典.

1802. PEN-LÜ 本律 The proper law

The pertinent law.

[Amended, p. 144:] There is an appropriate provision in the code to be followed in case of a crime.

1803. T'I HSING 提刑 Brought for [interrogation with] torture

To bring forth a prisoner for interrogation with the use of torture.

1804. HSING PI 刑辟 Criminal trial; trial of a criminal case

To try and sentence a person according to the Criminal Code.

Punishments

1805. K'U HSING 酷刑 Harsh punishment [or torture]

Harsh and cruel punishment [or torture].

1806. CHI HSING 極刑 Extreme punishment [or torture]

Extremely heavy punishment [or torture].

1807. FEI HSING 非刑 Unlawful punishment [or torture]

Punishment not permitted by law.

1808. TS'AN HSING 惨刑 Cruel punishment [or torture]

Excruciatingly cruel punishments.

1809. CHIA-KUN 夾棍 Pressing sticks

The punishment using the three-foot sticks. [Cf. 1694, 1800.]

1810. CHIA-HAO 枷號 The cangue

An instrument used to confine [the movements of] the head. [Cf. 1725.]

1811. PAN-TZU 板子 The bamboo

A length of split bamboo used in administering the punishment of beating.

1812. TSAN-TZU 桚子 Hand sticks

These are pressing sticks used on women. While the [three-foot] pressing sticks are applied to the prisoner's feet, these are used on hands.

1813. SHOU-NIU 手扭 Handcuffs

An instrument used for restraining the criminal's hands.

1814. HSIEH-LIAO 械鐐 Manacles

The iron chain used to tie together a prisoner's hands.

1815. NAO-KU 腦箍 Head band

An instrument of punishment which may be tightened on a prisoner's head.

1816. CHIAO-LIAO 脚鐐 Foot fetters

The iron chain used to tie together a prisoner's feet.

1817. HSI LIEN 細鍊 Thin chain

A small iron chain.

1818. LAO-KU TING CHIEH 牢固釘觧 To transfer securely nailed

To nail and lock securely [the various pieces of impedimenta on] a criminal, and transfer him to another locality for interrogation and trial.

1819. JU-FA CHIA-NIU 如法枷杻 Cangued and handcuffed according to regulations

A prisoner's head is cangued and his hands manacled according to methods prescribed by law.

1820. HSING-SHU 刑書 Clerks of Punishments

Clerks serving in the Board of Punishments.

1821. CHIEN-YEN 檢驗 To inspect and examine

To inspect and examine a corpse and/or bodily injuries.

1822. YÜ-TSU 獄卒 Jailer

Government runner serving in a prison.

1823. WEN-P'O 穩婆 Woman coroner

A female coroner who examines corpses.

1824. WU-TSO 仵作 Coroner

A male coroner who examines corpses.

1825. YÜAN-HSIEN TSAI YÜ 寃陷在獄 Jailed on a false charge

A person is imprisoned due to a false charge unjustly lodged against him.

1826. PI-CHIEN MIEN-I 斃監免議 Cancellation of trial of one who has died in prison

The prisoner having died in jail, the [prospective] trial and sentencing of his crime will be cancelled.

Punishments

1827. YEN-CHIN CHIH SZU 淹禁致死 Death due to long
imprisonment

(A prisoner) has died from the effects of prolonged
imprisonment.

1828. T'U-CHIEH SUNG PU 圖結送部　Sealed deposition to be
dispatched to the Board

To release a prisoner on bail, a deposition should be
executed by the person posting the bail, with [official?]
seals afixed thereto, and [the document] sent to the
Board (of Punishments), there to be deliberated and acted
upon.

1829. PING-WU LING-NÜEH 並無凌虐 No question of
mistreatment

In the case of a criminal having died in prison, there is
no question of mistreatment or abuses by the jailers.

1830. FAN-YÜ TSAI-T'AO 反獄在逃 Has revolted and escaped
from prison

A prisoner rebels and escapes from prison; this is
punishable with the same penalty as for rebels.

1831. YÜEH-YÜ T'O-T'AO 越獄脫逃 Escaping from prison

(A prisoner) steathly makes his escape by scaling the
prison wall.

1832. CHÜ TSUI CH'IEN-T'AO 懼罪潛逃　Fleeing for fear of
punishment

A criminal, fearing arrest for his crime, has stealthily
fled to some other place.

1833. SU-TSUNG T'O-T'AO 疎縱脫逃 Escape resulting from
carelessness

Government agents making the arrest are careless, thus
enabling the criminal to escape.

1834. TSAI-T'U PING-KU 在途病故 Dies of illness en route

A prisoner has taken ill and died while being transferred
[to another locality].

1835. PU-CHÜEH SHIH CH'IU 不覺失囚 Not aware of the escape of a prisoner

The guard(s) escorting a prisoner who is being transferred are negligent, and have unknowingly allowed him to escape.

1836. HSIANG-CHI CHIU-CH'IN 相繼就擒 Captured one by one

A large number of robbers being captured successively.

1837. YEN-CHI WU-TSUNG 嚴緝無踪 A thorough search [or hunt] yielding no clue

Although a thorough search has been conducted, the criminal is still at large and his whereabouts unknown.

1838. LE-HSIEN YEN-CHI 勒限嚴緝 To conduct a thorough search within a given time limit

To order the search for and seizure of a criminal within a given time limit.

1839. HU-TSEI KUO-PAN 獲賊過半 More than half of the bandits are taken

Of the many escaped criminals, more than half have been recaptured.

1840. KO-SHENG KUAN-T'I 隔省關提 Inter-provincial extradition

When a criminal from province A has fled to province B, an official request is addressed [by the authorities of A] to the local officials [of B], to ask for the extradition of the criminal.

1841. FAN-I JEN-TENG 番役人等 Policemen

Government runners whose duty it is to investigate or search for robbers [or thieves, bandits] are called "policemen," also known as fan-tzu 番子 [the police]. [Cf. 1843, 1844.]

1842. PU-TAO T'UNG-CHIH 捕盜同知 Sub-prefect in charge of police affairs

A t'ung-chih 同知 (sub-prefect) who is specially in charge of the capture of thieves and robbers.

Punishments

1843. FAN-TZU 番子 Police

See above [1841].

1844. PU-I 捕役 Policemen, constables

Government runners whose duty it is to capture thieves and robbers. [Cf. 1841.]

1845. TU-CHI 督緝 To superintend the search [or hunt, for criminals]

The government authorities supervising and urging on the policemen in their effort to apprehend the thieves and robbers.

1846. K'UAI-SHOU 快手 Police agents

Government runners who with their own hands capture the thieves and robbers. [Cf. 1841, 1844.]

1847. TS'UI-CHI 催緝 To urge on the search [for a criminal]

For interpretation see above [1845].

1848. HSIEH-CHI 協緝 To assist in search

The policemen of one locality assisting those of another to jointly capture the thieves and robbers.

1849. CHUI-CHI 追緝 To pursue and capture

Escaped criminals are pursued and retaken. [Cf. 1853.]

1850. FANG-NA 訪拿 To arrest following investigation

To locate the criminal through investigative work, and seize him.

1851. AI-NA 挨拿 To arrest following door-to-door [investigation]

To seize a criminal after having ascertained his movements [or whereabouts] by conducting a door-to-door investigation.

1852. PIEN-CHI 遍緝 Wide search

To hunt (for the criminal) in every place, and capture him.

1853. CHU-NA 逐拿 To chase and seize

To capture (a criminal) by pursuing him. [Cf. 1849.]

1854. HSI-NA 躧拿 To seize by following

To capture (a criminal) by following his movements.

1855. CHI-HU 緝獲 Captured after a search

(*Chi 緝 "search" is missing in the Chia-ch'ing edition; it appears in the annotated edition as na 拿 "seize" or "arrest.")

The criminal has already been seized.

1856. WU-NA 誤拿 Arrested by mistake

A law-abiding citizen is erroneously apprehended as a criminal.

1857. CH'U JENG CH'IH LE-HSIEN YEN-CHI PING I YÜAN-CHI CH'A-NA WAI 除仍飭勒限嚴緝並移原籍查拿外 In addition to ordering a thorough search [for the criminal] within a time limit, and requesting [the officials] at his native district to assist in the investigation and arrest...

A criminal has escaped. The superior official orders a thorough search for him within a set time limit, and also addresses a written request to the authorities of (the criminal's) native district, asking them to conduct an investigation and help bring about his arrest. In addition, there are other measures to be taken [in dealing with this problem].

[[5]]   The major crimes and felonies
          A. Homicide and sexual crimes.   Nos. 1858-1897

1858. KU-SHA 故殺 Killing with an intent to kill

To kill a man intentionally.

1859. MOU-SHA 謀殺 Murder by conspiracy; premeditated homicide

Two or three persons plotting together to kill a man.

1860. CHU-SHIH 主使 To instigate

To conceive the scheme oneself, but ask others to carry it out.

1861. CHU-MOU 主謀 To incite

Same meaning as above [1860].

1862. TS'UNG ERH CHIA-KUNG 從而加功 To participate [in the crime] by being an accomplice

An "accomplice" is one who helps. This phrase means to help another person in perpetrating a murder.

1863. HSI-SHA 戲殺 Manslaughter resulting from [practical] joking; accidental homicide

Unintentionally killing a man through practical joking [or rough play].

1864. CHEN-SHA 鴆殺 Murder by poison

To kill a man by the use of poison.

[Amended, p. 144:] Chen 鴆 is a kind of bird whose blood, if drunk, is poisonous enough to kill a man. It was often used [as a lethal potion] in ancient times. In the present entry the word chen is employed to denote posion in general.

1865. TZU-WEN 自刎 Cutting one's own throat

To die by cutting one's own throat.

1866. TZU-I 自縊 Hanging oneself

To die by hanging (oneself) with a rope.

1867. TZU-CHIN 自盡 Suicide

The general term for [various manners of] taking one's own life.

1868. WU-SHA 誤殺 Killing by mistake

To kill a man without having so intended.

1869. KUO-SHIH-SHA 過失殺 Killing by accident

To kill a man due to a slip of the hand.

1870. PI-SHA 逼殺 To bring about suicide through ill-use

To drive a person to death [by suicide] through oppressive treatment.

1871. YEN-SHA 淹殺 Drowning

To die through submersion in water.

1872. PENG-SHA 綳殺 To kill through trussing

To truss up a person and thus cause his death.

1873. HO-SSU 嚇死 Frightened to death

To frighten a person, thus causing his death.

1874. YA-SSU 壓死 Crushed to death

To die from bearing [an overload of] heavy things.

1875. WEI-LI CHIH-FU JEN 威力制縛人 To control others through intimidation

To tyrannize over others by force, so as to deprive them of freedom.

1876. HSIA-CHIH CHIUNG-JU 挾制窘辱 To oppress by coercion and insult

To presume upon one's powerful position, and coerce and insult others.

1877. FENG-PING SHA-SHANG JEN 瘋病殺傷人 To kill and/or injure others due to insanity

To injure another person as a result of mental derangement.

1878. CH'AN-YEN TSO-SHIH SHA JEN 讒言佐使殺人 To incite murder through slanderous lies

To tell a slanderous falsehood to a person, thus rousing his rage and causing him to kill someone.

1879. YUNG-I SHA-SHANG JEN 庸醫殺傷人 Death and/or injury caused by an incompetent [or a quack] physician

A person is injured [or harmed] because of the incorrect medication prescribed by the physician.

1880. T'UNG-CHIEN 通姦 Adultery

A man and a woman having illicit sexual relations.

1881. HO-CHIEN 和姦 Adultery by mutual consent

A man and woman mutually agreeing to have adulterous relations.

1882. CH'IANG-CHIEN 强姦 Rape

A man forcing adulterous relations on a woman in spite of her objections.

1883. TIAO-CHIEN 刁姦 Seduction

To cheat and coerce, so as to violate other people's womenfolk.

1884. LUN-CHIEN 輪姦 To rape by turns

Several men taking turns in raping the same woman.

1885. CHI-CHIEN 鷄姦 Sodomy

Fornication carried on between two men.

1886. CHIEN-WU 姦污 Rape
YIN-JU 淫辱 Assault

[Both these terms mean] to violate other people's womenfolk.

1887. YIN-YEH 寅夜 Late at night

In the middle of the night.

1888. MOU-HO JUNG-CHIH 謀合容止 Plotting for an overnight stay

[A man and a woman] plotting together to commit adultery, with the one allowing the other to stay overnight.

1889. YIN-CHIEN CHIH-SHA 因姦致殺 Homicide resulting from adultery

Homicide is committed over the issue of adultery.

1890. CH'IANG-HSING CHI-CHIEN 强行鷄姦 Forced sodomy

To commit sodomy by coercion.

1891. FAN I-CHÜEH YING-LI 犯義絕應離 The criminal has violated the proper principle and should be divorced

The woman having committed a serious crime, the proper principle between husband and wife no longer obtains, and she ought to be divorced forthwith.

1892. LI-I FU TSUNG 離異婦宗 Divorce and return to own family

A woman divorced by her husband will return to her own family. [Fu 婦 "woman," misprint for kuei 歸 "return"?]

1893. TS'UNG-FU CHIA MAI 從夫嫁賣 To be married off or sold, as the husband disposes

A woman who has been convicted of adultery may be either sold or married off, in accordance with her husband's wishes.

1894. CHIEN-CHIU CH'ING-MI 姦久情密 Close attachment arising out of a long liaison

With the passage of time a close sentimental attachment has arisen between an adulterous couple.

1895. SSU-T'U YUNG-HAO 思圖永好 Wishing to make their relation permanent

[The couple] want to become husband and wife permanently.

1896. SUI MOU-SHA FU 遂謀殺夫 Thereupon have murdered the husband

A woman, wishing to live permanently with her lover, has schemed for the murder of her legal husband.

[Amended, p. 144:] Mou-sha ch'in-fu 謀殺親夫 , murder of one's own husband. A woman commits adultery with another man, and together with him brings about the murder of her husband. The statutory punishment for this most heinous crime is death by slicing.

1897. TI-SSU PU-TS'UNG PEI-SHA 抵死不從被殺 Killed in resistance to assault

A woman is killed because of her stubborn resistance to being raped.

-291-

[[5]] (continued)
      B. Disorderly conduct, felonious assault and battery.
      Nos. 1898-1975

1898. TOU-OU 鬥毆 Assault and battery; a brawl

    Two persons attacking and fighting each other.

1899. CHENG-CHIAO 爭角 Contention

    To argue and fight.

1900. FEN-CHENG 忿爭 Heated argument

    An argument caused by anger.

1901. CHIAO-K'OU 角口 Quarrel

    Verbal argument.

1902. LI-MA 詈罵 To revile

    To insult another with base language.

1903. JU-MA 辱罵 Abuse, scold

    HUI-MA 毀罵 Curse, vilify

    Both terms meaning the same as above.

1904. CH'ÜN-OU 羣毆 Mob fracas, mob violence

    Many persons assembling and fighting each other.

1905. HEN-OU 狠毆 Severe beating

    To strike [or beat] someone with great force.

1906. CHIEH-OU 截毆 Ambush

    To waylay an enemy and beat him.

1907. CHU-OU 助毆 To assist in beating

    To help a person beat another.

1908. K'UN-FA 髡髮 Hair-shaving

    To cut off another person's hair. [Cf. 1956.]

1909. TSO- T'AN 左袒 To shield

To be partial and give protection to one individual.

1910. CHIU-HU 救護 To rescue

To give succor and protection to a person.

1911. CHIAO-SO 教唆 To instigate

To manipulate behind the scenes and cause crimes to be committed against others.

1912. HO-LING 喝令 To roar an order

To shout out loudly an order to beat up others.

1913. YÜAN-MOU 原謀 Instigator

The person who had originally instigated [a crime].

1914. T'U-LAI 圖賴 Aiming to put the blame

Planning to put the blame on some other person.

1915. SA-P'O 撒潑 Tantrum, hysteria

Creating disturbances unreasonably.

1916. CH'ENG-SHANG 成傷 Resulting in injury

Injuries have resulted from the beating [or the fight].

1917. TA-SHANG 打傷 To injure [or wound] by beating

To beat a person so that his bones are dislocated or broken.

1918. TSU-TANG 阻當 To halt, stop

To stop a man from hitting or beating another.

1919. CH'ÜAN-CHIEH 勸解 To make peace by persuasion, to pacify a quarrel

To calm [the contestants] with gentle words and thus disengage them.

1920. SHENG-SHIH 生事 To start trouble

To initiate a contention.

1921. CH'I-YU 起由 Cause of contention

The reason behind the trouble.

1922. MI-SHIH 彌事 To quiet down the matter

To pacify the affair.

1923. YANG-CHAN YIN 養贍銀 Damage for injury

The person inuured [in a fight] should receive money from the offender as living allowance.

1924. PAO KU 保辜 Liability time limit

A man wounded by another person is examined by the officials as to the seriousness of his injury, after which a time limit is accordingly set. If he dies within the time limit, [the assailant] pays with his own life; if the man dies after the expiration of the time limit, then the penalty is to be reduced. This is known as the "liability time limit" [cf. 1965].

1925. HO-HSI 和息 Peace-making

A law suit being stopped through the efforts of intermediary peace-makers.

1926. SSU-HO 私和 Privately settled, settled out of court

The two parties to a law suit settling the affair privately between themselves instead of waiting for a court decision.

1927. SHANG-HEN 傷痕 Scars of wounds

Scars showing the places where one has been wounded.

1928. T'O-LEI 拖累 To embroil, involve

To draw an innocent person into [the case] on account of some involvement.

1929. MAI-TSANG YIN 埋葬銀 Burial or interment cost

The cost for burying a man dead from wounds is paid by the killer's family.

1930. WAN-YEN 剜眼 Gouging of eye(s)

To gouge out the eyeballs.

1931. CHIH-CHIEH JEN 支解人 Dismemberment

To hack off the four limbs of a man and cut him into pieces.

1932. CHE-KO JEN 折割人 Mutilation

To break a man's limbs or body, or to cut off his hands, feet, ears, nose, etc.

1933. TS'AI-SHENG 採生 Abortion [literally, "to snatch a life"]

(*Sheng 生 "life" is erroneously given as ch'ü 出 "out" in the annotated edition.)

To cut open a pregnant womb by evil methods, and take out the foetus.

1934. TSAO-CH'U TU-TU 造畜蠱毒 Turning into animals, creating venomous snakes

By the exercise of sorcery a man is turned into an animal; or, mixing a poisonous drug with food and inducing a man to eat it, to create venomous snakes in his bowels.

1935. YA-MEI 壓魅 A sorcerous curse

By exercising sorcery a man is cursed with incantations according to the year, month, [date], and hour of his birth, so as to bring about his death.

1936. KU TZU SHANG-TS'AN 故自傷殘 Purposely self-inflicted wound

To wound oneself intentionally, with a view to blaming it on another person.

1937. JOU CHAN KU P'O 肉綻骨破 Torn flesh and broken bones

To beat another person so severely as to result in torn flesh and broken bones.

1938. JOU-HSIA SHUANG-MU 揉瞎雙目 Blinding both eyes by rubbing [lime into them]

To blind another person by rubbing powdered lime into his eyes.

1939. SSU ERH FU-SU 死而復甦 To revive from unconsciousness

To beat a man until he becomes unconscious, but later is revived.

1940. FENG TS'UNG SHANG JU 風從傷入 Draft penetrating the wound

Death has resulted from the penetration of the wound by drafty air [or wind].

1941. HSIA-SHOU CHIH JEN 下手之人 The one who sets hands on [a victim]

The criminal who actually sets hands on a man and injures him.

1942. CH'UI-SHIH TA-SHOU 搥師打手 Professional strongmen or fighters

Professional fighters who are skilled in the military arts.

1943. SSU-HSING TIAO-TA 私行弔打 Privately hanging up and beating [a thief]

When one catches a thief [or burglar], the latter should be turned over to the government authorities for interrogation. It is prohibited by statute to [truss him,] hang him up and give him a beating privately.

1944. LIANG CHIEN HSIANG-OU 良賤相毆 Good and base battering each other

A melee in which fighting breaks out between persons of good families and those of lower classes.

1945. T'AI-JEN LUAN-TA 抬人亂打 Abduction and mob beating of a victim

To take a man to a certain spot, where a mob gives him a beating.

1946. WEI-JAO FANG-WU 圍繞房屋 Encircling the house, surrounding the house

To assemble a mob and [force] open a man's house, with the intention of starting a fight.

1947. NEI-SUN T'U-HSIEH 內損吐血 Blood-spitting caused by internal injuries

To injure a person's internal organs through beating, thus causing him to spit blood.

1948. CH'I-HUI SSU-SHIH 棄毀死屍 To abandon and destroy a corpse

To destroy [or mutilate] a corpse and then abandon it.

1949. CH'I ERH PU-SHIH 棄而不失 Abandoned but not lost

The corpse, though abandoned, has not been lost.

1950. P'AO-SA SSU-SHIH 抛撒死屍 To scatter corpses

To discard and disperse corpses at random.

1951. P'ING-CHIH T'A-JEN FEN-MU 平治他人墳墓
Razing of others' graves or tombs

To raze and level off other people's graves or tombs, with a view to encroaching on that land.

1952. PU-WEN SHOU TSU T'A-WU CHIN-JEN PING CHIAO 不問
手足他物金刃並絞　Death by strangulation is mandatory whether [the killing is done] with hands, feet, other tools or metal blades

In the case of involuntary manslaughter [1868, 1869] the sentence should be death by strangulation regardless of whether the killing is accomplished by the use of hands, or feet, or other instruments including metal blades. For murder by conspiracy and premeditated murder [1859, 1858, respectively] the penalty is decapitation.

1953. P'ING-CH'Ü JEN I SHIH 屏去人衣食　Depriving a person of clothing and food

To bring about a person's death by stripping him of all clothing and starving him.

1954. PA-FA FANG-TS'UN I-SHANG 拔髮方寸以上 The hair pulled exceeds one square inch [in area]

It is a criminal offense to pull off another person's hair to as much as one square inch in area or more (*Misprint here).

1955. I SUI-WU WU JEN T'OU-MIEN 以穢物污人頭面
Soiling a man's head and face with refuse

To insult a person by smearing or soiling his head and face with filthy stuff.

1956. CHIN K'UN-CH'Ü FA 盡髡去髮 Cutting off the hair completely

To cut off all the hair on a person's head [cf. 1908].

1957. CHE-LEI TO-T'AI 折肋隨胎 Breaking a rib and [causing] miscarriage

To beat a pregnant woman until her ribs are broken, thus causing a miscarriage.

1958. HSIA JEN I-MU 瞎人一目 To blind an eye

To damage [and blind] one of the eyes of a person.

1959. TUAN JEN SHE HUI-PAI I YIN YANG 斷人舌毀敗一陰陽 Cutting a tongue, damaging a female or male organ

To cut a person's tongue with a knife, or to damage the sex organ of a man or woman.

1960. CHE JEN I-CH'IH CHI SHOU TSU I-CHIH 折人一齒及手足一指 Breaking a tooth, or a finger, or a toe

To break (off) a person's tooth, or a finger or toe.

1961. MIAO JEN I-MU CHÜEH-HUEI JEN ERH PI 眇人一目抉毀人耳鼻 To blind one eye, or damage an ear and/or nose

To cause a person to lose sight in one eye [cf. 1958], or to damage his ear and/or nose so that they can no longer function.

1962. JO P'O JEN KU CHI YUNG T'ANG-HUO T'UNG-T'IEH-CHIH SHANG-JEN CHE CHANG 若破人骨及用湯火銅鐵汁傷人者杖一百 One hundred blows for the criminal who has broken the bone(s) of another man, or has injured others with boiling water, fire, or liquid copper or iron

Such should be the penalty for a person who has broken the bone(s) of another, or has caused injury to others by pouring boiling hot liquids over them.

1963. I SUI-WU KUAN-JU JEN K'OU-PI-NEI CHE TSUI I JU-CHIH 以穢物灌入人口鼻內者罪亦如之
Same [penalty] for pouring refuse into another person's mouth and/or nose

The penalty is the same as [1962; i.e., one hundred blows] for forcing a person to take filthy things through the mouth and/or nose.

1964. SUN JEN ERH-SHIH I SHANG TU-CHI FEI-CHI 損人二事 以上篤疾廢疾 Injuring a person in more than two places [causing] severe illness or crippling

To injure a person's mouth, nose, etc., or hands and feet, up to two or more places, so that the victim becomes seriously ill or crippled, and is therefore unable to work.

1965. KU-HSIEN NEI WAI 辜限內外 Within or beyond the liability time limit

The seriousness of the crime is decided on the basis of whether a fatally injured person dies before or after the date set as the liability time limit. [See 1924.]

1966. SU-WU HSIEN-HSI 素無嫌隙 No hostile feeling had existed

There never had been any enmity between two given persons.

1967. WEI-FAN CHIAO-LING 違犯教令 Disregarding and violating the instructions and orders

To act deliberately contrary to [parental] instructions [or good precepts] and orders, and end up by committing a crime.

1968. TSAI-CH'ANG PU-HSING CH'ÜAN-TSU 在場不行勸 阻 Those present did not persuade [the contestants] to stop

Companions present at a fracas, from which fighting and manslaughter resulted, had not attempted to persuade the contestants to stop the fight.

1969. WU-KAN SHENG-SHIH 無干省釋 The innocent party is released

An innocent party who gets inadvertently involved in a case is released upon examination.

1970. YA-TZU HSIAO-FEN 睚眦小忿 Angry eyes

Slight resentment expressed [to the extent of] showing anger in one's eyes.

1971. PU-P'ING CHIH CH'I 不平之氣 Enraged by injustice

To feel outraged upon seeing something unjust.

1972. PU-MU CHIH T'IAO 不睦之條 Article(s) on discord

To violate the statutory articles pertaining to discord.

1973. YU PU-YÜ PING[-LI] CHIH SHIH 有不欲并[立]之勢 Appearing as if unable to coexist

The mutual feeling [between two litigants, or contestants, etc.] is such that they cannot coexist together.

1974. TS'AN-TU CHIH CHUANG PU-SHENG FA-CHIH 慘毒之狀不勝髮指 The cruelty [of the crime] makes one's hair stand on end

[The criminal] has made his victim suffer in such cruel ways, that even a bystander's rage is so aroused so as to make his hair stand on end.

1975. CH'ING CH'IH CHUNG SHANG YUAN CH'ANG HSIEH CHENG 青赤腫傷圓長斜正 A blue, red, or swollen wound, round, long, slanting, or centrally placed

All these words are descriptive of the color and shape of wounds.

[[5]] (continued)
C. Extortion, oppression, fraud, drunkenness, gambling. Nos. 1976-2020

1976. SHIH-SHEN 勢紳 Powerful gentry

Influential members of the gentry.

1977. T'U-HAO 土豪 Local despots

Strong-handed or overbearing men of the locality.

1978. KUANG-KUN 光棍 Scoundrel

A swindler, a lying lawbreaker.

1979. LA-HU 喇唬 Hoodlum

Same as above [1978].

1980. CHI-TU 積蠹 Inveterate offender

A criminal with a long lawbreaking record [literally, "with a collection of evil deeds"].

1981. P'ING-MIN 平民 The common people; civilian population

Law-abiding people.

1982. PO-TAO TZU 悖道子 An unfilial son; a contrary son

A bad son who behaves contrary to the principles of filial piety.

1983. FENG-YANG YU- CH'ÜEH 奉養有缺 Lacking in attendance and support [of one's parents]

An unfilial son who has neither attended his parents enough nor provided them with sufficient support.

1984. HSÜN-CH'I SHIH-HAO 勳戚勢豪 High aristocracy, imperial relatives, and powerful magnates

Families of prominent and old nobility, of the Empresses' relatives, and of those who possess domineering power...

1985. CII'IN-SHU NEI-CH'I 親屬內戚 Clan members and relatives

...as well as clan members or relatives of a powerful family.

1986. SHIH-HAO TA HU 勢豪大戶 Big powerful families

Such people as belong to a powerful and numerous family [or clan].

Punishments

1987. SHIH-YAO CHIH CHIA 勢要之家 A powerful and influential family

A family that is powerful and possesses great influence.

1988. HAO-HUA KUEI-LI 豪猾規利 Profit seeking

Strong-handed and dishonest blackguards seeking to profit themselves through victimizing good people.

1889. E-SHAO HSIUNG-WAN 惡少凶頑 Intractable delinquent youths

Unprincipled youths who are cunning, intractable, and cruel.

1990. JEN-JEN TS'E-MU 人人側目 Silently hated [literally, "regarded with oblique glances"] by everyone

[A person] being feared as well as hated by all the people, who dare not look him directly in the eye.

1991. CH'IANG-TO CHIEN-CHAN 强奪奸占 To seize and seduce by force

To seize other people's womenfolk by force, then seduce and possess them.

1992. TIAO-TENG YUNG-CH'IANG 刁蹬用强 To force unreasonable arguments

To dispute unreasonably by resorting to specious and dishonest arguments.

1993. I-SHIH CH'I-LING 依勢欺凌 To bully others on borrowed power

To bully or abuse law-abiding citizens on the strength of one's connection with a powerful family.

1994. PA-CH'IH CHA-HAI 把持詐害 To extort and oppress through domination

To dominate in the local affairs and thus extort and oppress the law-abiding people.

1995. KUEI-CHI YIN-MOU 詭計陰謀 Dishonest schemes and nefarious plots

To victimize others with dishonest schemes and nefarious plots.

1996. MAO-JEN K'UANG-CHUAN 冒認誆賺 To defraud by false identification

Falsely to identify [other persons as one's own relatives] with a view to defrauding the latter of money.

1997. HSIUNG-CHIU TZU-HSING 酗酒恣性 Disorderly conduct while intoxicated

To behave without restraint while drunk.

1998. HSIUNG-CHIU SA-P'O 酗酒撒潑 Offensive conduct while intoxicated

To behave wildly while drunk.

1999. PU WU SHENG-LI 不務生理 Having no proper occupation

To idle the days away and not attend to a proper means of livelihood .

2000. SAN WU CH'ENG-CH'ÜN 三五成群 In groups of threes and fives

Delinquent youths gathering together to start trouble.

2001. TA-KU T'I-CH'IU 打鼓踢球 Beating the drum and kicking a ball

Engaging in useless pastimes.

2002. YEN-YÜ AO-MAN 言語傲慢 Insolent in speech

To be arrogant in speech, showing scorn for others.

2003. CH'Ü-MI YUNG-CH'IEN 取覓用錢 To exact money as a reward

To perform an errand for another person, and then exact money [from the latter] as reward.

2004. HSÜ-CHANG SHENG-SHIH 虛張聲勢 To make false display of power and influence

To pretend to have authority and influence, and so intimidate others with false appearance.

Punishments

2005. CH'IEN-CHAI PEN LI 錢債本利 Principal and interest of a debt

The amounts of money owed in principal and interest.

2006. HSI-SHANG CHIA-HSI 息上加息 Double interest; interest charged on the interest

To double the gain on interest.

2007. SHU-CHIEH HO-CHA 書揭喝詐 Blackmail through [threatened?] publicity

To write down on paper some person's secret affair and display it to the public, with a view to extorting bribe money from the person concerned.

2008. T'OU NI-MING CHIEH 投匿名揭 To send anonymous information

To write down on paper some person's secret affair, and send it to the government authorities without giving one's own name.

2009. MING WEI WO-FANG 名為窩訪 Under pretext of making an investigation

Under the name of conducting a personal investigation for smuggled goods (an official) acts with a view to extorting [money from the persons investigated].

2010. CHA-MAO KUAN-YUAN HSING-MING 詐冒官員姓名 Falsely assuming the name of an official

Falsely to assume the name of a high official, so as to obtain money and goods from others.

2011. CHA-WEI CHIA-KUAN 詐為假官 Pretending to be an official

Same as above [2010].

2012. CHA YÜ-JEN KUAN 詐與人官 Making false official appointments

To make and distribute illegal credentials to office, in order to exact money payments [from those who obtain them].

2013. T'AO-HUA YA-TZU 套畫押字 Forgery of signature

> To make a false document and forge the signature of another person, and use this as certificate or evidence.

2014. MIAO-MO YIN-HSIN 描摸印信 Forgery [or illegal duplication] of seal

> To fashion a false official paper, and forge the impression of the official seal on it.

2015. WEI-TSO CHIN YIN 偽作金銀 Producing simulated gold or silver

> To make false gold or silver so as to defraud others with it.

2016. YEN-KO HUO-CHE 閹割火者 To castrate [into] a eunuch

> [...] To castrate a boy and sell him into government service.

2017. TZU-CHI CHING-SHEN 自己淨身 Self-cleansing; self-castration

> To perform castration on oneself.

2018. HSIA CHI TU-PO 挾妓賭博 Gambling in the company of prostitutes

> To summon prostitutes and gamble together.

2019. K'AI-CHANG TU-FANG 開張賭房 Opening a gambling house

> To set up a gambling house.

2020. K'AI-CH'ANG CH'OU-T'OU 開場抽頭 Operating a gambling house and obtaining premiums

> To set up a gambling house and profit by the premiums obtained [from the gamblers].

[[5]] (continued)
    D. Heresy. Nos. 2021-2065

2021. SHA-HSIEH MENG-SHIH FEN-PIAO 歃血盟誓焚表
Taking the blood oath and burning the manifesto

(*Sha 猷 is given as ch'a 插 in the Manchu-Chinese editions, and as ch'a 喢 in the annotated edition.)

When plotting an uprising, rebels first kill a [sacrificial] animal for confirmation of the group, then take an oath, and a manifesto is burnt as prayer to heaven.

2022. CH'AN-WEI YAO SHU 讖緯妖書 Evil books of phrophecy

Books that delude the people by foretelling the portents of the stars, and prophesying on the future of the empire.

2023. CH'UAN-PU WEI-YEN 傳布譌言 Rumor-mongering

To create rumors and spread them among the people to mislead them.

2024. NIEH-TSAO LI-KO 捏造俚歌 Creating vulgar songs

To create vulgar songs and verses, using them falsely to prophesy on the future.

2025. K'AN-K'O CH'UAN-SUNG 刊刻傳誦 Publication and circulation

To publish evil books and vulgar songs, and circulate them for all to read and learn.

2026. YEN CHIEH CH'ANG-HO 沿街唱和 Being sung all over town

The whole town singing to the tune of the vulgar songs.

2027. PAN-TSO TSA-CHÜ 扮做雜劇 Presented as drama

To dramatize [e.g.] immoral stories [or bad deeds] and act them out in the theater.

2028. HSIEH-TU SHEN-MING 褻瀆神明 Profanation of the deities

To act irreverently and thus be guilty of profanation of the deities.

2029. KAO-T'IEN PAI-TOU 告天拜斗 Praying to Heaven and worshipping the stars [literally, the Dipper]

To pray to Heaven, and worship the stars and constellations, on account of one's wish to carry out improper schemes.

2030. FEN-SHAO YEH-HSIANG 焚燒夜香 Burning the midnight incense

To gather a group in a midnight meeting, for the purpose of burning incense [for some purpose]. [Cf. 2031, 2052].

2031. TSUNG-LING SHAO-HSIANG 縱令燒香 Allowing [them to convene] incense-burning [sessions]

The head of a family allowing members of his household to gather in groups and conduct incense-burning sessions without restraint. [Cf. 2030, 2052.]

2032. NAN NÜ HUN-TSA 男女混雜 Men and women intermingling

Men and women indiscriminately gathered together for an incense-burning session.

2033. SHIH WU HSIEH-SHU 師巫邪術 The sorcery of wizards and witches

Male and female sorcerers deluding the people with their evil magical arts.

2034. CHIA-CHIANG HSIEH-SHEN 假降邪神 A fraudulent trance

Male and female sorcerers deluding the people by pretending to be the medium for some heterodox spirit.

2035. SHU-FU CHOU-SHUI 書符咒水 Magical signs and waters

A sorcerer draws magical signs and recites incantations over water, which people then swallow as medicine to cure their ailments.

2036. FU-LUAN TAO-SHENG 扶鸞禱聖 To invoke the spirits by sand-writing seances

A sorcerer writes words in a tray of sand and claims they are done by a spirit that has been invoked. This is called a "sand-writing seance."

2037. WU I T'IAO-SHEN 巫覡跳神 Sorcerers' spirit dance

A sorcerer performs a [ritual] dance and falsely claims he is moved by a spirit that has been invoked.

2038. TSO-WEI I-TUAN 作為異端 Unorthodox conduct

To commit any deed that is strange and misleading.

2039. CHUANG-PAN SHEN-HSIANG 粧扮神像 Decked out as a divine image

A sorcerer made up to appear as the image of a divinity.

2040. MING-LO CHI-KU 鳴鑼擊鼓 Beating the gong and the drum

A sorcerer makes music while invoking the spirits.

2041. YING-SHEN SAI-HUI 迎神賽會 Religious processions and fairs

Sorcerers conducting processions for divine images and organizing religious meetings, thus to delude the people and get their money.

2042. CH'UN CH'IU I-SHE 春秋義社 Spring and autumn sacrificial societies

To organize a sacrificial society, worshipping the spirits (that roam unclaimed); in the spring and autumn fees are collected from the people for the sacrifices to these spirits.

2043. SHAO-LIEN TAN-YAO 燒煉丹藥 Distilling the elixir

Taoist priests distill the elixir pills, falsely claiming that they will confer immortality on those who eat them.

2044. P'EI T'I KUAN TSAN 披剃冠簪 Robed and shaven; capped and hairpinned

In becoming a Buddhist monk one wears a monk's robe and has the hair shaven off; in becoming a Taoist priest one dons a tall cap and has one's hair [knotted and] secured with a pin.

2045. WANG-YEN TU-HUO 妄言蠱惑 To delude with heresy

To fabricate fantastic talk and mislead the people.

2046. CH'IU-T'AO PU-SHIH 求討布施 Begging for alms

A monk begging for money.

2047. LIEN-CH'IEN HAO-FO 斂錢號佛 To collect money for prayers

To demand money from people and use it to pay the cost of sutra recitations and prayers.

2048. JAN T'IEN-TENG CH'I TENG 燃天燈七燈 To light the seven celestial lamps

(*Ch'i teng 七燈 "seven lamps" are given as ch'i-chan 七盞 "seven" in the annotated edition.)

These lamps, seven in number, are made of red paper and mounted on a long pole in the form of the Great Dipper. They are called "celestial lamps."

2049. CH'I- JANG HUO-TSAI 祈禳火災 Praying to avert a fire disaster

To allege that a catastrophe of fire is about to occur, and that it is to be averted through the recitation of sutras.

2050. TSO-TAO LUAN-SHIH 左道亂世 Heterodoxy menacing the age

To advocate heretical beliefs so as to create disturbances in the way of orthodoxy.

2051. YIN-NI T'U-HSIANG 隱匿圖像 Concealed [worshipping of] an image

To worship in secret the image of a heretical god and not let others know about it.

2052. CHI-CHUNG SHAO- HSIANG 集衆燒香 Gathering a group to burn incense

To gather a group of persons together and conduct an incense-burning session.

[Cf. 2030, 2031.]

2053. YEH-CHÜ HSIAO-SAN 夜聚曉散 To gather at night and disperse at dawn

[A group that] foregathers in the night, but disperses during the day.

2054. YANG HSIU SHAN-SHIH 佯修善事 Pretending to do good deeds

To obtain money under the pretext of doing a charitable deed.

2055. SHAN-HUO MIN-JEN 煽惑民人 Inciting and misleading the common people

To incite and delude the people with heretical talk, with a view to starting a rebellion.

2056. HSIU-CHAI SHE-CHIAO 修齋設醮 Observing fasts and setting up altars

A meeting where fasts are observed and sutras are recited.

2057. PAI SHAO PIAO-WEN 拜燒表文 To worship, and to burn a manifesto

Praying to Heaven by burning a manifesto and performing the rituals of worship.

2058. TZU HAO TUAN-KUNG T'AI-PAO SHIH-P'O MING-SE 自號端公太保師婆名色 Self-styled Proper Lord, Grand Guardian, Grand Instructress, etc.

These are names and titles assumed by male and female sorcerers.

2059. HSIA-CHIH KUAN-FU YU-SHOU-HAO-HSIEN CHIH JEN 挾制官府游手好閑之人 Idlers who intimidate officials

Men having no proper occupation and spending their time in idle vagrancy, who often use public affairs as a means to establish connections with the officials as a step toward the use of coercion in the future.

2060. WU-YEH YU-SHOU LAI-LI PU-MING CHIH JEN 無業游手來歷不明之人 Men without occupation whose past is unclear

Idlers and vagrants who have no proper occupation, and whose past histories are not known.

2061. WU-LAI HAI MIN MAO-TSEI 無賴害民蟊賊 A worthless pest who harms people

Mao 蝥 is a poisonous insect. A worthless fellow who starts troubles, causing others to suffer, is just like a poisonous insect.

2062. CHIH-MEI WANG-LIANG CHIH HSING 魑魅魍魉之行 The acts of hobgoblins and water ghosts

These [i.e., chih-mei wang-liang] are the names of malicious demons. This phrase describes a man's cruel, diabolic deeds.

2063. CHIEN T'UNG KUEI YÜ HSING JO HU SHU 奸同鬼蜮 行若狐鼠 Treacherous as a ghost and the yü-toad, and foxy and ratty conduct

This means a person is as treacherous as a ghost or the malicious yü-toad, and in conduct equals the fox or the rat in cunning.

2064. CHA-WEI JUI-YING 詐為瑞應 False prophecy of good fortune

Falsely forecasting good fortune in order to cheat the ignorant people.

2065. TSAI HSIANG 災祥 Catastrophe or good luck

An auspicious or an evil omen.

[[5]] (continued)
    E. Larceny, banditry. Nos. 2066-2146

2066. FAN-JEN 犯人 Criminal

One who has committed [or is guilty of] a crime or offense.

2067. CHUNG-FAN 重犯 Major criminal

One who is guilty of a major crime.

2068. SHOU-FAN 首犯 Ringleader, principal criminal

The person who is the leader in the crime.

2069. WEI-TS'UNG 為從 Accomplice, abettor

The person who has a secondary role in the crime.

Punishments

2070. TAO-FAN 盜犯 Larcenist

One who is guilty of robbery or theft.

2071. YÜAN-MOU 元謀 Instigator

The person who is the chief planner [of a crime].

[Cf. 1913.]

2072. SHOU-TAO 首盜 Robber chief

The head of robbers or thieves.

2073. HUO-TAO 夥盜 Robber band

The rank and file of a group of robbers or thieves.

2074. CHIEN-FAN 監犯 Prisoner [literally, "imprisoned criminal"]

A criminal who is incarcerated in a jail.

2075. I-FAN 逸犯 Escaped prisoner [or escaped criminal]

A criminal who has escaped.

2076. HSIUNG-FAN 凶犯 Criminal charged with homicide

A murderer among the criminals.

2077. TU-FAN 蠹犯 Criminal charged with oppression

A criminal who has abused and caused suffering to law-abiding people.

2078. I-TAO 逸盜 Escaped robber [or thief]

A robber or thief who has escaped.

2079. SHUI-TANG 水黨 River pirate

A robber who plunders along river routes.

2080. HSIEN-TSEI 線賊 Robber spy

The robber or thief who acts as the guide for the group.

2081. CH'IANG-TAO 強盜 Brigands, bandits

Powerful bandits who waylay and rob people by force.

2082. HSIANG-MA 響馬 The "horse-bells" [or mounted bandits]

(*Hsiang 響 "noisy" is given as hsiang 嚮 "direction" in the Manchu-Chinese editions.)

Riding on horseback, powerful bandits in North China equip their mounts with bells that announce their approach from a distance. Hence they are known by this name.

2083. HSIANG-MA CH'IANG-TAO 響馬强盜 Horse-bell bandits; [or mounted bandits]

Same as above [2082].

2084. CH'IEH-TAO 竊盜 Thief

A petty thief who steals from people.

2085. CH'IANG-CH'IEH 强劫 Robbery, banditry, brigandage

A big bandit who robs by force [cf. 2089].

2086. T'AO-MO 掏摸 Burglary

A thief who steals by breaking into a house through a hole in the wall.

2087. YAO-CH'IEH 邀劫 To waylay and rob

To stop a traveller on the way and rob him of his money.

2088. CHIEH-TO 截奪 To ambush and rob

Same as above [2087].

2089. TA-TO 打奪 Robbery, banditry, brigandage

(*To 奪 "to seize" is given as chieh 劫 "to rob" in the annotated edition.)

A big bandit who robs by force [cf. 2085].

2090. CH'AO-CH'IANG 抄搶 Plundering and looting

To plunder and loot or rob a place.

2091. HSING-CHIEH MOU-CHIA 行劫某家 A certain household is robbed

(*Mou 某 "a certain" is given as ch'i 其 "his" in the annotated edition.)

The valuables of this household have been seized by robbers.

2092. CHIEH CH'IU 劫囚 Breaking the jail for a prisoner

To seize [and carry away] a jailed prisoner.

2093. WO-CHU 窩主 Harborer

A man who harbors and hides robbers or thieves.

2094. YÜ-I 羽翼 Accomplices, assistants, followers

Members of a robber band.

2095. CHEN-CHIH 偵知 To gather information

To detect and learn [the facts in preparation for a crime].

2096. CHIU-HUO 糾夥 Assembling a group

To gather together a gang of robbers.

2097. HSI-P'AN 躧盤 Scouting the place

To investigate [the physical environments of] a certain locality or house, preparatory to staging a robbery.

2098. SHANG-TAO 上盜 Has been robbed

The robbery has already been committed.

2099. YÜEH CH'IANG 越墻 Over the walls

To enter [a house] by scaling the walls.

2100. JU YUAN 入院 Into the courtyard

To enter the courtyard of a house.

2101. CH'UANG MEN 撞門 Battering the door

To knock on the door.

2102. CH'IAO MEN 撬門 Forcing the door

To break open the door with a knife.

2103. JU SHIH 入室 Into the rooms

To enter into the chambers of a house.

2104. K'UN-TA 綑打 To tie and beat up

To tie up the master [of a house] and beat him.

2105. HUO HSIEH 火械 With lights and weapons

Committing robbery openly with the help of lights
and weapons.

2106. HUO-K'AO 火烤 Roasting with fire

To roast the master [of a house] with fire, thus forcing
him to give up his money and valuables.

2107. YU-SHAO 油燒 Scalding with oil

To heat oil, and use it to scald the victim of the robbery.

2108. K'AO-TA 拷打 Inquisition with beating

To beat the master [of a house] in order to find out where
he has hidden his money and valuables.

2109. TAO-CHA 刀扎 Stabbing

To pierce with a knife.

2110. YU-HUO-CHIH 油火紙 Oiled paper torch

To kindle oiled paper and use as light.

2111. TAO-TA 刀打 To hit with a knife

To beat a person with the back of a knife blade [or sword].

2112. K'UNG-HO 恐嚇 To threaten

To frighten.

2113. CHÜ-PU 拒捕 To resist arrest

To offer armed resistance to government troops who have
come to apprehend the robbers.

[Amended, p. 145:] Instead of being submissive, robbers
offer resistance to the government forces when being
arrested by the latter.

2114. CHÜ-TI 拒敵 To resist by force

Same as above [2113].

2115. CH'U-SHOU 出首 To inform

A partner in crime turns to inform the authorities of the deed.

2116. KOU-YIN 勾引 To induce

Thieves and bandits inducing others to join their band.

2117. PU-FU 不扶 To give no aid

Refusing to be an accomplice.

2118. HSÜ TSANG 虛贓 Untruthfully [identified] loot

Loot that has been falsely identified or claimed [cf. 1794].

2119. YEN-TSEI 鹽賊 Salt smuggler

A law-breaker who sells illegal salt.

2120. YEN-T'U 鹽徒 Salt smuggler

A man who sells illegal salt.

2121. CH'I-I HSING-CHIEH 起意行劫 Plotting a robbery

Bandits foregathering to plan a robbery.

2122. KUNG-MOU WEI-TAO 共謀為盜 Scheming together for a robbery

Same as above [2121].

2123. LIN-SHIH PU HSING 臨時不行 Last-minute withdrawal

To join the robbers at first in plotting, but to withdraw from the venture when the time of action arrives.

2124. I YAO MI-JEN 以藥迷人 To drug a person

To poison a person with drugs so as to defraud him of his valuables.

2125. FEN-PU PA-FENG 分佈把風 To deploy look-outs

To station at various spots members of the robber band, who are to be on guard and gather intelligence and information.

2126. FANG-HUO YEN-SHAO 放火延燒 Arson; to set afire

Bandits setting fires to and burning other people's houses.

[Appendices, p. 145:] [A] Sha-jen fang-huo 殺人放
火 Murder and arson. Both are things done by bandits.
[B] Tsung-huo t'u-chieh 縱火圖劫 To commit arson
with intention to rob. Bandits setting a man's house afire,
with a view to robbing it during the ensuing confusion.

2127. SHIH-CHU SHIH-SHIH 失主失事 Victim of robbery

The owner whose valuables have been robbed. [The
second pair of characters here probably should be
shih-chu 事主.]

2128. PEI-CHIEH PEI-HAI 被劫被害 The robbed house; the
suffering party, the victim

(*Hai 害 "suffering" is given as kao 告 "to indict" in the
annotated edition.)

The family that has been robbed by bandits.

2129. SHANG I P'ING-FU 傷已平復 The wound has healed

[A person] injured by the robbers has recovered from
his wounds.

[Appendix, p. 145:] Chü-shang shih-chu 拒傷事主
Wounding the victim of a robbery

In the course of robbing a house, the robbers have
wounded the owner when the latter offers resistance.
This additional offense will increase the seriousness
of the crime by one degree.

2130. PIAO-FEN ERH SAN 傀分而散 To disperse after
distribution of loot

After a robbery, the loot is equally divided among the
bandits, who will then disperse.

2131. WO-SU CHU-LIU 窩宿住留 To harbor overnight

To harbor robbers in one's house and give them lodgings.

2132. WO-TS'ANG JUNG-YIN 窩藏容隱 To harbor and conceal

To harbor and hide robbers in one's house.

2133. T'UNG TAO WANG-LAI 通盜往來 Maintaining contact with robbers

To maintain clandestine contacts with robbers.

2134. TS'AO-K'OU SHENG-FA 草寇生發 Bandits on the rise

Bandits are rising all over the countryside.

2135. TSEI-TAO TZU-MAN 賊盜滋蔓 Bandits on the increase

More and more bandits have appeared.

2136. TAO-TSEI CH'UNG-CH'IH 盜賊充斥 Full of bandits

A [certain] place is full of bandits.

2137. HSIAO-CHÜ PU-SAN 嘯聚不散 Have gathered, refusing to disperse

Bandits have gathered in answer to each other's call, and will not disperse.

2138. LÜ-LIN TA-TAO 綠林大盜 A big bandit of the greenwood

A powerful bandit who has his hideout in a mountainous forest.

2139. HUAN-FU CHÜ-SOU 萑苻聚藪 Gathering ground of brigands

[...] That is, a given locality is the camping and gathering place of bandits.

2140. TA-SSU CH'ANG-CHÜEH 大肆猖獗 On a wild rampage

The bandits giving full vent to their ferocity.

2141. TZU-TSU PU JU 趑趄不入 Hesitantly hanging back

Government agents on a mission to capture bandits become frightened, and are unwilling to penetrate more deeply into the robbers' lair.

2142. YANG-SHUN YIN-WEI 陽順陰違 Pretending to abide by the law but actually disobeying it

[E. g.] Robbers putting on an appearance of being submissive subjects, while they clandestinely violate the law and engage in banditry. [This is a common phrase the use of which is not limited to bandits, but which may be applied to an official or any other person who pretends to obey an instruction but does not implement it.]

2143. CH'AO SHA TA-YÜAN 抄殺大寃 The great wrongs of robbery and murder

Valuable possessions of law-abiding citizens are robbed and they themselves are killed: they have suffered these great wrongs at the hands of robbers.

2144. TAO WU SHIH-CHÜ 盜無實據 No substantial evidence of robbery

There is no substantial proof of [a man's] having committed robbery.

2145. TSAO-I TE-TS'AI YU CHÜ 造意得財有據 There is evidence of [their] conspiracy for robbery

There is substantial proof that [the given persons] have plotted to rob others of money or valuables.

2146. TS'ANG-NI YIN-SUNG 藏匿隱送 To conceal, to transmit

To conceal a robber or thief in one's house, or clandestinely to transmit and deliver stolen goods for him.

[[5]] (continued)
F. Kidnapping. Nos. 2147-2161

2147. LÜEH-MAI 略賣 To seize and sell

To seize other people's children [tzu nü 子女 , literally, "son and/or daughter"] by force, and sell them.

2148. LÜEH-YU 略誘 To lure and seize

To entice other people's children out of their house and seize them.

2149. KUAI-P'IEN 拐騙 To kidnap through deception

"To kidnap" is to take away. This phrase means to
lure others' children out of their house with sweet talk,
and then take them away in flight.

2150. CHÜ-P'IEN KUAI-TAI 局騙拐帶 To entrap and abduct

To devise a plot whereby other people's children are
kidnapped and taken away in flight.

2151. CH'IN-CH'I KUAI-P'IEN 侵欺拐騙 To embezzle and
abscond

To embezzle and steal others' money and valuables, and
abscond with them.

2152. KUAI-TAI PU-MING 拐帶不明 Suspected to be kidnapped

The story of the children in [a man's] company is highly
suspicious; they have obviously been kidnapped.

2153. SSU-CHIN T'U-CHIAO 私禁土窖 Private dungeon

A powerful family digs its own private dungeons [literally,
"cellars"], in which its captured enemies are imprisoned.

2154. YIN-YU T'AO-TSOU 引誘逃走 To lure and flee

To entice others' children by deception, and take them
away in flight.

2155. PEI JEN WEI-PI 被人威逼 Under duress; by coercion

A child [or girl] is coerced by the law-breaker to commit
adultery, or to flee with him. [The character wei 威
preceding chien 姦 in the text is obviously a misprint for
ch'eng 成.]

2156. YU PI CHUAN-MAI 誘逼轉賣 [To kidnap by] inducement
or coercion, and to sell

At first to kidnap a child either by enticement or by coercion, and then to sell him [or her] to another person.

2157. YAO-PING P'U TING 藥餅撲頂 To touch the head with
a drug pellet

There is an evil technique whereby one hits the crown of

a person's head with a drugged pellet, whereupon the victim will walk away following [the kidnapper].

2158. SHIH PU YU-CHI 事不由己 Involuntary act

A child was compelled by a law-breaker to flee with him; since this act is not voluntary, he [or she] is not adjudged guilty.

2159. MI-SHIH TZU-NÜ 迷失子女 A child is lost

A child has been kidnapped by law-breakers employing evil arts.

2160. HSIEH-SHU MI-KUAI 邪術迷拐 To kidnap with evil arts [sorcery]

To kidnap children using evil [magical] methods.

2161. HO-YU 和誘 To persuade and lure

To persuade and lure the children with a view to abducting them.

[[6]] Miscellaneous offenses. Nos. 2162-2199

2162. KUEI-FU KO-T'ENG 詭負葛藤 Unscrupulous swindle and [legal] entanglement

(*Kuei 詭 "unscrupulous" is given as kuei 鬼 "devilish" in the Manchu-Chinese editions.)

"Unscrupulous swindle" means to defraud others of money through a cunning scheme; "entanglement" denotes some-thing unending. Law-breakers first swindle others out of money, causing litigation to arise; then the latter becomes an endless suit lasting a long time.

2163. I-T'U MIEH-K'OU 以圖滅口 In order to eliminate witnesses

When a nefarious deed of law-breakers becomes known to another person, they kill him for fear that he might tell others about it. Thus the danger of witnesses is eliminated.

2164. HSING-MING PU-K'O 星命卜課 Horoscope and fortune-telling

To tell others' futures by casting horoscopes, and telling fortune by examining birth dates or the analysis of words; all such talk is liable to mislead the people and is prohibited by statute.

2165. KUO-FANG CH'I-YANG 過房乞養 To be foster parents, to adopt

A childless couple may become foster parents to one of their brothers' children, or adopt a son from a family of a different surname.

2166. CHAO-HSÜ YANG-LAO 招婿養老 To have a living-in son-in-law for old age

A couple having daughter(s) but no son may have a son-in-law marry into their family, so as to have support in old age.

2167. T'UNG-CHÜ 同居 Extended household; living together

Father, sons, brothers and relatives all living within the same household.

2168. PU T'UNG-CHÜ 不同居 Separate households; not living together

[Members of a given extended family] living in different places.

2169. WU-FU TSU-CHIH 無服族姪 Younger generation clansmen without mourning obligations

"Without mourning obligations" means no mourning is to be worn for a given person's death--that is, his distant relatives. [The present entry] denotes distant cousins [literally, "nephews"] many times removed. [Cf. 2181.]

2170. CHAO MU LUN-HSÜ 昭穆倫序 The proper order of elder and younger branches

The designation for the elder branch [of a clan] is

"luminous" 昭 , and that for the younger branches is
"solemn"楊 . Each has its proper place in the order
[of the affairs of the clan] which must not be disturbed.

2171. TSUN PEI SHIH-HSÜ 尊卑失序 Rule of precedence is
upset

The proper order of precedence pertaining to members
of a family or clan, and to the different sibling orders and
generations, must not be disregarded.

2172. TI-SUN CH'ENG-CHUNG 摘孫承重 The grandson being
the heir

When a man's son dies, his grandson by direct descent
should be the heir.

2173. PING-WU KUO-CHI 並無過繼 [A given person] is by
no means an adopted child

That is, the man is the true son of his father, and no
adoption had ever taken place.

2174. I WU NIEH-SANG 亦無捏喪 No fraudulent report
of [parent's] death

At times a criminal might falsely testify that his father
or mother has just died, hoping thus to win clemency for
his crime.

2175. NI-SANG PU CHÜ-AI 匿喪不舉哀 Concealing a
[parent's] death and not announcing it

At news that his father or mother has died an official should
obtain leave for a parent's death, and vacate his post. Any
official who conceals the death and does not leave his post
is to be severely punished according to statute.

2176. PING-WU I TZ'U CH'ENG-TING 並無以次成丁
There is no junior adult [at home]

According to statute, a criminal who has aged parents but
no adult brothers may, upon being sentenced to remote
garrison duty [see 1748] or permanent banishment [see
1737], appeal for the remission of the banishment, and
be allowed to remain at home, so that he may support his
parents.

2177. K'EN-CH'I LIU-YANG 懇乞留養 To appeal for [permission to] stay and support

Same as above [2176].

2178. PU-FU YIN-CHIEH 不扶印結 Without sealed bond

When an official arrives at his post, or a licentiate takes his examinations, he is to have metropolitan officials from his own province execute sealed bonds to vouch for the authenticity of his mission, which otherwise cannot [be accomplished].

2179. PU WEI CHIEH-T'IEH 不違揭帖 No illegal petitions

The petitions presented contain only proper sentiments without any illegal statement.

2180. CHI CH'IN WAN-CHÜ 給親完聚 Returned to family for reunion

A woman [prisoner] is sentenced by the magistrate to be returned to her kin, so that the family may be reunited.

[Cf. 1742.]

2181. TA-KUNG HSIAO-KUNG SSU-MA T'AN-WEN 大功小功總麻袒免 Second, third, fourth, and fifth degree of mourning, respectively

There are five degrees of mourning to be observed among people of the same patrilineage. They are, [1] the first degree [tzu-ts'ui 齊衰], to last for one year; [2] the second degree [ta-kung 大功], five months; [3] the third degree [hsiao-kung 小功], three months; [4] the fourth degree [ssu-ma 總麻], one month; and [5] the fifth degree [t'an-wen 袒免], the mourning period expires with the completion of the funeral.

Known as "the five mourning degrees" 五服, these are determined on the basis of the closeness of the kinship involved. When a person suffers at the hands of another who belongs to the same lineage, the penalty for the crime is determined according to the degree of mourning relationship between the parties. [The five categories of mourning

given in the present entry vary considerably from those
listed in the late Ch'ing Hui-tien, which are as follows:
(1) first degree [chan-ts'ui 斬衰], mourning period three
years; (2) second degree [tzu-ts'ui 齊衰], the period
varies from one year to five months to three months,
(3) third degree [ta-kung 大功], nine months; (4) fourth
degree [hsiao-kung 小功], five months; and (5) fifth
degree [ssu-ma 緦麻], three months. KHHT, 38:3b-4.
Traditional usage does not include t'an-wen in the five
mourning degrees.]

2182. TI T'ANG-CHIH 嫡堂姪 First-cousin nephews

That is, one's nephews who belong to the second mourning
degree [in relation to oneself].

[Cf. 2181.]

2183. YU-AI FENG-SHUI 有碍風水 Damaging the natural
environment [of a given locality]

Feng-shui ["geomancy"] refers to the [foretelling of] good
or bad fortune as determined by the natural enviornment.
This phrase means that the construction of a canal or the
building of a house [at a specific spot] will adversely affect
the people of the entire area.

2184. CHIEN-T'A T'IEN-HO 踐踏田禾 Trampling field crops

To allow one's own cattle and horses to trample and
destroy the crops in other people's fields.

2185. MU-FANG NIU YANG 牧放牛羊 Pasturing cattle and
sheep

To pasture cattle and sheep [or to let cattle and sheep
graze on the loose] so that they damage other people's
fields.

2186. TS'AI-CH'IAO KENG-CHUNG 採樵耕種 Wood cutting
and cultivation

To cut wood and cultivate the land illegally in the government [-owned or -occupied] hills and fields.

2187. TZ'U CHIH PEN-MO 詞之本末 The body and the conclusion of the argument

There is a beginning and an end to a litigation argument.

2188. CHUN CH'I LI CHU 准其離主 Permitted to leave his master

If in the purchase of a slave the laws are infracted, the magistrate will sentence [the slave] to leave his master and be set free.

2189. KU CH'U-JU JEN TSUI 故出入人罪 Purposely lighten or add to the penalty

It is a grave infraction of the law to purposely mete out a light sentence for a major crime, or to give heavy punishment for a minor one.

2190. AN-LIN CH'Ü-CH'U 按臨去處 The inspected area

Place(s) visited by a superior official in the course of his inspection.

2191. YEN-CH'A TS'AN-CHIU 嚴查參究 Strict investigation, impeachment, and examination

To investigate strictly the violations of the law, and to impeach and interrogate.

2192. PEI-CHU T'OU-YING 背主投營 Deserting one's master and enlisting in the army

A servitor deserting his master and clandestinely enlisting himself in the army.

2193. KAO-CHUANG PU SHOU-LI 告狀不受理 Rejection of a plaint

A common citizen brings an issue to court, but the presiding official rejects the complaint and refuses to try the case.

2194. I-FA CHÜEH-FA 依法決罰 To punish according to law

To pass sentence according to law, thus to punish a man's crime.

2195. CHÜ-CHUNG I KAI-CH'ING 舉重以概輕 To judge [a man] on the important crime, thus encompassing the lesser ones

When one person is tried [simultaneously] for several crimes, judgment should be made on the basis of the heaviest crime, and he is to be punished as the law prescribes. The lesser counts are dismissed.

2196. SHAN-JU HUANG-CH'ENG 擅入皇城 Unauthorized entry into the Forbidden City

To enter the imperial palace illegally.

2197. SHAN-YUNG PING-CHANG HSIANG-CH'I 擅用兵仗 响器 Unauthorized use of weapons and band instruments

To make illegal use of army weapons, and drums and bugles, in an altercation.

2198. SHEN-KAO SO-TSAI KUAN-YUAN 申告所在官員 Complaint against local officials

Subjects bringing to court a complaint against the official(s) of their own locality.

2199. CHIH-FU KO-SHAN- CHIN WEI-CH'IN CHE PING-HSING CHIN-CHIH 指腹割衫襟為親者並行禁止 Prohibition of marriage contracts made through prenatal promise and slashing of a gown

Among the ignorant people children are often betrothed to each other before they are actually born, as earnest of which the lapels of the [respective parents'] gowns are cut off and used as proof of the betrothal. Both practices are prohibited by law.

CHAPTER VI

THE BOARD OF WORKS

[[1]] River conservancy work. Nos. 2200-2283

2200. HO-KUNG 河工 River works; river conservancy; conservancy works

Work done on river channels and embankments.

2201. TA-HSIU CHUNG-HSIU HSIAO-HSIU 大修 中修 小修
Major repairs, secondary repairs, minor repairs

According to statute, river works should undergo major repairs once every ten years, secondary repairs once every five years, and minor repairs once every three years. Fixed sums are appropriated for these works, exclusive of [the emergency work needed] in case of a flood. [The late-Ch'ing Hui-tien lists only four major types of repair work: sui-hsiu 歲修 (annual repairs, cf. 2202), ch'iang-hsiu 搶修 (rush repairs, cf. 2206), ling-an 另案 (special work), and ta-kung 大工 (major project). KHHT, 60:2a-b.]

2202. SUI-HSIU 歲修 Annual repairs

In addition to the "three repairs" 三修 [see 2201], the incidental repair work done each year is called "annual repairs."

2203. LÜEH-HSIU 略修 Light repairs

Repairs done in a general way.

2204. PAO-HSIU 保修 Guaranteed repairs; to guarantee repairs

A deposition is to be written by the official [in charge of] the repair work [or construction], guaranteeing the work done for a certain period of years. If it deteriorates before the end of the period, the repair of the damage should be paid for by that official. [Cf. 2334.]

2205. WAN-HSIU 挽修 Emergency repairs

The critical point is about to be passed in a river work, and the repairing work is hastened in order to restore [the river to a safe state].

2206. CH'IANG-HSIU 搶修 Rush repairs

The critical point has been passed in a river work, and the repairing work is carried out with all possible effort and speed, in order to avoid [a flood].

2207. CH'UANG HU 創護 To initiate a protective device; to devise and protect

To initiate a new device for the protection of the river channel.

2208. HSIU-CHU 修築 To construct

To build.

2209. LEI-CH'I 壘砌 To build with masonry

To build a dyke with bricks and stones, because they are more durable.

2210. HSIU-CHÜN 修濬 To dredge

When a river channel has become silted and shallow, the silt is removed by dredging, so that [the water] can flow freely.

2211. TA-CHÜN CHUNG-CHÜN HSIAO-CHÜN 大濬中濬小濬 Major dredging, secondary dredging, minor dredging

The same as the "three repairs" [see 2201]. [KHHT, 60:2b, lists only two types of dredging: sui-chün 歲濬 (annual dredging) and ta-chün 大濬 (major dredging). The annual undertakings are financed by regular appropriations.]

2212. T'IAO CH'IEN 挑淺 Cleaning out a shallow [channel]

A silted river channel is deepened by scraping out [the silt].

2213. HSÜAN-HSIEH 宣洩 To flush out

The impeded flow of the river is made free again by having [the obstructions] flushed out.

2214. YÜEH-K'AI 越開 To by-pass

An obstructed river channel is by-passed [by the current?].

2215. HSIA-SAO 下埽 Lower embankment

An additional earthen embankment built below the river dyke is known as the "lower embankment."

2216. CHIA-PANG 加幫 Extra bulwark

Extra layers of reeds, wood, and stones added onto the sides of a river dyke, in order to strengthen it further.

2217. KUO-T'OU 裹頭 Source enclosure

A dyke built around the source of a river is called a "source enclosure."

2218. TUNG-KUNG 動工 To begin work

To commence work [on construction or repairs].

2219. KUNG-CHÜN 工竣 Work completed

The [construction or repair] work has been finished.

2220. PI HUNG 閉泓 Closure of channel

To stop (the flow of) the water at the source, in order to facilitate work [in the river].

2221. HO LUNG-MEN 合龍門 Closing the "dragon's gate"

In closing a breach, a gap called the "dragon's gate" is left in it. When work is finished this gap also is closed, and this is known as "closing the dragon's gate." [Cf. 2429.]

2222. HSIANG-TIEN YEN-CH'IH 廂墊鴈翅 Wing-shaped side embankments

To protect the river banks, earthen mounds in the shape of [spread] wild goose wings are built along both sides of the river.

2223. KU-CHI 估計 To estimate

To estimate the sum of money needed for a river works undertaking.

2224. LÜEH-KU 略估 Rough estimate

To estimate the approximate sum.

2225. CHÜ-KU 據估 According to the estimate

To proceed on the basis of the sums estimated by the officials.

2226. TSOU-HSIAO 奏銷 Rendering a financial account

To memorialize on the sums of money spent, and close the matter.

2227. PAO-HSIAO 報銷 Making a financial report

To report to the Board [of Works] the sums of money spent.

2228. CHIEH-SHENG 節省 Sum(s) saved

The money saved through economizing in the offices.

2229. HAI CHIEN 核減 Reduced upon deliberation

The Board [of Works] examines and reduces the excessive amounts in expenditures.

2230. FOU-TO 浮多 Excessive expenditures

Too much money is being spent on fraudulently reported expenditures [or padded accounts].

2231. FOU-MAO 浮冒 Dishonest accounting

To make a fraudulent report on expenses, and claim to have spent such sums.

2232. YU- CHIEN WU-FOU 有減無浮 Only reduction and no increase permitted

In making an estimate of the amounts to be expended, only reductions and no increases [over previous estimates?] are to be permitted .

Works

2233. FU-HAI WU I 覆核無異   No discrepancy is found upon auditing

No discrepancies [or errors] have been found in a financial report when it is audited by the Board [of Works].

2234. HSÜ-SHU K'AI-PAO 虛數開報 Making a padded account

The sums reported in a financial account as having been spent are found to be false and untrue.

2235. NO-CH'IEN PU-HOU 挪前補後 To shift funds around

To shift a surplus sum of money under item A to item B, in order to make up for a deficiency in the latter.

2236. LAO TI 老堤 Old dykes; existing dykes

The dykes that have existed since [or were built in] previous years.

2237. SHIH TI 石堤 Stone dyke

A dyke that is built of stones.

2238. T'U TI 土堤 Earthen dyke

A dyke that is built of earth.

2239. LÜ TI 縷堤 Slim dyke

A narrow, small dyke.

2240. YÜEH TI 越堤 Spanning dyke

A dyke that spans [the river] to reach the opposite bank.

2241. KENG TI 埂堤 Path-dyke

To make earthen paths serve as dykes.

2242. YÜEH PA 越壩 A spanning dam or weir

A large, thick dyke is called a dam [or weir]. The present term denotes a large dam that spans [the river] and reaches to the opposite bank.

2243. LUNG-MEN TA PA 龍門大壩 The large dragon's gate dam

In repairing a breach along the river, future breaching is prevented with the construction of a large dam at the spot where the "dragon's (gate)" gap is closed [cf. 2221]; this is known as the "large dragon's gate dam."

2244. YAO TI 遙堤 Distant dyke

A dyke built at some distance from the river.

2245. TA TUN 大墩 Great mounds

Earth is piled up into mounds along the river bank, to be used as material in repair or construction work [on dykes].

2246. PA-T'AI 壩臺 Dam terrace or tower

High terraces [or towers] for look-out are built on the dams.

2247. LAN-HO PA 攔河壩 Mid-channel dam

A large dam that stands athwart the river channel.

2248. KUN-SHUI PA 滾水壩 Diversion dam

To build a dam alongside the fields, so that it will contain the water [of a flood] and guide its flow into the river.

2249. T'IAO-SHUI PA 挑水壩 Deflection dam

A large dam that divides the powerful flow of the river.

2250. CHIEN-SHUI PA 減水壩 Detention dam

A large dam that cuts down the force of the river's flow.

2251. YIN-HO 引河 Diversion channel

A tributary that leads the water off in a given direction.

2252. YÜEH-HO 越河 Alluvial river

A large river that flows across a plain.

2253. HAN-TUNG 涵洞 Reservoir; tank

A water storage basin.

2254. CH'ING-K'OU 清口 Sluice gate [?]

The point where clear water flows in and out [of a reservoir?].

2255. YÜN-K'OU運口 Canal junction; transport port

A port where transport boats [or canal traffic運船] come and go. [A few of the terms in the present section may be found in the maps in D. Gandar, Le Canal Impérial: Etude Historique et Descriptive (Shanghai, 1894). In the case of yün-k'ou (literally, "canal entrance"), the term appears as the designation for the junction of the Yangtse and the Grand Canal in ibid. , Plate XII; it is also used to indicate the spot where Hung-tse Lake joins the Grand Canal, in Plates XIV, XV, and XVI.]

2256. LIU SAO 柳埽 Willow fence

A low fence woven of willow branches, erected to hold back the water.

2257. LUNG-WEI SAO龍尾埽 Dragon-tail dyke

A long, narrow dyke that twists and turns like a dragon's tail.

2258. T'U-NIU SAO 土牛埽 Earthen-ox dyke

An "earthen ox" is a mound of earth. The present term refers to a dyke constructed of such earthen mounds.

2259. SHA-CHOU 沙洲 Sandbar; shoal

A strip of sand located in the middle of the river that was formed as a result of silting is called a "sandbar" or "shoal. "

2260. T'AN-SHA 灘沙 Sandy beach

A strip of sand along the bank of the river that has resulted from silting is called a "sandy beach. "

2261. LIEN-YÜEH連越 To link, to be adjacent across [a river]

To link together by water, or to be adjacent by being on the opposite banks of the same river.

2262. T'AN-CHIA 灘價 Beach tax [literally, beach price]

The amount of tax paid on reeds grown on the sandy beaches.

2263. T'AN CHIA 攤價 Allocated costs

(*T'an 攤 "allocate" is given as t'an 灘 "beach" in the Manchu-Chinese editions.)

The costs for river works are estimated in terms of the materials and labor needed, and are levied from the people by allocation.

2264. FENG SAO 風埽 Windbreak dyke

A dyke that serves as protection against the wind.

2265. CHI-TSUI SAO 磯觜埽 Rock point dyke

A dyke built at the approach to a rock in mid-channel.

2266. YÜ-TSUI SAO 淤觜埽 Sand point dyke

A dyke built at the approach to a sandbar in the river.

2267. CHIEN-SHIH TI-MIEN 堅實地面 Firm earth

Where the earth is thick and firm, and the soil solid.

2268. TI-SHIH KAO WA 地勢高窪 High or low terrain

To be situated either on high ground or on lowland.

2269. KUNG-LIAO 工料 Labor and materials

The costs of wages and materials.

2270. T'U-FANG 土方 Cube of earth

A cubic foot of earth. ["A cube 方 of earth measures one chang (10 Chinese feet or ch'ih) long by one chang wide by one ch'ih high. " KHHT, 60:3.]

2271. CH'AI-LIAO 柴寮 Lumber storage

The place where lumber or wood is stored.

2272. HUI-LIAO 灰寮 Lime storage

The place where lime is stored.

Works

2273. SHENG-CH'ANG 繩廠 Rope factory

Workshops where hemp ropes are manufactured.

2274. TANG-TS'AO 蕩草 Marsh grass

Grass produced in reedy marshes.

2275. WEI-CH'AI 尾柴 Terminal lumber

The wood used to spike the terminal point of a dyke
is called the "terminal lumber."

2276. CHIN-SHU 斤數 Number of catties

The materials used in the construction of a river dyke,
stated in terms of catties.

2277. CHUANG CHÜEH 椿橛 Stakes, pegs

The wooden pegs used in dyke construction; the large
ones are called stakes or piles, and the small ones pegs.

2278. HSIU-KUO TI-KUNG 修過堤工 Dyke work already done

New dyke construction that has been completed.

2279. TS'AI-MAI WU-LIAO 採買物料 To purchase materials

To shop for and purchase materials for river works.

2280. HSIN CHIU WU-LIAO 新舊物料 New and old materials

Same as above [2279]; and below [2281].

2281. HSIA-KUO TI-KUNG 下過堤工 Dismantled dykes

Materials that have already been dismantled from
old dykes.

2282. HSIEN-YIN TS'AI-MAI 現銀採買 Cash purchase

To buy materials with ready money that was issued by
a government treasury.

2283. K'UEI-TUAN CHIA-CHIH 虧短價值 Short payment
on the cost

The costs of construction materials are withheld and not
paid in full by the person(s) in charge of the project.

[[2]] Floods and emergency work. Nos. 2284-2346

2284. T'AO-HUA SHUI 桃花水 Spring floods [literally, "peach blossom waters"]

Also known as peach [blossom] floods. Rivers usually rise in the second month [ca. early March to early April] when the peach trees are in bloom, and special precautions must be taken [against floods].

2285. FU-HSÜN 伏汛 Summer floods

The hot summer season is a time when rivers will rise.

2286. CH'IU-HSÜN 秋汛 Autumn floods

Rivers also rise around the time of the moon festival in the eighth month [ca. mid-September]. Together with the two previous floods [2284, 2285], they are known as the "three flood periods" 三汛.

[Cf. 2449.]

2287. FU CH'IU SHUI-FA 伏秋水發 High water in Summer-autumn

End of summer and beginning of autumn: the season when the level of the rivers is on the rise.

2288. PO-T'AO 波濤 Waves and billows

When rivers are in flood, the water will roll up in great waves just like the sea.

2289. SUI CHANG SUI HSIAO 隨長隨消 Subsides as soon as it rises

Although the sea rises very quickly [i. e., in tides?], it also subsides quickly, therefore will not cause a catastrophe.

2290. CHIAO-CHANG 交漲 Simultaneous [or joint] flooding

Both the Yellow River and the Grand Canal are in flood at the same time.

2291. MAN-LIU 漫流 Overflowing

The river has risen to a high point where it overflows the dykes.

2292. TING-CH'UNG 頂衝 Sweeping straight down

The (flooded) river roars down straight at [the dykes, etc.].

2293. CH'UNG-CHÜEH 衝決 Breached by flood

The floodwaters break the dyke and continue to flow onward.

2294. CH'UNG-SHUA 衝刷 Scoured by flood

The water of a flooded river scouring the bottom of the channel as if to sweep it completely bare.

2295. SHUA HUANG 刷黄 Scouring the Yellow River

The [floodwaters] sweeping down and scouring the Yellow River.

2296. CH'ING-CH'I 傾圯 Collapsing; about to collapse

The collapse of a river dyke.

2297. I-HSIEH 欹斜 Inclining at an angle

A river dyke being battered by water into a leaning position.

2298. CHUNG-HSÜAN 鐘懸 Hanging like a bell

(*According to the Manchu text, chung 鐘 "bell" should read hu 壺 "a jar.")

A river dyke has been destroyed by flood with only one section remaining, looking like a bell suspended all by itself.

2299. T'AN-T'A 坍塌 To collapse

A river dyke is damaged and collapses.

2300. CHIH-HSIEN 蟄陷 Sinking in

A river dyke sinks into the ground, like an insect

proceeding to its place of hibernation. [The reference to an insect here is a very unusual figure of speech. 蟄 is possibly an error for tien 墊 , in which case the present phrase will simply mean "to settle and sink in."]

2301. TUAN LIU 斷流 To halt the stream

To stop the flow of the river in its course.

2302. YÜ-TSU 淤阻 Siltation

The silting of a river channel by mud, thus making it shallow.

2303. SHUI HSIAO 水消 The water recedes

The river water subsides and recedes.

2304. SHUI HO 水涸 The water dries up

The river has dried up.

2305. TA-LIU TING-CH'UNG 大溜頂衝 Great rollers sweeping straight down

A flooded river forms long rollers and sweeps down straight ahead--the breaching of the dykes is imminent.

2306. CHIANG-K'OU HENG-CHANG 江口橫漲 Backing up of a risen river

Floodwaters at the mouth of a river backing up into the main channel.

2307. TING-CH'UNG YÜN-K'OU 頂衝運口 Flooding straight into the Canal

The [flooded] river rushing straight into the channel of the [Grand] Canal.

2308. WANG-YANG TSE-KUO 汪洋澤國 A great watery expanse

The flooded river has created a vast watery expanse, and turned dry land into a sea.

2309. HAI-HSIAO CH'AO-YUNG 海嘯潮涌 The onrush of a tidal wave

A sudden onrush of the tide is known as a "tidal wave."

2310. TZU PI KUA-K'OU 自必掛口 Naturally will merge at the juncture

Although the river is flooded, the water will not rise exceedingly high, and will flow into [a main river or lake?] at its mouth; this is a natural principle of things. [The character sui 遂 "thereupon" is apparently a misprint for sui 雖 "although."]

2311. CHIEN-LING ERH HSIA 建領而下 Cascading down

The river flowing by stages from a high point downward, presenting a stair-like pattern similar to that of roof tiles [laid one upon another].

2312. HSÜ FU K'UNG-CHI 需夫孔亟 Urgently in need of laborers

The river has made a breach [in the dyke], and laborers are most urgently needed for stopping the breach and doing repair work.

2313. JEN-LI NAN-CHENG 人力難爭 Beyond human ability to prevent

The flood-wrought devastation is a calamity of nature which human efforts cannot prevent.

2314. CHIANG-KUNG SUI FU YIN 江工歲夫銀 Annual labor costs

The money needed each year for wages and food costs paid to laborers working on river conservancy works.

2315. SHANG-PAN-CHIEH TAO-T'A 上半截倒塌 The upper portion [or section] has collapsed

The upper portion of a river dyke has collapsed.

2316. SHANG-WU-TS'ENG SHIH-KUNG 上五層石工 Masonry for the five upper layers

The five upper layers of a river dyke ought to be constructed of stone.

2317. YING HSIA SHIH-KUNG I-TUAN 應下石工一段
Let a [given] section be of masonry

A certain section of a river dyke occupies a very critical
spot, and ought to be constructed of stone.

2318. KEN-CHIAO CHÜ I FOU-TUNG 根腳俱已浮動
The foundations are loose and shaky

The foundations of a river dyke have become loose and
are no longer firm.

2319. LIANG-T'OU HSI-CHIEH CHANG-LIEH 兩頭悉皆漲
裂 Both ends have burst

Both ends of a river dyke are breached by water and have
burst open.

2320. CHAO TS'AO-KUEI CHIA-CHIH HSIAO-SUAN 照漕規
價值銷算 The accounts are to be rendered according
to the regulations governing grain transport

The accounting for all money spent for river works is to
be done according to the regulations and statutes governing
grain transport.

2321. T'A-HSIEH TAO-TI WU-SHIH-YÜ CHANG 塌卸到底
五十餘丈 Has collapsed to the bottom for over five
hundred feet

That is, for such a distance a river dyke has collapsed and
fallen from top to bottom.

2322. I-TAI SHIH-KUNG 一帶石工 A stretch consisting of
masonry

The dyke from point A to point B is constructed entirely
of stone.

2323. SSU-WANG MI-MAN HAO-HAO WU-YA 四望瀰漫
浩浩無涯 A watery panorama vast and boundless

The flood is extensive. No land is in sight in any
direction and [the water] appears to be boundless.

2324. CHIAO-KUNG CHIH SHIH YU-JU LEI-NUAN 交攻之
勢猶如纍卵 A joint onslaught of [the floods] makes

the situation precarious [literally, like piling eggs one upon another]

With the flood waters of both the Yellow River and the Grand Canal rising and reaching the dykes simultaneously, the latter are about to be breached, making the situation very dangerous.

2325. HO-SHUI CH'IEN-HO CH'UAN CHIH NAN-CH'IEN 河水 淺涸船滯難前 The progress of boats is being delayed by the shallowness of the river

The water in the river has fallen so low that boats are held up and cannot make progress.

2326. FOU-SHA I CH'IEN TSOU-SHUI I CH'UNG 浮沙易淺 驟水易衝 Shifting sand tends to decrease the depth [of a river], while a sudden onrush of water easily breaches [a dyke]

When there is loose sand in the river bed the current is liable to become shallow; and when the water rises suddenly in the river it will easily breach the dykes.

2327. HUANG-LIU PIEN-CH'IEN CHIH-SHE TI-KEN 黃流 變遷直射堤根 The Yellow River, changing its course, charges straight at the base of the dykes

The Yellow River has suddenly changed its course, rushing straight into the Grand Canal and beating against the base of the dykes. A breach is imminent.

2328. CH'UNG-SHAN T'AN-HSIEH WEI-HSIEN CHIH-CHI 衝汕 坍卸危險至極 [A dyke is] extremely dangerously battered and about to collapse

Having been battered by [flood] waters, a river dyke is about to collapse; the situation is extremely dangerous.

2329. LING CHU YUEH-PA HAN-YÜ HU-SHUI 另築越壩 捍禦湖水 Building another spanning dam to fend off the lake water

The water in the lake has risen and threatens to back out into the river. Another dam spanning the river should be built to fend off the flood.

2330. CHU-KUO YUEH-PA CH'AI-CH'I CHIU-CHUANG 築過
越壩 拆起舊椿 A spanning dam has been built and
the old stakes are pulled up

As the [new] spanning dam has been constructed, the
old wooden stakes ought to be pulled up and removed.

2331. SO-YUNG CHUANG-CHÜEH HSI I-MU SSU-CHIEH 所用椿
橛係一木四截 The stakes and pegs used are
quarter-lengths of wood

The stakes and pegs used in the dyke construction are
quarter-lengths of wood [or lumber].

2332. HUO-YEN FEI-T'ENG CH'ING CH'ENG HUI-CHIN 火焰
飛騰頃成灰燼 Within a moment [the dyke] was
burnt to ashes in the soaring flames

A very fierce fire has reduced the dyke to ashes within
a few moments.

2333. CHIU-SAO TIEN-HSIU CHIA-T'AO CH'ENG PU JUNG-I
舊埽墊朽加套誠不容已 Circumstances
dictate the speedy shoring up and refacing of old dykes

All the dykes and embankments are old. They should be
inspected for decayed spots, which are to be repaired with
wood and stones, and an extra facing is to be added to the
surface. The matter is urgent and allows of no delay.

2334. TZU-HSING KU-MU CHUANG-SHOU CHIA-CH'I SHIH
I-TS'ENG 自行催募椿手加砌石一層
To hire dyke laborers privately, and add one more layer
of stone

A dyke is in disrepair. The official in charge of river
works [ho-kuan 河官] will at his own expense hire dyke
laborers [literally, stake drivers 釘椿人] and have an
additional [layer] of stone slabs paved on to the old dyke.
[Cf. 2204.]

2335. CHUAN-CH'ENG CH'UNG-T'A CHIN-TS'UN TUAN-CH'ENG
JO-KAN 磚城衝塌僅存斷城若干 All that
remain of the toppled brick city walls are only so many
broken ruins

(*In the Manchu-Chinese editions the words jo-kan 若
干 "so many" or "a certain number of" follow t'a 塌
"toppled. ")

The river has burst its dykes, and destroyed the walls
of the cities [in the path of the flood]. All that remain are
so many broken walls.

2336. PI-CHIN CH'ENG-CH'IH YÜN-TAO CHIN-SHIH I-HSIEN
    T'U-TI 逼近城池運道僅恃一綫土堤
    [The river] is close to the city and the Canal, the only
    protection [against it] being a narrow earthen dyke

    The river at a given locality is very close to a certain
    city, and it is not far from the canal traffic. The only
    protection [against floods] is an earthen dyke. The
    situation is highly precarious.

2337. WAI TSE HUANG-LIU TING-CH'UNG NEI TSE T'ING-LAO
    MI-MAN 外則黃流頂衝内則停潦瀰漫
    A rampaging Yellow River without, and an accumulation
    of excess water within

    Beyond the dykes bordering the Grand Canal the flooded
    Yellow River is rushing onward, while within the Canal
    channel there is a large accumulation of rain water: the
    catastrophe of dyke breaching and of floods can be expected
    shortly.

2338. CH'ING-K'OU CH'ING-SHUI SHEN-TA 清口清水甚
    大 Large volume of clear water at Ch'ing-k'ou

    A very large body of clear water is joining the flow at the
    junction with a clear-water river. [Ch'ing-k'ou 清口
    and Ch'ing-chiang 清江 in 2338 and 2339 are interpreted in
    the text as "clear-water junction" and "clear-water river, "
    respectively. While this is literally correct, the two
    phrases might still have a more specific frame of reference
    that can be properly understood only when these terms are
    interpreted as a place name, i.e., Ch'ing-k'ou (or Ch'ing-
    chiang-k'ou, also Ch'ing-chiang-p'u), near Huai-yin 淮
    陰 in northern Kiangsu, where up to 1856 the Yellow
    River joined the River Huai and followed the course of the

latter to the sea. These two entries therefore refer to conditions before 1856, when the Yellow River once more changed its course, and thus ceased to be a matter for concern at Ch'ing-k'ou. See under Ch'ing-k'ou, Huai-ho, and Huang-ho kai-tao 黃河改道 in Tz'u-hai; and plates XIV, XV, XVI in Gandar, Le Canal Impérial: Etude Historique et Descriptive.]

2339. TI HUANG YU-YÜ 敵黃有餘 More than adequate to counter the Yellow River with

The water from the clear-water river is more than sufficient to match [or fend off] the Yellow River current. [See note under 2338.]

2340. CHÜEH-WU TAO-KUAN 絕無倒灌 There is absolutely no backwashing

The river flows smoothly, and there should be no danger of backwashing [into a canal, a lake, or another river, etc.].

2341. CHI-YU SAO-SHUA CH'UNG-SHE CHIH HUAN 既有掃刷衝射之患. Not only is there the harm of [the water] sweeping, scouring, and battering...

(*Sao-shua 掃刷 or "sweeping and scouring [the channel]" are given as sao-k'ua 掃塝 "to sweep and topple" in the Manchu-Chinese editions.)

There are already four harms [caused by flood water]: sweeping, scouring, battering, and charging [against the dykes].

2342. YU-YU TAO-TS'UI YÜ-CHI CHIH YÜ 又有倒攉淤激之虞 ...but there is also the danger of the [dykes] collapsing and the [channel] silting up

Furthermore, there is the danger of [a river] bringing about the collapse of dykes and the silting of the channel, thus to cause breaches by the backwashing of the water.

2343. HU-CH'ENG TA-TI P'ING-JIH NENG HSIU-CHU KAO CHIEN HO-CHIH JU-TZ'U LUN-MO 護城大堤平日能修築高堅何至如此淪没 If only the great protective dykes were built high and sturdy in normal times, there would not have been such inundations (now)

Had the large dykes, erected for the protection of [these] cities, been constantly kept in good repair, and kept high and sturdy in normal times, then the inundations and drownings of people today would not have taken place.

2344. SO-CHU TI-KUNG YU I-CH'U HANG-O PU-CHIEN CH'ENG-SHUI CHI LOU 所築堤工有一處夯硪不堅 盛水即漏 On a dyke one single spot of earth not solidly tamped will cause the dyke to leak

To "tamp" the earth means to pound the earth and stones in building a dyke, so as to make it hard and firm. If any spot in a dyke is not tamped firmly, the dyke will leak and cannot hold back the water.

2345. PI-HSÜ T'IEN SAO HSIANG-HU MU FU PANG-CHU FANG K'O I-TZU HAN-YÜ 必須添埽廂護募夫幫築 方可以資捍禦 In order to avoid disaster, auxiliary embankments must be built, and laborers recruited to help construct them

If a dyke is found to be weak, additional earthen embankments must be built along its side to protect it. In order to avert the disaster of a flood, laborers must be recruited to help complete the construction soon.

2346. KUNG-CH'ENG CHIN-CHI TANG-CH'AI YUAN-YÜN PU-CHI SHIH-I CHIU-CHIN KOU-YUNG WEI-CH'AI 工程緊急、 蕩柴遠運不及是以就近購用尾柴 The construction is too urgent to await the shipment of marsh grass and wood from a distance, therefore terminal lumber has been bought from sources at hand

While the dyke work is very urgent, the place is far from any reedy marsh, making it difficult to obtain the grass and wood. For expediency it has been decided that the coarse terminal wood used to strengthen the ends of dykes [2275] should be bought locally, thus meeting the need.

[[3]] The construction of buildings. Nos. 2347-2375

2347. SHANG-LIANG 上樑 To place the beams in position

In building a house, the great cross beams are now placed in position.

2348. SHU-CHU 竪柱 To erect the posts [or pillars]

The wooden pillars are erected.

2349. MA-SANG 碼磉 To build the pillar bases

Constructing the bases for the pillars.

2350. FAN-TSAO 番造 To remodel

(*Tsao 造 "to construct" is given as chiu 究 "to examine" in the Manchu-Chinese editions--probably a misprint for 瓦.)

To alter a building.

2351. KUAN-CHIANG 灌漿 To seal with liquid mortar

To pour a lime and water mixture into the crevices between roof tiles as a binder, so as to keep them firmly [in place].

2352. KOU-MIN 勾抿 Plastering

To paint a wall with lime.

2353. TA P'ENG TSU-YIN 搭蓬租銀 [Ground] rent for sheds

Where workmen have gathered, money must be issued to rent land from the local people, there to erect sheds where the workers are to be quartered.

2354. SSU-CHIH 四至 The four boundaries

The four boundaries of a site [or a plot of land].

2355. SAN-TSO-TUNG MENG 三座洞門 Triple-arch gate

The gates of the [imperial] palace are all constructed in the design of three arched doorways standing one next to another.

2356. TOU-KUNG HSIEH-SHAN 斗拱斜山 Brackets, sloping walls [literally, sloping hills]

The roof ridge of a principal palace is carved in the

design of stars and is called the "bracket." The walls
flanking the palace are shaped to incline outward and
downward, and are termed "sloping walls" [or literally,
"sloping hills"]. [Tou-kung, usually written 斗栱 or
枓栱 , is the bracket placed between the top of a pillar
and the beam to spread the weight of the roof. It is an
old Chinese architectural device dating from the Chou
period, and has nothing to do with carved roof ridges.
See Ito Chuta 伊東忠太 , Chung-kuo chien-chu shih
(History of Chinese architecture), tr. Ch'en Ch'ing-ch'uan
(Shanghai, 1937), pp. 132-134, 137.]

2357. CHENG-TIEN 正殿 Principal palace

The principal hall of a palace.

2358. HSIANG-TIEN 香殿 Incense hall

A palace for the burning of incense and the worship of
the deities.

2359. TI-CHI 地基 The site

The site chosen to build a palace on.

2360. KAI CHI 改基 Change of site

The site first decided upon being unsuitable, a change is
made and another one is chosen.

2361. P'U-MIEN LIN-CHIEH FANG 舖面臨街房 Shop fronts,
houses facing the street

Shops and houses on downtown streets.

2362. P'U-HU 舖戶 A shop; store

A house of business.

2363. TSO-KUAN 作官 Workshop foreman

The head of [a group of] artisans; or the head of a
crafts workshop.

2364. YEN-LIAO 顏料 Paints

The plaster and coloring used to paint houses.

2365. CH'AO-TSAO CHIH-CHANG 抄造紙張 The manufacture of paper; paper-making

To make paper; commonly called the "lifting of paper" 抄紙.

2366. TZU-CH'Ü FAN-LAN 咨取泛濫 Wasteful requisitioning

"Wasteful" means being excessive in amount. The official in charge of construction has asked for excessive amounts of materials in his requisitions.

2367. HUANG-HUA CHU 黃花竹 Yellow spotted bamboo

A bamboo that is yellow and displays a spotted pattern.

2368. HSÜN-CHU 熏竹 Smoked bamboo

A bamboo that has been turned into a dark color through a smoking process.

2369. T'AO CHIN 淘金 Gold washing

To wash for placer gold.

2370. TS'AI MU 採木 Purchase of lumber

To buy lumber.

2371. TS'AO-MU 漕木 Grain boat lumber

The lumber used in constructing the grain transport boats.

2372. T'UNG-P'I KAO 桐皮槁 T'ung-bark fir

Fir logs that are slender and long are known as slim firs [shan-kao 杉槁]; of these, the best display a bark as fine-grained as that of the t'ung tree [Aleurites cordata], hence the present name.

2373. CHIA-MU 架木 Frame lumber

The lumber used in building the framework of a house.

2374. T'UNG-SHAO CHIA-MU 通梢架木 Through-length frame lumber

A long piece of lumber that reaches from the ground to the top [of the framework].

2375. CH'ANG-TUAN CHIA-MU 長短架木 Uneven-length frame lumber

The framework [of a house] is constructed by lashing together wood of various lengths.

[[4]] Ships, sailors, and related labor force. Nos. 2376-2422

2376. CHAN-CH'UAN 戰船 Warship

Naval boats used in warfare.

2377. SHUI-CHÜ 水艍 Small watercraft

A sampan.

2378. KAN-TSENG 趕䑪 Pursuer

A small, fast boat.

2379. LI-CH'UAN 犁船 Spiked boat

A boat with spikes affixed to its bow.

2380. CHÜN-CH'UAN 軍船 Troop boat

A boat used to transport troops.

2381. SHAO-CH'UAN 哨船 Patrol boat

A boat used for patrolling.

2382. CH'IEN-CH'UAN 淺船 Flat boat

A flat-bottomed boat for plying in shallow waters.

2383. HUNG TSO-CH'UAN 紅座船 Red boat

A red-painted boat used by officials.

2384. HUNG PO-CH'UAN 紅剝船 Red tender

Government boat used to transfer tribute grain [from the big transport boats to the shore]; it is also painted red.

The above two categories of boats are commonly referred to as man-chiang hung 滿江紅 "a riverful of red."

2385. CHÜN LIU-CH'UAN 濬柳船 Willow dredging boat

A boat built of willow wood; it is used to dredge the rivers.

2386. TU-CH'UAN 渡船 Ferry boat

A boat for ferrying passengers.

2387. TU-MA CH'UAN 渡馬船 Horse-ferry boat

A boat used specially to ferry horses and carriages.

2388. HUA-CHIANG TU-CH'UAN 划槳渡船 Multi-oared ferry boat

A high speed ferry boat powered by several oarsmen.

2389. CHIANG-CHI HUNG-CH'UAN 江濟紅船 Red ferry boat

A red boat [2383] that is used in ferrying.

2390. KUNG-CHÜ 貢具 Tribute [boat] furnishings

Furnishings needed in a boat. [Cf. 818.]

2391. TO 舵 Rudder

The rudder of a vessel.

2392. P'ENG-TS'O 蓬錯 Sail winch

The iron winch used to pull the sails.

2393. CHIANG LU 槳櫓 The oar and the scull

The oar and the scull which are used to move the boat along.

2394. KAO-TZU 篙子 The pole

The pole used for punting a boat.

2395. T'AN-SHENG 簹繩 Mooring rope

The rope used for tying up a boat [at the mooring].

2396. HAO-PAN 號板 Cabin planks; the deck

The [floor or wall] planks of a boat cabin.

2397. PU HSIU 補修 Mending and repairing

To repair and mend boats.

2398. CH'E-TSAO 拆造 To remodel; to dismantle and reconstruct

    [Interpretations are missing from entries 2398-2401.]

2399. SHUI-MIEN T'AN-LIANG 水面探量 Survey and sounding of water from the surface

    [See note in 2398.]

2400. CH'UAN-CHIA 船家 Boat master; captain

    [See note in 2398.]

2401. SHUI-SHOU 水手 Sailor

    [See note in 2398.]

2402. CH'IEN-FU 縴夫 Boat puller; tracker

    Laborers who pull boats [along the shore].

2403. TO-KUNG 舵公 Helmsman

    The man who takes charge of the tiller.

2404. LAN-T'OU 攔頭 Fore-guard

    The man on watch at the fore deck or bow of a boat.

2405. LIU-FU 溜夫 Current watcher

    The man who keeps check on the force of the current.

2406. T'I-LIU 提溜 Current checker

    Same as above [2405].

2407. CH'IEN-FU 淺夫 Dredge-man; dredger

    A man who does dredging work.

2408. SHUI-FU 水夫 Boatman

    Same as sailor [2401].

2409. KENG-FU 更夫 Night watchman

    The man in charge of the night watchers on board a boat.

2410. TU-T'OU 渡頭 Ferry master; [ferry]

    The head man in charge at a ferry crossing.

2411. K'ANG-FU 摃夫 Bearer

A laborer who bears and carries the baggage.

2412. HANG-FU 夯夫 Pile-driver

Laborer who drives the piles. [...]

2413. CH'ANG-FU 長夫 Long-distance labor duty

A laborer who serves the entire distance [of the transport service] without changes en route. [See 659, 1583.]

2414. TUAN-FU 短夫 Short distance [or relay] labor duty

Laborers who are changed at every station. [See 659, 1584.]

2415. CHUANG-FU 壯夫 Able-bodied laborer

A laborer in the prime of life.

2416. MA-FU 馬夫 Groom

(*Ma 馬 "horse" is given as k'ua 骒 "equestrian" in the Manchu-Chinese editions.)

A laborer who tends the horses.

2417. CHIAO-FU 轎夫 Chair bearer

A laborer who bears the sedan-chair.

2418. YAO-FU 徭夫 Laborer on duty

A civilian laborer who is serving on government duty.

2419. CH'ANG-CHIEH K'UAI-SHOU 長接快手 A runner serving as long distance greeter

A k'uai-shou 快手 "dexterous hands" is a type of government runner, who is dispatched to greet official visitors on the way.

2420. JEN-FU HSÜAN CHIEH HSÜAN T'AO 人夫旋解旋逃 Laborer(s) escaping en route [from government duty]

A laborer who has been assigned government service escapes on the way.

2421. **LAO-CH'IEN P'U-FU** 撈淺舖夫 Dredgers at a station

In each section of a river-works project a station house is provided as lodging for the dredgers, who clear the channel of sand when the water is low.

2422. **TO-LIAO TOU-TING [sic] PING-TING** 舵瞭斗艇兵丁 Tiller guard and look-out soldiers

(*Ting 艇 "skiff" is given as wei 桅 "mast" in the annotated edition.)

Soldiers who guard the tiller of the boat, and those who serve as look-outs in the crow's-nest.

[[5]] Further river engineering terms. Nos. 2423-2474

2423. **CH'IN-CHAN CHIEH-TAO** 侵佔街道 Encroaching on the street

Private houses and shop buildings encroaching on the right-of-way of public streets.

2424. **TSO-CHIEN CHIEH-TAO** 作踐街道 To deface the street

Making a public street dirty.

2425. **CHÜEH-CH'ENG K'ENG-K'AN** 掘成坑坎 To dig holes into [the street]

The inhabitants obtain earth by digging into the street, thus making it uneven.

2426. **YÜ-SAI KOU-CH'Ü** 淤塞溝渠 Silting of ditches

Drainage ditches being silted with earth or dirt, so that water cannot flow through.

2427. **SHUI-KOU LANG-WO** 水溝浪窩 Drainage ditch; wave-formed eddies

A ditch for the drainage of water; and eddies of sand that have been formed by the action of waves.

2428. **SHAN-SUN T'AN-T'A** 汕損坍塌 Collapsing due to water damage

The base of a dyke is washed over and battered by water, which thus causes the dyke to collapse.

2429. CHIN-LIU K'OU-MEN 僅留口門　Leaving only [one] gap

In repairing a breach, only one gap or sluice gate is left open for the runoff of water.

[Cf. 2221.]

2430. TS'ENG-TS'ENG HANG O 層層夯硪 To tamp and roll layer by layer

To "tamp" means to pound down the earth with a wooden stake; and to "roll," to press down the earth with a stone roller. In building a dyke the earth is tamped and rolled down layer after layer, so as to achieve solidness and strength.

2431. TI-TING TOU-T'AN [sic] 堤頂陡坦　Dyke-top wall

(*T'an 坦 "level" is given as yuan 垣 "wall" in the annotated edition.)

A high wall erected on the top of a river dyke.

2432. HSING-O I-PIEN 行硪一遍　Rolled once

To roll over an entire [section or area] once.

2433. HANG-CH'U SAN-PIEN 夯杵三遍　Tamped down three times

To tamp down the earth three times.

2434. CHI SHA-PA T'IAO-CHÜN 即煞壩挑濬 Immediately to dam up and dredge

When silting has made a river channel shallow, a dam is to be erected to stop the flow of water, so that the river bed can be dredged.

2435. I-CHANG CHIH SHUI 異漲之水　Extraordinarily high water

Water that has risen to an unusually high level.

2436. CHIANG-CH'AO 江潮 River tide, [tidal basin?]

Tidal water of a river.

2437. CH'Ü-CH'U T'IAO-WA SHIH CHIH 曲處挑挖 使直
To straighten a twisting [channel] by digging

Where the course of the river twists and bends, it is
dug up so that [the channel] becomes level and straight.

2438. P'IAO-MO CHI-SUI 漂没擊碎 Wrecked and lost

A boat encounters a storm on its voyage, is damaged
and made adrift.

2439. HUAI-SHUI TUNG-HSIA 淮水東下 Eastward flows the
Huai

The water of the Huai River flows down toward the east.

2440. TAO-KUAN 倒灌 To back up; a back flow or backwash

Water flowing up against the current.

2441. P'ANG-CHÜEH 旁決 Overflow

Water spilling over [the retaining dykes] and flowing out
over the sides.

2442. PANG-CHU T'IAO-CHÜN 幫築挑濬 To assist in
construction and dredging

To help in the building of dykes and dredging the shallow
[channels].

2443. TI-AN TAN-PO 堤岸單薄 The dykes are flimsy

The dykes along the river are not solidly built.

2444. CH'UNG-MEN CHIH CHANG 重門之障 Multiple
protection

Having several [or a series of] protective spillways 口
門 located one behind another.

2445. SHA-T'U YÜ-CH'IEN 沙土淤淺 Made shallow through
silting by sandy earth

The river bed is becoming smooth and shallow as a
result of silting by sandy earth.

2446. LIU CH'UAN CHI-YUNG 流湍激涌 A rushing torrent

An unchecked rampaging onrush of water.

2447. HUI-WO 迴渦 Whirlpool; eddy

(*Wo 渦 "eddy" is given as wo 窩 "nest" in the annotated edition.)

The recoil swirl of waves or currents.

2448. MAN-CHÜEH CH'UNG-T'A 漫決冲塌 Overflowing a breach and causing the collapse [of a dyke]

(*Ch'ung 冲 "to wash" is given as ch'ung 衝 "to charge" in the Manchu-Chinese editions.)

The river water overflows through a breach in the dyke, thus forcing it to collapse.

2449. CH'IU CHANG 秋漲 The rise [of water] in the autumn

The river rise high in the autumn. [Cf. 2286.]

2450. SU-SHUI KUEI-TS'AO 束水歸漕 Guiding the water back to the Canal

To build high embankments along both shores, so as to control the water and guide it back to the Grand Canal.

2451. CH'UNG-CHÜEH 衝決 To breach

[Water] breaching a gap in the dyke and flowing through it.

2452. CH'UAN-CHI 湍急 Fast-flowing

(*Chi 急 "fast" is given as liu 流 "current" or "flow" in the annotated edition.)

Fast-flowing water.

2453. FEN-SHA CHANG-I 分煞漲溢 To divert the surplus water

To dig lateral ditches in order to divert the excess water.

2454. CHÜN-TI TIEN-SHA 濬滌墊沙 To dredge and scour silted sand

When the river bed has become sand-filled through silting, it is to be dredged and flushed clean.

2455. P'EI PO TSENG PEI 培薄增卑 To strengthen the flimsy
and raise the low

To add [material] to the dyke and increase its thickness,
and to build it further so as to increase its height.

2456. CH'IH-CHIN YING-LIU CHIH CH'U 喫緊迎流之處
A critical spot facing the current

An important dyke situated at a spot where it bears the
brunt of the current.

2457. HSIUNG-YUNG HUAN-MAN 洶涌澴漫 Roaring flood
water

Water rushing on with great force and spreading in all
directions.

2458. WU-FANG TSA-CH'U CHIH TI 五方雜處之地
A place of heterogeneous population

An area where people from many different places
congregate and live.

2459. YÜN-LIAO HO 運料河 River for the transport of
materials

A lateral river or channel plied by the small boats that
transport materials.

2460. LAN-NI CH'IEN 爛泥淺 Muddy shoals

River shoals formed by the silting of mud.

2461. SAO-T'AI 埽臺 Dyke terrace or tower

A terrace or tower built upon a dyke that serves as
look-out point [on which to check] water conditions.

2462. PIEN-MIN CHA 便民閘 Irrigation water-gate

[Such a water-gate] is set up for the storage and
freeing of water as a means to benefit [the common
people's] agriculture.

2463. LAN-MA HO 攔馬河 Halt-horse river

To open [a ferry over?] a river or ditch so that horses
can be ferried across.

2464. KUEI-JEN TI 歸仁堤 Return-to-kindness Dyke

The name of a dyke.

2465. CH'IEN-CHIH WAN-P'AI 千支萬派 Thousands of branches and myriads of tributaries

That is, there is a large number of branch streams.

2466. CHIH-HO 支河 A branch river or stream

A small tributary river.

2467. TS'AO-PA 草壩 Reed dam or weir

A dam [or weir] constructed of reeds.

2468. P'ING-HUAN 平緩 Smooth and slow

The current flows very smoothly without much speed.

2469. SHUN-KUEI 順軌 Following the course

The river flows down its original course.

2470. KENG-SAI 梗塞 Obstructed

The flow of water is stopped [by an obstruction].

2471. CH'ANG-TI 長堤 Long dyke

A major [or large] dyke.

2472. CHÜEH-K'OU 決口 A breach

A hole or gap [in the dyke] burst open by river water.

2473. P'ING-FU 平阜 Plateau

A level area on a mountain or highland.

2474. HSIEN-KUNG 險工 Critical [river] work

A critically important [river] work or construction.

[[6]] Bookkeeping and administration. Nos. 2475-2503

2475. SHE-FA 設法 To devise a way

To make a plan.

2476. CHI-CH'IH TAI-WAN 稽遲怠玩 To delay and idle away the time

To manage river works negligently, handling them in an indolent and procrastinating manner.

2477. SO-SSU HO-SHIH 所司何事 What are the duties [of a given official]?

What are the responsibilities of river works officials? They are the matters pertaining to river works.

2478. HO-KUNG LIU-PI 河工流弊 Abuses incidental to river works

Many abuses have arisen in connection with the administration of river works.

2479. K'AN-JEN HO-WU 堪任河務 Capable of directing river affairs

A [given] district magistrate can be entrusted with the [administration of] river works.

2480. FOU-MAO CHIH PI 浮冒之弊 The abuses of padded accounts and fraud

The abuses of padding the accounts for river works expenditures, and of receiving funds under false pretexts.

2481. YAO TZU SHUN CHING 堯咨舜警 The seekings of Yao, and the alertness of Shun

This phrase describes the solemn attention given by the Emperor to river works. It is comparable to the Emperor Yao's seeking [of advice] from all the people, and to the Emperor Shun's alertness and self-warning.

2482. LIANG TS'AI 量材 To evaluate [a man's] ability

To estimate a man's ability and employ him accordingly.

2483. HSIEN-SHIH YÜ-T'U 先事豫圖 To make preparation beforehand

In all matters there should be preparations beforehand.

2484. FANG-AI YÜN-TAO 妨礙運道 Obstruction of the waterway

The waterway has been obstructed and is not suitable for grain transport.

2485. CH'E-TI CH'ING-SUAN 徹底清算 A thorough accounting

To count up all the funds expended, making every item clear.

2486. TS'AI SHOU K'AN-WEI 才守 堪委 Worthy to be appointed, as to both ability and conduct

Both the ability and the moral conduct of a given person qualify him to the appointment [to a certain post].

2487. T'UNG-JEN I-SHIH 同仁 一視 Equal treatment

To regard (all) with the same good will without discrimination.

2488. T'A-K'AN 踏勘 Field inspection; to inspect personally

To make an inspection on foot [or in person].

2489. FANG SHOU 防守 To protect and guard

To take precaution and guard [as a dyke].

2490. T'I-KU 題估 To memorialize an estimate

To estimate the funds to be expended, and memorialize it to the throne.

2491. T'I-HSIAO 題銷 To memorialize a financial account

To present to the throne a final financial account.

2492. TU-HSIU 督修 To direct repairs

To lead the workers in repairing and maintaining river works and the like.

2493. CHING-HSIU 經修 In charge of repairs

To handle the matters relative to river repair work.

2494. CH'ENG-HSIU 承修 To undertake repairs

To contract for the river repair work.

Works

2495. CHIEN-HSIU 監修 To supervise repairs

To supervise the work on river repairs.

2496. HSIANG-TU CH'ING-HSING 相度情形 To gauge
the condition or circumstances

To inspect and estimate the condition [or progress] of
river works.

2497. I-FANG WEI-JAN 以防未然 To guard against mishaps

To guard against future disaster.

2498. LIN-YÜEH 臨閲 Inspection

To go about and inspect the river works.

2499. CH'ENG-SHIH TS'UN-CHUANG 城市村庄 Urban, rural

In the city, and in the country.

2500. LÜ-YEN HSIU CH'I 閭閻休戚 Joy and grief of all the
households

The happiness and sorrow of all the common people.

2501. KUAN-FENG WEN-SU 觀風問俗 Observing the customs
and seeking the traditions

To investigate and find out about the local customs.

2502. HUI-AI YUAN-YUAN CHIH CHIH-I 惠愛元元之至
意 The unexcelled intention of universal benevolence

The Emperor's kind thought of dispensing benevolence to
all the people.

2503. FU-HSIEH PIEN-MANG 撫恤編氓 Compassion for the
masses

Kind and compassionate treatment of all the people.

[[I.]] The Board of Civil Appointment. Nos. 2504-2535

2504. CHIN HSIEN-CH'IEN PU-YUNG PAN 儘先前補用班
Expectant officials' top priority list

The names on the expectant officials' priority list
[see 15] should have precedence over all others in
obtaining appointment to vacant posts. The expectant
officials' top priority list comprises names that are
given precedence within the priority list.

2505. HUA-YANG 花樣 Categories

This refers to the designations for the various lists,
such as: immediate appointment 即補 , expectant
候補 , priority 儘先 , top priority 儘先前 , and
so on.

2506. WEI-SHU WEI-CH'AI 委署委差 Appointed by
provincial authorities to either an acting or an ad hoc post

All appointments to substantive posts in the provinces must
first be memorialized [for approval]. However, in the
case of an acting official, or of one who is to serve on a
specific mission, the governor-general and/or governor
may make the appointment on their own authority.

2507. LUN-WEI TAO-PAN 輪委到班 Having reached one's
turn for appointment

Each person awaiting appointment in the provinces for an
acting or ad hoc position is to wait for his own turn in
a rotating list. "Having reached one's turn" means a given
official's name is next on the list, and that he will shortly
receive an appointment.

2508. CHIH-FEN 指分 Assignment by choice

[In the appointment of] officials both metropolitan and

provincial, it is the custom for the Board of Civil
Appointment to assign the appointees, by drawing lots,
to their respective provinces and offices. However, a
person who has obtained his rank by purchase and has
contributed money [to the government] may specify the
province or the office of his own choice, and will be
assigned accordingly.

2509. CHIEN-SHU 兼署 Concurrently acting

An official in one post serving as the acting official in
another capacity.

2510. CHIEN-CH'AI 兼差 In concurrent posts

An official holding other posts concurrently.

2511. TU-PAN TSUNG-PAN 督辦總辦 Director-general or
superintendent; manager, or office chief

A director-general [or superintendent, B. 188] directs
the conduct of public affairs from above. A manager
[B. 102] or office chief [B. 369A] has general supervision
[over a given matter]. Of the two, the position of the
director-general or superintendent is the higher.

2512. PANG-PAN HSIANG-PAN 幫辦襄辦 Assistant or
deputy superintendent; assistant

To be an assistant [or deputy] superintendent [B. 232] is
to help in the conduct of public affairs. An assistant
[B. 102] also means one who assists or helps.

2513. HSIEN-CH'I KUNG-CH'U 先期公出 Absent on a prior
mission

A local official happens to be absent from his post on a
prior mission when some incident occurs in the area
under his jurisdiction.

2514. YEN-CHIA I-CH'U 嚴加議處 To be severely penalized

[An official's] common, minor offenses are considered by
the Board (of Civil Appointment), where a decision is
reached on the penalty [cf. 112]. In the case of a major
offense the penalty should be more severe.

2515. CHIANG-CHI CHUN TI-HSIAO PU-CHUN TI-HSIAO 降級
准抵銷不准抵銷 Revocable and irrevocable
demotions of rank

In deliberating on the case of an official who is guilty
of an offense, the Board (of Civil Appointment) may
decide to impose the penalty of demotion of rank. If
the official has previously won an advancement of rank
on account of meritorious service, his demotion and
advancement may be permitted to cancel each other. In
the event of a major offense, however, the demotion must
actually remain in effect, and is not to be cancelled [by
the advancement].

[Cf. 147.]

2516. CHU-CHENG 主政 Second Class Secretary

The chu-shih (second class secretaries 主事 B. 292) of
the Six Boards.

2517. K'AI-CH'ÜEH 開缺 To vacate a post

An official in a substantive post who is guilty of an offense
not sufficiently serious to cause his demotion or dismissal,
is asked to vacate his present post. If he is a minor
functionary he will await future appointment by his
superiors; if a high official, he will await reappointment
by order of the throne.

2518. K'AI-CH'ÜEH LAI-CHING 開缺來京 To vacate [his]
post and proceed to the capital

If a high official has had to vacate his post on account of
some offense, but the Emperor wishes to observe him
further in order to determine his suitability for re-employ-
ment, he is ordered to "vacate his post, and proceed to the
capital to await reappointment by the throne 簡用 ."

In case it has been decided that (the official) should not
be re-employed, he is then ordered simply to "vacate
his post," without the phrase "and proceed to the capital
to await reappointment by the throne."

2519. **KO-CHIH YUNG-PU HSÜ-YUNG** 革職永不敍用
To be dismissed and permanently barred from government
employment

In the case of an official who has committed a grave offense
and must not be employed again, an edict will order that he
"be dismissed and permanently barred from official recommendations and government employment."

2520. **CH'Ü-CHU HUI-CHI** 驅逐回籍 To be deported to [his]
native province [or locality]

If an official is guilty of infraction of the law and other
immoral conduct while serving in some province, the
government not only will dismiss him from his post, but
will order that he be deported to his native place, and be
forbidden to tarry in the said province and create [further]
trouble.

2521. **CH'IN-CH'AI** 欽差 By imperial commission

[An official] who is sent to the provinces to conduct a
[specific] affair by special order of the Emperor is known
as serving "by imperial commission" [or as an imperial
commissioner]. [Ch'in-ch'ai ta-ch'en 欽差大臣 ,
often abbreviated to ch'in-ch'ai.]

2522. **CH'IN-AN** 欽案 A case [or matter] by imperial command

All matters being conducted following an order of the
Emperor are known as "cases or matters by imperial
command."

2523. **CHIA-CHI SUI-TAI PU SUI-TAI** 加級隨帶不隨帶
Conveyable and non-conveyable promotion in rank

A meritorious official may be rewarded with an advancement in rank, which may be in one of two categories:
conveyable and non-conveyable. A conveyable advancement
goes with [the grantee] regardless of any change of post;
a non-conveyable advancement is granted for the duration
of his present tenure only, and becomes null if he is
transferred to another post.

2524. PU-FA 不法 Illegal; unlawful

The acts of an official are contrary to the laws and regulations.

2525. CHU-KAO 主稿 [a] The composer of a memorial; [b] A writer of drafts

[a] The one who composes a memorial. When several high provincial officials jointly memorialize on a subject, the name of the one who has written the memorial must be noted at the end of the document.

[b] Also, those among the administrative staff of the Six Boards, who are usually in charge of drafting the official correspondence and memorials for their respective Boards, are likewise known as chu-kao 主稿 [writers of drafts]. [For chu-kao Brunnert gives Keeper of the Drafts (495A).]

2526. CHIEH-TANG YING-SSU 結黨營私 To form cliques for personal ends

An official gathering a clique or sect about himself to carry out his own business.

2527. WANG-SHANG HSING-SSU CH'ING T'UNG SHIH-K'UAI 罔上行私情同市儈 Cheating [his] superiors and working for private gain like a business shark

An official cheats his superiors and goes about exercising his personal ambitions; his conduct is so base that it resembles that of a greedy broker in the marketplace.

2528. KUNG ERH WANG-SSU 公爾忘私 Forgetting one's private welfare in one's devotion to public duties

This describes an official who neglects his personal affairs due to attention to his public duties.

2529. KUO ERH WANG-CHIA 國爾忘家 Forgetting one's family in one's devotion to the country

This describes an official who neglects his own family as he gives full-hearted service to the country.

2530. CHŪN ERH WANG-SHEN 君爾忘身 Forgetting one's self in one's devotion to the Emperor

This describes an official who forgets about his own person [or life] in his loyalty to the Emperor.

2531. CHUNG-AI HSING CH'ENG 忠愛性成 By nature loyal and patriotic

This means that an official is naturally endowed with these qualities: loyalty to the Emperor, and patriotism for the country.

2532. CHI-KUNG FENG-SHANG 急公奉上 Being public minded in order to serve the throne

This means that an official eagerly keeps all public affairs to heart so as to serve the Emperor well.

2533. HUI-CHIA SHU-NAN 毀家紓難 Sacrificing the family [fortune] to relieve the [national] distress

To break up one's family fortune and donate the property for relief of the country in distress. This was done by Minister Tzu-wen 子文 of Ch'u 楚 in the Spring and Autumn period. In later ages this phrase usually is used to describe one who has made financial contributions to help the country.

2534. HSÜN-CH'ANG LAO-CHI, I-CH'ANG LAO-CHI 尋常勞績,異常勞績 Ordinary merit; extraordinary merit

Merits achieved by officials are divided into two classes, ordinary and extraordinary. "Ordinary" denotes minor merits, and "extraordinary," major ones. For minor merits the rewards are small, while for the major merits the rewards are correspondingly large.

2535. CHAN-HSÜN HUI-HU 瞻徇迴護 To shelter with partiality

Chan means to gaze [elsewhere]; hsün, to follow one's personal wishes; hui, to be round-about; and hu, to protect. This phrase means that a high official chooses to be partial to his own subordinates, and if they commit mistakes he will disregard or defend rather than impeach or punish them

[[II]] The Board of Revenue. Nos. 2536-2552

2536. YU-CHU CHIH K'UAN 有著之款 Dependable funds

Funds that have a definite source and can be relied upon for use. [Items 2536 and 2537 are identical with the two entries [1199a, 1199b] appearing at the end of Chapter II, The Board of Revenue, marked [p. 143].]

2537. WU-CHU CHIH K'UAN 無著之款 Undependable funds

Funds that have no definite source and cannot be relied upon for use. [See note under 2526.]

2538. K'U-T'ANG 庫帑 Treasury funds

Monies that are stored in government treasuries. [...]

2539. WEI-CHENG CHIH KUNG 惟正之供 Principal national revenues

The taxes paid by the people are the principal source of supply for the government.

2540. T'U-CHU 土著 Natives

Local inhabitants who have lived and settled in an area. [Cf. 865.]

2541. K'O-CHI 客籍 Visitors or temporary residents

Persons from other places who are visiting or temporarily residing [in a locality]. [Cf. 865.]

2542. JU-KUAN TS'AI-WU 入官財物 Government-confiscated property

The property of a criminal is inventoried and confiscated by the government.

2543. KUAN-PI SSU-PI 官鐅私鐅 Government pan; illegal pan

A pan 鐅 is a salt-making apparatus. According to statute, it must be manufactured and issued by the government to the salt producers for use. Pans not cast by the government are called "illegal pans," of which the use is prohibited.

2544. CHIEN-CHIA TI-SSU 減價敵私 Reducing the price to combat illegal [salt]

To lower the price of government salt as a means to combat illegal salt.

2545. WAI-HSIAO CHIH K'UAN 外銷之款 Extra-account funds

An account must be rendered to the Board of Revenue for all expenditures of government funds. Those funds that need not be accounted for, but are used by the provincial officials at their own discretion, are known as "extra-account funds."

2546. YEN-TU CHUNG-PAO 嚴杜中飽 Strict prohibition of the middleman's squeeze

A "middleman's squeeze" consists of government funds that have been neither paid into government treasuries above, nor [spent for] the populace below, but have gone to line the pockets of the men in between who handle them. That is, the men in the middle have squeezed the money for their own gain. [An official] with fiscal responsibilities should strictly prohibit and eradicate such conduct.

2547. LIU-WANG WEI-FU 流亡未復 Refugees have not returned [or been rehabilitated]

In the wake of famine or warfare the people of a locality have scattered and fled, and the population has not yet returned to normal.

2548. LIANG-CH'UAN 糧串 Tax receipt

The receipt issued as a certifying document by the government to the taxpayer, when the latter has paid the [land] taxes

2549. CH'OU-LI CHI-HSIANG 抽釐濟餉 Levying likin to meet military needs

In the old days only customs duties were levied [by the the government]. Since the reigns of Hsien-feng and T'ung-chih, however, China has been continually in upheaval, and military funds ran low. Tariff barriers therefore were set up, and <u>likin</u> is levied on merchandise [in transit] as a means to help meet military needs.

2550. AN-MU K'O-P'AI 按畝科派 Payments assessed according to acreage

If a local public event occurs and there should be insufficient government funds to defray the costs, the people will be asked to contribute, each person being assessed a sum according to the acreage of the land he possesses. The assessment must be done on the basis of acreage in order that all may be justly treated.

2551. TU-HSIAO 督銷 To supervise the sale; salt sales superintendent

The government, fearing that the salt merchants might engage in unfair practices in selling salt after they have obtained the salt certificates, has established a bureau 局 in each salt sales area, in which an official is commissioned to supervise the sales.

2552. TIEN-SHANG LING T'IEH 典商領帖 A pawn-broker obtains his license

A merchant desiring to open a pawn shop must obtain a license at the Board (of Revenue) before he is allowed to open and operate [such a shop].

"To pawn" means to mortgage one's possessions in return for money.

[[III]] The Board of Rites. Nos. 2553-2557

2553. HSIEN-K'AO 縣考 District examination

A student 童生 is examined by the district magistrate and sent on to the prefect.

2554. FU-K'AO 府考 Prefectural examination

A student is examined in the prefecture and sent before the <u>Hsüeh-yüan</u> 學院 (Literary Chancellor, B. 827A) or provincial Director of Studies. [See 1315.]

2555. TAO-K'AO 道考 Circuit examination

Before the office of the provincial Director of Studies 學政 was established, a licentiate 秀才 was examined by the intendant of the circuit, therefore [this stage of the public examinations] was called "circuit examination." Nowadays under the provincial Director of Studies this examination is known as the "chancellor's examination," but the old term "circuit examination" is still occasionally used.

[Cf. 1315.]

2556. HSIANG-SHIH 鄉試 Provincial examination

Licentiates taking the examinations in [the capitals of] their respective provinces for the degree of provincial graduate 舉人.

2557. HUI-SHIH 會試 Metropolitan examination

The provincial graduates taking the examinations in Peking for the degree of metropolitan graduate 進士.

[[IV]] Board of War. Nos. 2558-2562

2558. TS'AO FANG 操防 To drill, to guard

To drill the troops, and [using the troops] to guard the defenses.

2559. CHÜN-CHENG 軍政 Inspection of military personnel

This takes place once every three years, similar to the great accounting 大計 for the civil officials.

[Cf. 1398.]

2560. TA-YÜEH 大閱 Grand inspection

A general inspection by the governor and governor-general of the training of all the military units under their jurisdiction.

2561. LÜ-YING 綠營 Green Standard

The old Chinese regular army.

2562. MU-YUNG募勇 Braves; militia

Soldiers recruited as needed since the outbreak of the [Taiping] wars, such as the Hunan and Anhwei armies.

[[V]] The Board of Punishments. Nos. 2563-2580

2563. T'OU-SHOU投首 To turn oneself in

A criminal voluntarily goes to a government office and admits to having committed a crime, without waiting for others to accuse him or for the government to arrest him. [Cf. 1653.]

2564. PI-CHAO 比照. To use a comparable [provision]

In the event that a crime does not fit into any provision in the code, then in judging the case a provision pertaining to crimes of a similar character should be used through comparison.

2565. CH'ING SHIH 情實 The guilt is established

The criminal has been clearly and unequivocally interrogated, and his guilt has been established.

2566. SHIH-CH'U失出 Lightly sentenced by mistake

A man guilty of a serious crime is mistakenly given a light sentence.

2567. SHIH-JU失入 Heavily sentenced by mistake

A man guilty of a light crime is mistakenly given a heavy sentence.

2568. MOU-SHA謀殺 Premeditated murder

To kill a man with previous intent. [See 1859.]

2569. CH'IANG-CHIEN CHIH-MING 强姦致命 Death due to rape

To commit manslaughter as a result of the fight caused by a woman's resistance to rape. [Cf. 1897.]

2570. CHIH-MING SHANG 致命傷 Fatal injury

In a homicide case the inspecting official(s) [i.e., the coroner?] must examine carefully all of the [dead person's] bodily injuries, and determine which are the ones that have caused the death.

2571. CHUANG SHANG 裝傷 Faking an injury

A cunning person has initiated a litigation on trumped up charges. Fearing that the magistrate might doubt his word, he inflicts fake wounds on himself and blames them on his opponent, hoping thus to cheat [the court]. [Cf. 1936.]

2572. CHENG-HSIUNG 正兇 The principal murderer; the killer

The criminal who is the killer.

2573. PANG-HSIUNG 幫兇 Accomplice; accomplice in murder

The man who helps the principal murderer to kill.

2574. T'UNG-CHI 通緝 A general search or hunt

Lest the criminal escape to a distant place, [the authorities concerned] will notify the officials in all the localities, asking them to make a concerted effort to search for, and capture, him. [Cf. 1848.]

2575. SO-SHIH 唆使 To instigate

Skilfully talking another person into committing a crime. [Cf. 1911.]

2576. CHUNG-CHENG CH'ÜEH-TSAO 眾證確鑿 Irrefutable evidence of witnesses

According to statute, the passing of sentence in a case before the court must be based on the true testimony of the criminal. However, in the case of a crafty criminal who refuses to confess, the testimony of witnesses, if truthful and bearing upon the facts, can also be used as

the evidence upon which the verdict is given. In such
an event the confession of the criminal is not necessary
[for sentencing].

2577. NI-LUN 逆倫 To violate the principles of human
relationships

A subordinate or younger person, who causes injury
to one in a higher position or more advanced in age,
is called a violator of human relationships, because
he acts contrary to the principles of human obligation.

2578. MING-HUO CHIH-CHANG 明火執仗 With lights and
weapons

Those who dare to rob a house at night with the aid of
lights and weapons are called robbers. [Cf. 2105.]

2579. HSIAO-CH'IEH 小竊 Petty thief; burglar

Those who slip into a building unseen and steal things
are called petty thieves [or burglars]. [Cf. 2084.]

2580. YAO-YEN HUO-CHUNG 妖言惑衆 Misleading the
people with heresy

To confuse and mislead the people with heretical and
fantastic talk.

[[VI]] The Board of Works. Nos. 2581-2586

2581. CHENG KUNG 鄭工 The Cheng-chou works

The river works at Cheng-chou [Honan].

2582. LING KUNG 陵工 Mausoleum work

Construction work at the imperial mausolea. The
tombs of the Emperors and Empresses are called
"mausolea."

2583. YEN-SHOU 驗收 To inspect and terminate [a public
works project]

The work on every major public works project is

supervised by an official. Upon the completion of the work an official is also sent to inspect it, and thus terminate the project.

2584. I-KUNG TAI-CHEN 以工代賑 To institute work relief in place of dole

In a year of disaster--such as that caused by a great flood or other catastrophe--when the hungry masses have nothing to live on, the government may put these people to work on some public project that is needed in the locality. The wages so earned will take the place of relief doles.

2585. CHUAN-KUNG 磚工 Brickwork; masonry

Some parts of the dykes along the Yellow River are constructed of bricks.

2586. T'ANG KUNG 塘工 Sea wall work

Work concerned with the repair and/or construction of sea walls.

LIST OF SOURCES AND MONOGRAPHS CONSULTED

INDEX OF ENTRIES

INDEX OF SUBJECTS

LIST OF SOURCES AND MONOGRAPHS CONSULTED

B.: Brunnert, H.S. and V.V. Hagelstrom. Present Day Political
  Organization of China, trans. from the Russian by A.
  Beltchenko and E.E. Moran. Shanghai: Kelly and Walsh,
  1912.

Boulais, Guy, S.J. Manuel du Code Chinois (Variétés Sinologiques
  No. 55). Shanghai: Imprimerie de la Mission Catholique,
  1924.

Brunnert, H.S. and V.V. Hagelstrom, see B.

Chang Chung-li. The Chinese Gentry: Studies on Their Role in
  Nineteenth Century Chinese Society. Seattle: University
  of Washington Press, 1955.

Ch'ien Tuan-sheng. The Government and Politics of China.
  Cambridge, Mass.: Harvard University Press, 1950.

Ch'ing shih-kao, see CSK.

CSK: Ch'ing shih-kao 清史稿 (Draft history of the Ch'ing dynasty).
  Peking: Bureau of Ch'ing History (Chao Erh-hsün,
  director), 1927.

CTTS: Hsiao I-shan 蕭一山. Ch'ing-tai t'ung-shih 清代通史
  (A general history of the Ch'ing dynasty), Vols. 1 and 2.
  Shanghai: Commercial Press, 1932.

Escarra, Jean. Le Droit Chinois. Peiping: Henri Veitch, 1936.

Fairbank, John K. and Ssu-yü Teng. Ch'ing Administration: Three
  Studies (Harvard-Yenching Institute Series No. 19).

Cambridge, Mass.: Harvard University Press, 1960.

Gandar, Domin., S.J. Le Canal Impérial, Etude Historique et
Descriptive (Variétés Sinologiques No. 4). Shanghai:
Imprimerie de la Mission Catholique, 1894.

Hinton, Harold C. The Grain Tribute System of China (1845-1911).
Cambridge, Mass.: Harvard University, Center for East
Asian Studies, 1956.

Hoang, P. Notes Techniques sur la Propriété en Chine (Variétés
Sinologiques No. 11). Shanghai: Imprimerie de la Mission
Catholique, 1897.

Hsiao I-shan, see CTTS.

Hu-pu tse-li 户部則例 (Regulations and precedents of the Board
of Revenue). 1851 ed.

KHHT: Ta-Ch'ing hui-tien, Kuang-hsü 大清會典, 光緒
(The institutes of the Ch'ing dynasty, Kuang-hsü edition).
Shanghai: Commercial Press, 1908.

Liang Fang-chung. The Single-Whip Method of Taxation in China,
trans. Wang Yü-ch'üan. Cambridge, Mass.: Harvard
University, Center for East Asian Studies, 1956.

Lin Yutang. A History of the Press and Public Opinion in China.
Chicago and Shanghai: University of Chicago Press, 1936.

Mayers, William Frederick. The Chinese Government. 3rd ed.,
rev. by G. M. H. Playfair; Shanghai: Kelly and Walsh, 1896.

Morse, Hosea Ballou. The Trade and Administration of the
Chinese Empire. Shanghai: Kelly and Walsh, 1908.

Oda Yorozu 織田萬 . Ch'ing-kuo hsing-cheng fa 清國行政
法 (Administrative laws of the Ch'ing dynasty), trans.
from the Japanese by Cheng Ch'ih et al. Shanghai:
Kuang-chih Book Co. , 1906.

Powell, Ralph. The Rise of Chinese Military Power, 1895-1912.
Princeton: Princeton University Press, 1955.

SCYC: Wang Ch'ing-yün 王慶雲 . Shih-ch'ü yü-chi 石渠餘
紀 . 1890 ed.

Shimizu Taiji 清水泰次 . Chūgoku kinsei shakai keizai shi
中國近世社會經濟史 (Social and economic
history of early Modern China). Tokyo: Nishino Shoten,
1950.

Ta-Ch'ing hui-tien, Kuang-hsü, see KHHT.

Wang Ch'ing-yün, see SCYC.

Yang Lien-sheng. Money and Credit in China: A Short History.
Cambridge, Mass.: Harvard University Press, 1950.

INDEX OF ENTRIES

Numbers refer to entries, not to pages.
Where a number is preceded by "in," the entry
has been abbreviated in this index to its key
words.

Chang-ch'u, 991.

Chang-fang lo-kuo, 1557.

Chang-liang, 990.

Chang-liu chun t'u, 1737.

Chang-tseng, 992.

Ch'ang-cheng, 607.

Ch'ang chieh, 659, 1585.

Ch'ang-chieh k'uai-shou, 2419.

Ch'ang-ch'uan shou-shao, 1546.

Ch'ang-ch'uan tai feng, 136.

Ch'ang-fu, 1583, 2413.

Ch'ang-jen tao, 385.

Ch'ang-luan, 1512.

Ch'ang-ti, 2471.

Ch'ang-tuan chia-mu, 2375.

Chao-chi (kei), 652.

Chao-chi liu-i, 920.

Chao-chi tiao pieh-hsiang tsa-
chih yung, 84.

Chao-chi (-kei) yin, 526.

Chao chieh, 1709.

Chao-fu, 1503.

Chao-fu ch'ien-i fu-yeh hsin-
tseng Chuang-ting, 1086.

Chao-fu min-ting ch'i-fen ling,
886.

Chao-hsü yang-lao, 2166.

Chao-li chun ch'u che-hao, 736.

Chao-li t'u-chüeh shu-k'o pi-ku,
1765.

Chao mu lun-hsü, 2170.

Chao-na ch'eng kang, 1056.

Chao nei, 1711.

Chao shang chung hsia tse ch'i-
k'o, 982.

Chao-tan tao fei, 435.

Chao-t'an yeh pu-shou, 1543.

Chao ts'ao-kuei chia-chih
hsiao-suan, 2320.

Chao tu-po chih hsin-li, 1774.

Chao-tui, 801.

Chao wen-ming erh hsi shou-
shih, 1392.

Ch'ao-ch'iang, 2090.

Ch'ao-chin, 1231.

Ch'ao fu, 1479.

Ch'ao-kung, 1232.

Ch'ao-mieh, 1480.

Ch'ao sha ta-yüan, 2143.

Ch'ao shen, 1687.

Ch'ao-tsao chih-chang, 2365.

Ch'ao t'ui, 9.

Che-hsi, 587.

Che jen i-ch'ih chi shou tsu
i-chih, 1960.

Che-ko jen, 1932.

Che-lei to-t'ai, 1957.

Che-se, 586, 587, 777; ... yin,
512.

Che-ts'an, 110.

Che yin, 121.

Ch'e (ch'ih)-ch'ien, 47.

Ch'e-chu yin, 489.

Ch'e-ti ch'ing-suan, 2485.

Ch'e-tsao, 2398.

Ch'e yin, 1038.

Chen-chih, 2095.

Chen hsieh, 1354.

Chen-sha, 1864.

Chen-shou, 1458.

Ch'en-ni kung-wen, 1596.

Ch'en pu-pi hsien yuan, 387.

Cheng-chiao, 1899.

Cheng-ch'ih ying-wu, 1362.

Cheng ch'u-k'o, 1255.

Cheng-hsiang ch'ien-liang, 417.

Cheng-hsiung, 2572.

Cheng jun yin, 559.

Cheng kung, 2581.

Cheng-kung, 465; ... tao-mi,
718.

Cheng-lien ying-wu i-shih Ts'ao-
yen, 1380.
Cheng ma, 1612.
Cheng-mi, 695.
Cheng shai, 761.
Cheng-shui, 455.
Cheng ssu erh hao, 721.
Cheng-tien, 2357.
Cheng-ting, 590.
Cheng-ting, 871.
Cheng-t'u ch'u-shen, 190.
Cheng-t'u pan, 11.
Cheng-yin kuan, 186.
Ch'eng-ch'ai, 199.
Ch'eng-chao, 1708.
Ch'eng-chui i-nien hsian-man,
689.
Ch'eng erh-ch'ien-shih chih
liang-che, 234.
Ch'eng-hsing shu-pan, 200.
Ch'eng-hsiu, 2494.
Ch'eng-p'an, 1050.
Ch'eng-shang, 1916.
Ch'eng-shen ch'uan-ts'o, 305.
Ch'eng-shih ts'un-chuang, 2499.
Ch'eng-shun feng-ying, 349.
Ch'eng-ting, 877.
Ch'eng-tsai pu-ch'eng-tsai, 1013.
Ch'eng-ts'ui, 608.
Ch'eng-yü fu-yü wu, 1238.
Chi-chien, 1885.
Chi-ch'ih tai-wan, 2476.
Chi ch'in wan-chü, 1472, 2180.
Chi-chu, 772.
Chi-chuang t'ien, 942.
Chi-chung shao-hsiang, 2052.
Chi hsing, 1806.
Chi hsüan, 2.
Chi-hu, 1855.
Chi-i, 1211.
Chi-kuan, 1645.
Chi-kung feng-shang, 2532.

Chi-lu, 37; ... wu-tz'u, 38.
Chi-mi ta-shih, 1422.
Chi-mo ju-kuan, 1745.
Chi neng ju-ch'i ts'ao-lien keng
shih hu-sung wu-yü, 1379.
Chi-pien liang-min, 337.
Chi-pu wu t'ao-pu chih huan, 1377.
Chi sha-pa t'iao-chün, 2434.
Chi-tien, 93.
Chi t'ien, 923.
Chi t'ien, 957.
Chi-ts'an, 102.
Chi-tsui sao, 2265.
Chi-tu, 1980.
Chi-wen, 1212.
Chi yu, 50.
Chi-yu sao-shua ch'ung-she
chih huan, 2341.
Ch'i-chia, 796.
Ch'i-chieh, 657; ... yin, 516.
Ch'i-cheng yin, 504.
Ch'i erh pu-shih, 1949.
Ch'i-fu, 159.
Ch'i-hui ssu-shih, 1948.
Ch'i-i hsing-chieh, 2121.
Ch'i-jang huo-tsai, 2049.
Ch'i jen tsang-wu, 1684.
Ch'i-sha ti, 956.
Ch'i tien, 1230.
Ch'i-ting, 795.
Ch'i-ts'ao, 1609.
Ch'i-wei, 1148.
Ch'i-yu, 1921.
Ch'i-yün, 805.
Chia ch'a, 1110.
Chia-ch'an chin-chüeh, 1791.
Chia-ch'eng pu ju-fa, 1636.
Chia-chi, 36; ... sui-tai pu
sui-tai, 2523.

Chia-chiang hsieh-shen, 2034.
Chia-ch'ou na-sung, 1660.
Chia-hao, 1810; ...i-ko yüeh,
  1725.
Chia-hao heng-cheng, 376.
Chia-hao yin, 491.
Chia hsi, 781.
Chia hsien, 30.
Chia hsün, 1694.
Chia i-chi chiang erh-chi chin
  chiang i-chi tai-tsui t'u-kung,
  147.
Chia-kun, 1809.
Chia kung chi ssu, 365.
Chia-liu chun-t'u pu-wang, 1766.
Chia-mu, 2373.
Chia-pang, 2216.
Chia-p'ao yeh pu-shou, 1544.
Chia-tai, 813, 1331.
Chiang-ch'ao, 2436.
Chiang-chi, 124; ...chun ti-
  hsiao pu-chun ti-hsiao, 2515.
Chiang-chi hung-ch'uan, 2389.
Chiang-chih erh-chi, 143.
Chiang ch'ih, 1048.
Chiang-feng, 131; ...erh-chi,
  135.
Chiang-k'ou heng-chang, 2306.
Chiang-kung sui fu yin, 2314.
Chiang lu, 2393.
Chiang tiao, 127.
Chiang-ts'ai, 1352.
Ch'iang-ch'ieh, 2085.
Ch'iang-chien, 1882.
Ch'iang-chien chih-ming, 2569.
Ch'iang-hsing chi-chien, 1890.
Ch'iang-hsiu, 2206.
Ch'iang-tao, 2081.
Ch'iang-to chien-chan, 1991.
Chiao-chang, 2290.

Chiao-chieh p'eng-tang, 322.
Chiao-fu, 2417.
Chiao-hsi kung-sheng, 192.
Chiao-k'ou, 1901.
Chiao-kung chih shih yu-ju lei-
  nuan, 2324.
Chiao-liao, 1816.
Chiao p'an, 68.
Chiao-so, 1911; ...hsien-hai,
  1662.
Chiao-su yüan-ch'ü, 1672.
Chiao-tai, 67.
Chiao-t'ung ch'u-ju, 339.
Ch'iao ch'ien, 711.
Ch'iao-ch'üeh pu-mao , 973.
Ch'iao-kung, 1681.
Ch'iao-li ming-se, 361.
Ch'iao men, 2102.
Chieh-cheng, 603.
Chieh-ch'i, 94.
Chieh-ch'i, 1151.
Chieh-chiao t'ui yin, 1058.
Chieh ch'iu, 2092.
Chieh-hsiang wu-su, 243.
Chieh-hsiao, 1321.
Chieh jen, 64.
Chieh jen, 123.
Chieh-kao, 1652.
Chieh-k'uang yin, 486.
Chieh-li chi-kung chi-chih i
  chen, 233.
Chieh-liu, 669; ...yin, 555.
Chieh nan ch'ien-liang, 419.
Chieh-ou, 1906.
Chieh-p'in tiao-pu, 81.
Chieh pu, 26.
Chieh-sheng, 1165, 2228; ...
  ching-fei ch'ing-ch'u chi-yü,
  1084.
Chieh-shu, 72.
Chieh-tai niu-chung, in 917.
Chieh-tang ying-ssu, 2526.

Chieh-to, 2088.
Chieh tsui ling-ch'ih, 1761.
Chieh-yin, 1519.
Ch'ieh-tao, 2084.
Chien-ch'ai, 2510.
Chien-chan kuan, 1780.
Chien-chia ti-ssu, 2544.
Chien-chiu ch'ing-mi, 1894.
Chien-chŭ, 109.
Chien chung-ping ku-yung
    hsin-huang k'ou-tun, 1442.
Chien-fan, 2074.
Chien fang, 1253.
Chien-hou ch'iu-hou ch'u-chŭeh
    chŭn-wu wang tsung, 1771.
Chien-hsi, 1518.
Chien-hsiu, 2495.
Chien-hsŭ hua-li, 384.
Chien hsŭan, 25.
Chien-hsŭan chŭ-jen, 191.
Chien-hsŭan k'an chung, 1615.
Chien-jang k'o-cheng yin, 563.
Chien-k'uang yin, 1625.
Chien-kung pu-i, 1675.
Chien-liang, 750.
Chien-lin, 382, 1295.
Chien-ling erh hsia, 2311.
Chien mi, 694.
Chien-ming, 1180.
Chien pu, 8.
Chien shen, 1696.
Chien-shih, 1296.
Chien-shih ti-mien, 2267.
Chien-shou [tao], 385.
Chien-shu, 2509.
Chien-shui pa, 2250.
Chien-t'a t'ien-ho, 2184.
Chien-teng fa-lo, 1722.
Chien-teng t'u ch'eng, 1741.
Chien-t'iao pei-fu i-mi tu-jih,
    1068.
Chien-ts'ŭn, 670.

Chien-tui t'ing, 798.
Chien t'ung kuei yŭ hsing jo hu
    shu, 2063.
Chien-wu, 1886.
Chien-yen, 1821.
Chien yu ch'i-se, 907.
Ch'ien-chai pen li, 2005.
Ch'ien-ch'ai pu-shen, 303.
Ch'ien-chi (kei) ti-chui mi, 726.
Ch'ien-chih wan-p'ai, 2465.
Ch'ien-ch'iu ling-chieh, 1222.
Ch'ien-ch'uan, 2382; ... kung-
    chŭ yin, 564.
Ch'ien-ch'ŭ ping-fu, 1591.
Ch'ien fa, 1098.
Ch'ien-fan ch'ing cheng, 1103.
Ch'ien-feng, 1486.
Ch'ien-fu, 2402.
Ch'ien-fu, 2407.
Ch'ien jen, 63.
Ch'ien-p'ai, 1470.
Ch'ien-po yin, 543.
Ch'ien sha, 952.
Ch'ien-tao ma-t'ou, 1592.
Ch'ien-ts'an, 105.
Ch'ien-t'ung, 48.
Ch'ien-yŭn, 808.
Chih-chai, 1204; ... yŭ nei, 1207.
Chih-chang yin, 479.
Chih-chao, 1128.
Chih-cheng yu-fang yŭn-k'an
    pao-chŭ, 27.
Chih-ch'eng hsiu-li, 375.
Chih-chieh, 40.
Chih-chieh jen, 1931.
Chih-ch'ien, 1099.
Chih-chin ch'ao-i, 1240.
Chih erh pu-chŭ, 321.
Chih-fen, 2508.
Chih-fu ko-shan-chin wei- ch'in
    che ping-hsing chin-chih, 2199.

Chih-ho, 2466.

Chih-hsiao, 773; ...yin, 553.

Chih-hsien, 28.

Chih-hsien, 2300.

Chih-jih, 1471.

Chih kung-chü kuan, 1290.

Chih-mei wang-liang chih hsing, 2062.

Chih ming, 31.

Chih-ming shang, 2570.

Chih-ping, 1531.

Chih-shen, 1692.

Chih-shih, 167.

Chih-shu yin, 484.

Chih-su, 1472.

Chih ts'ang chih t'un, 768.

Ch'ih-chih, 1047.

Ch'ih-chin ying-liu chih ch'u, 2456.

Ch'ih-ch'ü, 1510.

Ch'ih-i chiu-tao, 1602.

Ch'ih-ling yen chia fang-fan pu-ti tsai-ssu, 1395.

Ch'ih wu-shih, 1724.

Ch'ih-yen, 610.

Ch'ih yen, 1049.

Ch'ih-yen su-fang, 330.

Chin ao, 756.

Chin ch'uang, 1507.

Chin hsien-ch'ien pu-yung pan, 2504.

Chin-hsien pu-yung pan, 15.

Chin-hua yin, 480.

Chin k'un-ch'ü fa, 1956.

Chin-liu k'ou-men, 2429.

Chin ping, 1534.

Chin-shih kuan, 172.

Chin-shou chin-chieh, 684.

Chin-shu, 2276.

Chin tan, 742.

Chin tou, 741.

Ch'in-an, 2522.

Ch'in-ch'ai, 2521.

Ch'in-chan chieh-tao, 2423.

Ch'in-chan t'ien-ti, 1005.

Ch'in-ch'i, 641; ...kuai-p'ien, 2151; ...no-i, 374.

Ch'in-fei, 617.

Ch'in-k'o, 635.

Ch'in-kung, 42; ...t'u-ts'e, 205.

Ch'in-lin shang-ssu, 175.

Ch'in-lou, 631.

Ch'in pu an-chien, 331.

Ch'in-shih, 616; ...yin, 533.

Ch'in-shu nei-ch'i, 1985.

Ch'in-tao ch'ien-liang, 371.

Ch'in-t'ien hung-tan, 1124.

Ch'in tsang, 1790.

Ch'in-yü, 618.

Ching-ch'a, 91.

Ching-cheng, 600.

Ching-chi, 1089.

Ching-chih, 201.

Ching-fei yin, 476.

Ching hsiang shen chung, 247.

Ching-hsiu, 2493.

Ching i yu-tz'u, 1707.

Ching-jui chih ping, 1535.

Ching-kuan, 70.

Ching-lüeh, 1465.

Ching min ch'iang kan, 219.

Ching-pei yen-mi, 1452.

Ching-pi, 1451.

Ching-piao, 1252.

Ching-shou, 599; ...yin, 510.

Ching-shu ch'i i, 1277.

Ch'ing-chang, 989.

Ch'ing-chen, 1704, 1718.

Ch'ing-chi, 586, 587; ...yin, 492.

Ch'ing-ch'i, 2296.

Ch'ing ch'i chien ts'ung, 1601.

Ch'ing ch'ih chung shang yuan ch'ang hsieh cheng, 1975.

Ch'ing-fou, 259.

Ch'ing-ho piao ch'ien, 1223.

Ch'ing-hsiao, 592; ... ti-chu chia-hao yin, 581.

Ch'ing huang pu-chieh chih hou, 1028.

Ch'ing-k'ou, 2254; ... ch'ing-shui shen-ta, 2338.

Ch'ing kuan, 264.

Ch'ing-nien ch'ang-chi, 1358.

Ch'ing pi-chien, 90.

Ch'ing-shang tsun-hao, 1225.

Ch'ing shen ch'in chin, 226.

Ch'ing sheng wu-i chih fan-wen shih, 214.

Ch'ing shih, 2565.

Ch'ing shih tsao-pao ping-ma ch'ien-liang i-pien chi-ho shih, 1199.

Ch'ing tsui lüeh-chieh, 1714.

Ch'ing-yao pai-chi mi, 723.

Ch'ing-yüan ti-ch'ang, 1677.

Chiu-ch'ien yin, 542.

Chiu-hu, 1910.

Chiu-huo, 2096.

Chiu-kuan, 1155.

Chiu-sao tien-hsiu chia-t'ao ch'eng pu jung-i, 2333.

Chiu-shih hu-k'ou, 898.

Chiu-ts'an, 108.

Ch'iu-chang, 839.

Ch'iu chang, 2449.

Ch'iu-hsün, 2286.

Ch'iu liang, 703.

Ch'iu shen, 1686.

Ch'iu-t'an, 1203.

Ch'iu-t'ao pu-shih, 2046.

Ch'iung-k'un wu-i, 897.

Cho i, 218.

Cho-p'ai, 627.

Cho-po, 649.

Cho-ting, 115.

Chou hsüeh-cheng, 1283.

Chou lu hsien-chieh, 836.

Chou-sui o-pan, 1065.

Ch'ou hu, 771.

Ch'ou-li chi-hsiang, 2549.

Ch'ou p'an, 1659.

Ch'ou-ts'ai, 1473.

Chu-cheng, 2516.

Chu-chi, 1210.

Chu-ch'ih, 118.

Chu-chou chen-chiu, 910.

Chu feng, 129.

Chu-hsiao k'ai-fu, 687.

Chu huan, 1268.

Chu-i fen-hsi, 1187.

Chu-i teng-ta pao pu, 1188.

Chu-kao, 2525.

Chu-kuo yueh-pa ch'ai-ch'i chiu-chuang, 2330.

Chu-lien shou-lei, 1666.

Chu-mou, 1861.

Chu-na, 1853.

Chu-ou, 1907.

Chu-shih, 1860.

Chu-shou, 382.

Chu wu ts'ung-ts'o, 223.

Ch'u chao kung-t'u yu-i chi yu chih-shih, 1685.

Ch'u chen-fan ssu-tsui wai, 1738.

Ch'u-ch'en i-hsin, 787.

Ch'u chi, 1228.

Ch'u fan-chü chih jen, 224.

Ch'u-fen, 111.

Ch'u feng, 133.

Ch'u-hsi, 1216.

Ch'u-ju pu-ch'ang, 310.

Ch'u-ming wei-chih chih shu, 1184.

Ch'u na, 646.
Ch'u pang, 1322.
Ch'u-shih, 1257.
Ch'u-shou, 2115.
Ch'u-t'iao fei-mi, 719.
Chuan-ch'eng ch'ung-t'a chin
  ts'un tuan-ch'eng jo-kan, 2335.
Chuan-kung, 2585.
Chuan-wen mo-hu tzu-hua mo
  pien, 1271.
Chuan-yen chih chien, 1022.
Ch'uan-ch'ao hsien-yü, 426.
Ch'uan-chi, 2452.
Ch'uan-chia, 2400.
Ch'uan-hsüan, 1523.
Ch'uan-p'iao, 1138.
Ch'uan-pu wei-yen, 2023.
Ch'uan-ti, 1333.
Ch'uan-t'ou hao-p'iao, 1122.
Ch'uan-t'ou wu-chang, 797.
Ch'uan-yü chao-lai, 905.
Chuang chüeh, 2277.
Chuang-fu, 2415; . . . kung-chia,
  440.
Chuang-pan shang-pai, 714.
Chuang-pan shen-hsiang, 2039.
Chuang-shang, 2571.
Chuang-ting, 869.
Ch'uang-hu, 2207.
Ch'uang-kao, 406.
Ch'uang-men, 213.
Chui-chi, 1849.
Chui-kan, 1493.
Chui-p'ei yin, 539.
Chui-pen chu-pei, 1448.
Ch'ui-shih ta-shou, 1942.
Chun ch'i li chu, 2188.
Chun-kung, 1288.
Ch'un ch'iu i-she, 2042.
Chung-ai hsing ch'eng, 2531.
Chung chang, 1723.

Chung-ch'en lieh-shih, 1246.
Chung-cheng ch'üeh-tsao, 2576.
Chung-chih chu mo chuan, 1234.
Chung-chung hsü-so, 1416.
Chung-chün, 2211.
Chung-fan, 2067.
Chung fan lüeh-chieh chao-ts'e,
  1717.
Chung hsing p'ing po, 197.
Chung-hsiu, 2201.
Chung-hsüan, 2298.
Chung ma, 1614.
Chung pu-yen ch'i so-ch'ang,
  1384.
Chung ssu, 1201.
Chung-t'u tou-liu, 327.
Chung-yang, 144.
Chung-yen lai-li, 1064.
Ch'ung-ch'ih tzu-man, 1437.
Ch'ung-ching, 1754.
Ch'ung-chüeh, 2293, 2451.
Ch'ung-k'ai, 1177.
Ch'ung-men chih chang, 2444.
Ch'ung-shan t'an-hsieh wei-
  hsien chih-chi, 2328.
Ch'ung-shua, 2294.
Ch'ung-tsu t'ien, 947.
Ch'uo tai, 766.
Chü-chung i kai-ch'ing, 2195.
Chü ho, 97.
Chü hsien, 1498.
Chü-ku, 2225.
Chü-p'ien kuai-tai, 2150.
Chü-pu, 2113.
Chü-shou chia-o, 1226
Chü-ti, 2114.
Chü tien li-ch'eng, 1224.
Chü tsui ch'ien-t'ao, 1832.
Chü yü, 1698.
Ch'ü-chang, 840.
Ch'ü-chu hui-chi, 2520.

Ch'ü-ch'u t'iao-wa shih chih, 2437.

Ch'ü-mi yung-ch'ien, 2003.

Ch'ü shih ch'in ch'ü, 1373.

Chüan-chi chien ku, 722.

Chüan-chu t'ien, 944.

Chüan pan, 14.

Ch'üan chao, 1710.

Ch'üan chao fang-ts'e, 1713.

Ch'üan cheng, 98.

Ch'üan-chieh, 1919.

Ch'üan-feng kuan, 178.

Ch'üan heng, 10.

Ch'üan-k'en, 995.

Ch'üan-tan, 1134.

Chüch-ch'eng k'eng-k'an, 2425.

Chüeh-fa, 1727.

Chüeh-k'ou, 2472.

Chüeh-kuo jih-ch'i, 1779.

Chüeh-wu tao-kuan, 2340.

Ch'üeh-chih, 615.

Ch'üeh kuan feng-yin, 433.

Ch'üeh-o yin, 558.

Chün-cheng, 2559.

Chün-chi chung-wu, 1423.

Chün-ch'uan, 2380.

Chün erh wang-shen, 2530.

Chün-hsü k'ung-chi, 1428;
 ...ts'ang-ts'u li-pan, 232.

Chün-hsün, 1511.

Chün jung shu-lien, 1371.

Chün liu-ch'uan, 2385.

Chün-san an-chia hsien-ting, 885.

Chün-shih pu ch'üan, 1409.

Chün-ti tien-sha, 2454.

Chün t'ien, 933.

Chün-ting, 874.

Chün-tsui, 1752.

Ch'ün-ou, 1904.

E-shao hsiung-wan, 1989.

En-jung yen, 1347.

Erh-chia tz'u chin-shih ch'u-shen, 1273.

Erh-teng ch'in-chih, 78.

Erh-tou t'ien, 941.

Fa feng, 126.

Fa k'o, 1337.

Fa pieh-ti chi-pien wei ch'ung-chün, 1768.

Fa pien-wai wei min, 1747.

Fa yen-chang ch'ung-chün, 1767.

Fan-cheng, 1505.

Fan-i, 854.

Fan i-chüeh ying-li, 1891.

Fan-i jen-teng, 1841.

Fan-jen, 2066.

Fan-tsao, 2350.

Fan-tsui tai-tui, 1679.

Fan-tzu, 1843.

Fan-yü tsai-t'ao, 1830.

Fang-ai yün-tao, 2484.

Fang-ch'ien yin, 545.

Fang-fan, 1461.

Fang fu ch'ai p'in, 893.

Fang-huo yen-shao, 2126.

Fang-k'ao, 1298.

Fang-mien kuan, 187.

Fang-na, 1850.

Fang-shou, 1458, 2489.

Fang-tse, 1218.

Fang-wu, 1074.

Fei-fa hsing-shih, 307.

Fei hsing, 1807.

Fei-pao chün-ch'ing, 1425.

Fei-lao sheng-hsi, 1424.

Fei-sa, 632.

Fei t'ien, 922.

Fei-yüan chia-hai, 1661.

Fen-cheng, 1900.

Fen-kuan ch'eng-ch'ih i-tu ch'ü-
pi, 1081.
Fen-pu pa-feng, 2125.
Fen-sha chang-i, 2453.
Fen-shao yeh-hsiang, 2030.
Fen-teng, 1167.
Fen-yung teng-shan she-fa
chi tse (tsei), 1378.
Feng-hsien kuan, 184.
Feng-hsin ching-fei yin, 576.
Feng-hsin yin, 477.
Feng kung yin-liang, 423.
Feng mi, 707.
Feng-ping sha-shang jen, 1877.
Feng pu pien-chi, 1594.
Feng sao, 2264.
Feng-ts'ai kai-tiao, 80.
Feng ts'ung shang ju, 1940.
Feng-wei kung-ch'u, 153.
Feng-yang yu-ch'üeh, 1983.
Fou-mao, 639, 2231; . . . chih
pi, 2480.
Fou-sha i ch'ien tsou-shui
i ch'ung, 2326.
Fou-to, 2230.
Fou-tsao, 258.
Fou-tsao ch'ien-lu ts'ai-li
pu-chi-che chiang-chi tiao
wai- yung, 392.
Fu-cheng t'i-min, in 228.
Fu-chi fu-yeh, 911, 996.
Fu chiao-shou, 1282.
Fu chieh, 662.
Fu-chien, in 987.
Fu ch'iu shui-fa, 2287.
Fu chu-k'ao, 1292.
Fu-ch'üeh, 158.
Fu-hai wu i, 2233.
Fu-ho, 1164.
Fu-hsieh pien-mang, 2503.
Fu-hsün, 2285.

Fu-hui ting-k'ou, 880.
Fu-i ch'üan-shu, 1114.
Fu-k'ao, 2554.
Fu ku, 1497.
Fu-kuan chih liu-p'in teng
shih, 210.
Fu-kuo huan-chih, 137.
Fu-li, 1401.
Fu-luan tao-sheng, 2036.
Fu ma, 1617.
Fu mi, 696.
Fu mi, 702.
Fu-sheng, 1280-A.
Fu-shih, 1166.
Fu shou tzu-chao, 1676.
Fu-shui, 461.
Fu-t'ou, 1088.
Fu tso, 182.
Fu-tu, 411.
Fu tz'u ling-tui, 831.
Fu-wei, 1466.
Fu-yeh, 996; also in 911.
Fu-yuan, 1259.
Fu yü wu-fang, 335.
Fu-yün, 811.

Hai-chiang, 1403.
Hai chien, 2229.
Hai-fen wei ching, 1454.
Hai-hsiao ch'ao-yung, 2309.
Hai-t'an yü-sha ti, 975.
Han pa, 851.
Han-pa wei nüeh, 1011.
Han-tung, 2253.
Han-yü, 1462.
Hang-ch'u san-pien, 2433.
Hang-fu, 2412.
Hang-shui, 454.
Hao-fang, 1316.
Hao-hua kuei-li, 1988.
Hao-ling sen-yen, 1456.

Hao-lu yen, 1053.

Hao-mu shih-hsiang wei-nan teng shih, 1195.

Hao-pan, 2396.

Hao-pan fu-ch'uan mi, 735.

Hao-shu, 1576.

Hao-tai, 1556.

Hei-tan huang-tan, 1009.

Hen-ou, 1905.

Heng-ch'ung i-wang ch'ien-lai, 1440.

Ho-cha ch'iu-so, 369.

Ho-chi ping min, 1363.

Ho-chien, 1163.

Ho-chien, 1881.

Ho-ch'u fu-ch'a chih min, 913.

Ho-hsi, 1925.

Ho-hsiao, 1162.

Ho-kung, 2200; ... liu-pi, 2478.

Ho-ling, 1912.

Ho lung-men, 2221.

Ho shao ch'ao ts'uo, 733.

Ho shui ch'ien-ho ch'uan chih nan-ch'ien, 2325.

Ho-ssu, 1873.

Ho-suan, 1159.

Ho-t'an ti, 964.

Ho tang k'ung-tao fang-pien ying i ch'ou-miu, 1394.

Ho-yu, 2161.

Hou ch'üeh, 6.

Hou hsüan, 5.

Hou-k'ou yin, 544.

Hou pu, 7.

Hsi kai wen-ch'üan, 316.

Hsi ku, 709.

Hsi lien, 1817.

Hsi-na, 1854.

Hsi-p'an, 2097.

Hsi-sha, 1863.

Hsi-shang chia-hsi, 2006.

Hsia chi tu-po, 2018.

Hsia-chih chiung-ju, 1876.

Hsia-chih kuan-fu yu-shou-hao-hsien chih jen, 2059.

Hsia jen i-mu, 1958.

Hsia-kuo ti-kung, 2281.

Hsia-ma yen, in 1350.

Hsia-sao, 2215.

Hsia-shou chih jen, 1941.

Hsia-tse ko chiu-huang t'un-yü kung shui wu-pai mu, 986

Hsiang-chi chiu-ch'in, 1836.

Hsiang-chien, 1213.

Hsiang-ch'ü pu-yuan, 1024.

Hsiang-ma, 2082; ... ch'iang-tao, 2083.

Hsiang-pan, 2512.

Hsiang-shih, 2556; ... lu, in 1350; ... wai-lien wu-so kuan, 1274.

Hsiang-tien, 2358.

Hsiang-tien yen-ch'ih, 2222.

Hsiang-tu ch'ing-hsing, 2496.

Hsiang yin-chiu li, 1235.

Hsiang-yüeh, 844.

Hsiao-chiao, 775.

Hsiao-ch'ieh, 2579.

Hsiao-chien yin, 485.

Hsiao-chü pu-san, 1436, 2137.

Hsiao-chün, 2211.

Hsiao-feng, 597.

Hsiao-hsiu, 2201.

Hsiao-hu ch'i-ling mi, 731.

Hsiao-kung, 2181.

Hsiao-suan, 1160.

Hsiao-tzu shun-sun, 1248.

Hsieh-chi, 1848.

Hsieh-chi ch'ien-liang, 420.

Hsieh-chi ma, 1610.

Hsieh-chi pen-k'o t'ung-jung teng shih, 1198.

Hsüan-hsieh, 2213.
Hsüeh chi t'ien, 945.
Hsüeh tsu, 708.
Hsün-ch'ang lao-chi, 2534.
Hsün-ch'i shih-hao, 1984.
Hsün-chu, 2368.
Hsün-huan pu, 1120.
Hsün li, 217.
Hsün-liang chou-mu, in 388.
Hsün-lien p'o ch'in, 1375.
Hsün-lien shih-tsu, 1364.
Hsün-nan, 1506.
Hsün-p'i nieh-chieh, 379.
Hsün-shih kuan, 1299.
Hsün-ti, 1524.
Hsün tien pu-yen, 1411.
Hu-ch'eng ta-ti, in 2343.
Hu-fu, 747.
Hu-hsiang fang-hai chün ch'eng
   pu-lan, 1381.
Hu-k'ou jih fan, 912.
Hu-li, 73.
Hu-ping, 1533.
Hu-po, 961.
Hu-shui kuan-t'ien, 1007.
Hu-sung, 1588.
Hu tan tou sheng, 732.
Hu t'ien, 925.
Hu-ting, 872.
Hu-tsei kuo-pan, 1839.
Hu-ying pu-ling, 301.
Hu-yu chih-chao, 895.
Hua-chiang tu-ch'uan, 2388.
Hua-min, 867.
Hua-ming ts'e, 1127.
Hua-yang, 2505.
Hua-yin, 473.
Huai-kuan ssu-shui yin, 569.
Huai-shui tung-hsia, 2439.
Huai-tai, 1332.
Huan-chih, 138.

Huan-ch'iu, 1217.
Huan-chüeh, 1703, 1718.
Huan-fu chü-sou, 2139.
Huang-ch'ien, 1008.
Huang-hua chu, 2367.
Huang-huang wu-ts'o, 902, 1430.
Huang-k'uai ting-yin, 428.
Huang-kung, 1681.
Huang-liu pien-ch'ien chih-she
   ti-ken, 2327.
Huang-niu, 1342.
Huang ti, 950.
Huang t'ien ch'eng-shu ti, 976.
Hui-ai yuan-yuan chih chih-i,
   2502.
Hui-chia shu-nan, 2533.
Hui-chiao chung jen, 864.
Hui chieh, 661.
Hui-chün jih-ch'i, 1426.
Hui-fu, 1521.
Hui-i, 113.
Hui k'ung, 823.
Hui-liao, 2272.
Hui-lo kung-hsing, 358.
Hui-ma, 1903.
Hui-pi, 139.
Hui-shih, 1307, 2557; ...chü-
   jen, 1279.
Hui shu, 57.
Hui-shu, 1154.
Hui-t'i, 407.
Hui-t'i, 408.
Hui-tien, 1801.
Hui-ts'e, 1172.
Hui tz'u, 824.
Hui-wo, 2447.
Hun-jen man-tsang, 1794.
Hung-hsien, 1136.
Hung hsiu, 758.
Hung-i niao-ch'iang, 1558.
Hung-p'i chao-p'iao, 1123.

Hung po-ch'uang, 2384.

Hung-pu ch'ih-ts'e, 1119.

Hung-tan, 1144.

Hung t'ien, 934.

Hung tso-ch'uan, 2383.

Huo-cho, 1485.

Huo-fu, 1287.

Huo-hao yin, 490.

Huo hsieh, 2105.

Huo-k'ao, 2106.

Huo ma, 1613.

Huo mi, 698.

Huo-mien, 683; ...yin, 547.

Huo-p'ai, 1565.

Huo-p'iao, 1565.

Huo-ping, 1532.

Huo-shui, 458.

Huo-tao, 2073.

Huo-t'ung, 1556.

Huo-yen fei-t'eng ch'ing
    ch'eng hui–chin, 2332.

I-chan chieh-chih yin, 1629.

I-chan shih-cheng hsieh-chi
    ch'ien-liang, 1632.

I-chang chih shui, 2435.

I-ch'ang lao-chi, 2534.

I-chia tz'u chin-shih chi-ti,
    1272.

I-chia yin, 556.

I ch'iang-tao li lun pu-fen
    shou ts'ung chü-chan, 1772.

I-chih yu-tan, 1121.

I-ch'iu chin-ch'ü, 324.

I-ch'iu huan-tuan, 1004.

I-ch'u, 112.

I chuan-i chien, 1023.

I erh san yün, 835.

I-fa chüeh–fa, 2194.

I-fan, 2075.

I-fang wei-jan, 2497.

I-fu, 1582.

I-fu chieh-fu, 1249.

I hsiang-tang yuan-ch'üeh
    lüeh-chia sheng-yung, 85.

I-hsieh, 2297.

I-hsü, 34; ...pan, 13.

I-ku k'o p'o, 1434.

I-kuan, 114.

I-kung tai-chen, 2584.

I-lan, 759.

I-li k'ung-ho, 372.

I ma, 1604.

I ma chung-na chih ch'a, 1635.

I mou-jen pu-yung, 1391.

I-o yin, 557.

I pa, 850.

I (yeh) po (pai), 1327.

I-shih ch'i-ling, 1993.

I-shu chien-sung, 342.

I sui-wu kuan-ju jen k'ou-pi-nei
    che tsui i ju-chih, 1963.

I sui wu wu jen t'ou-mien, 1955.

I-tai shih-kung, 2322.

I-tao, 2078.

I-teng ch'en-chih, 77.

I-ti, 1577.

I ts'ai ying-ch'iu, 356.

I-ts'o kuo-shih, 328.

I-tsu yuan-o, 1020.

I-t'u mieh-k'ou, 2163.

I-tzu shih, 409.

I-wan, 612.

I wu nieh-sang, 2174.

I yao mi-jen, 2124.

I yin, 782.

I yuan-chi ch'a-na, in 1857.

Jan t'ien-teng ch'i teng, 2048.

Je shen, 1688.

Jen ch'i hsiao-hsiao, 1680.

Jen-fu hsüan chieh hsüan t'ao,
    2420.

K'en-ch'i liu-yang, 2177.

K'en en hsiang-ch'ing t'i fu hsing-shih i tun pen-yuan shih, 213.

K'en en hsiang-t'i sheng-pu teng shih, 212.

K'en-fu yen-che, 1057.

K'en-fu yen-ch'eng wang-hang tu-ch'uan teng-hsiang yin-liang, 585.

K'en-huang chi feng yü-chih teng shih, 1197.

K'en-kuo chung hsia tz'u san-tse t'un-t'ien, 984.

K'en-kuo min-fu keng-ming t'ien-ti, chi kuei-ping t'un-t'ien, 983.

K'en-kuo t'ien-ti, 971.

Keng-chiu yü-san chih ku, 1029.

Keng-fu, 2409.

Keng-ming t'ien-ti, in 983.

Keng-sai, 2470.

Keng ti, 2241.

Ko-ch'ien, 825.

Ko-chih, 119.

Ko-chih yung-pu hsü-yung, 2519.

Ko-mo [ti], 965.

Ko-sheng kuan-t'i, 1840.

Ko so-tang ko, 1027.

K'o-ch'ao, 400.

K'o-chi, 2541.

K'o-chia, 1317.

K'o-ching, 1705, 1718.

K'o-chü, 1310.

K'o-i, 1706, 1718.

K'o-k'ao, 1311.

K'o-lien, 636.

K'o-liu tao-tsang, 1793.

K'o-lo. 633.

K'o-p'ai, 630.

K'o t'ien, 931.

K'o t'ien, 937.

K'o-tse, 1130.

K'o yen, 1052.

Kou-min; 2352.

Kou so lo-chih, 314.

Kou-sung pu-hsi, 1669.

Kou-yin, 2116.

K'ou-chien yüeh-liang, 344.

K'ou-li, 471 .

K'ou-liang, 705, 1571.

K'ou-liu cheng-hsiang yin, 567.

K'ou ts'an, 1515.

K'ou-yin, 469.

Ku-chi, 2223.

Ku ching tiao-huan, 1278.

Ku ch'u-ju jen tsui, 2189.

Ku-hsien nei wai, 1965.

Ku-kung, 847.

Ku lei, 1496.

Ku-p'in k'ou-liang, 720.

Ku-p'in tien-lien, 888.

Ku-sha, 1858.

Ku-sheng chih-chieh, 313.

Ku-sheng hsien-hsien, 1247.

Ku tzu shang-ts'an, 1936.

K'u hsing, 1805.

K'u-t'ang, 2538.

Kua-fa, 1170.

Kua-hao, 1168.

Kua-mien chiu-hsing, 899.

Kua-p'i, 1169.

Kua pu, 414.

Kua tuo ts'o-chu, 1182.

Kuai-p'ien, 2149.

Kuai-tai pu-ming, 2152.

K'uai-shou, 1846.

Kuan-chi (kei), 764.

Kuan-chiang, 2351.

Kuan-chieh, 1330.

Kuan-chieh, 1587.

Kuan-chien, 415.

Kuan-chuang po-shih-k'u, 883.

Lao-ch'eng lien-ta, 1369.

Lao-ch'ien p'u-fu, 2421.

Lao-ku ting chieh, 1818.

Lao-ping, 274; . . . -che hsiu-chih, 389.

Lao-shui, 457.

Lao ti, 2236.

Le-hsien yen-chi, 1838, and in 1857.

Lei-ch'i, 2209.

Lei ping, 1538.

Li-chang, 845; . . . kung-ying fu ma ch'ien-liang, 579.

Li-chieh nan-chih, 1017.

Li-chieh wang-lai, 348.

Li-ch'uan, 2379.

Li-chüeh cheng-fa, 1776.

Li-fan chih-chü, in 228.

Li fu-feng, 179.

Li i-fa chi-yu i-pi, 1030.

Li-i fu [sic, kuei] -tsung, 1892.

Li jen, 122.

Li-lien chih ts'ai, 220.

Li-ma, 1902.

Li pei chien tz'u, 338.

Li pien-feng, 179.

Li shen, 1695.

Li-sheng, 1285.

Li shou kuan yün, 834.

Li-tai ling-ch'in, 1244.

Li-ting, 873.

Li-wu, 1233.

Li yu chan-kung, 1439.

Li-yü hsün-hsin, 295.

Liang chien hsiang-ou, 1944.

Liang-ch'ien yin, 497.

Liang-ch'uan, 817.

Liang-ch'uan, 2548.

Liang ch'uan hsiang-ti, 830.

Liang-i chü-tsou, 1720.

Liang-p'ing chiao-i, 1096.

Liang-tan, 1149; 1566.

Liang t'ou hsi-chieh chang-lieh, 2319.

Liang-t'ou shui-yin, 427.

Liang ts'ai, 2482.

Liang-tsao, 1650.

Liao-pien, 450.

Liao-wang, 1540.

Lieh chi, 101.

Lieh-fu, 1250.

Lieh-nü, 1251.

Lien-ch'ien hao-fo, 2047.

Lien-ming t'ang-pao, 1569.

Lien-yüeh, 2261.

Lin-chi, 1571.

Lin-ch'ing cha hsieh-tsai chih-chia shui-yin, 583.

Lin-shih pu hsing, 2123.

Lin-yüeh, 2498.

Ling-ch'i ling-chien, 1550.

Ling chu yüeh-pa han-yü hu-shui, 2329.

Ling-chuang, 1139.

Ling-hsing t'iao-mai pu-hsü cheng-t'un shou-chu, 791.

Ling-hu jen, 881.

Ling k'ai pien-men, 341.

Ling kei yu-t'ieh, 1059.

Ling kung, 2582.

Ling p'ing, 49.

Ling-shan-sheng, 1281.

Ling-yin, 472.

Ling yin chieh-fei, 441.

Ling-yün, 806.

Liu-chieh, 673.

Liu ch'uan chi-yung, 2446.

Liu-fu, 2405.

Liu jen, 128.

Liu kuan, 180.

Liu-nan, 769.

Liu-nien sheng-k'o, 1000.

P'i-hui, 1143.

P'i-juan, 276; ... wu-neng chi su hsing pu-chin-che chü ko-chih, 391.

P'i-t'ieh, 1150.

P'i t'ieh k'uei-chia, 1560.

P'i-wan, 277.

Piao-fen erh san, 2130.

Piao-ying, 1525.

P'iao-mo, 829; ... chi-sui, 2438.

Pieh-ching fan chieh huo-mai, 1076.

Pien-ch'an p'ei-pu, 1787.

Pien-chi, 1852.

Pien-chia yin, 515.

Pien-chiang, 1399.

Pien-li, 1699; ... sheng-shih, 1673.

Pien-min cha, 2462.

Pien-shen min-ting, 879.

Pien-yüan ch'ung-hsü, 1753.

P'ien-jen hsi nu, 320.

Pin-hai yao hsün, 1405.

Pin-hsing, 1306.

P'in-ch'ang yü shan, 1237.

P'in-chi k'ao, 396.

P'in-nan hsia hu, 891.

Ping-chan pu-wang, 1763.

Ping-hsiang chih ch'üeh-o jih-shen teng shih, 1196.

Ping huang, 1514.

Ping mi, 706.

Ping-p'ai, 1570.

Ping-pao ta-shang t'ien-ho, 1012.

Ping tsang chih-tsui, 1743.

Ping-wu i tz'u ch'eng-ting, 2176.

Ping-wu kuo-chi, 2173.

Ping-wu ling-nüeh, 1829.

P'ing-chih t'a-jen fen-mu, 1951.

P'ing-ch'ü jen i shih, 1953.

P'ing-fan, 1487.

P'ing-fu, 2473.

P'ing hsi, 1508.

P'ing-hsing, 140.

P'ing-huan, 2468.

P'ing-liang, 751.

P'ing mi, 693.

P'ing-min, 866, 1981.

P'ing t'iao, 785.

P'ing t'ung, 1340.

Po-chi wu-ku, 1663.

Po-ch'uan, 816.

Po-hsieh yin, 517.

Po-hsing, 116.

Po-ping, 1536.

Po-pu, 647.

Po-shang, 1092.

Po-tao tzu, 1982.

Po-t'ao, 2288.

Po wan, 814.

P'o-i, 650.

Pu-ch'en-chih, 270.

Pu-chih, 269.

Pu-chin, 261.

Pu-chui yin, 540.

Pu-chüeh shih ch'iu, 284, 1835.

Pu fa, 588.

Pu-fa, 2524.

Pu-fu, 2117.

Pu-fu yin, 530.

Pu-fu yin-chieh, 2178.

Pu-hsi t'ung-ch'eng, 196.

Pu-hsiao, 271.

Pu-hsing k'ai-pao, 309.

Pu hsiu, 2397.

Pu-i, 1844.

Pu-k'an shui-shih hsiao ts'ao, 746.

Pu-lang, 171.

Pu-li, 611.

Pu-mu chih t'iao, 1972.

Pu-na tzu-li, 677.
Pu-nien ho-ko, 1417.
Pu-ping, 1530.
Pu-p'ing chih ch'i, 1971.
Pu-shen yu-ai, 250, 1025.
Pu-tan, 1133.
Pu-tao t'ung-chih, 1842.
Pu-t'ung, 1343.
Pu t'ung-chü, 2168.
Pu wei chieh-t'ieh, 2179.
Pu-wen shou tsu t'a-wu chin-
   jen ping chiao, 1952.
Pu-wu i-chia chiu-i chih yü, 1032.
Pu-wu sheng-li, 1999.
Pu-ying chung chang, 1730.
Pu-ying chung li, 1729.
Pu yün, 799.
P'u-hu, 2362.
P'u-mien lin-chieh fang, 2361.
P'u-ping, 1528.
P'u-tien yin, 482.

Sa-p'o, 1915.
San chai, 1206.
San ch'ang t'i-ko, 1276.
San-chia tz'u t'ung-chin-shih
   ch'u-shen, 1275.
San-ch'ih, 1800.
San fu-tsou, 1719.
San shang k'en-huang wei-chin
   teng shih, 1193.
San-sui, 591.
San-teng p'ing-chih, 79.
San-t'ing chün-shao, 1547.
San-tso-tung men, 2355.
San wu ch'eng-ch'ün, 2000.
Sao-t'ai, 2461.
Sha-chou, 2259.
Sha hsieh, 1516; ... meng-shih
   fen-piao, 2021.
Sha min, 849.

Sha-t'u yü-ch'ien, 2445.
Shai yang, 762.
Shai yang, 763.
Shan-ch'ang, 960.
Shan ch'ih ying-wu, 1368.
Shan-hsien, 474.
Shan-huo min-jen, 2055.
Shan-ju huang-ch'eng, 2196.
Shan-kou shu-kuan, 333.
Shan-sun t'an-t'a, 2428.
Shan t'ien, 924, and in 988.
Shan-yung ping-chang hsiang-
   ch'i, 2197.
Shang cheng chü-ch'üeh, 1678.
Shang-hen, 1927.
Shang i p'ing-fu, 2129.
Shang-kang, 1040.
Shang-kung, 1073.
Shang-liang, 2347.
Shang-ma yen, in 1350.
Shang-pan-chieh tao-t'a, 2315.
Shang-ssu, 168.
Shang-tao, 2098.
Shang ts'ang, 755.
Shang-wu-ts'eng shih-kung, 2316.
Shao-che wu-fan erh-mi chia yin,
   578.
Shao-ch'uan, 2381.
Shao-k'ai, 1176.
Shao-lien tan-yao, 2043.
She-ch'ien, 1701.
She-chü chu-ch'ien, 1102.
She-fa, 2475.
She-hou, 1702.
She-li ming-se, 786, 1186.
She liu, 202.
She-pa, 861.
She-ting, 878.
She-ts'ang, 740.
Shen-kao so-tsai kuan-yuan, 2198.
Shen kung, 1697.

Ta-shang, 1917.
Ta-sheng, 1492.
Ta-shui ch'ung-ni, 1010.
Ta ssu, 1200.
Ta-ssu ch'ang-chüeh, 1432, 2140.
Ta-tang, 749.
Ta-tao ch'ang-ch'iang, 1554.
Ta-tien shih-fei, 362.
Ta-to, 2089.
Ta tun, 2245.
Ta-yüeh, 2560.
Ta-yün, 812.
T'a-hsieh tao-ti wu-shih-yü chang, 2321.
T'a-jung, 281.
T'a-k'en, 2488.
Tai-cheng, 605; ...yin, 505.
Tai-feng ch'ai-ts'ao, 1447.
Tai-man wu-shih, 289.
Tai-na yin, 538.
Tai t'ieh-so san-t'iao, 1764.
Tai-tsui cheng-shou, 686.
Tai-wan, 278.
T'ai-jen luan-ta, 1945.
Tan ma, 1611.
T'an-chia, 2262.
T'an chia, 2263.
T'an-chiang t'ien-ti, 969.
T'an-hsi yin, 499.
T'an-k'u, 254; ... -che ko-chih t'i-wen, 390.
T'an-lan, 262; ...pai chien, 297.
T'an-li, 255.
T'an-lieh, 256.
T'an-p'ai, 628.
T'an-sa yin, 508.
T'an-sha, 2260.
T'an-sha ch'i-tsao, 1061.
T'an-sheng, 2395.

T'an-shih pu-shih, 311.
T'an-t'a, 2299; ...t'ien-ti, 968.
T'an-ts'an, 257.
T'an-tsang huai-fa, 354.
T'an-tui, 596.
T'an-wen, 2181.
T'an-ya, 1463.
Tang-ch'ai, in 2346.
Tang-chih hsün-lo, 1455.
Tang-p'ing, 1502.
Tang-t'ang, 51.
Tang-ts'ao, 1095.
Tang-ts'ao, 2274; ... pu-sheng tsao k'u kung-chien, 1078.
T'ang-cha, 397.
T'ang kung, 2586.
T'ang-pao, 402.
T'ang-ping, 1527.
Tao-cha, 2109.
Tao-fan, 2070.
Tao hu, 748.
Tao jen, 53.
Tao-k'ao, 1315, 2555.
Tao-kuan, 2440.
Tao-ma ts'ai-k'uang yin, 1628.
Tao-ta, 2111.
Tao-tsei ch'ung-ch'ih, 2136.
Tao tsei tzu-man, 2135.
Tao-tsei tzu-man, 2135.
Tao wu shih-chü, 2144.
T'ao chin, 2369.
T'ao-hu chou-chih wen-ts'e, 896.
T'ao-hua shui, 2284.
T'ao-hua ya-tzu, 2013.
T'ao-mo, 2086.
T'ao shou, 1759.
T'ao ta chih yin, 1060.
Te-shou chih-pi chih hsiao, 1387.
Teng-chieh, 1220.
T'eng-lu shu-shou, 1305.
T'eng-lu so, 1303.

Ti-an tan-po, 2443.
Ti-ch'ao, 399, 1568.
Ti-chi, 2359.
Ti-chia mai-wu, 345.
Ti-chu, 593; ...yin, 488.
Ti-chüeh, 1728.
Ti-fang, 841.
Ti Huang yu-yü, 2339.
Ti-hui, 1590.
Ti-ma kung-liao ch'ien-liang,
    572.
Ti ma pien-chia yin, 1630.
Ti-pao, 1568.
Ti-pei pu yen, 1408.
Ti-shih kao wa, 2268.
Ti-ssu pu-ts'ung pei-sha, 1897.
Ti-sun ch'eng-chung, 2172.
Ti t'ang-chih, 2182.
Ti-ting ch'ien-liang, 416.
Ti-ting tou-t'an, 2431.
Ti tuo huang-wu, 974.
T'i-chiang yin, 496.
T'i-hsiao, 2491.
T'i hsing, 1803.
T'i-ku, 2490.
T'i-liu, 667.
T'i-liu, 2406.
T'i-ming lu, 1325.
T'i-po, 1478.
T'i pu, 18.
T'i-t'ang, 198.
T'i-tiao, 1294.
Tiao-chien, 1883.
Tiao pi, 1517.
Tiao-po, 1477.
Tiao pu, 17.
Tiao-sang wen-chi, 1243.
Tiao sung, 1655.
Tiao-teng, 770; ...yung-ch'iang,
    1992.
Tiao-ts'an chi-po chih ti, 978.

Tiao-tu kuai fang, 1410.
T'iao ch'ien, 2212.
T'iao-ma yin, 1624.
T'iao-pien hsiang-yin, 449.
T'iao-shui pa, 2249.
T'ieh-chieh yin, 495.
T'ieh ch'u, 1336.
T'ieh-fang, 1460.
T'ieh tuan, 1757.
Tien chieh, 665.
Tien-chu wo tun, 1069.
Tien-fa, 656; ...yin, 521.
Tien-hsüan, 1469.
Tien-hu, 846.
Tien-mai shui-ch'i, 1125.
Tien-mao, 45.
Tien-p'ei, 674.
Tien-shang ling t'ieh, 2552.
Tien-shih, 1308.
Tien-shih, 1468.
Tien-shui, 463.
Tien-yung-kuo, 1575.
T'ien-chieh hsiang-lien, 1006.
T'ien pang, 1320.
T'ien-p'ing, 589.
T'ien-she tao hsien an-i chih-
    shih kung-shih, 1289.
T'ien-ti, 921.
T'ien-wen, 1254.
T'ien yü, 739.
Ting-ch'ai, 848.
Ting-ch'ung, 2298.
Ting-ch'ung yün-k'ou, 2307.
Ting hsüan, 4.
Ting-kung hsü-shui, 442.
Ting-kung t'ien, 940.
Ting ming, 1334; ...tai-kao,
    1657.
Ting nei-chien, 157.
Ting-pei tsung-t'u tsung chih
    t'u-ts'e, 206.

Tsang-fa k'u, 1783.
Tsang-fa yin-liang, 1784.
Tsang kuan, 263.
Tsang-pien yin-liang, 1786.
Ts'ang-ch'u, 692.
Ts'ang hu, 745.
Ts'ang-ni yin-sung, 2146.
Ts'ang-shou, 1141.
Tsao-ch'u tu-tu, 1934.
Tsao feng, 828.
Tsao-hu, 1041.
Tsao-i te-ts'ai yu chü, 2145.
Tsao-ting, 1042.
Ts'ao cha yin, 1626.
Ts'ao-chieh yin, 493.
Ts'ao fang, 2558.
Ts'ao i-su, 738.
Ts'ao-k'ou sheng-fa, 2134.
Ts'ao-liang, 713.
Ts'ao mi, 699.
Ts'ao-mu, 2371.
Ts'ao-pa, 2467.
Ts'ao-t'a ti, 966.
Ts'ao-tan, 1131.
Tse-ch'eng chih fa, 251.
Tse-jen, 58.
Tse-li, 1129, 1799.
Tse (tsei)-shih pu-ti, 1433.
Tse-ts'an, 110.
Ts'e-ying, 1491.
Tseng-ch'u jen-ting hu chieh
    t'ao-jen shih-chi, 245.
Tseng-hao, 780.
Tseng mi, 700.
Tseng-t'ich p'an-chiao mi, 727.
Tseng-yin, 470.
Ts'eng-ts'eng hang o, 2430.
Ts'eng yü ch'ao-ni li yu chan-
    kung, 1382.
Tso-chien chieh-tao, 2424.
Tso-erh kuan, 183.

Tso-kuan, 2363.
Tso-t'an, 1909.
Tso t'ang, 1539.
Tso-tao luan-shih, 2050.
Tso-tsang chih-tsui, 1744.
Tso ts'e-lun, 1644.
Tso-wei i-tuan, 2038.
Ts'o-k'u ju hsi, 1063.
Ts'o shu, 1035.
Tsou-chiao, 1573.
Tsou-hsiao, 666, 1161, 1574,
    2226; ...an-nei pu po ko-
    k'uan, 1189; ...yin, 525.
Ts'ou-chih yin, 520.
Tsu-chia, 467.
Tsu-huai yen fa, 1071.
Tsu-mu lin-feng kung-chieh,
    207.
Tsu-shui, 459.
Tsu-tang, 1918.
Tsu t'ien, 930.
Tsu-yin, 466.
Ts'u-meng niu-lei, 1344.
Ts'u-o sui-mi, 715.
Tsuan-tsao, 1173.
Ts'ui-cheng pu-te yin, 566.
Ts'ui-chi, 1847.
Ts'ui fu-k'o erh su-pi p'o-ch'ing,
    236.
Ts'ui [sic]-kung, see Ku-kung.
Tsun-chih chu-chien, shih, 209;
    ...teng shih, 1190.
Tsun pei shih-hsü, 2171.
Ts'un-ch'i t'iao-san, 788.
Ts'un-hsieh san-ko yüeh, 1638.
Ts'un-k'u yin, 560.
Ts'un-liu, 668; ...pei-chih yin,
    568; ...yin, 554.
Ts'un-sheng yin, 561.
Tsung-ch'e wei-shu, 1153.
Tsung-chia, 842.

Tsung-fang chün-hen hsieh-i,
    1446.
Tsung-ling shao-hsiang, 2031.
Tsung-pan, 2511.
Tsung-pu, 792.
Tsung-yün, 810.
Ts'ung-chen mao-ts'ao chih
    ch'ü, 979.
Ts'ung-ching lei-chi chih ti, 980.
Ts'ung erh chia-kung, 1862.
Ts'ung-fu chia mai, 1893.
Tu-chi, 1845.
Tu ch'i, 1561.
Tu-ch'uan, 2386.
Tu-fan, 2077.
Tu-hsiao, 2551.
Tu-hsiu, 2492.
Tu-k'en huang-ti, 244.
Tu-li, 75.
Tu-ma ch'uan, 2387.
Tu-pan, 2511.
Tu-t'ou, 2410.
Tu-ts'ui, 609.
T'u-chieh, sung pu, 1828.
T'u-chih ch'eng-hsi, 204.
T'u-chu, 2540; ... ti, 953.
T'u-hao, 1977.
T'u-hsiang ch'an-wei chih shu
    chan chih-luan, 1266.
T'u-i, 1075.
T'u-jen hsin-fu ch'in chih t'u-she
    ch'eng-hsi, 208.
T'u-lai, 1914.
T'u-min, 865.
T'u-mu, 860.
T'u-niu sao, 2258.
T'u pien, 1355.
T'u-she, 859.
T'u-ssu, 858.
T'u ti, 2238.
T'u t'ien, 927; ... yin, 548.

Tuan chieh, 660, 1586.
Tuan-fu, 1584; 2414.
Tuan-hou, 1501.
Tuan jen she hui-pai i yin-yang,
    1959.
Tuan liu, 2301.
Tuan-p'ai, 629; ... yin, 509.
T'uan-lien, 1467; ... huo-ch'i,
    1365.
Tui-hsing, 803.
Tui-liu, 802.
Tui-p'in tiao hsien-san yung, 83.
Tui-p'in tiao-yung, 82.
Tui-tu so, 1304.
Tui-yüeh ling p'ing, 52.
Tui-yün, 804.
T'ui-pu ts'e-yen chih shu chan
    hsiu-chiu, 1265.
Tun-t'ai, 1542.
T'un-liang, 447.
T'un mi, 754.
T'un po-shih-k'u, 884.
T'un t'ien, 932, and in 984.
T'un-ting, 870.
Tung-fang ch'ien-pen yin, 562.
Tung-kung, 2218.
Tung-shih ch'ü fa, 315.
Tung-tso chi-shih ch'iu-ch'eng
    wu-wang, 1015.
Tung-tsu, 826.
T'ung ch'eng kuan-yüan, 195.
T'ung-chi, 2574.
T'ung-chien, 1880.
T'ung-chü, 2167.
T'ung-fang, 2270.
T'ung-hsia, 1353.
T'ung-hsing tse-li, 1116.
T'ung-hui ch'i-mieh, 353.
T'ung-jen i-shih, 2487.
T'ung-jung po-chi (kei), 688.
T'ung-jung po-hsieh chan yin,
    574.

T'ung-k'ao kuan, 1297.
T'ung-kuan, 1152.
T'ung-liao, 169.
T'ung-o hsiang-chi, 360.
T'ung-p'i kao, 2372.
T'ung-shao chia-mu, 2374.
T'ung tao wang-lai, 2133.
T'ung-t'ung t'o-fang, 364.
Tuo-k'ai, 1175.
Tzu ch'en, 1397.
Tzu-chi ching-shen, 2017.
Tzu-chin, 1867.
Tzu-ch'ü fan-lan, 2366.
Tzu hao tuan-kung t'ai-pao
    shih-p'o ming-se, 2058.
Tzu-hsin kai-t'u shang k'o-i
    ts'e-li, 240.
Tzu-hsing ku-mu chuang-shou
    chia-ch'i shih i-ts'eng, 2334.
Tzu-i, 1866.
Tzu-jen pu-wei, 1674.
Tzu-li, 601; ... shu-huan, 1785.
Tzu-li, 999; ... yin, 514.
Tzu ma, 1608.
Tzu mu tao-pi, 1627.
Tzu-pei an ma, 1600.
Tzu pi kua-k'ou, 2310.
Tzu-shou mien tsui, 1746.
Tzu-tsu pu ju, 2141.
Tzu-wen, 1865.
Tzu-wen nei, 410.
Tzu-wu chieh-tz'u no-pi chih pi,
    1031.
Tz'u chih pen-mo, 2187.
Tz'u-tzu, 1733.
Tz'u yen, 1234.

Wai-ch'ao, 401.
Wai chuan, 21.
Wai-fan se-mu jen teng, 863.
Wai-hsiao chih k'uan, 2545.

Wai li, 176.
Wai-p'ai yin, 506.
Wan-fa cha-tsang, 1788.
Wan-hsiu, 2205.
Wan-pan yin, 528.
Wan-shou sheng-chieh, 1221.
Wan t'ien, 704.
Wan-yen, 1930.
Wang-kao hsün-shao chih jen,
    1545.
Wang-ming ch'i p'ai, 1548.
Wang-nieh chih-shih, 312.
Wang-shang hsing-ssu ch'ing
    t'ung shih-k'uai, 2527.
Wang-sheng i-i, 317.
Wang-yang tse-kuo, 2308.
Wang-yen tu-huo, 2045.
Wei-ch'ai, 2275, and in 2346.
Wei-cheng chih kung, 2539.
Wei-ch'ien, 622.
Wei-chin hsia-hai, 1418.
Wei-fan chiao-ling, 1967.
Wei-hsien, 329.
Wei-jao fang-wu, 1946.
Wei-i kung-shih, 424.
Wei-li chih-fu jen, 1875.
Wei-p'ai, 398.
Wei pang, 822.
Wei-shu wei-ch'ai, 2506.
Wei-tso chin yin, 2015.
Wei-ts'ung, 2069.
Wei-wan, 621; ... yin, 527.
Wei-wan pu-chi i-fen i-shang
    i shih-fen wei-lü, 690.
Wen-fu, 154.
Wen-li yu t'ung lieh-wei i-teng,
    1338.
Wen-p'ing, 394.
Wen-p'o, 1823.
Wo-chu, 2093.
Wo-su chu-liu, 2131.

-413-

-415-

INDEX OF SUBJECTS

Numbers refer to entries, not to pages.

Huai River, 2439.

Impeachment, 97–110, 116, 149, 311.
Imperial commission, 2521.
Imperial mausolea, 1244, 2582.
Imperial pasturages, 972.
Imperial Student, 192, 1280, 1288.
Infantrymen, 1457, 1530.
Inspection of officials, 44–45. See also Scrutiny of officials.
Institutes of the Ch'ing Dynasty, 1801.
Irrigation water-gate, 2462.

Labor service, 573, 659–660, 1579–87, 1591–92.
Land, agricultural settlement, 447, 932, 983–986; Banner, 967; cultivation of, 994–999, 1007–09; legal categories of, 921–980; malfeasance concerning, 1002–05; surveying of, 989–993; taxes on, see Taxes.
Land record books, 1126.
Law officers, 1820–24.
Law suits, initiating, 1647–73; judgment and verdict of, 1700–07, 1718–22, 2564–67; and testimony, 1694–97, 1708–11, 1717, see also Confrontation in court; trial procedures of, 1674–99, 1708–17.
Legal documents, types of, 164–165, 1119–51, 1565–71, 2552.
Liability time limit, 1924, 1965.
Likin, 2549.
Local constable, 841.

Marriage contracts, 2199.
Master of Ceremonies, 1285.
Meltage fees, 376.
Merits, recording of, 37–38. 149, 236.
Metropolitan examinations, see Examinations.
Metropolitan graduates, banquet for, 1347; classes of, 1272–73, 1275.
Military courier station messenger-soldiers, 1527–28, 1539.
Military district, 1524.
Military equipment, 1548–52, 1557, 1559–63.
Military intelligence, 1422–25, 1543, 1545–46.
Military officials, 1352–56, 1383–98; demerits of, 1407–21; inspection of, 1398–2559; meritorious acts of, 1358–75.
Military post system, 572, 577; credentials used in, 1564–67, 1570; courier reports of, 402; and government dispatches, 1593, 1594–1602; management of, 1577–92.
Militia, 1467, 1531, 2562.
Mourning, degrees of, 2169, 2181–82; observance of, 154–163.

National College of Letters, 722.

Official adviser, 188.
Official documents, 394–410.
Official posts, 53–68, 180–202, 1352–57; absence from, 151–53; of an assistant nature, 84, 183; in charge of, types, 66, 69–76; minor, 84, 189;

HARVARD EAST ASIAN SERIES

25. *China's Struggle for Naval Development, 1839–1895.* By John L. Rawlinson.
26. *The Practice of Buddhism in China, 1900–1950.* By Holmes Welch.
27. *Li Ta-chao and the Origins of Chinese Marxism.* By Maurice Meisner.
28. *Pa Chin and His Writings: Chinese Youth Between the Two Revolutions.* By Olga Lang.
29. *Literary Dissent in Communist China.* By Merle Goldman.
30. *Politics in the Tokugawa Bakufu, 1600–1843.* By Conrad Totman.
31. *Hara Kei in the Politics of Compromise, 1905–1915.* By Tetsuo Najita.
32. *The Chinese World Order: Traditional China's Foreign Relations.* Edited by John K. Fairbank.
33. *The Buddhist Revival in China.* By Holmes Welch.
34. *Traditional Medicine in Modern China: Science, Nationalism, and the Tensions of Cultural Change.* By Ralph C. Crozier.
35. *Party Rivalry and Political Change in Taishō Japan.* By Peter Duus.
36. *The Rhetoric of Empire: American China Policy, 1895–1901.* By Marilyn B. Young.
37. *Radical Nationalist in Japan: Kita Ikki, 1883–1937.* By George M. Wilson.
38. *While China Faced West: American Reformers in Nationalist China, 1928–1937.* By James C. Thomson Jr.
39. *The Failure of Freedom: A Portrait of Modern Japanese Intellectuals.* By Tatsuo Arima.
40. *Asian Ideas of East and West: Tagore and His Critics in Japan, China, and India.* By Stephen N. Hay.
41. *Canton under Communism: Programs and Politics in a Provincial Capital, 1949–1968.* By Ezra F. Vogel.
42. *Ting Wen-chiang: Science and China's New Culture.* By Charlotte Furth.
43. *The Manchurian Frontier in Ch'ing History.* By Robert H. G. Lee.
44. *Motoori Norinaga, 1730–1801.* By Shigeru Matsumoto.
45. *The Comprador in Nineteenth Century China: Bridge between East and West.* By Yen-p'ing Hao.
46. *Hu Shih and the Chinese Renaissance: Liberalism in the Chinese Revolution, 1917–1937.* By Jerome B. Grieder.
47. *The Chinese Peasant Economy: Agricultural Development in Hopei and Shantung, 1890–1949.* By Raymond H. Myers.
48. *Japanese Tradition and Western Law: Emperor, State, and Law in the Thought of Hozumi Yatsuka.* By Richard H. Minear.
49. *Rebellion and Its Enemies in Late Imperial China: Militarization and Social Structure, 1796–1864.* By Philip A. Kuhn.
50. *Early Chinese Revolutionaries: Radical Intellectuals in Shanghai and Chekiang, 1902–1911.* By Mary Backus Rankin.
51. *Communication and Imperial Control in China: Evolution of the Palace Memorial System, 1693–1735.* By Silas H. L. Wu.
52. *Vietnam and the Chinese Model: A Comparative Study of Nguyên and Ch'ing Civil Government in the First Half of the Nineteenth Century.* By Alexander Barton Woodside.
53. *The Modernization of the Chinese Salt Administration, 1900–1920.* By S. A. M. Adshead.